The Young Offenders Act:
A Revolution in Canadian Juvenile Justice

One of the most controversial social policies in Canadian history is the Young Offenders Act of 1984. To some it represents a more enlightened and more humane approach to the rights of young persons before the law; to others it offers unwarranted protection to those who least deserve it – those who commit crimes. Still others feel the new legislation strikes a resounding chord for the necessity of making offenders responsible and accountable for their behaviour.

The essays in this volume explore the impact of this legislation on Canadian juvenile justice from the perspective of lawyers, policy-makers, researchers, and other professionals involved in the court system. Among the areas discussed are the theoretical framework for the policy; the impact on law and social-service practitioners; and the impact on clients.

Mr Justice Archambault, who wrote the foreword, was appointed by the federal government in the late 1960s to review the juvenile justice system as it was then operating. His investigation laid the groundwork for the Young Offenders Act; his perspective, and the essays that make up the body of the volume, provide a comprehensive overview, not only of the current legislation, but of the legal and social-service systems that it supports.

Alan W. Leschied is Adjunct Assistant Professor, Department of Psychology, University of Western Ontario, and Assistant Director of the London (Ontario) Family Court Clinic.

Peter G. Jaffe is Associate Professor (Adjunct) in the departments of Psychology and Psychiatry, University of Western Ontario, and Director of the London Family Court Clinic.

Wayne Willis is a Child and Family Worker at the London Family Court Clinic.

The Young Offenders Act:

A Revolution in
Canadian Juvenile Justice

edited by

Alan W. Leschied

Peter G. Jaffe

Wayne Willis

UNIVERSITY OF TORONTO PRESS
Toronto Buffalo London

© University of Toronto Press 1991
Toronto Buffalo London
Printed in Canada

ISBN 0-8020-2623-0 (cloth)
ISBN 0-8020-6714-X (paper)

Canadian Cataloguing in Publication Data

Main entry under title:
The Young Offenders Act

ISBN 0-8020-2623-0 (bound)   ISBN 0-8020-6714-X (pbk.)

1. Canada. Young Offenders Act. 2. Juvenile
Justice, Administration of – Canada. 3. Youth
Legal status, laws, etc. – Canada. 4. Juvenile
delinquents – Canada. I. Leschied, Alan Winfield,
1952–   . II. Jaffe, Peter, 1948–   . III. Willis,
Wayne.

KE9445.Y68 1991   345.71'08   C90-095935-5
KF9779.Y68 1991

The editors wish to dedicate the book to our parents, from whom we have drawn our commitment to balancing compassion and rational thinking in the justice community.

Contents

Foreword

The Young Offenders Act, which came into effect on 2 April 1984, profoundly altered the course of the juvenile-justice system in Canada. Although the extensive debate and discussion that preceded the new legislation did not produce a unanimity of views, the act, in the main, did garner a high degree of consensus for its approach and was hailed as a major and necessary reform. Unfortunately, despite the best intentions of its authors and our legislators, this act, like many others, is imperfect and has fallen victim to the law of unintended consequences.

Admittedly the inherent tensions resulting from the blend of diverse and sometimes conflicting principles on which the law is based make its application all the more difficult. Two particularly serious problems have emerged during the first six years of its existence. First, while the act was intended to provide a better balance between the protection and interest of society and the rights and needs of young persons, it strikes me, on the one hand, that the 'justice' and 'legal' objectives of the act are being effectively realized while, on the other hand, the 'needs' and 'treatment' aspects thereof leave much to be desired. Second, while the research is perhaps not yet complete and conclusive, it is becoming abundantly clear that there has been an overuse of custodial dispositions since the implementation of the Young Offenders Act.

In shifting our juvenile-justice system from the treatment- and welfare-oriented model, which prevailed under the Juvenile Delinquents Act, to the more justice-oriented model of the Young Offenders Act, one could, of course, reasonably anticipate that a good deal more emphasis would be placed on public protection and the rights and responsibility of young persons. However, this should not occur to such an extent that it becomes a serious detriment to our resolve and ability to cater to the needs and rehabilitation of young persons who run afoul of the law.

It is no surprise that the 'legal' and 'rights' aspects of the act are being adequately met. Two circumstances have contributed significantly to this development. The 'legal' professionals, including the police, who had long felt hard done by under the Juvenile Delinquents Act, saw the opportunity with the Young Offenders Act to claim new turf that had long been elusive. They were not only ready, but enthusiastic about the new legislation and hence wasted little time in staking their territory. As well, given the major shift in the legislation, a lot of resources were made available to ensure implementation of the 'justice' aspects of the new law (e.g., legal aid and new custodial institutions).

Most unfortunately, in my view, professionals in the social and behavioural sciences failed to tackle the new law with the same degree of enthusiasm and vigour. It appears to me that many of them spent too much time and energy lamenting lost ground and not enough ensuring that the new law be implemented in a balanced way. Others devoted much of their energy to criticizing the act and characterizing it as a 'pure justice,' or essentially 'offence'-based model with the result that they are convincing themselves and everyone else (much like a self-fulfilling prophecy) that, under the Young Offenders Act, the treatment and rehabilitation of young offenders are out the window. May I suggest that they would better serve the system by spending more effort on showing and emphasizing the essential difference between the Young Offenders Act and the ordinary criminal law than by building the case for their similarity.

The undue emphasis placed on public protection over the needs and treatment of young offenders has undoubtedly contributed to the overuse of incarceration. With the advent of the Young Offenders Act far too many people fell into the error of equating public protection with harsh treatment and severe sanctions. In addition, the problem was, in my view, further exacerbated by the decisions of the courts of appeal of a number of provinces to the effect that general deterrence was one of the principles governing the determination of a disposition. There is no doubt that public protection and the responsibility of young persons call for the need to deter young offenders from committing further crimes, i.e., specific deterrence. However, with all due deference, in my opinion, the emphasis on the individual and the needs of the young person under the new act mitigate against the adoption of the principle of general deterrence in dealing with young offenders. That has to be one of the essential differences between the Young Offenders Act and the sentencing of adult offenders under the ordinary criminal law. One hopes the Supreme Court of Canada will see it that way when called upon to adjudicate on the matter.

I have a sinking feeling that open custody is being resorted to where a young offender is in need of a residential placement to provide the guidance, discipline, and control required. In many instances the young person's needs in this regard could be satisfied by a residential placement as a condition of a probation order. Why is so little use being made of the residential placement available by virtue of paragraphs 23(2)(e) and (f) of the act? It appears to me that we are escalating young persons much too rapidly through the system with the result that custody and transfer to adult court are being resorted to prematurely.

For all that, all is not lost. I remain firmly convinced that the act has the scope and mandate to address individual needs and welfare considerations in dealing with young persons. What must occur is a correction in the course we have chartered since the 1984 launching of the new legislation. Fortunately, many social- and behavioural-science and mental-health professionals are fighting back and doing battle to reclaim and retain what was almost lost by default.

The editors of *The Young Offenders Act: A Revolution in Canadian Juvenile Justice* have gathered together a number of learned articles showing the diversity of views and providing much-needed information on, and insight into, the Young Offenders Act and its operation; these articles will assist all of us in our continuing efforts to properly apply this law. The many scholarly presentations that follow contain valid criticisms of the new act and its implementation, as well as valuable suggestions for the improvement of our juvenile-justice system, that will assist in bringing together social- and behavioural-science and mental-health professionals, on the one hand, and the legal and justice professionals, on the other, to work together for the betterment of our juvenile-justice system. Professionals from all disciplines involved with young offenders must become sensitized to one another's role and responsibility and be prepared to work together as members of a partnership rather than as adversaries.

In order to rectify the current imbalance there is a need to shore up the social, psychological, medical, and mental-health services available to the Youth Court in dealing with young offenders. The legal professionals have an obligation to get involved and pitch in to ensure that a better balance is established between the protection and interest of society as a whole and the needs and rehabilitation of young persons in particular.

This collection of articles will go a long way in demonstrating to the reader that the Young Offenders Act is not solely 'offence'-based, but that it is as well clearly 'offender'-based (therein lies one of its essential differences from the ordinary criminal law); that the need to protect society is not to be equated with harsh sentences or custodial dispositions; that in dealing with young persons, treatment and rehabilitation are still valid and necessary objectives and that they have their place in the Young Offenders Act; and that an effective juvenile-justice system is one of the most powerful crime-prevention strategies. It is clear that the Young Offenders Act is intended to recoup young offenders as law-abiding and productive members of society – the time to work with these young persons is while they are young, malleable, and responsive to treatment and rehabilitative measures.

I believe that the Young Offenders Act, although not perfect, and capable of improvement, is still a realistic and effective blueprint for our juvenile-justice system. We must, however, be prepared to take stock now and again and not be hesitant to correct our course when we are straying. In order to make the best of it, all actors in the system must work together and co-operate closely to ensure that all aspects of the system are considered and the contributions of the various professionals are respected and supported by all. My congratulations to the editors, P. Jaffe, A. Leschied, and W. Willis, whose work not only is a testimony to their interest and expertise in and ongoing concern for juvenile justice, but, I am sure, will make a significant contribution to the improvement of our system of justice for young persons.

Judge J.R. Omer Archambault
Provincial Court of Saskatchewan
Prince Albert

Preface

Few issues raised in the Canadian media arouse public concern in the way that criminal-justice matters do. It is little wonder, since this issue prompts two seemingly contradictory instinctive responses: one is natural apprehension regarding personal safety and security; the other, our capacity for compassion.

This conflict becomes heightened when the criminal-justice matters relate to youth. The Canadian public has, in the past eighty years, displayed considerable latitude in our views of the offending behaviour of youths in our country. In 1908, with the passage of the Juvenile Delinquents Act, there was a clear indication that the Canadian public was ready to consider young persons not as criminals, but rather as youths requiring the firm and 'wise' parental hand of the court to provide guidance and assistance. With changing political perspectives, the public's view of the role of the court has shifted, seeing it now only as a means to control youth crime. Increased emphasis on individual civil rights for youths, as well as a belief that our crime-control measures have not been effective in the past, has led, over the last several decades, to a reconsideration of juvenile-justice policy.

In 1984, Parliament proclaimed the Young Offenders Act to provide a new perspective for juvenile justice. This legislation signalled a considerable departure from seeing the court as a caring parent to viewing the court as a forum for ensuring protection of individual civil liberties while meting out justice in a fair and equitable manner. The implications of this swing in attitude have been the focus of considerable attention. Canada has followed other major Western industrialized nations, such as the United States and Great Britain, in revising statutes pertinent to juveniles in conflict with the law. Whether Canada's experience after these revisions will be unique, or whether Canada, like the other countries, will see increasing incarceration of young offenders remains an open question. These are the serious matters. They require serious attention not only from policy makers, judges, lawyers, and persons involved in direct service with young persons, but also from the Canadian public.

The Young Offenders Act: A Revolution in Canadian Juvenile Justice addresses some of the major issues raised by new juvenile-justice legislation in Canada. Particularly, it underscores the dynamic tension between treatment issues and the demand for accountability in response to juvenile crime. The Canadian juvenile-justice system is, and will be, confronted with: increasing rates of incarceration of young persons, decline in the emphasis given to rehabilitation and treatment, renewed emphasis on due process and legal representation, as well as demand by the Canadian public that young persons be held more accountable and responsible for their behaviour. Each of these themes is explored in a different way by the contributors to this volume. The book is organized in a manner that portrays the shift in juvenile-justice legislation from the macro level of societal expectations of juvenile-justice systems to the micro level of practice within the courtroom and its impact upon young persons and their families. All of the principal disciplines are represented and, while some overlap exists between chapters, this, in itself, represents the high level of integration across disciplines and between practices, within both a social-science and a legal perspective.

Acknowledgments

We have attempted to bring together in this collection perspectives on the Young Offenders Act and on its implications for the Canadian juvenile-justice system and those persons who have been most outspoken in addressing juvenile-crime issues. Representatives from a full range of professions, from practitioners of criminology and law to academics and persons involved in direct service, have been included. We are extremely grateful for the considerable time, effort, and expertise each has devoted to his or her contribution.

Before commencing to put together this book, we could never have anticipated the amount of energy that would be required to meet all of the needs and demands for a comprehensive outline of juvenile-justice matters in Canada. This challenging task was made less daunting by virtue of the support provided by the University of Toronto Press, especially by Virgil Duff. We also acknowledge the helpful suggestions of reviewers, whose comments assisted us in giving direction to this text. In addition, we came to appreciate the extensive organizational effort that was required in orchestrating the submissions of all of the contributors, and for this we owe a debt of thanks to Ms Bonnie Henderson, Ms Elizabeth Timmermans, and Ms Suzanne Bell, who performed the task not only of retyping manuscripts, but also of administering these submissions. Bonnie and Liz taught us that the road to a final manuscript is littered with hundreds of interim drafts that we thought were final.

Finally, we would like to thank the many persons who have helped us in our own formulation of the very important part that juvenile justice plays in the life of a community. In this regard, we wish to acknowledge our appreciation to the staff and board of the London Family Court Clinic, both past and present, whose richness and diversity of opinion have promoted our own interest in juvenile-justice matters. This acknowledgment is also extended to the larger juvenile-justice community in Ontario. We specifically acknowledge the support of the Ontario Ministry of Community and Social Services in assisting the development of the London Family Clinic over the past decade. Support from the London Foundation also assisted in the production of this book.

The Editors
London, Ontario

Contributors

His Honour Judge J.R. Omer Archambault, Provincial Court of
Saskatchewan, Prince Albert, Saskatchewan

George A. Awad, MD, FRCP(C), Toronto Family Court Clinic, Toronto,
Ontario

Nicholas Bala, BA, LLB, LLM, Queen's University, Kingston, Ontario

His Honour Judge L.A. Beaulieu, Judicial District of York, Toronto,
Ontario

Jeannette J. Cochrane, BA, Clarke Institute of Psychiatry, Toronto, Ontario

Carol M. Crealock, PhD, University of Western Ontario, London, Ontario

Jim Hackler, PhD, University of Alberta, Edmonton, Alberta

Peter G. Jaffe, PhD, London Family Court Clinic, London, Ontario

Mary-Anne Kirvan, BA, LLB, Department of Justice Canada, Ottawa,
Ontario

Alan W. Leschied, PhD, London Family Court Clinic, London, Ontario

P.G.R. Patterson, MD, FRCP(C), Child and Adolescent Centre, London,
Ontario

John C. Pearson, BA, LLB, LLM, Director of Prosecutions for the Province
of Nova Scotia, Halifax, Nova Scotia

Susan Reid-MacNevin, MA, University of Guelph, Guelph, Ontario

Marge Reitsma-Street, PhD, Laurentian University, Sudbury, Ontario

Joy M. Rogers, MSc, Clarke Institute of Psychiatry, Toronto, Ontario

Ira M. Schwartz, PhD, University of Michigan, Ann Arbor, Michigan

Stanley Stylianos, BSc, Central Toronto Youth Services, Toronto, Ontario

Christopher D. Webster, PhD, Clarke Institute of Psychiatry, Toronto,
Ontario

Gordon West, PhD, University of Toronto, Toronto, Ontario

Wayne Willis, BA, London Family Court Clinic, London, Ontario

PART ONE

Theoretical Overview

Part I offers the reader a theoretical overview of the major factors involved in the development of new juvenile-justice legislation in Canada. West explores the concept of state response to youthful offenders: he warns of the worrisome role played in the past by the 'child-savers' and voices his fears that a rebirth of 'child-saving' is made possible under the current Young Offenders Act. Reid-MacNevin offers a theoretical overview of the historical development of the Young Offenders Act. Hackler completes this first section with the suggestion that perhaps a new youth-justice law in Canada was unnecessary, and develops this theme in asserting that organizational failure and lack of vision in the law have created a cumbersome juvenile-justice system in Canada. He contrasts this Canadian system with its French counterpart and concludes that a less formal, less adversarial system may provide greater flexibility in addressing the causes of youth crime.

1 Towards a more socially informed understanding of Canadian delinquency legislation

Gordon West

'The importation of children taken from the reformatories, refuges and work-houses of the old world,' the commissioners concluded, was 'fraught with much danger and ... calculated, unless conducted with care and prudence, to swell the ranks of the criminal classes in this country,' ... 'these street Arabs' speedily returned 'to their old habits, on arriving in Canada, and, as a consequence, became a burden and an expense upon the taxpayers of the Dominion in our reformatories, gaols, and penitentiaries.' (Sutherland 1976: 30)

In 1889, Kelso estimated that Toronto had 'between six and seven hundred boys and about one hundred girls' who were sent out on the streets 'by drunken and avaricious parents to earn money by the precarious selling of newspaper, pencils, etc.,' but who more frequently used their work 'as a cloak for begging and pilfering.' (Sutherland 1976: 103)

One cannot begin to appreciate the significance of the recent passage and continuing implementation of the Canadian Young Offenders Act without some historical perspective on how we have dealt with 'youth in conflict' (usually, in conflict with some adults). While the young often seemed most threatening, but also the most amenable to reform, in the general concern about public disorder in the burgeoning nineteenth-century Canadian cities, before the passage of the Juvenile Delinquents Act (JDA) in 1908, there was no such thing as juvenile delinquency in the law, but only crime by young persons, which was generally responded to within the same legislation as was crime by adults.

This introductory chapter will offer an admittedly selective socio-historical background that provocatively aims to raise questions about some contemporary issues. The earlier child-savers' concerns regarding our young continue to echo in Canadian debates about birth control and abortion, falling demographic/reproduction statistics, day-care provision, and immigration, as well in debates specifically concerning legal issues surrounding juvenile misbehaviour. The young have figured prominently not only in official police statistics, but also in self-report surveys of misbehaviour, popular images of deviance, and moral panics.

As will become evident, these historical facts suggest a feminist-informed political-economy perspective, critical of the Canadian state's attempts to manage our young through coercive legislation – while systematically maintaining their social disadvantage. Leaving more thorough expositions of theories specifically related to delinquency and legal issues to later chapters, I will try to provoke by offering a critically appreciative overview of the historical development of juvenile-delinquency legislation, and conclude that we are seriously in need of a more sophisticated sociopolitical analysis of policies and actions legislating juvenile delinquency in Canada.

The Historical Status of Children and Youth in Canada

Unfortunately, little written material exists from before the last couple of centuries of European conquest regarding the situation of 'deviant' native children in the geographic territory now claimed by the Canadian state. Clearly, however, before the agricultural and public-health revolutions, life at the end of the Middle Ages in Western Europe and its new colonies (as in the Third World today) was often short, brutish, and nasty: child and infant death rates were very high, with perhaps a quarter or third dying in their first year and only half surviving to age twenty-one, the average life expectancy being thirty (Gillis 1974: 10–11). However, Ariès argues (1962) that children in medieval Europe were treated as small adults, and accepted within adult activities: games and social events, economic endeavours – even sexuality!

Musgrove (1964) strongly supports the argument that change from this medieval status coincided quite directly with the Industrial Revolution, and the accompanying urbanization, resulting in the passage of factory acts (for instance, in Britain in 1833 and 1847) restricting child labour. Universal compulsory-education acts followed in Britain in 1870, 1876, and 1880 (Musgrove 1964: 76–7), as much to control as to educate, meeting stiff opposition from working-class families dependent on their children's income. Whereas, during early industrialization, children were exploited grossly for low wages, their partly humanitarian exclusion from the labour market had, by the end of the nineteenth century, made them an expendable surplus population.

By the middle and late 1800s, the larger Canadian cities experienced many of the same problems as did French, British, and American ones (Sutherland 1976), but with a foreshortened 'time-lag,' as they grew almost instantly within the 'prehistoric' wilderness. In advocating the establishment of a universal compulsory public-school system, Egerton Ryerson, the 'father' of Ontario public-school education, opined in 1848 that the immigrants from the Irish famine 'accompanied by disease and death' were possible 'harbingers of a worse pestilence of social insubordination and disorder' (Prentice 1977: 56). Moreover, the Canadian urban youth problem was greatly accentuated during the late 1800s by the arrival of some 75,000 homeless British waifs and street urchins. Sutherland's quote ''doption, sir, is when folks gets girl to work without wages' (1976: 10) indicates the mixing of humanitarian and economic motives and concerns. We hear contemporary restatements of racist attitudes towards immigrants, although officially we recognize the necessity of further immigration to fuel an expanding economy whose consumer-demand and labour-force needs are not being satisfied by the declining local birth rate.

In 1871, Ontario made school attendance compulsory; questions of organization and discipline preoccupied the early educators, especially as concerns about a perceived growth in crime became widespread (Houston 1972). The schools offered an institution whereby the state could control and exercise surveillance over not just all children, but almost all families too (Fitz 1981a). Sutherland (1976: 12, 18) and Leon (1978: 40ff) document that notions about the 'good family' had become so clearly articulated by the end of the nineteenth century that Children's Aid Societies felt morally justified in breaking up families that did not conform. We are still debating what constitutes proper child care, not only in the obvious case of universally funded child-care provision, but also regarding runaways 'precocious' childhood sexuality, and so on.

In spite of the rather negative aspects of social control that are being emphasized in this discussion, it must also be acknowledged that the child-savers did succeed in achieving many of their more worthwhile humanitarian goals: establishing on the political agenda the needs of children; attempting to provide practical employment skills; offering common schooling (and communication); and – perhaps most unquestionably valuable of all – establishing noticeably better standards of public health.

Yet, British law had already traditionally held young people as accountable for their criminal actions as adults. In most cases involving young offenders, this view was mercifully tempered: the ancient common-law necessity of demonstrating mental capacity regarding knowledge of right and wrong by those between ages seven and fourteen gradually became enshrined as courts and juries were increasingly reluctant to impose harsh penalties on young malefactors. Periods favouring institutionalized-reformatory treatment of young offenders, industrial-school treatment, and probation treatment had preceded by decades the formal passage of the Juvenile Delinquents Act (Leon 1978). But, besides establishing a legal calculus of punishments to deter whenever the public schooling system failed, it was deemed essential to *reform* those who none the less offended: in hospitals, reformatories, and prisons (Foucault 1977; Prentice 1977).

It must be understood, then, that, from the beginning, the child-savers' interests went far beyond preventing, punishing, or correcting criminal-code violations by the young. Juvenile crime and misbehaviour were seen as not only evils linked to working-class and immigrant parents' drunkenness, sexual immorality, laboural sloth, and resultant poverty, but also as a challenge to a moral crusade for the construction of a New Jerusalem on this 'virgin' continent.

After passage of the new delinquency legislation, however, critical analyses and reforms of the overall social system (which had been acknowledged, by at least some of the child-savers, as fundamentally underlying the miseries of the families of the youngsters that concerned them) largely faded from their view. It is against this background series of specific nineteenth-century Canadian demographic changes and political concerns about children that one must view changes in their formal legal criminal-code status.

The Canadian Juvenile Delinquents Act, 1908

The passing of the Canadian Juvenile Delinquents Act in (JDA) 1908 formally redefined the legal status of the young, established a formal legal category of delinquency, and allowed for setting up organized systems of probation and juvenile courts. The act (as revised in 1924) defined as a 'juvenile delinquent' 'any child who violates any provision of the Criminal Code or of any Dominion or provincial statute, or of any by-law or ordinance of any municipality, or who is guilty of sexual immorality or any similar form of vice, or who is liable by reason of any other act to be committed to an industrial school or juvenile reformatory under the provisions of any Dominion on provincial statute.'

It should be noted immediately that the common-law understanding that age seven was a minimum for knowledge of right from wrong was retained; the upper age limit has varied (sometimes by sex) from province to province. Key terms such as 'sexual immorality' or 'any similar form of vice' were nowhere explicitly defined. With such undefined, sweeping powers, trials involving juveniles were conducted by special judges, in separate courts, and in private. Judges and probation officers were given special investigatory powers, including access to hearsay evidence and no necessity to reveal confidential information to defendants; procedural rules were minimal. No automatic right to appeal was present, and dispositions ranged from warning and release to indeterminate sentences, with the guilty remaining under the courts' jurisdiction until age twenty-one. dispositions were not linked to the gravity of the offence, but were tailored to the child's supposed 'needs.' The vagueness of this legislation, its lack of due process, the inclusion of a wide range of new juvenile-status offences (e.g., truancy), and wide dispositional powers left the treatment of juveniles open to administrative arbitrariness. In winning this legislative reform, the child-savers partly detached juvenile justice from the adversarial legal system, making it part of an administrative welfare program, and subsequently allowed much of its humanitarian potential to be undermined in its implementation.

Training-school placement became the ultimate sanction of the juvenile law. By the provisions of the Ontario Training Schools Act, in conjunction with the JDA, youngsters who were neglected by parents, had no community facility able to take them, and were sent to training school were also legally delinquent. The same institution provided for 'good' children who were victims, and for 'bad' children who were victimizers – on the grounds that the former were delinquents in the making. 'The distinction between *neglected* and *criminal* in effect translated as *potentially* vs. *actually* criminal' (Houston 1972: 263).

Sutherland presents evidence that the number of youngsters incarcerated in various types of institutions kept pace with the population growth (1976: 146–9), contrary to the child-savers' espousal of decreased incarcerations. That two-thirds of our juvenile females sent to training schools were incarcerated in Ontario under section 8 of the Training Schools Act attests eloquently to the extension of jurisdiction (as do the 25–35 per cent of the incarcerated boys). The disproportionate representation of native Indian youngsters is an equally eloquent testimony to the institutionalized racism of the system. Probation sentences were used increasingly to allow 'informal' 'counselling/interviews,' which must be understood as the real exercise of increasing state control over the young. Leon (1978) and

Sutherland (1976: 14–15, 112, 120) clearly establish connections between the leading moral entrepreneurs, such as Kelso and Scott; judges, ministers, cabinet members, and senators; as well as newspaper editors, doctors, clergy, and other very solid and respectable community members.

The circle of special provision for rearing of the young was extended in the activities of the family court's jurisdiction over a range of provincial social legislation (e.g., the Children's Protection Act, 1927; Deserted Wives' and Children's Maintenance Act, 1927; Adoption Act, 1927, for Ontario) (see Chunn 1983). Various federal commissions initiated changes endorsing a more 'corrective' official policy during the 1940s and 1950s. More 'facilities' were built, and a somewhat pleasant, professionally non-conflictive era espoused that, if only more therapeutic services were available, our delinquency problems would be solved (see Ratner 1985).

Yet, the corrective effects of such resourceful treatment as could be administratively mustered by the liberal-democratic Canadian state were not impressive. Not atypically, for instance, the *Annual Report* of the Ontario Department of Corrections for 1972 acknowledged that a third of the annual admissions to training schools were repeaters, somehow 'uncured.' Half those released became unemployed; three-quarters returned to the 'detrimental home conditions' that supposedly caused their problems in the first place. Numerous alternative, usually psychologically based 'talk-oriented,' therapies sprang up, claiming spectacular successes and private consultant fees. Yet, most of these proved, upon serious research study, seldom to be more effective than 'leaving the kids alone' (see, e.g., Schur 1973; Hackler 1978); few of the more demonstrably successful were competently organized administratively.

On the balance of the historical evidence, it is difficult to deny that the Juvenile Delinquents Act exemplified the legal domination of some groups over others: upper- and middle-class old, white, Protestant (and Catholic) males dominated; their opposites were subordinated. This domination continues today; it is bluntly evident in whatever statistical analysis is made of delinquency.

A more potent agent of change than any research evaluation was the action of lawyers who began to question the inadequacy of legal safeguards (perhaps partly inspired by children's rights movements [see, e.g., Berkely, Gaffield, and West 1978]). Middle-class parents and 'new left' social workers – indeed, anyone sympathetic to children – could not help but be troubled, upon even a casual visit to training schools, by the conditions in which young inmates were maintained.

Hence, by the 1970s, by almost all objective accounts, the system established in 1908 to prevent, correct, and contain youthful offenders really did not work very well, from whatever dominant perspective – whether conservative repressive control or liberal rehabilitation – and a seemingly endless parade of government commissions on deviant youth behaviour proposed various changes. The policies based on the child-savers' corrections movement (subordinating the young) seemed to have failed. Is the contemporary debate regarding the new Young Offenders Act a signal of the rebirth? For, as a century ago, Canadian streets are disturbingly filled with errant youths; but, now, in addition to the traditional mainstay of petty property crime (West 1979), instead of selling newspapers and pencils, they offer 'speed,' 'crack,' and their bodies – if not their very souls and lives (Visano 1987; Ng, 1982).

The More Recent Social History of Youth in Canada

Again, to understand contemporary delinquency and delinquency legislation, we must contextualize these issues by examining the socio-political situation of young people living in Canada. Canada, in particular, experienced the largest post–Second World War baby boom of all the Western First World countries. As a result, by the 1960s a tidal wave of young persons swamped all Canadian institutions. Although the Canadian federal state (and its supporters) has continued to maximize profit by promoting various export staples dependent upon cheap youthful labour, the boom has been followed by an indigenous demographic 'bust': for any even mildly calculating adult in Canada, it is clearly economically now personally disadvantageous to birth and rear children. Not without consequence, the Canadian welfare state has been as severely shaken as any Western society by the ending, in the 1970s, of the long economic boom that began with the Second World War.

Adolescents have been required to attend school until they are sixteen years of age, and feeble employment prospects encouraged most to remain in school even longer. Consequently, the education systems in Canada have expanded enormously, to become one of the largest Canadian 'industries.' By 1970, they consumed 8 per cent of the GNP, occupied 6.5 million students and teachers, and consumed 20 per cent of the total government spending (over $6 billion). Now they must reorganize and fight for contracts. Labour regulations effectively prohibited employment of those under sixteen years of age. In terms of training and experience, then, they stand at a disadvantage to other workers; even when they are legally eligible for jobs, their pay is differentially lower. Massive structural

unemployment remains: whereas the overall 1970 Canadian unemployment rates for males and females were 6.6 and 4.5 per cent, respectively,
for fourteen- to nineteen-year-olds, they were 15 and 11.4 per cent; and for
twenty- to twenty-four-year-olds, they were 10.5 and 5.1 per cent (Committee on Youth 1971). Young people consequently must rely to an unusual
extent on alternative sources of income (e.g., parents or theft).

During the last couple of decades, criminal-justice-system costs expanded remarkably (Waller 1979). Official crime rates soared as the post-
war baby boom reached adolescence, although increases in self-reported
delinquency are much less clearly documented. Most delinquents engage
only in minor nuisance behaviour; yet, our young are seen as unapprecia-
tive of our past, unsocialized, menacingly strong and healthy, and seduc-
tively sexy – the quintessential strangers in our midst. With crime and
delinquency as the third-ranking issue of concern to Canadians, after
inflation and unemployment, moral reproduction becomes fertile material
for reconstruction of domination: for repression against threatening boys,
for protection of errant girls.

Contemporary Legislative Responses
for the Control of Our Young: The Young Offenders Act

Partly in response to these issues, many of the provinces introduced some
changes in implementing legislation without the federal Canadian government changing the JDA itself. Among the most touted of the last decade are
police discretion, court diversion, and decarceration from training schools
by alternative community group-home placement. Yet, although there have
been piecemeal administrative changes during the debate, provincial
reluctance has indicated variable and delayed implementation.

Some of these issues were articulated in more general policies regarding
youth; for instance, those regarding the finding that school failure affects
delinquency (West 1984). But, while some reforms were tried in the 1960s
and early 1970s, the last half of the 1970s saw a resurgence of traditional
pedagogies and curricula and retreat of the new. Moreover, these attempted educational reforms only obliquely addressed one key factor that
research identified as precipitating delinquency: the ranking of students
into race-, gender-, and class-bound streams. For schools to succeed (in the
ranking demanded of them by corporations and universities), some students *must* fail.

Legally, many of the worst abuses of sexist, racist, classist, and agist
social oppression through inequities were formally addressed in the last

few decades. Ontario, for instance, introduced legal-aid and duty-counsel lawyers to juvenile courts over the last two decades, so that due process was more encouraged. In revoking section 8 of the Training Schools Act, Ontario ended the practice of allowing dependent children (who may have committed no crime) to be incarcerated. Similarly, the Quebec Youth Protection Act, passed in 1977 and put into effect in 1979, institutionalized diversion of young offenders as well as neglected children (Frechette and Leblanc 1987).

The federal government's parliamentary Committee on Juvenile Delinquency recommended sweeping legal changes in 1965, but three bills had to be introduced before enough support was gained to finally pass the new Young Offenders Act in 1982.

The new Canadian Young Offenders Act has eliminated all status offences from the federal code (e.g., truancy and 'sexual immorality'), confining delinquency to federal crimes. Maximum three-year sentences replaced the former indefinite terms. The new act also provided for administrative review of any special treatment, and the addition of some safeguards in the trial stage, such as the right to legal counsel, stricter rules of evidence and proof, press access, and appeals (Leon 1978: 167). These are combined with the encouragement of screening or diversion procedures. The upper limit of juvenile age was also raised from sixteen to eighteen across the country.

Consequently, sixteen- to eighteen-year-olds are protected against the relative harshness to which adults are subjected, but they also lose those adult rights that are not extended to juveniles. In some sense, the subordinated age group is expanded to older youths. Below age twelve, children lose all vestiges of responsible personhood in being basically deprived of the opportunity for a court trial: they are relegated to the same types of welfare bureaucracies that have so obviously failed to uplift the old, the native peoples, the poor, and the previously delinquent (Schur 1973).

Yet, while potential cost-savings, combined with additional federal revenues, are tempting, strong opposition to these legislative changes has existed both provincially and federally. Police (especially in Toronto) have expressed 'law and order' concerns about legalistic restrictions on pursuit of those under age twelve. The Canadian Mental Health Association and Canadian Corrections Association (mainly comprising social workers, psychiatrists, and criminologists) have claimed that the professional definition of the treatment 'needs' of the young should take precedence over formal legality, while child-welfare organizations seek more adequate government financing for the new programs.

One of the most salient characteristics of juvenile status in Canada has been *denied adulthood*. Young people have been deemed to be of a fundamentally different nature from adults (e.g., immature, dependent, ignorant, frivolous, happy). In our society, young people often are such little outcasts; but we fail to recognize the self-fulfilling, vicious-circle nature of this oppression until we learn that children of other societies and times act much as adults do when they are allowed and expected to (Ariès 1962). In our society, it has become *illegal* for a person under eighteen to, in some instances, act maturely (i.e., as an adult).

Towards a Critical Theory of Legislating Delinquency in the Canadian State

Almost daily, one reads about reform bills, increased police efforts, new school disciplinary measures, and so on. Why are the problems concerning errant youth still with us? How are our attempts at reforms frustrated? Doubtless, moral issues in child care and the rearing of our young are complicated.

Having outlined the social status of children and youth within the Canadian social formation, and sketched the advent of the Juvenile Delinquents Act, it is now time to try to understand these events and situations theoretically. What determined the historically evolving legal status of Canadian young people? Why and how did social and political forces combine to change it? How are we to understand the legal regulation of the young?

An alternative explanation to conservative and liberal offerings regarding juvenile delinquency (which espouse, basically, that youths need either more control or more therapy), contemporary neo-Marxists argue that the social relations of production (see West 1984b) include the production of art, language, and culture in general, not just economic activities narrowly defined. Feminists, in particular, have challenged Marxists by arguing that gender is as fundamental a concept in understanding the organization of human society as is class, that gender cannot simply be reduced to class (e.g., Barrett and McIntosh 1982). Furthermore, we may extend the arguments put forward by feminists and ask whether age is not also an equally fundamental concept (see, e.g., Fitz 1981a, 1981b; Gaffield and West 1978).

The relations of reproduction and production seen as underlying delinquency neither exist naturally nor are maintained without considerable effort. One cannot ignore the central role of the contemporary state in influencing both material conditions and an ideological climate. The state clearly acts as a regulatory mechanism, adjusting economic, educational, and family policies, while responding to popular opinion (which it, not infrequently, has a large hand in manipulating). Power does not simply reside in the economic élite alone, or in 'males in general,' but is articulate in and through other institutional sectors, including the political. The neo-Marxist belief interpretation of the contemporary liberal-democratic capitalist state would suggest that the state functions to maintain business prosperity, ensure social integration through coercion, and maintain order through engendering legitimacy.

It is not necessary to assume a severely reductionist position or to regard the state as directly responsive to the needs of capital. Juvenile-justice policy and wider legislation regarding the rearing of the young have been as concerned with the constitution and reproduction of gender and age relations as with reproducing capital relations (Land 1980; Gavigan 1981; Donzelot 1979; Fitz 1981b). Thus, although the economic system might best be seen as the creator of youth as a problem population, the intervention of the state to create institutions (schools and reformatories) to deal with it provides an example of government attempts to ameliorate contradictions, simultaneously assisting in the accumulation of profit, the engendering of legitimacy, and the exercise of coercion. It would follow, therefore, that Canadian governments have been less concerned with justice and the prevention of delinquency than with maintaining their control and legitimacy by managing youth.

Bourgeois interest and the Canadian state must amalgamate widespread support within a power bloc in order to control mass democratic struggle and continue ruling. The securing of consent is maintained through key political terms that guarantee formal legal equality while deflecting attention from substantive (real or economic) inequality. The mass media are a key site for ideology (Ng 1982) (so are professionally enclosed debates about caring for the proper needs of our young).

But, while analyses of such uses of ideological discourse in moral panics about youth are important, more attention must be paid to the concrete operation of the legal system itself. Internal contradictions within Canadian law have caused recent outspoken discontent over juvenile-delinquency legislation. Class, race, and gender divisions are reconstituted as legal conflicts and welfare problems (Pashukanis 1979.) Although the juvenile-justice system has justified itself as a general advocate to effect positive social change on behalf of troubled youth, it still has almost never moved beyond the traditional liberal attribution of individual guilt and punishment. Such contradictions need to be analysed for specific instances of delinquency and law. The moral panics over juvenile delinquency, coupled with legal concerns for children's rights and the further displacement of the young from the mainstream of Canadian life, have led to renewed attempts to reform juvenile justice during the past two decades. Such policies as diversion represent an attempt by the state to 'save' the liberal notion that each violation not only should be, but can be punished. This assertion is in contrast to self-report studies conclusively indicating there is far too much delinquency for the legal apparatus to deal with (Morton et al 1980).

The contemporary concern with children's rights seems to have taken a similar turn from issues of children's freedom to issues of children's (adult-defined) needs for protection – with, of course, accompanying adult supervisors to regulate erring families. Somehow, what seemed, and some have deemed to be, a revolution in juvenile justice has perhaps turned out to be not even great reform, but more like a century-long trickle-down – to oppressed children (especially from minorities and ethnic immigrants) and their caretakers (especially women) from the professionals in the bureaucracies upon high, which remain overwhelmingly staffed by white, male, North Western-European descendants. The liberal-democratic/bureaucratic solutions to our delinquency problems show few solutions after a century of efforts.

Acknowledgments

Parts of this chapter are vastly condensed and updated versions of material that previously appeared in West (1984a), reprinted here with the permission of Butterworths. In addition to the contribution of so many 'students'/teachers, I would like to thank personally Grant Lowery, of Central Toronto Youth Services, and Mary E. Morton, of Queen's University, who have taught me so much about legislative changes regarding young offenders. Of course, only a few of the above analyses are attributable to any of them: it is our continuing arguments regarding the raising of our 'revolting' young that I so deeply appreciate.

References

Ariès, P. 1962. *Centuries of Childhood*. New York: Random House
Barrett, M., and M. McIntosh. 1982. *The Anti-Social Family*. London: Verso/New Left

Berkeley, H., C. Gaffield, and W.G. West. 1978. *Children's Rights: Legal and Educational Issues*. Toronto: OISE Press

Chunn, D. 1983. 'Social control through the family courts: The reorganization of summary justice in Ontario, 1888–1938.' Paper presented to the Annual Meeting of the Canadian Sociology and Anthropology Association, Vancouver

Committee on Youth. 1971. *It's Your Turn: A Report to the Secretary of State*. Ottawa: Information Canada

Department of Corrections. 1971. *Annual Report*. Toronto: Ontario Department of Corrections

Donzelot, J. 1979. *The Policing of Families*. New York: Random House

Fitz, J. 1981a. 'The child as a legal subject,' in R. Dale, G. Esland, R. Fergusson, and M. MacDonald, eds, *Education and the State*, vol ii: *Politics, Patriarchy, and Practice*, 285–302. Milton Keynes, UK: Open University Press

– 1981b. 'Welfare, the family and the child,' in J. Fitz and J. Shaw, *Education, Welfare, and Social Order*, 7–45. Milton Keynes, UK: Open University Press

Foucault, M. 1977. *Discipline and Punish*. Harmondsworth, UK: Penguin

Frechette, M., and M. Leblanc. 1987. *Délinquances et délinquants*. Chicoutimi, PQ: Gaetan Morin Editeur

Gaffield, C., and W.G. West. 1978. 'Children's rights in the Canadian context,' in H. Berkeley, C. Gaffield, and W.G. West, eds, *Children's Rights: Legal and Educational Issues*, 3–14. Toronto: OISE Press

Gavigan, S.A.M. 1981. 'Marxist theories of law: A survey, with some thoughts on women and law,' *Canadian Criminology Forum* 4 (1): 1–12

Gillis, J.R. 1974. *Youth and History*. New York: Academic

Hackler, J. 1978. *The Prevention of Delinquency: The Great Stumble Forward*. Toronto: Methuen

Houston, S. 1972. 'The Victorian origins of juvenile delinquency,' *History of Education Quarterly* 12: 254–80

Land, H.J. 1980. 'The family wage,' *Feminist Review* 6: 55–77

Leon, J. 1978. 'Children's rights revisited,' in H. Berkeley, C. Gaffield, and W.G. West, eds, *Children's Rights: Legal and Educational Issues*, 35–58. Toronto: OISE Press

Mies, M. 1986. *Patriarchy and Accumulation on a World Scale*. London: Zed

Morton, M., W.G. West, et al. 1980. *A Research Evaluation of the Frontenac Juvenile Diversion Project* Ottawa: Solicitor General

Musgrove, F. 1964. *Youth and the Social Order*. London: Routledge and Kegan Paul

Ng, Y. 1982. 'Ideology, Media and Moral Panics: An Analysis of the Jacques Murder.' MA thesis, Centre of Criminology, University of Toronto

Pashukanis, E. 1979. *Law and Marxism*. London: Ink Links

Prentice, A. 1977. *The School Promoters*. Toronto: McClelland and Stewart

Ratner, R. 1985. 'Inside the liberal boot,' in T. Fleming, ed, *The New Criminologies in Canada*, 13–26. Toronto: Oxford

Schur, E. 1973. *Radical Non-intervention: Rethinking the Delinquency Problem*. Englewood Cliffs, NJ: Prentice-Hall

Sutherland, N. 1976. *Children in English-Canadian Society: Framing the Twentieth-Century Consensus*. Toronto: University of Toronto Press

Visano, L. 1987. *This Idle Trade: The Occupational Patterns of Male Prostitution*. Concord, ON: Vita-sana

Waller, I. 1979. *Selected Trends in Canadian Criminal Justice*. Ottawa: Solicitor General

West, W.G. 1979. 'Serious thieves: Lower class adolescent males in a short-term deviant occupation,' in E. Vaz and A. Lodhi, eds, *Crime and Delinquency in Canada*, 247–69. Scarborough, ON: Prentice-Hall

– 1984a. *Young Offenders and the State: A Canadian Perspective on Delinquency*. Toronto: Butterworths

– 1984b. 'Phenomenon and form in interactionist and neo-Marxist ethnography,' in L. Barton and S. Walker, eds, *Social Crisis and Educational Research*, 256–87. London: Croom Helm

2 A theoretical understanding of current Canadian juvenile-justice policy

Susan Reid-MacNevin

> One cannot change a law, enforce it, ignore it, or enact any form of our collective enterprise without starting a chain of events, many of which are bound to be undesirable. (Nettler 1974: 62)

> ... the problem of designing an effective and humane system for the future is not a question of not knowing what to do or in which directions we must turn ... The problem is, that in taking those steps, we must impinge upon a network of political, professional and bureaucratic relationships now so deeply imbedded as to make the very notion of basic change sound revolutionary. (Miller 1979: 103)

When one attempts to analyse shifts in social policy, a paradox concerning the way in which the problem is defined and dealt with is readily apparent: reforms may appear to present a radical shift in orientation to the problem, but there is also a considerable degree of stability and changelessness. For example, it is easy to criticize the Victorian 'child-savers' in the drafting of the first Canadian juvenile-justice legislation, Juvenile Delinquents Act (JDA) (RSC, C. J-3), for their lack of scientific data to support their policy assertions. However, the legislation that replaced the 1908 JDA as recently as 1984, the Young Offenders Act (YOA) (SC, 1981–82–83, c.110), while based on a carefully considered theoretical analysis, still does not provide clear guidance on the amelioration, treatment, or control of youthful crime in Canada. While reforms through history have often been considered as attempts to eradicate the problems of youth crime and criminality, it is important to remember that, despite such a lofty aim, the elimination of these problems would infringe upon a whole network of socio-political groups and professionals. Rather, reforms should be seen as a reflection of the attitudes and beliefs of society regarding the most appropriate means of dealing with young offenders. In order more clearly to delineate the ambiguity present within the Young Offenders Act, the discussion will address four ideological perspectives or models of juvenile justice: community change, welfare, justice, and crime control. The approach to the young offender regarding the etiology of his or her criminal conduct, the purpose of disposing of the young offender through the juvenile-justice system, and the type of disposition most preferred under each of the models will be discussed. This background will provide a basis for an analysis of the difficulties facing professionals in delivering services to young persons who come in contact with the law, as well as suggest some implications regarding the 'unintended' consequences of the new federal legislation for young offenders.

Juvenile Justice in Canada: A Brief Overview

Leon (1977) suggests that the reformers responsible for the development of the Juvenile Delinquents Act (1980) were as much concerned with sociopolitical factors as with the humanitarian concerns of protecting children from the harsh, adult criminal-justice system. He argues that the development of the Juvenile Delinquents Act was the result of a 'diverse' reform movement that was involved in 'rescuing' children from what were perceived to be the harmful effects of life in an increasingly urbanized and industrialized society (1977: 72).

The former JDA was philosophically grounded in the doctrine of *parens patriae*, which held that the state could intervene as a 'kindly parent' in those cases where the family was unable to provide for the 'needs' of their offspring. While this philosophy might be seen as a humanitarian gesture on the part of the new juvenile court to ensure the 'care' of young persons who came in contact with the law, the tenets of this approach provided enormous discretion to the professionals who were entrusted to deliver services to young offenders. *Parens patriae* was used as a 'legal bridge between the troubled child and the agencies of amelioration' (Faust and Brantingham 1974: 552).

Much controversy surrounded the lack of procedural safeguards for youth under the Juvenile Delinquents Act (Gandy 1971; MacDonald 1971; Catton and Leon 1977; Justice for Children 1981, 1983; Marshall and Thomas 1983). In many instances, there was little if any relationship between the disposition or sentence imposed and the offence that was committed. Intervention with youth was based on the assumption that 'professionals' within the juvenile-justice system had some body of theory or 'superior expertise' that could justify placing the offender's needs over his or her legal rights (Cousineau and Veevers 1972: 256).

The contradictions and injustices for youth under the Juvenile Delinquents Act led to extensive consultation and discussion regarding the nature and purpose of the juvenile-justice system over a twenty-five-year period until the Young Offenders Act was proclaimed in April 1984. While maintaining the welfare notion of the *parens patriae* doctrine of the Juvenile Delinquents Act, the Young Offenders Act also attempts to meet the competing interests of the youth, the larger society, and the professionals entrusted to 'care' for and 'control' youth who come under their jurisdiction. The Young Offenders Act is an attempt to balance the responsibility that young persons must bear for their criminal conduct with the rights of society and the special needs and rights of individual youth. The YOA also acknowledges the responsibility of the community to take reasonable measures in the prevention and control of youthful crime.

This combination of philosophical perspectives has been applauded by a number of commentators as being a more balanced system of juvenile justice (Kaplan 1982; Wilson 1982; Archambault 1983; Nasmith 1983; Lilles 1983). This positive interpretation should, however, be considered with caution. While the extremes of any one perspective are avoided, as was the case with the welfare approach of the former JDA, the inclusion of a variety of ideological perspectives without a clear understanding of the priority to be taken in dealing with criminal offences committed by youth may create even more tension and conflict between and among juvenile-justice practitioners. While the combined ideological orientation of the legislation calls for a 'delicate balancing act by the court' (Nasmith 1983: 10), a lack of stated priority within the principles may further enhance the discretion, influence, and power already held by juvenile-justice practitioners.

The Influence of Ideology on the Development of Social Policy for Young Offenders

According to Dror (1971), social policy is most concerned with issues of social control. However, when on considers social policy in relation to young offenders, there has always been a blurring of social-control and welfare concerns (Shichor 1980; Higgins 1980; Yelaja 1978; Lerman 1977; Kassebaum 1974). Rein (1976: 16) suggests that, by examining the beliefs and assumptions, or ideologies, that direct any given social policy, the dual and often contradictory functions of social control and welfare may be

delineated. Such an analysis can be seen as integral to a clearer understanding of the intended and unintended consequences of any new social
policy (Gil 1976: 34).

Pisciotta (1981: 118) suggests that adherents to various ideological
perspectives within the criminal-justice system differ in the assumptions
they make about: 1 / the purpose of law enforcement, the courts, and
correctional institutions; 2 / the origin and purpose of laws; 3 / the definition of the criminal or delinquent; 4 / the nature and accuracy of
criminal statistics; 5 / the motivation and results of the actions of reformers, legislators, and correctional administrators; 6 / the perception of
capitalist society; and 7 / recommendations given for humanizing and
improving the criminal-justice system. Similarly, Reid (1964) suggests that,
within any human-service organization, there are two levels of philosophical orientation; he distinguishes between 'general ideological goals,' which
have been stated in 'official declarations,' and 'operational goals,' which
guide the activities and programs of agencies involved in the implementation of services. Hassenfeld and English (1974) argue that explicit
'service ideologies' develop within human-service organizations that are
used by agency personnel to bring order, coherence, and legitimation to
their day-to-day activities. By way of summary, then, there appear to be
three levels of guiding assumptions regarding the implementation of social
policy affecting young offenders: 1 / the stated philosophy as declared in
the legislation; 2 / the translation of the stated philosophy into program
goals and objectives; and 3 / the ideological orientation of the professionals responsible for delivering service to young offenders.

There are two major orientations regarding beliefs about human nature
and the social order as they relate to criminal behaviour that could be
placed on a perspectival continuum with opposing poles. Such a dichot-
omy has been labelled by a number of commentators as: conservative right
versus socialist left (Miller 1973); residual versus institutional (Wilensky
and Lebeaux 1965: 138–40); anti-collectivist versus collectivist (George and
Wilding 1976: 21, 62); and order/functionalist/liberal versus conflict/
dialectical/Marxist (West 1984: 15; Hagan and Leon 1977; Marchak 1975).

These various perspectives can perhaps best be explained in terms of
four theoretical models of juvenile-justice procedure, namely, the crime-
control model, the justice model, the welfare model, and the community-
change model (Reid and Reitsma-Street 1984). Much of the criticism of the
former JDA was levelled at the relative ineffectiveness of the 'rehabilitative
ideal' or treatment approach taken under the welfare model. While the YOA
retains the position that young persons require guidance and assistance,

as coined in the welfare approach, the provisions for 'treatment' under the YOA follow more precise rules and procedures, which can be seen as associated with the justice model. Under the justice model, it is argued that a humane system of juvenile justice requires treatment services for those individuals who wish to participate in them rather than services that are forced on unwilling 'clients.' There are also provisions within the YOA that are derived from the crime-control model. The crime-control model is based on the belief that the 'rehabilitative ideal' has resulted in the 'coddling' of offenders and has left society severely victimized. In order to ameliorate the situation, proponents of the crime-control model argue that young offenders should be held accountable for their transgressions. In an attempt to further balance the focus of the YOA on a variety of approaches, the YOA includes provisions from the community-change model. This model suggests that 'treatment' is merely another piecemeal reform that encourages the abuses of power already existing in the juvenile-justice system. The emphasis, according to this perspective, should be placed on activities that strengthen communities, to bring about dramatic social change throughout the wider society.

Four Models of Juvenile-Justice Procedure

These four models of juvenile-justice procedure can also be viewed as falling on a continuum with polar dichotomies; the community-change model falls on the radical or extreme-left ideological position, while the crime-control model falls at the conservative or extreme-right position. The welfare and justice models vie for a middle ideological position, with the welfare model lying more to the left and the justice model lying more to the right. Each of these models will be analysed in more detail below.

Community- or Societal-Change Model

The community-change model perceives the roots of youthful crime as determined by forces beyond the control of the individual. In the extreme, this orientation assumes that the 'primary responsibility for criminal behaviour lies in the conditions of the social order rather than in the characteristics of the individual' (Miller 1973: 144). The major socializing agents for youth – the family, the school, and the neighbourhood – are seen to be significantly influenced by the norms that are developed and differentially applied by the political, economic, and social ruling class (Reid and Reitsma-Street 1984: 4). Krisberg and Austin (1978: 1) argue that society is plagued with crime and delinquency because offenders form a subservient class that is alienated, powerless, and prone to economic manipulation. In the case of youthful offenders, such economic alienation is further accentuated as they are virtually removed from economic participation in the wider society by their age and lack of educational or vocational credentials to qualify for employment. Chambliss (1975: 152) argues that 'crime is a reaction to the life conditions of a person's social class.' Following this line of reasoning with respect to young offenders, the community-change model would suggest that, as a result of the alienation of youth from the economic sector of the wider society, their behaviour is merely a reaction to the circumstances of their lower-class 'life' in the school system and wider community, which are 'ruled' by middle-class administrators and public officials.

Proponents of this approach would dispel any attempts to 'correct' the offender, arguing that, unless there is an overall change within society, little can be accomplished through reforms aimed at changing individual offenders (Chambliss 1974, 1975; Quinney 1977; Krisberg 1977). While radical criminologists adhering to this ideology position would argue for the use of political activism in bringing about a complete restructuring of the capitalist system (Turk 1969), Miller (1973: 144) sees the potential of taking short-term measures that can ameliorate the situation without a major social revolution. He argues that increased local control in the community through a decentralization of power and more citizen involvement are steps that would assist in decreasing the abuses of power of the ruling class.

The aim of policies based on the community-change model, then, is to change the very processes that lead to inequality, poverty, and youthful crime by promoting the welfare of all individuals. The u.s. President's Commission on Law Enforcement and the Administration of Justice (1967) recognized the value of this perspective by making strong recommendations with respect to reintegrating offenders back into mainstream society. The recommendations clearly indicated a preference for community-based corrections over the use of 'fortress-like' institutions to incarcerate offenders. The main objectives of such recommendations were to provide opportunities for the offender to build or rebuild 'solid ties' with the family and the wider community through education, training, and employment (u.s. President's Commission 1967: 7). The commission recognized the dual responsibilities of both the community and the offender required to implement such recommendations. The attitudes of citizens in the community must change in order to accommodate the reintegration of offenders. Similarly, offenders must learn how to effectively utilize community resources and supports (u.s. President's Commission 1967: 7). The commission also recommended that custodial dispositions be limited to the few, serious offenders who pose a threat to society. When incapacitation was necessary, it was strongly recommended that the institutions provide a variety of educational and vocational programs to facilitate community reintegration upon release (u.s. President's Commission 1967: 7).

In the principle of the yoa, subsection 3(1)(b) states: '[Society] has the responsibility to take reasonable measures to prevent criminal conduct.' This phrase is clearly indicative of the tenets of the community model (Reid and Reitsma-Street 1984). Similarly, when one examines the disposition section of the yoa (*viz.* s. 20), there is also a strong emphasis on community-based alternatives to incarceration. Perhaps the most important implication of this emphasis on the community within the yoa is that it alerts the 'experts' within the juvenile-justice system to their public accountability. This accountability is exemplified by the fact that, while young-offender proceedings are confidential (*viz.* s. 38), they are no longer held in camera but are open to public scrutiny, with a few minor exceptions delineated in section 39.

Welfare Model

The welfare or family model (Griffiths 1970) is founded on the positivist school of criminology, which assumes that young offenders commit offences as a result of factors that are beyond their control. In its infancy, the welfare model drew heavily on the medical model, which assumed that delinquency was a manifestation or symptom of an illness (MacNamara 1977). Perhaps the best example of this orientation is found in the guiding philosophy of the former jda, in section 38, which states: 'every juvenile delinquent shall be treated, not as criminal, but as a misdirected and misguided child, and one needing aid, encouragement, help and assistance.'

Proponents of this ideological orientation argue that there are criminogenic factors indigenous to the individual young offender and that it is by 'doing something for, to, or with him [or her] that rehabilitation can be affected' (MacNamara 1977: 440). In terms of the preferred intervention, then, proponents of this view do not see the need for a determinant sentence as long as the professionals who are working with the troubled youth are 'treating' the problem (Wyman 1977). In order to fully understand the criminogenic conditions that prompted the display of the 'state of delinquency,' it is necessary to carefully assess all of the psychological and social variables related to both the offender and his or her environment. Once such a comprehensive examination has been conducted, an individualized treatment plan, or disposition, can be created to match the changing needs and circumstances of the young person.

While the validity of the medical model has been negated by a number of individuals in the field (MacNamara 1977), the rehabilitative philosophy of the welfare model continues to show prominence in the field of juvenile justice. Bartollas and Miller (1978) suggest that, while offenders may not be able to alter the social or emotional deprivations of their past, they can be shown that their negative attitudes, maladjustive behaviour, and inappropriate interpersonal relationships at present interfere with their ability to live a crime-free life. Proponents of this view concentrate their efforts through a variety of therapeutic-community approaches and variations of behaviour modification to help young offenders cope more effectively with their personal problems, peers, family situation, and wider community. Like that of the earlier medical model, this focus emphasizes a broad legal definition of criminal behaviour, with considerable discretion and power granted to 'experts' who make decisions regarding the most suitable treatment for the young offender.

The guiding principle of the YOA, as mentioned, retains a number of the tenets of the welfare model, which was paramount under the former JDA. For example, subsection 3(1)(c) states that, because of a young offender's 'state of dependency and level of development and maturity,' she or he also has 'special needs and require[s] guidance and assistance.' This focus on the special needs of a youth who comes in conflict with the law is also exemplified in other phrases within the principle section that stress the importance of 'special guarantees' of a young person's rights (s. 3[1][e]), reduced accountability and responsibility (s. 3[1][a]), and the provision for alternative measures from formal judicial proceedings (s. 3[1][d]). Also in line with the tenets of the 'family model' is the emphasis within the principle section of the YOA on the best 'interests' of the young person's family (s. 3[1][f]) and the responsibility ascribed to parents 'for the care and supervision of their children' (s. 3[1][h]).

While the YOA has replaced the much-criticized indeterminant sentence of the former JDA with determinant dispositions, the emphasis on the social history of the youth with respect to the provisions regarding predisposition reports (s. 14) is very much a part of decisions related to custodial placements. While a predisposition report is mandatory only in cases where the youth court is considering custody, there have been a number of documented cases where the youth-court judge has requested such social histories for less serious offences.

Justice Model

The justice or 'due process' model (Packer 1964; Catton 1975) is based on the assumption of an equal balance of the rights of society to protection from criminal behaviour and the rights of the individual charged to fair treatment under the law. Many of the injustices created through the single-focused view based on the 'rehabilitative ideal' under the former JDA raised a number of questions regarding the discretionary power granted to 'experts' within the juvenile-justice system. Fogel and Hudson (1981: viii) elucidate this perspective by arguing that if it cannot be shown that treatment is reliable, 'we can at least be fair, reasonable, humane and constitutional in practice.'

Unlike the community-change and welfare models, the justice model is premised on the belief that the young person has volition and free will and is therefore responsible for his or her actions (Schafer 1974). Viewed in this way, offenders are seen to deserve punishment, or their 'just desserts,' if they violate the law. Punishment under this model is not determined according to the offender's needs, but rather is based upon the penalties he or she deserves for the act (Von Hirsh 1976: 98). The justice model sees the imposition of treatment as an infringement on the offender's rights and questions the rationale, methodology, and coerciveness of the reha-bilitative focus espoused by proponents of the welfare model. Fogel (1979: 227) claims that agents of the criminal-justice system abuse the power they are granted over citizens by denying them due-process rights. He argues that 'one of the most fruitful ways to teach the non–law-abiders to be law-abiding is to treat them in a law-abiding manner' (Fogel 1979: 204). The concept of 'justice-as-fairness' insists upon procedural safeguards to reduce capricious and arbitrary discretion by 'experts' within the juvenile-justice system. Such safeguards include provisions for a fair, open trial; an opportunity for legal counsel; and all of the challenges and appeals provided in the adult system of criminal justice. To compensate for the age of the young person, proponents of the justice model recommend adoption of diminished responsibility and accountability for the young person, the use of additional adult assistance throughout the trial process, and proportionately lighter sentences than those that would be meted out for an adult (Reid and Reitsma-Street 1984: 3).

While it was pointed out that diminished responsibilty and reduced accountability are tenets of the welfare model, these notions also tie in with the framework of the justice model. The philosophy of the YOA incorporates additional guide-lines with respect to the provision of guarantees of the youth's rights, including the right to the 'least possible interference with freedom' (s. 3[1][f]). The YOA also provides for a variety of other 'special guarantees,' such as the right to appeal (s. 27), the right to have a review of the disposition imposed (ss. 28–34), the right to counsel without delay in all proceedings affecting the young person (s. 11), and insistence upon consent of the young person with respect to treatment (s. 22 [1]).

Crime-Control Model

The crime-control model (Packer 1964; Horton 1981) is primarily concerned with the maintenance of order within society. Laws are designed to attach criminal sanctions and punishment to any behaviour that is perceived to be immoral or threatening to the collective social order. Social defence, deterrence, retribution, and punishment are seen as essential justifications for the use of criminal procedures, with such proceedings being weighted in favour of the interests of society rather than the individual offender (Van den Haag 1975). Proponents of this view, like those who adhere to the ideological orientation of the justice model, believe individuals are volitional and freely choose to violate the law. However, the crime-control model is premised on the social utility of punishment rather than on a 'just desserts' philosophy. A youth is seen as a 'miniature adult' who freely chooses to engage in disapproved conduct and thereby poses a threat to society (Reid and Reitsma-Street 1984: 3).

Like the welfare model, the crime-control model is based on laws that are flexible and broad, with little opportunity for procedural challenge. The process of apprehension, fact-finding, adjudication, and disposition is swift and efficient, utilizing both informal and routine procedures. Proponents of this model suggest that, if treatment or rehabilitation has not proved to be effective in improving offenders, society can be assured that incarceration will remove criminals from mainstream society and will attempt to deter others from committing offences (Conrad 1981: 157). The lack of evidence in support of the rehabilitation of offenders forms the corner-stone of the ideological stance taken by the law-and-order advocates of the crime-control model. While Wilson (1975: 172) urged that the rehabilitative theory of sentencing be abandoned, he did point out that 'experiments with new correctional and therapeutic procedures' should be continued and expanded when they have been shown to be less 'costly and more humane while still providing reasonable security.' The main focus for the proponents of the crime-control model appears to be that offenders should be treated in a punitive manner. Wilson (1977: 110) indicates that 'prisons and jails are not intended to be pleasant places ... the level of amenity there must always be less than its level in society at large or else people outside will envy those inside and perhaps even try to break into prison.'

With respect to the guiding philosophy of the YOA, there are a number of phrases that also address the tenets of the crime-control model. Subsection 3(1)(b) clearly states that 'society must ... be afforded the necessary protection from illegal behaviour.' Further, subsections 3(1)(d) and (f), while addressing welfare and justice issues related to the youth's age and stage of development and his or her right to the least possible interference with freedom, also include the phrase 'that is not inconsistent with the protection of society.' While the YOA does not include provisions for minimum sentences, as is the case under the Criminal Code (RSC 1985, C. c-46), there are clear parameters to deal with more serious offenders with regard to the transfer of the young person to adult court (s. 16) as well as the provisions regarding detention (ss. 7–8) and secure-custody dispositions (s. 24).

The main tenets of each of the four models discussed are summarized in table 1.

Implications of the Contradictions of Four Models of Juvenile-Justice Procedure

The foregoing discussion has outlined the contradictory tenets of the four models of juvenile-justice procedure. It was also shown that the YOA contains elements of each of these models, both in the guiding philosophy and in the more substantive aspects of the legislation. At the outset of this discussion, it was pointed out that the JDA was not based on a carefully considered theoretical approach and that this lack of attention to such issues led to inconsistencies and injustices within the juvenile-justice system. The carefully considered provisions of the YOA are based on a theoretical analysis of the essential components of a juvenile-justice system that provides something for everyone. Miller (1979: 102), in discussing the necessary elements of a 'more humane' juvenile-justice system, draws upon the research of Ohlin et al (1978), who suggest that such a system should:

TABLE 1
Assumptions of the four models of juvenile justice

Community change	Welfare	Justice	Crime control
–main tenet is that society is responsible for the promotion of the welfare of its citizens and must work to prevent crime and delinquency	–main tenet is that the needs of the young person and his or her family must be attended to	–main tenet is that interference with freedom is limited and procedures are based on consent as much as possible	–main tenet is that it is the responsibility of the state and the courts to maintain order in society
–youth behaviour is seen as being determined by life conditions	–youth behaviour is seen as being determined by social/psychological forces	–youth behaviour is seen as freely determined	–youth behaviour is seen as freely determined
–focus on collective society rather than the individual youth as being responsible for criminal conduct	–focus on criminal conduct as being part and parcel of social events	–focus on the repression of crime with a qualification that there is a high probability of error in informal fact-finding	–focus on repression of criminal conduct
–focus on changing social processes that lead young people to engage in criminal conduct and to improve the quality of life	–focus on evaluation of whole youth and his or her life circumstances	–focus on the formal adversarial system	–focus on screening process that diverts innocent out of the courts
–offences are unspecified prior to occurrences	–offences are unspecified and young person is brought to court to be aided and assisted		–offences are specific and defined prior to their occurrence

1 / follow the principle of the least restrictive alternative consonant with public safety; 2 / stress support to the family; 3 / provide residential care in the most family-life setting possible; 4 / establish strong community linkages for all group-living situations; 5 / make secure custody an alternative of last resort; and 6 / apply the definition of 'dangerous' or 'in need of care' only when all other avenues have been exhausted. The principles and provisions with the YOA seem to have addressed these essential components and, thereby, to have followed through on the research evidence available. However, the lack of priority in the assumptions and principles of the legislation does not provide any points of resolution for individuals and bureaucracies responsible for the day-to-day implementation of the act. Since the principles offer a rationale or justification for every possible direction, it is highly likely that factors other than the 'best interests' of either the young offender or society will take precedence. Rather, such factors as bureaucracies' access to funding and resources as well as the individual ideologies of the practising professional are more likely to be given a higher priority than is the implementation of the theoretical premise of the principles of the act.

Miller (1979: 98) indicates that the juvenile-justice system operates under both 'manifest' and 'latent' functions. Manifest functions include those items that justify the existence of the system, such as the philosophical tenets of law and order, public safety or child welfare, and proper treatment or rehabilitation. Latent functions are seen as much more mundane concerns, such as employment in remote areas, political patronage, contracts with vendors for services, arrangement between specific institutions and courts, and the self-interests of professional and custodial groups. Harris and Webb (1987: 66) argue that the 'politicians, civil servants, law officers, academics, judges, barristers, social workers and the like whose status and identity depend on their being experts in a subject in which they are persistently unable to make advances' must be maintained under the rhetoric of criminal-justice reform so that 'success' is not achieved at the expense of eliminating the bureaucratic interests of socio-political groups. The conflict and contradiction, as espoused in law and by individuals' ideological orientations, may serve to further the bureaucratic machinery of the juvenile-justice system. Foucault (1977: 272) argues that, while the prison fails to eliminate crime, one should not expect reformers to eliminate this expensive and inhumane system, as it has been extremely successful in producing delinquency.

In addition to the ambiguity and vagueness of the legislation, there is also the problem of a lack of a firm knowledge base, technology, and any agreed-upon criteria of success or failure regarding the most appropriate interventions with offenders throughout the criminal-justice system (Cohen 1985: 164). Despite a plethora of literature regarding correctional intervention (Gendreau 1981; Ross and Gendreau 1980; Palmer 1983; Garrett 1985; Gendreau and Ross 1987), it is almost impossible to predict what intervention will work under what circumstance (Wyman 1977). Perhaps it is this ambiguity in the status of knowledge that further entrenches the contradictions and inconsistencies within the juvenile-justice system as professionals are freed from simple accountability. Harris and Webb (1987: 4) point out that the lack of accountability is promoted through a constant enforcement of such notions as 'professional values,' 'confidentiality,' 'self-determination,' and 'professional opinion,' which, once expressed, is 'notoriously immune to close examination.' They argue that a lack of homogeneity of purpose among juvenile-justice practitioners, themselves, reinforces conflicting abstraction of such concepts of care and control, deterrence and rehabilitation, welfare and justice. This diversity ensures that the juvenile-justice system continues to seek professional advice and thereby promotes the vested interests of the various professional groups. Harris and Webb (1987: 5) state that 'if simplicity, lucidity and unambiguity were possible in the supervision of young offenders, there would not be any need to have the professionals: lowly paid functionaries would do the job very much better.' While ambiguities lead to a variety of uncertainties regarding 'professional judgment,' such ambiguities also provide the professionals with considerable power and discretion, which allow them to operate with an extraordinary degree of freedom.

Harris and Webb (1987: 9) suggest that the juvenile-justice system 'exists as a function of the child care and criminal justice systems on either side of it, a meeting place of two otherwise separate worlds.' They suggest that by humanizing the juvenile-justice system and 'blurring the boundaries between the delinquent and non-delinquent young,' the nexus of state control over the young has been substantially expanded (1987: 13). Cohen (1985) concurs with this notion, indicating that, by making the system appear less harsh, professionals are encouraged to use it more often. Further, he argues that, rather than slowing down the career of delinquency, 'each benevolent intermediate option ... facilitates, promotes and accelerates it by making each consecutive decision easier to take' (p. 98).

The discretion of professionals in interpreting vague and ambiguous legislation for young offenders has been evidenced in England after the passage of the Children and Young Persons Act in 1969. Harris and Webb (1987: 5) point out that the plethora of theories available to account for the etiology of youthful crime merely serve to justify professional actions. With no one 'right answer,' ideological preferences of the various professionals may take precedence, with decisions being 'determined arbitrarily and explained post hoc by reference to almost any convenient theoretical justification for the action selected.' Parker et al (1980: 236) suggest that ambiguity in legislation simply provides for enhanced diversity and dissonance as the various practitioners 'vie for influence and tilt decisions towards their own ideological and organizational preference.' The variety of theoretical approaches embodied in the Young Offenders Act while seen by many as a positive feature of the new legislation, may further promote the ambiguity and contradictions that have always existed within the juvenile-justice system.

The continuation of such ambiguity under the YOA has been reported by a number of individuals during the initial phases of implementation over the past four years. Judge Bennett (1985) suggests that, while the YOA provides a philosophical base for ensuring that youth who need extra guidance and supervision receive such help, the practice within the family courts is quite different. Rather than diverting the former 'good kids' away from the juvenile-justice system, he suggests, such youth are much more easily identified, charged, and more likely to plead guilty. The 'real criminal types' which the crime-control provisions of the legislation were intended to address, 'cover their tracks better,' insisting on their 'right to counsel at every stage of the proceedings' and thereby causing problems with investigations and subsequent bottle-necks in the system. He goes on to strongly suggest that family courts are perhaps better described as 'M.A.S.H.' units, as the likelihood of 'straightening out' the youth who are most in need of extra help is long removed as a result of the delays in the court proceedings (Bennett 1985: 18).

Kirvan (1987) points out that the YOA retains the belief that young persons have special needs, from the standpoint both of adolescents as a collective group and of a subgroup of adolescents who may be suffering from such problems as a physical or mental illness or disorder, a psychological disorder, or a learning disability. She goes on to indicate, however, that guide-lines for procedural fairness must be carefully adhered to in considering a treatment disposition. She cautions that 'care must be taken to ensure that the special needs of a young person do not result in a more onerous disposition than one which is commensurate with the offence' and suggests that specific special needs should be addressed outside of the criminal law 'once a disposition commensurate with the offence has been satisfied' (Kirvan 1987: 25). In practice, it appears that the courts are, in fact, assuming that such special needs should be dealt with outside of the criminal law because of the reticence on the part of the court to order a treatment disposition (Weiler and Ward 1986; Leschied and Jaffe 1986). Leschied and Hyatt (1986) report that only five orders for treatment under subsection 22(1)(l) were given as dispositions during the first year of YOA implementation. Two of these five dispositional orders were terminated when the youth withdrew consent. While the YOA has made strides in ensuring that the disposition imposed is consonant with the seriousness of the offence committed, the data regarding the implementation of the new legislation indicate that the justice and crime-control provisions may be taking precedence over the more welfare-oriented provisions of the act. Leschied and Gendreau (1986: 316) argue that the thrust towards 'justice' for young offenders has 'signalled the advent of proceduralism which ... stripped the juvenile court of its intended purpose to service young offenders, leaving the system with a miniature criminal court duplicating adult court.' Weiler and Ward 1986: 7519) provide evidence that programs for sixteen- and seventeen-year-olds under the YOA are simply modified versions of children's and adults' services. They suggest that 'we are apparently a long way away from recognizing that Canada has reformed juvenile justice in a fundamental way and that neither the former JDA nor the current adult system provides the experience and models on which to build.'

The lack of a stated priority in the principle of the YOA provides an outlet for the continuation of such ambiguity and diversity of professional groups within the juvenile-justice system. In addition, this lack of direction in legislative mandate encourages the reliance on professional judgment at the local level. While a priority in the principal or guiding philosophy of the act would at least provide some direction for juvenile-justice practition-ers in local communities, the problem still remains regarding what the stated priority should be. Reid and Reitsma-Street (1984: 13) suggest that, without a priority in the principles of the legislation the mandatory justice provisions may be honoured in form, but the crime-control provisions will be stressed in practice. They go on to suggest that 'formal court proceed-ings, fines, probation and custodial dispositions will take precedence over more welfare-oriented proceedings' (1984: 13). The reason for such a direction, they suggest, is related to the amount of flexibility, creativity, and time required to implement and develop community-change and welfare-oriented dispositions, with crime-control and justice alternatives being much more expeditious with respect to human resources.

The rhetoric will undoubtedly continue to reflect the tension between proponents of rehabilitation and punishment, with the bureaucracies and political constituencies continuing to debate their salient concerns. Whether the 'visionaries' quest for truly progressive juvenile justice legislation in Canada' (Leschied and Jaffe 1986: 321) will ever materialize can be speculated upon only in light of a tense struggle over ideological perspectives both in the stated philosophy and within individual juvenile-justice bureaucracies at the local level. Rather than a compromise and balancing of the somewhat contradictory principles of the legislation, it may be that the yoa will be interpreted primarily by standard operating procedures at the local level. It is argued that the latent functions of the juvenile-justice system, as reflected in the struggle to access funding and resources, will, in the end, be the means by which guidance and interpretation of the philosophy regarding care and control of young offenders in Canada will be made.

References

Archambault, O. 1983. 'Young Offenders Act: Philosophy and principles,' *Provincial Judges Journal* 7 (2): 1–20

Bartollas, C., and S.J. Miller. 1978. *The Juvenile Offender: Control, Correction, and Treatment*. Boston: Holbrook Press

Bennett, J.F. (Judge). 1985. 'Concerns about the Young Offenders Act,' *Provincial Judges Journal* 8 (4): 17–19

Catton, K. 1975. 'Models of procedure and the juvenile courts,' *Criminal Law Quarterly* 18: 181–201

Catton, K., and J. Leon. 1977. 'Legal representation and the proposed young persons in conflict with the law act,' *Osgoode Hall Law Journal* 15: 107–24

Chambliss, W.J. 1974. 'Functional and conflict theories of crime,' *MSS Modular Publications* 17: 1–23

– 1975. 'Toward a political economy of crime,' *Theory and Society* 2 (2): 149–70

Cohen, S. 1985. *Visions of Social Control*. New York: Oxford University Press

Conrad, J.P. 1981. *Justice and Consequences*. Lexington, MA: D.C. Heath

Cousineau, D.F., and J.E. Veevers. 1972. 'Juvenile justice: An analysis of the Canadian Young Offenders Act,' in C.L. Boydell et al, eds, *Deviant Behaviour and Societal Reaction*, 243–61. Toronto: Holt, Rinehart and Winston

Dror, Y. 1971. *Public Policy Making Re-examined*. Scranton, OH: Chandler

Empey, L.T. 1978. *American Delinquency: Its Meaning and Construction*. Homewood, IL: Dorsey

Faust, F.L., and P.J. Brantingham. *Juvenile Justice Philosophy*. St Paul, MN: West

Fogel, D. 1979. *We Are the Living Proof: The Justice Model for Corrections*, 2nd ed. Cincinnati: Anderson

Fogel, D., and J. Hudson, eds. 1981. *Justice as Fairness: Perspectives on the Justice Model*. Cincinnati: Anderson

Foucault, M. 1977. *Discipline and Punish*. Harmondsworth, UK: Allen Lane

Gandy, J.M. 1971. 'Rehabilitation and treatment programs in the juvenile court,' *Canadian Journal of Criminology* 13 (1): 9–23

Garrett, C.J. 1985. 'Effects of residential treatment on adjudicated delinquents: A meta-analysis,' *Journal of Research in Crime and Delinquency* 22: 287–308

Gendreau, P. 'Treatment in corrections: Martinson was wrong,' *Canadian Psychology* 22: 332–8

Gendreau, P., and R.R. Ross. 1987. 'Revivification of rehabilitation: Evidence from the 1980's,' *Justice Quarterly* 4 (3): 349–408

George, V., and P. Wilding. 1976. *Ideology and Social Welfare*. Boston: Little Brown

Gil, D. 1976. *Unravelling Social Policy*. Cambridge, MA: Schenkman

Griffiths, J. 1970. 'Ideology in criminal procedure or a third model of the criminal process,' *Yale Law Journal* 79: 359

Hagan, J., and J. Leon. 1977. 'Rediscovering delinquency: Social history, political ideology and the sociology of law,' *American Sociological Review* 42: 587–98

Harris, R., and D. Webb. 1987. *Welfare, Power and Juvenile Justice: The Social Control of Delinquent Youth*. London: Tavistock

Hassenfeld, Y., and R.A. English. 1974. *Human Service Organizations*. Ann Arbor, MI: University of Michigan Press

Higgins, J. 1980. 'Social control theories of social policy,' *Journal of Social Policy* 9: 1–23

Horton, J. 1981. 'The rise of the right,' *Crime and Social Justice* 15: 7–17

Justice for Children. 1981. *Brief on the* Young Offenders Act, *Bill C-61*. Toronto: Canadian Foundation for Children and the Law

– 1982. *Response to Ontario Consultation Paper on Implementing Bill C-61*, Young Offenders Act. Toronto: Canadian Foundation for Children and the Law

Kaplan, R. 1982. *Highlights of the Young Offenders Act*. Ottawa: Ministry of the Solicitor General, Canada

Kassebaum, G. 1974. *Delinquency and Social Policy*. Englewood Cliffs, NJ: Prentice-Hall

Kirvan, M.A. 1987. 'Commentary on the implications of the *Young Offenders Act* for treatment and rehabilitation,' *Provincial Judges Journal* 11 (3): 18–27

Krisberg, B. 1977. 'Gang youth and hustling: The psychology of survival,' *Issues in Criminology* 9: 115–29

Krisberg, B., and J. Austin. 1978. *The Children of Ishmael*. Palo Alto, CA: Mayfield

Leon, J. 1977. 'The development of Canadian juvenile justice: A background for reform,' *Osgoode Hall Law Journal* 15: 71–106

Lerman, P. 1975. *Community Treatment and Social Control: A Critical Analysis of Juvenile Correctional Policy*. Chicago: University of Chicago Press

Leschied, A., and P. Gendreau. 1986. 'The declining role of rehabilitation in Canadian juvenile justice: Implications of underlying theory and the Young Offenders Act,' *Canadian Journal of Criminology* 28 (3): 315–22

Leschied, A., and C. Hyatt. 1986. 'Perspective Section 22(1): Consent to treatment order under the Young Offenders Act,' *Canadian Journal of Criminology* 8(1): 69–78

Leschied, A., and P.G. Jaffe. 1986. 'Implications of the Young Offenders Act in modifying the juvenile justice system: Some early trends,' *Young Offenders Service* 3 (2): 7525–32

Lilles, H. 1983. 'Beginning a New Era,' *Provincial Judges Journal* 7 (3): 21–6

MacDonald, J.A. 1971. 'A critique of Bill C-192: The Young Offenders Act,' *Canadian Journal of Criminology* 13 (1): 166–80

MacNamara, D.E.J. 1977. 'The medical model in corrections: Requiescat in pace,' *Criminology* 14: 439–54

Marchak, P. 1975. *Ideological Perspectives in Canada*. Toronto: McGraw-Hill

Marshall, I.H., and C.W. Thomas. 1983. 'Discretionary decision-making and the Juvenile Court,' *Juvenile and Family Court Journal* 34 (3): 47–9

Miller, J.G. 1979. 'The revolution in juvenile justice: From rhetoric to rhetoric,' in L.T. Empey, ed, *The Future of Childhood and Juvenile Justice*, 66–111. Charlottesville, VA: University Press of Virginia

Miller, W.B. 1973. 'Ideology and criminal justice policy,' *Journal of Criminal Law and Criminology* 64: 141–62

Nasmith, A.P. 1983. 'Paternalism Circumscribed,' *Provincial Judges Journal* 7: 16–20

Nettler, G. 1974. *Explaining Crime*. London: McGraw-Hill

Ohlin, L.E., R.B. Coates, and A.D. Miller. 1978. *Reforming Juvenile Corrections: The Massachusetts Experience*. Cambridge: Ballinger Press

Packer, H. 1964. 'Two models of the criminal process,' *University of Pennsylvania Law Review* 113: 1–69

Palmer, T. 1983. 'The effectiveness issue today,' *Federal Probation* 47: 3–10

Parker, H., M. Casburn, and D. Turnbull. 1980. 'The production of punitive juvenile justice,' *British Journal of Criminology* 20 (3): 236–60

Pisciotta, A.W., 1981. 'Theoretical perspectives for historical analyses: A selective review of the juvenile justice literature,' *Criminology* 19(1): 115–29

Quinney, R. 1977. *Class, State and Crime*. New York: David Mackay

Reid, S.A., and M. Reitsma-Street. 1984. 'Assumptions and implications of new Canadian legislation for young offenders,' *Canadian Criminology Forum* 7: 1–19

Reid, W. 1964. 'Inter-agency co-ordination in delinquency prevention and control,' *Social Service Review* 38: 418–28

Rein, M. 1976. *Social Science and Public Policy*. Harmondsworth, UK: Penguin

Ross, R.R., and P. Gendreau. 1980. *Effective Correctional Treatment*. Toronto: Butterworths

Rothman, D.I. 1980. *Conscience and Convenience*. Boston: Little Brown

Schafer, S. 1974. *The Political Criminal: The Problem of Morality and Crime*. New York: Free Press

Shichor, D. 1980. 'Some issues of social policy in the field of juvenile delinquency,' in D. Shichor and D.H. Kelly, eds, *Critical Issues in Juvenile Delinquency*, 35–50. Lexington, MA: D.C. Heath

Turk, A.T. 1969. *Criminality and the Legal Order*. Chicago: Rand McNally

U.S. President's Commission on Law Enforcement and the Administration of Justice. 1967. *Task Force Report: Corrections*. Washington, DC: GPO

Van den Haag, E. 1975. *Punishing Criminals: Considering a Very Old and Painful Question*. New York: Basic

Von Hirsch, A. 1976. *Doing Justice: The Choice of Punishments*. New York: Hill and Wang

Weiler, R., and B. Ward. 1986. 'A national overview of the implementation of YOA: One year later.' *Young Offender Service* 3 (2): 7517–24

West, W.G. 1984. *Young Offenders and the State: A Canadian Perspective on Delinquency*. Toronto: Butterworths

Wilensky, H.L., and C.N. Lebeaux. 1965. *Industrial Society and Social Welfare*, 2nd ed. New York: Free Press

Wilson, J.Q. 1975. *Thinking about Crime*. New York: Basic

– 1977. 'The political feasibility of punishment,' in J.B. Cederblom and W.L. Blizek, eds, *Justice and Punishment*, 108–25. Cambridge, MA: Ballinger

Wilson, L.C. 1982. *Juvenile Courts in Canada*. Toronto: Carswell

Wyman, M. 1977. *Comments on Juvenile Delinquency*. Report #3. Calgary: Alberta Provincial Courts

Yelaja, S.A. 1978. *Canadian Social Policy*. Waterloo: Wilfrid Laurier University Press

3 Good people, dirty system: The Young Offenders Act and organizational failure

Jim Hackler

Organizational Characteristics That Make Good People Do Poor Work

More than two decades ago, Everett Hughes wrote an influential article entitled 'Good People and Dirty Work' (1964). One of the themes in that article was that, when people work with stigmatized clients, such as the handicapped or the insane, some of that stigma 'rubs off.' In a larger sense, individuals cannot function independently of the organizational setting in which they are found. I would like to expand on these ideas to suggest that various aspects of organizations, the setting, and the nature of the interaction surrounding their activities will, in fact, 'rub off' on the people involved. The juvenile-justice system is staffed by many talented and well-intentioned people. It is my contention, however, that the juvenile-justice system in Canada works badly, despite valiant efforts on the part of many within the system. Part of the problem, it is proposed, is the increased emphasis on legal procedures. Although such procedures are intended to protect juveniles, I argue that they have done more damage than good. The emphasis on proceduralism not only 'rubs off,' it captures the people involved. They may complain, and at times become frustrated and quit, but frequently they will have difficulty modifying a system that is performing badly. Alternatively, they may become complacent and accept the system as it is.

The picture is not completely dismal, however. Occasionally we see instances where people have been able to overcome some of the deficiencies in the system and accomplish a good deal despite the severe handicaps imposed on them by an extremely inefficient structure. One goal of this chapter, then, is to provide both positive and negative examples of experiences and situations that have been observed.

Readers may well question the methodology that has led to some of these conclusions. Some of my early work in juvenile justice emphasized traditional data-gathering approaches. In Vienna, I utilized question-naires, which were translated into German and administered to more than 300 people serving in eleven different roles throughout the Viennese juvenile-justice system. These data were analysed and presented in one of the longest and driest articles I have ever written (Hackler, Brockman, and Luczynska 1977). In addition to administering the questionnaires, I interviewed many people. These interviews not only answered most of my questions more effectively than did the data analysis, but also moved quickly from my initial questions to greater insights about the system. My questionnaire data permitted the use of statistics but lacked the sensitivity to deal with complex questions.

In recent years I have been relying more heavily on intelligent people who work in the system and have insights that I consider superior to many of the ideas that come out of some of our more formal research. I describe this strategy more thoroughly under the label 'the local-wisdom approach' (Hackler 1983–4).

Although this chapter tries to get its message across with anecdotes rather than formal logic, I have definitely been influenced by those sophisticated scholars who use an organizational approach to the crimi-nal-justice system (e.g., Hagan 1983), particularly those who have pointed out that informal structures operating throughout the criminal-justice system are quite capable of evading, absorbing, or blunting any reforms imposed on them by legislation (Feeley 1983). The Canadian scene has suffered in attempts to modify a bureaucratic system by passing detailed legislation without trying to gain a better understanding of the informal dynamics of the subsystems within Canadian juvenile justice. Studies of the 'court-room work group' (Eisenstein and Jacob 1977) should have warned us that many of the activities of juvenile justice are extremely difficult to legislate in a predictable way.

It is interesting that we are beginning to recognize that the interaction of technology with the larger world leads to accidents and damage: oil rigs catch fire in the North Sea; CFCs damage the ozone layer; and pollution is leading to the destruction of forests, and so on. What is less obvious is that some of these same calamities also represent organizational failures, the inability of bureaucracies and other institutions in society to interact successfully. When failures are dramatic, such as the burning of an oil-rig or the explosion of a space shuttle, both technological and organizational failures come to light. However, when a juvenile-justice system imposes an additional burden on the lives of young people already facing a decreased chance of success, it does not undergo the same scrutiny. In fact, the movement from child-saving to child-blaming has provided a rationale for the continuation of destructive practices (Haveman 1986). Such practices will probably eventually lead to young people being less successful citizens in the future and contributing as adults to more than their share of child abuse, wife abuse, and crime. My more radical colleagues provide scathing criticisms of the system, which are frequently appropriate, based on faults in capitalism. I agree that there are great injustices in society, which require changes at the societal level. In the meantime, some smaller changes could be introduced relatively easily. My approach is to see if moderate changes in the system could be achieved by using an organizational approach. If we view juvenile justice as a 'loosely coupled system,' it may be easier to identify areas where change is possible.

Juvenile Justice as a Loosely Coupled System

There are a number of organizational models that can be used to study juvenile justice. John Hagan has utilized the concept of 'loosely coupled systems' to study the criminal-justice system (Hagan, Alwin, and Hewitt 1979; Hagan, Nagel, and Albonetti 1980). Earlier, Reiss spoke of American criminal justice as a 'loosely articulated hierarchy of subsystems' (1971: 114–20). This approach also makes sense for juvenile justice, where different subsystems vary in the tightness or looseness of this coupling (Hagan 1983: 5). Youth-court judges, probation departments, prosecutors' offices, and the police are responsive to one another in varying degrees but still maintain considerable independence.

It is quite possible that there are many advantages in having loosely coupled rather than tightly coupled systems, but the Young Offenders Act was introduced without taking into account the realities of such a system. According to Peter Solomon, the behaviour of professionals, such as the police and crown attorneys, derives as much from occupational and organizational influences as from the influence of the law and the rules that are supposed to define their roles (1983: 5). In addition, the law and the rules provide these actors not only with constraints, but with resources that enable them to achieve their own goals and justify their actions. The argument I wish to make here is that this loosely coupled system has satisfied the needs and goals of some components of the system while, in fact, damaging juveniles. Furthermore, I will argue that this does not have to be the case. The juvenile-justice system in France is also a loosely coupled system but has been adapted to serve the society more effectively.

How does the Young Offenders Act fit into this picture? It is also the product of 'loosely coupled systems,' but because of the agreement that was finally produced in Parliament, some people assume that it produced a consensus.

The Myth of Agreement in the Young Offenders Act

Prior to the 1984 Young Offenders Act, several attempts to draft new legislation met with failure. The new legislation was long and involved, and entailed many compromises. Those who worked so hard on drafting this legislation sincerely believed that they had achieved something positive because they were able to satisfy a variety of conflicting interest groups and organizations. In this respect, the law succeeded. However, the result is that the YOA sends confusing messages.

Maria Los writes that the new legislation did not reject the treatment philosophy outright in favour of the 'just desserts' model (1987: 26). In fact, the law was designed to satisfy a number of influential groups who were not in agreement. In her study of the media during this period, Los points out that the different parts of the country were also preoccupied with different concerns. For example, the press in Quebec was primarily interested in the province's legislation, which preceded the federal law. The result was concealed messages in the legislation that were contradicted by statements presented more openly. In practice, the YOA has led to much proceduralism and inefficient patterns of behaviour that reflect concerns of the different components of the system. For example, the YOA has been a boon for young lawyers needing to gain court-room experience; however, this may not have been in the interest of young offenders. According to Los, other concerned groups, such as adolescents, parents, social workers, and researchers, had little chance to express their opinions (1987: 3). The law was the product of 'paper' not 'people' specialists.

In this chapter, it is not my goal to argue for revisions in the law. It is regrettable that the legislation was drafted without taking into account the flexibility and ingenuity displayed by people who work in these systems, and with fear rather than appreciation of the extensive variability that exists in the system. At present it is more reasonable to accept this legislation as a given. A simpler system that did not try to plug so many loopholes would have enabled the realities of loosely coupled systems to operate by utilizing the considerable talent that we see at the local level. But it is also important to point out that the Young Offenders Act is not the primary culprit. Under the Juvenile Delinquents Act, we had similar problems. Some parts of the system worked out ingenious and effective ways of coping with the problems. At other times, the needs of powerful players in the system were favoured over the needs of the juveniles and society. This situation has also arisen under the Young Offenders Act, but now it takes more skill and ingenuity to overcome some of the procedural requirements.

Let us now turn to three models of juvenile justice as a way of organizing some other arguments.

The Welfare, Legal, and Negotiated Models of Juvenile Justice

It has been argued that the Juvenile Delinquents Act reflected a welfare model of juvenile justice, whereas the Young Offenders Act shifted to a legalistic model. Since this debate is well known, I shall not elaborate, but suggest instead that a 'negotiated' model, which might describe juvenile justice in France, could be seen to have certain advantages.

Under the French system, a juvenile can be recorded and released or sent to the *procureur*, who is similar to our prosecutor. The police can hold a juvenile overnight, but most cases are seen by the *procureur* and sent on to the judge the same day. The *procureur* can screen out the case or send it to the *juge des enfants*. While the *procureur* might recommend that an offender be held in secure custody, only the judge can actually approve such a placement. When a juvenile is confined, it is in a juvenile wing of an adult prison. Such detentions are rare, with the result that very few juveniles are in custody in France relative to the numbers in Canada (Hackler et al 1987).

Most of the time, the judge handles cases informally in the office. However, if a trial is called for, the judge must follow certain formal procedures, including ensuring that a defence attorney is present. If the judge does not use the formal trial, the juvenile cannot be incarcerated. No punitive measure can be used. The juvenile can be assigned to supervision by a correctional social worker (an *educateur*); but, if the juvenile resists being supervised, being placed in a closed institution is not an alternative. When the judge decides not to use the formal court, the emphasis turns to meeting the needs of the juvenile. The judge does not make a decision as much as negotiate options and services. A very wide range of services, including residential facilities, is available. Being placed in a residence is not a sentence. If a juvenile leaves a facility, the judge cannot threaten him or her with prison. During my first visits to France, I was suspicious about judges being so persuasive without using punishment; but, as time went on, I began to understand that most of the judges felt that juveniles could not be helped unless they participated in the decision making. This philosophy and its consequences are developed in another paper (Hackler 1988).

Not only does the judge negotiate with juveniles, he also negotiates with residences. While some facilities operated by the government are obliged to accept juveniles, the majority are private and are free to accept or reject clients. However, most of the facilities are run by benevolent agencies that are dependent on clients and the concomitant funding for their support. Thus, these facilities must be sensitive to the judge's request. The judge can convince them to take a share of difficult cases.

Both North American and French judges are concerned about juveniles; however, the French judge is more effective because of his flexibility and knowledge of the case. After giving up his or her power to punish by using a trial, the French judge still has a great deal of influence as well as extensive information about the juvenile. Judges also have at least one social worker with whom they work closely. Unlike our judges, those in France even talk to people on the telephone about their cases.

By contrast, Canadian judges work hard to remain ignorant about their cases before deciding on guilt or innocence. Let us explore how this practice makes our system work badly.

Keeping Judges Ignorant

Under the former JDA, it was true that judges could abuse their power as they performed their welfare role. They could 'lock up children for their own good.' The French have avoided this dilemma by not providing the judge with punitive powers unless a formal trial is held. By contrast, the Canadian system seems eager to have trials for even the most trivial offences. During trials, we feel it is important to separate guilt from sentencing. Before finding a child guilty, judges must remain ignorant of family background and a whole variety of circumstances that are deemed irrelevant to judging guilt for a particular offence. Once finding the child guilty, which we do in the vast majority of cases, the judge must suddenly become well-informed, feverishly reading through pre-disposition reports that have been prepared anticipating a guilty finding. Or the judge can adjourn the case until enough information has been gathered. French judges and French juveniles find such a situation ludicrous. To them, and to me, it is obvious that background factors are relevant to the question of guilt. An anecdote may help explain this view.

A boy had run away from an open facility, and his Canadian judge had a rule that anyone leaving a non-custodial setting would spend six weeks in a custodial setting. While this reasoning makes a good deal of sense to many judges, I later learned that this boy was being beaten by larger boys in the non-custodial residence. In the court room, with other boys waiting in the audience, the defendant was not about to tell the whole story. Nor was the judge going to be on the phone talking to others who understood the situation better. Since the residence was fifty miles away, the psychologist at the facility could not spend half a day at court on the chance possibility that his information would be used. Certainly, a Canadian judge could not call up someone involved in the case and get information. Given our tendency to keep judges ignorant, many of them are trapped by their own informal rules. Otherwise sensitive judges say they wish to make an example of those juveniles who 'do not follow orders.' That anyone who leaves open custody automatically gets closed custody is a rule used by many judges. It makes sense according to the justice model but defeats any attempt to understand the roots of a problem. It also limits the options that can be used.

In France, juveniles cannot be placed in custody for breaking an administrative rule. As a French judge said, 'Leaving a residence without permission is not a crime. We lock up juveniles only for committing crimes.' In another interview, a judge said, 'Sometimes the kids make better decisions than we do.'

Although most Canadian judges realize that many of their decisions are unwise, most of them feel that even their stupid decisions should be obeyed. Our mentality insists that it would be terrible if authority were not obeyed, even when that authority makes a poor decision. Therefore, we sometimes punish youths for disobeying administrative decisions more severely than for committing crimes.

In another Canadian case, the boy had been picked up on a Friday evening and held in detention until Monday morning. He was charged with missing appointments with his probation officer, not seeking work, and not living with the family to whom he had been assigned. The crown attorney presented the case from the paperwork she had in front of her. However, no probation officer appeared, and there was some confusion as to which probation officer was currently handling the case. The boy's employer had not arrived. (Would having an employer be relevant to the charge of not seeking work?) The boy was staying at home, and his mother was in the court room, but evidently he was supposed to be staying in another home. There seemed to be some confusion about all three charges. Asked how he pleaded, the boy was confused, but pleaded guilty. The duty counsel was also confused. At that point, the judge accepted the guilty plea and adjourned the case until Thursday, when he would decide on the sentence on the basis of a pre-disposition report. In the meantime, the boy would go back to the detention centre. No thought was given to the possibility that this dangerous criminal could go home with his mother. The mother tried to speak, but the judge cut her off, saying that she would be able to speak on Thursday, at the disposition hearing.

During the break, the distraught mother approached the prosecutor, saying, 'I know my boy is a brat, but he shouldn't be shit on like that.' After further discussion, the prosecutor agreed to raise the matter with the judge when he returned to the court room. When the judge returned, and the prosecutor pointed out that the mother would like to say something about the case, the judge simply repeated that the boy had pleaded guilty and the mother would have adequate time to provide information at the time of sentencing. When the mother stomped out of the court room, the judge hurled threats of contempt of court at her as she disappeared through the doors.

In this case, a minor offender had two sessions in detention. It is most unlikely that he or his mother will have much faith in the justice, efficiency, or intelligence of the system. But even with skilled people handling such cases, structural barriers prevent an intelligent response.

First, we insist that juveniles plead guilty or not guilty. They cannot tell their story in their own way. They must conform to the rituals. Second, the prosecutor usually has limited information. The French *procureur* refers a case to the judge because it merits attention, but the Canadian prosecutor is already arguing that the juvenile is guilty. Third, the judge is inhibited about exploring confusing situations or discussing topics outside of their proper sequence. These conditions frequently make a mockery of the youth court as a setting for the sensitive handling of complex problems. Fourth, once we have botched a situation, it is harder to correct it. A judge cannot call up a detention centre and say that he made a mistake and that the mother will come by and pick up the kid. By contrast, French judges are more goal- than ritual-oriented.

Now, it is possible that if any of the actors in this loosely coupled system had displayed more skill, the situation might have been handled more smoothly; however, the organization of the system and the laws are also to blame. For example, any decision made by a French judge must be reviewed immediately by the *procureur*. If the *procureur* disagrees, there is an appeal. Admittedly, such appeals are rare, but the *procureur*'s role is to represent the interests of the public and provide a check on the judge.

The reader may have also noticed one other point in the case of this dangerous criminal who might have been missing appointments with his probation officer, who might not have been looking for work, and who was improperly living in the home of his concerned mother. Obviously, such a dangerous character could not be left to roam the streets before appearing in court, but why was the warrant served late on Friday? He would then have to stay in custody over the weekend. If a probation officer wants to give a juvenile a 'taste of the cells,' the timing of a warrant can be crucial. In this case, good communications between the probation officer and the police might have increased the likelihood that a warrant would be served on a Friday. But we have strayed somewhat from the question of keeping judges ignorant.

In my interviews, I sometimes ask the judges to comment on the following hypothetical situation. A girl has been rejected by her parents and is staying in a non-custodial facility on a charge of theft. The disposition was used, not because of the theft, which the judge and probation officers thought was minor, but because the parents would not accept the girl. After several months, relations with the parents had improved and the girl was to return home. However, she has contracted gonorrhoea and the social workers are afraid to tell the parents, feeling it would lead to another rejection. They would like to extend her stay in the residence until the girl can get medical treatment; the girl might not carry out this treatment if she stays at home. The dilemma is that, if this reasoning is explained in court, the parents might be shocked and whatever progress has been made towards reconciliation might be destroyed. My question to the judge is: would you talk to a social worker about such a case in private before the court-room hearing? All the judges agreed that this would be improper.

Saying Too Much in Court

While keeping judges ignorant is part of the problem, another aspect of it involves revealing too much. In one situation, a girl learned in court for the first time that she had been adopted. It was a traumatic experience for the girl, and it created pandemonium in court. In a legalistic court, information that is shared is screened according to rules of law, not according to the impact on human beings. Since youth courts convict 80 to 90 per cent of defendants, is our emphasis on the right concerns?

Another danger is having professionals testify in court if they have been striving to develop rapport with the juveniles (Lebel 1981). While it is important to provide the judge with useful information, how much should a psychologist or social worker tell in open court? Will divulging information damage rapport with the client and make the counsellor less effective in the future?

I am fully aware of the dangers of discussing cases in advance and prejudging them before the hearing, but the above situations illustrate our unwillingness to assume that judges often deal with sensitive issues. We do not trust them. In France, a magistrate is expected to have integrity, to handle extensive information in advance, and still to be able to make equitable judgments in the court room. One might argue that, if the judge recommends that a case go to trial and then sits the case, the cards are stacked against the defendant. Possibly, but I watched one trial where the defence counsel argued that there was some doubt in the evidence, and under such conditions the judge should acquit. The defendant was acquitted. Again we see the ability of magistrates to play different roles at different times. But more important is the basic assumption that judges in France should be well informed. Even the juveniles in France thought that our system must be unfair because we permit judges to make decisions without knowing everything possible about the case. French juveniles said they preferred to be sentenced by the judge who has followed their situation and misdeeds for years. Later, I will suggest that one might create a new role, that of 'social service' judge, which could avoid some of our present difficulties.

Illustrations of Organizational Failure in a Loosely Coupled System

Three anecdotes may help us to understand how loosely coupled systems can function badly. In the first case, a sixteen-year-old girl was in court for trespassing. She and a number of her friends climbed the fence of a community swimming-pool in the middle of the night and went swimming in the nude. This was a small town, and the juveniles were all related or grew up together. It was not clear why this case ended up in court. The judge suspected there was something behind the case but had no luck in getting an adequate explanation in court. The girl was found guilty of trespassing and fined ten dollars. She now had a juvenile record.

When I pursued this case out of court, I discovered that the manager of the swimming-pool was the brother of the mayor and was tired of juveniles climbing over the walls during warm summer evenings for a swim. His complaints to the mayor led to a 'stake-out,' using the majority of the six-man police force. After the juveniles climbed the fence and were frolicking about in the nude, the police sprang their trap and arrested them all.

One can sympathize with the manager of the pool, but is this the best way to utilize the court? Having engaged in such behaviour many decades ago, I suspect that, had I been caught in all my naked glory and been forced to dress under the flashlights of the police, I would not have been a repeat offender. If this loosely coupled system had a better communication network among the police, probation officers, and judge, such a case might never have appeared in court. I cannot imagine this type of case appearing in a French juvenile court.

When loose coupling is accompanied by inefficient information flow, different parts of the system may perform ineffectively, with each organization 'covering its ass.' Perhaps little damage was done in this case, but was it necessary to give a girl a record of delinquency?

The second case involved a girl in court for theft. The parents separated, and the mother and father lived in two different cities. The daughter lived in a small town with a family who treated her like one of their own. She had been in no trouble in the community and had done well in school. However, this fifteen-year-old girl began to date a twenty-year-old. The family did not approve. When the father heard of the situation, he drove to the small town, picked up his daughter, and moved her to his apartment in the larger city. The girl did not like the woman who lived with the father. She stole eleven dollars from her father's wallet to buy a bus ticket back to the small town to return to the family with whom she had been living. The father swore out a warrant for her arrest for theft, and the police picked up the girl, put her in the local detention centre, then brought her to the larger city and housed her in a second detention centre, pending her arrival in juvenile court on a charge of theft. The social worker who looked into the case found it difficult to recommend any specific action.

In court, the girl expressed her desire to return to the small town. The father, who had legal custody, was concerned about the older boyfriend, even though the girl said she was no longer seeing him. The charge of petty theft remained. Duty counsel recommended that the girl plead not guilty, and she did. Therefore, a trial had to be held. But what to do with the girl in the meantime? The judge did not wish to send her back to the detention centre, but the father refused to accept her in his apartment as long as she was pleading not guilty. The session adjourned with the girl being sent back to the detention centre. She turned to the social worker and said, 'Why did I plead not guilty?' After a couple of days in detention, the girl came back, pleaded guilty to the theft before a different judge, and was sent home with her father.

I do not know the best way of dealing with family squabbles, but three different stays in detention centres and a criminal record may not be the best way of handling an argument between a father and daughter. We also saw good people doing dirty work: a probation officer, a social worker, and two reluctant judges wishing there were a reasonable way to handle the situation. In France, a judge may have had difficulties as well, but the girl would not have ended up in detention.

The third illustration involved a girl who was accused of stealing a chocolate bar from a store that reported all incidences of shop-lifting. The police determined that she had no previous record and recommended her for alternative measures However, a mistake was made somewhere between the police station and the prosecutor's office, and the girl was summoned to appear in court. There the prosecutor recognized the minor nature of the offence and asked why she had not been placed on alternative measures. Misunderstanding the proceedings, the father and daughter thought the girl had been recommended for the program and left the court. When their absence was noted, the prosecutor insisted, against the judge's preference, that a warrant for arrest be issued. Different parts of this loosely coupled system blamed each other for the mistake, but the girl was finally put on the program and completed it quickly. The prosecutor, however, did not revoke the warrant until almost two weeks later. In the meantime, the girl and her parents suffered a great deal of stress, wondering if and when she would be arrested.

Here was an illustration of 'stealing conflicts' from those who are in a better situation to resolve them (Christie 1977). In this case, the girl's parents were not only concerned but also seemed to be capable of handling the situation. I have argued elsewhere that the YOA has encouraged more stealing of conflicts than in the past (Hackler 1987). One might argue that, under the Juvenile Delinquents Act, social workers were guilty of being 'professional usurpers' of other people's problems. Now they have been joined, or have even been pushed aside, by those with more legal training.

The reader should not assume that the illustrations provided above are particularly rare. Relatively minor cases get bogged down from time to time as our loosely coupled system struggles with all of the rules. Nor would we assume that cases that are run assembly-line fashion through the court are being handled well. Cases that are routinely given community-service orders or probation may not get the sort of attention that might reveal background problems. From the clients' perspective, sometimes they are relieved, many times they are confused (Wilks, Birnie, and Chamberlain 1979), but rarely do they feel the system has provided them with a valuable service. By contrast, French youngsters frequently feel they have been helped.

Liaisons and Linkages

There is no magic solution for some of the clumsy ways our current system operates, but efforts to build communication bridges between parts of the system may be helpful. In Victoria, juvenile probation officers ride with the juvenile police from time to time. There could be some negative aspects of this interaction. Some probation officers argue their role is quite different, that they should be helping clients rather than emphasizing social control, and that close contact with the police would blur that distinction. While we were walking and riding the beat one night, it was clear the policeman was in charge, even though he was much younger than the probation officer. The officer's 'harder' orientation towards juveniles, emphasized control of behaviour. I asked the probation officer if the police mentality, which tended to be negative towards most of their clients, might make probation officers less sympathetic. The probation officer agreed that this might be a concern, but an experience at the end of the evening suggested that two professionals can communicate effectively without forgetting that they have distinct roles to play. The policeman dropped the probation officer off at the end of the shift, and while he was driving me home, he commented, 'Mark does well by his people.' It seems that this policeman felt that probation officers should be bleeding hearts and should be helpers rather than controllers. Since he had established good rapport with the probation officer, he would probably be helpful if the probation officer were to ask for assistance regarding a client. Of course, he would tease the probation officer about being a softy and letting these juvenile thugs lead him around by the nose, but that was simply the way you played your role.

While it is not clear if linkages between juvenile probation and the police serve clients more effectively, police departments that have juvenile liaison officers seem to reduce some of the organizational problems in these loosely coupled systems. For example, in New Westminster, BC, one experienced probation officer handles all of the forty to fifty juvenile cases that are active at a given time. One experienced police officer is also responsible for all juveniles. Little goes on in the community that escapes the attention of these two men. Does this help to explain why relatively few cases end up in the New Westminster youth court? Are problems addressed in a more effective way before there is a need for a court appearance?

Two other illustrations of linkage creation are provided by the Burnaby and Richmond RCMP detachments in British Columbia. The Burnaby unit created a special counselling program, the Burnaby Youth Services program. The Richmond unit brought two social workers into the police department. The specific nature of these services is not the concern of this chapter, but the creation of communication networks that link the police with other agencies and community resources may be one way of helping loosely coupled systems to operate more effectively.

Variability and Flexibility

Juvenile justice in Canada displays a great deal of variability but not necessarily flexibility; that is, the organization of juvenile justice inevitably varies from place to place, because these loosely coupled structures will be connected in different ways. This situation could lead to flexibility, but the constraints created by legislation sometimes lead to illogical practices. For example, how does one detain a juvenile overnight in smaller communities? Large cities have regular detention facilities, but in smaller communities the police may travel long distances to place juveniles in appropriate places. Sometimes, police units try to create a small holding facility that would be adequate for a juvenile detained for a few hours in the police station. If it is 3:00 a.m. and the youth is to appear in court at 9:00 a.m., a long trip to a detention centre has clear disadvantages.

When the YOA was first implemented, detention was one of the areas of concern mentioned by police departments. Since then there has been an accommodation, and it would be interesting to see how innovative local agencies have been. Obviously, some rules are needed concerning detention, but one of the weaknesses of the Young Offenders Act is that it attempts to treat local systems as if they were quite uniform. The detention situation is only one of many where it is impossible to anticipate all the factors that will be relevant and to draft detailed rules that take all such factors into account.

This attempt to legislate variability becomes a farce when one notes that, in Ontario, different types of courts are maintained for those under age sixteen and those age sixteen and seventeen. Such was not the intent of the YOA. My argument is that good legislation would permit flexibility.

Unlike many who feel that uniformity is part of providing justice, I would argue that this variability may, in fact, enable local systems to adapt, to be flexible, and to serve their clients more effectively. The French system has built in a certain amount of flexibility. For example, in the French system the school for magistrates trains people who will serve as *procureurs* and judges, at either the adult or the juvenile level. A magistrate can also be a *juge d'instruction*, an investigating judge. These magistrates look for different positions that are open throughout the country, and occasionally move from one role to the other. Since the pay is the same, they base their career decisions on a variety of other factors. The important fact is that judges are aware of the distinct roles to be played in the system and, with each new role, integrity must be a requisite within the system.

A striking illustration of this type of flexibility was displayed in Vienna when I arrived in court and saw one of the judges playing the role of defence lawyer. Naturally, I was surprised; when I inquired afterwards, I learned that a woman defendant had travelled some distance to Vienna for the hearing, but her defence lawyer had not appeared. Since members of the Viennese judiciary sit as judges for some cases but perform investigations before recommending that other cases go to trial, a judge had reviewed this women's case in advance. At the last moment, he told her that he was very familiar with the case, having done the investigation, and if her lawyer did not arrive, he would act as her defence. This seems somewhat incredible to North Americans, but the response of the Austrian judge who was presiding over the hearing was that this was the best defence he had heard all year. In other words, the role must be played with integrity, but people can play different roles.

In France, the magistrates have the same status, even though they are playing different roles. In North America, we are concerned if the judge is too 'chummy' with the prosecutor, but in France, co-operation does not obscure the fact that the different roles are designed to be a check on each other. In one sense, our hierarchy, with a judge on top but not necessarily well tuned to the system, can lead to arrogance and arbitrariness. In many of my discussions with judges, I have suggested that it might be healthy if judges were to act as duty counsel one day a month. In addition, they might be permitted to defend an occasional case instead of sending the youth on to legal aid. The judges were amused, and none of them took the suggestion seriously.

Let me provide an illustration of variability without flexibility. The trial was to begin at a certain time, but the defence attorney was not there. The prosecutor had no other cases that could be presented at the time, and the judge was annoyed because things were not ready to go. He ordered the prosecutor to find the defence attorney (which she had been trying to do). Meanwhile the judge adjourned the case for fifteen minutes. After fifteen minutes, the judge returned to the court room and waited impatiently, because the prosecutor was not there. When she hurried into the court room, explaining that she had still not been able to reach the defence attorney, the judge was angry and berated the prosecutor. From the standpoint of loosely coupled systems, this judge did not understand the way these agencies interact.

A judge may insist that everyone perform according to a set schedule; however, anyone who has observed court rooms in operation is aware that there are many last-minute changes, with witnesses not appearing, charges being withdrawn, and defence counsel not appearing. Lawyers give lower priority to defending juveniles than to adults. Frequently, a lawyer can find himself or herself with a time conflict between adult and juvenile court.

While some defence lawyers can be negligent about their juvenile cases, the point is that last-minute changes are a normal part of court-room operation. Let me describe the court room in a western city that displayed considerable skill in responding to the normal chaos that characterizes any youth or family court.

This court has several court rooms, several judges, and several additional occasional judges. However, the scheduling of cases was in the hands of the clerks and prosecutors. The judges have learned to allow time for a variety of informal processes to operate. For example, during one case, the judge wanted some more information before proceeding. It was possible that a probation officer could provide that information. Instead of adjourning the case until a different day, the judge simply adjourned temporarily. In this system, personnel from the sheriff's office control the flow of cases into the court and have an effective communication network with the outside world. Therefore, while one of the sheriff's officers was looking for the liaison probation officer, the clerk and prosecutor were moving on to another case.

Frequently, many activities are being pursued at the same time. Sometimes another judge will come in with a different case, sometimes with a different clerk and different prosecutor. There are also times when the court-room action takes the case to a certain stage where an informal resolution is possible. Some perceptive judges will adjourn the case temporarily while the people involved see if they can work something out informally.

After I had observed this court room for a while, it was obvious that the system was adaptable and able to deal with a wide range of situations in a variety of ways. While some courts would attempt to resolve a case in one setting, or adjourn it until a later date, this particular system was able to use several techniques, such as temporary adjournments, more effectively. Judges learned to adapt to the system by staying in their offices until they were called. At times there was much scurrying around behind the scenes, with the judges occasionally involved in the informal dynamics, but the effective linkages between the different players in the system seemed to result in more effective resolution of problems. This court seemed less trapped by procedures and more able to adapt to the needs of clients. Instead of being aloof and isolated, as they are in many courts, judges were frequently a resource, giving advice outside the court room. There seemed to be less pressure to render a decision in awkward cases. Other justice professionals might become involved with problem resolution, with the judge deliberately stepping back until progress had been made.

Another court displayed the same type of flexibility during an incest case, which had many typical characteristics: the mother had difficulty believing that the father could behave in this way, the two young girls had difficulty talking about it in court. One girl refused to testify in court but was willing to talk to the judge privately. The judge took the stenographer and the girl to his office and took her testimony in private. It is not clear to me how such testimony could be used, but the judge was trying to understand the situation.

The defence attorney played a unique role in that he was trying to look after the interests of the family and not simply trying to get the father acquitted. The defence counsel questioned his client extensively, while the prosecutor remained silent. The judge adjourned the case at a certain stage, and, during the break, a number of things happened. For example, Social Services took the girls into custody. When the trial resumed, the mother now accepted the awful reality. One of the questions of concern to the judge was what would happen, as the family was preparing to move into a new home. As the proceeding reached a point where the reality was clear, but solutions were not, the judge adjourned the trial without attempting to render a verdict or bring the proceedings to a conclusion. He directed the defence attorney, who spoke the language of the immigrant father, to stay with the case and remain in touch with the prosecutor.

Notice that the judge used the trial to bring the problem to the surface. However, aside from simply punishing the father, it was not clear how to resolve other issues. The defence counsel was clearly in a key position to expedite solutions. The prosecutor also stepped back from the case to await further developments. A less-skilled judge may have attempted to force a conclusion to the case that same day.

While it is difficult to link lack of flexibility with the Young Offenders Act, my impression is that the type of communication that encourages the adaptability and flexibility displayed in the above case has been replaced by greater attention to rituals and procedures, as illustrated by the legal objection to adjourning cases *sine die*.

The Unfortunate Loss of Adjourned *Sine Die*

Since the passage of the Young Offenders Act, judges have been unable to adjourn cases *sine die*, that is, to adjourn the case without making a decision. This procedure was used very effectively in Winnipeg in the period prior to the YOA, particularly for first-time offenders. A typical situation would involve a first-time offender facing the prospect of being found guilty. The judge might stop the proceedings, adjourn the case *sine die*, and point out to the juvenile that, if he or she got into trouble again, this case could be reopened and the judge would render a verdict and decide on a sentence. Psychologically, the juvenile had been to the edge of the cliff, but at the last moment had been allowed to step back. There was no criminal record. If the offender stayed out of trouble, he or she would not receive the formal label 'delinquent.'

In my discussion of this matter with the clerk of the Ottawa court, who had just been clearing out many juvenile files, he could not remember any of the cases that had been adjourned *sine die* ever being returned to court. Unfortunately, our system prefers neatness. None of this wishy-washy business of adjourned *sine die*. If the kid is guilty, let us be sure to brand him or her. People with this sort of mentality would not have appreciated some strategies used by a Nova Scotia judge. A first offender might have found the judge hesitant about rendering a guilty verdict. Instead, the judge might suggest to the defendant that she or he talk to the person sitting in the court room who arranges a variety of community-service projects while the case was adjourned for a month. The next month the youth would return and explain to the judge that she or he had helped to paint an elderly person's house. The judge may decide not to make a decision for another month. Two months later the youth would return and describe another worthwhile community activity. The judge, in turn, would dismiss the charges. The youth has no criminal record. Of course, the legalists would argue that the juvenile had been punished without having been found guilty. True, but from the standpoint of the defendant, that seems to be a clear advantage. Adjourned *sine die*, an intelligent option, has been lost as a means to satisfy procedural neatness.

The Auditor versus the Contingency Model

Assuming that variability will continue in our system, how does one also encourage the flexibility that might maximize the returns? Assuming diversity, what administrative policies would best expedite the operation of juvenile-justice systems? One could argue that upper-level administrators would serve the long-term goals of juvenile justice by offering help to local judges, probation officers, and administrators as to how they might deal with particular issues. We refer to this as the contingency model. By providing intelligent options, perhaps by passing on information as to how other local units are dealing with particular problems, upper-level decision makers could expedite the work of the courts and juvenile-service agencies. Unfortunately, administrative policies for providing help from above are frequently less common than those emphasizing directives from above. This latter is the auditor model.

The YOA implicitly supports an 'auditor model' for court administration, with an emphasis on monitoring and controlling activities in the various jurisdictions (Gallas 1976). The goal of the auditor model is to achieve uniformity, but this model assumes that the actors at the line level in the juvenile-justice system need to be controlled. A contrasting argument is that the conditions effecting juvenile courts vary from place to place and are influenced by the context of the situation. Because of this diversity, the auditor model is inadequate and is understandably resisted at the local level.

The system might do much better under a 'contingency model,' which emphasizes the ability to adapt and would take advantage of the intelligent personnel who currently administer the system at the grass-roots level. This does not imply neglect or overlooking deficiencies, but it does recognize the reality that those who staff the courts and front-line services are usually just as talented as those at other levels in the bureaucracy or those who draft the legislation, and, in addition, probably have a better understanding of the problems in the local community. Under the contingency model, upper-level administrators would attempt to expedite the innovative procedures developed by local units and provide information regarding alternative practices elsewhere. This would increase the options available to local problem-solvers.

In France, the contingency model is explicitly recognized. Judges have much flexibility, as long as they are helping the juvenile. If they are punishing, they must adhere to careful procedures. The contingency model seems to characterize the prosecutors who organized and controlled the timing of court activities. In other places, the auditor model seems to be the accepted way of working, with the people at the line level resisting in order to maintain their autonomy. Young clients frequently get hurt while various players struggle for power under the auditor model. I would argue that an auditor model does not work well in a loosely coupled system.

Another illustration of the lack of flexibility in our system is provided by a boy who had spent five months in a group home as part of a six-month sentence. He was doing well in school; his family was located in another town and did not seem to be well equipped to provide an appropriate environment for him. The workers in the group home were trying to work out some sort of strategy for when he finished his six-month sentence. The French judge who was visiting the group home with me asked why the boy could not continue to stay in the group home. It was explained to him that the group home was only for boys serving sentences and that juveniles had to leave when their sentences were finished, even if they had made a good adjustment and were doing well in school. The French judge was puzzled; in France, the judge has the authority to adapt the system to the needs of the juveniles. In fairness, we see this type of flexibility in our system at times. Creating a few beds for social-service youths in a facility for 'delinquents' is one illustration. However, I would argue that encouraging line workers to be innovative is relatively rare in our system.

The last illustration of the loss of flexibility under the YOA that I will present here is the formalization of procedures in the docket court.

The Docket Court

As the youth court now resembles the adult court, we see the growth of the impersonal docket court. This court is where many of the minor cases pleading guilty are dealt with summarily. More difficult cases and those pleading not guilty establish dates for later hearings. But let us focus on some of the minor cases that are handled routinely with a lecture and perhaps a short community-service order. Given the impersonal nature of the setting and the fact that the judge usually has little information on the case, beyond the offence, there is little search into the conditions that might have led to this offence.

By contrast, the French judge talks to the juvenile in the office. Parents may or may not be there. The juvenile presents his or her story and the judge can explore questions involving the family. There may be another visit with the parents involved. If a juvenile is hesitant about talking with the parents present, the judge will excuse the parents while he talks to the juvenile privately. The goal is for the judge to become well informed about the situation as soon as possible. Notice that, if the case is deemed serious enough to appear in court, the same judge will preside over the trial. From the standpoint of the juveniles in France, this makes sense. They want to be judged by someone who really understands their situation. When I tried to explain how we try to keep the judge from knowing these background factors before rendering a verdict, the response was that our system would seem woefully inadequate to address the needs of young offenders.

To conclude this section, I would suggest that the extensive variability that characterizes our system has lost some of its adaptive qualities: 1 / because the YOA has unsuccessfully tried to reduce that variability, and 2 / because an auditor model usually prevails. Many well-meaning people hoped that uniform procedures would provide a better defence for juveniles. In the next section, I argue that this wish has not been realized.

The Pretence of Defence

While observing a trial in Austria, I noticed that the defence attorney did a very poor job when he concluded his case. He simply gave the normal 'weeping and wailing' approach, which typifies the level of defence in many of our juvenile cases. However, the Austrian *Staatsanwalt* (prosecutor) rose after the defence was finished and questioned the juvenile again, this time bringing out a number of issues that were more appropriate for the defence. I was surprised, and spoke with the prosecutor afterwards, saying that it appeared that he had provided the defence as well as the prosecution. His response was 'Of course. The defence did a poor job, and it was my obligation to bring all of the facts out so that the judge could come to an intelligent decision. I understand that in your country you have an adversary model, where the two different sides try to win. Aren't you people interested in the truth? In justice?'

Up until that time, I had taken the adversarial model for granted. Since then, I have developed grave reservations about the adequacy of the adversarial system in juvenile justice. For most of the cases appearing in youth court, the problem of guilt or innocence is not the major dilemma. Prosecutors are not interested in convicting juveniles where there is some doubt, but there is frequently a dilemma in knowing what to do with the juvenile in a constructive manner. When a defence lawyer does the 'weep and wail' routine, it is usually before a judge who is desperately looking for any constructive alternative. Pleas to be gentle are unhelpful, and, in the youth court, lawyers rarely develop a plan that would help a juvenile.

Although defence lawyers are supposed to be representing the client, there are times when one has reason to doubt that this is so. In one case, where a boy wished to plead guilty, the lawyer convinced the boy to go to trial. After losing the case (the boy was sent to a group home, where he made reasonable progress), his lawyer continued to appeal the case. Towards the end of the boy's sentence, after he had made a good adjustment to school and his outlook seemed promising, the lawyer was still appealing the original conviction. The major disruptions for the boy during his rehabilitation were those caused by the appeals, which pulled the boy out of school so he could appear in court.

One might well ask if the use of defence counsel has hindered rather than helped the juveniles. Prior to the YOA, I watched one court case where experienced prosecutors were regularly used, but defence attorneys rarely appeared. I have argued elsewhere that the prosecutors are more inclined to 'do the defence' as well when there is no defence lawyer present (Hackler 1984). However, when a defence lawyer is present, and does a poor job, the prosecutor is less inclined to fill in the gaps. To do so would imply criticism of a colleague. In general, I felt that youths were better defended when there was only a prosecutor who was well informed.

In a loosely coupled system, the defence counsels are another component who have needs to be met, and these needs may be different from those of the juveniles. With more lawyers being provided to juveniles by legal aid, one is beginning to see the legal-aid system being pressured by lawyers to provide them with work. Is it the goal of legal aid to provide work for lawyers or to provide service for clients? Some of the lawyers act as if the former were the case.

In fairness, in those jurisdictions that have more experienced defence attorneys, those who become somewhat specialized in youth-court cases may offer better services. In Montreal, for example, there seem to be more lawyers with a specific interest in juvenile work. I was able to watch a number of attorneys who provided a vigorous defence when they thought a youth was inappropriately charged; but when guilt was not really the question, they concentrated their efforts on the type of disposition the prosecutor was willing to recommend.

Eddie Greenspan, a well-known Toronto lawyer, argues that an advocate should look ahead for the client's interests. In one case, he acted for a lad who had committed a number of break-and-enter offences. The boy was on drugs, and his parents were fed up with him (Greenspan 1982). Greenspan worked with the parents to get the boy into a rehabilitation centre. Because of numerous upsetting incidents at the centre caused by his client, Greenspan kept adjourning the case, and after one year and three months, when things were finally going well for his client (the lad had cured his drug problem and restructured his life), they pleaded guilty before a judge, who quite coincidentally happened to be a director of the rehabilitation centre (1983: 206–7). The lad got probation.

Greenspan calls this 'constructive delay,' and while defence counsels are vilified for delaying trials, Greenspan points out that, if the lad he was defending had pleaded guilty soon after his arrest, abandoned by his parents, a drug user, with twenty-one charges and no prospects or hopes, he would have received a stiff term of incarceration.

I would argue that the above case demonstrates a success, but a flexible system might permit more such adjournments based on a shared communication system without the need for a high-powered lawyer.

The Use of a Public Defender

While Greenspan provided an illustration of 'constructive delay,' many of the delays in youth court create hardships for juveniles and their families. Parents sometimes make considerable sacrifices to get to court only to face a five-minute hearing and an adjournment. In his book *The Process is the Punishment: Handling Cases in a Lower Criminal Court*, Malcolm Feeley suggests that going through the youth-court procedures could be more traumatic than the sentence (1979). Some of this delay might be avoided if we utilized a public-defender system. At present, we use a duty-counsel system, which provides legal advice to a juvenile at first appearance; if the juvenile decides to go to trial, the duty counsel steps aside while the juvenile find a defence lawyer.

While visiting the juvenile court in Oakland, California, I was told by the prosecutors that public defenders seemed to be more effective than other defence lawyers. If public defenders felt that a juvenile was being railroaded by the system, they put up an extremely vigorous defence. Their familiarity with the system gave them an advantage over less-experienced defence counsel. By contrast, guilt was rarely the major issue, and the public defender, having more knowledge of and contacts with those who could provide services, was able to negotiate more rapidly and effectively for recommended dispositions that would be of assistance to the client. If this is called plea bargaining, so be it.

In arguing on behalf of a public defender, one should note that research in the 1960s and 1970s provided a somewhat negative image of both defence lawyers in general, and public defenders in particular (Blumberg 1967; Casper 1971; McIntyre 1987: 2). Later research, however, provides a much more adequate assessment of the pubic defender (Brantingham and Burns 1981; McIntrye 1987: 45–8) It seems they are just as effective as private lawyers, especially for those of low status and with less serious charges.

In many cases public defenders have entered this position with a certain amount of zeal, but after a while their morale drops. Others do not see how they could get much satisfaction out of constantly defending those who some consider to be 'scum.' In addition, public defenders get little appreciation from their clients. In the youth court, however, conditions might be different. The enthusiasm that brings a lawyer to this role might lead to more satisfaction. Although it sounds like a radical idea, why could we not have crown attorneys and public defenders who can interchange roles? In reality, we have people who have worked as prosecutors who have been, or will be, defence lawyers. If a Viennese judge can act as a defence counsel, why could not our crown attorneys play that role occasionally? In fact, would it not be interesting to have our judges defend a few cases each month? They might get a different perspective on the way the system operates.

At present, public defenders tend to get discouraged and leave the job. However, we could create a body of legally trained civil servants who performed the tasks of prosecutors, defenders, and judges, and who moved among these roles the way people move about in other bureaucracies, such as the way professors move into administrative roles and back again into scholarly tasks. Our system creates a gap in terms of salary and prestige between judges and prosecutors and public defenders. For obvious political reasons, it is unlikely that we can alter the present system for appointing judges. However, in the youth and family courts, particularly, would not the roles of prosecutor and public defender be equally important? An attractive career pattern for such legally trained civil servants might improve the quality of justice. In fact, requiring experience as a prosecutor and public defender might be a logical prerequisite for anyone becoming a family-court judge.

Let us now ask if the use of public defenders might modify another problem that may have increased since the introduction of the YOA: taking the conflict out of the hands of those most concerned and cutting youths out of the discussion of their problems.

Cutting Youths Out of the Dialogue

Allison Morris and Henri Giller have pointed out that, when legal representatives are involved, the possibility of foreclosing direct dialogue between the bench and the defendant is all the greater (1987: 173). This point was rather obvious in many of the Canadian hearings I observed. A lively discussion ensued among judge, prosecutor, and defence counsel while the defendant and parents were left to one side, wondering what it was all about. In some situations the defendant sits next to the defence lawyer, which allows the possibility of private communication. In other situations, the defendant is physically placed at the extreme far side of the court room. I heard a number of legally trained persons in youth court state their preference for a situation that leaves the defendant over to one side of the court room so that the professionals can get on with the business at hand without being bothered by the defendant. In England, Morris and Giller (1987: 173) suggest, current practices may provide the appearance rather than the reality of due process. This seems to be an appropriate comment for Canada as well.

One of the goals of the Young Offenders Act is to be sure that juveniles understand their rights. Previous work has shown that juveniles did not understand the process very well under the JDA (Smith 1985; Wilks, Birnie, and Chamberlain 1979). My impression is that young people are more confused today. However, it is not clear who provides the best information. In one American study, probation officers claim that they, not police or attorneys, are the primary source of juveniles' understanding of their rights. However, the juveniles said it was the lawyer who provided this information (Lawrence 1983-4). We do not have a comparable study in Canada.

One could argue that, even though every juvenile tried in France must have a defence lawyer, that defence is usually based on a brief preparation shortly before the trial. The difference is that such a defence is less crucial because of the infrequency of trials and the length of sentences, usually a few weeks. Normally, the French judge spends little time on the child's rights, unless the case goes to trial. Usually, the judge brushes this aspect aside. In one sense, the charges are dismissed immediately. There is nothing to defend, so judge and youth can concentrate on effective new steps.

Recommendations for Change

In a chapter on minor crime and the courts, Peter Solomon concludes that the court is a very expensive and unsatisfactory place to deal with crimes that are not very serious (1983: Ch. 5). One could extend that idea to the youth court. While there are some serious cases that justify the formal procedures of the court, the vast majority of cases are of a minor nature, often reflecting underlying problems of a family or personal nature. The court is an inefficient place in which to deal with these social issues. In this regard, the French judge has a considerable advantage. In France, the court room is simply not used for problem-solving. Instead, the court is used when other alternatives have failed. Before suggesting a strategy that might be compatible with our present system, let me provide one more anecdote that illustrates the problem-solving orientation of the French judge, which is so lacking in our system.

The setting was a small facility for temporary care. A fourteen-year-old girl was in conflict with her mother, who wanted her to continue in school. The girl wished to take a course in hair-styling. The stepfather was sympathetic towards the girl, but felt that he should not interfere. The girl ran away from home, stole some food, and ended up before the judge. The judge simply swept the crime aside and turned immediately to the problem behind it. Since the girl did not want to go home and the mother did not want her, the judge made arrangements for the girl to stay in the facility. However, the judge and the social workers were trying to get the girl to go back home and go along with the mother to a greater degree. If the girl had been sixteen, the judge might have been more sympathetic to the girl being on her own, but as she was fourteen, both social worker and judge were encouraging a family reconciliation. The judge did not pontificate and then issue an edict for everyone to obey. Instead, he accommodated the key actors in the situation without taking the conflict out of their hands (Hackler 1987). If a reconciliation developed with the parents, the girl would go home. There would be no court hearing, no formal proceedings. If the girl was later dissatisfied at home, she might come to see the judge again, since in France the judge is viewed as a source of help, unlike in North America, where most youngsters have a different view of judges.

It is important to emphasize that French judges have no advantage in compassion or training over their Canadian counterparts. However, the structure of the Canadian court puts an unreasonable demand on our judges. They must render a decision. Somehow they are supposed to bring closure to what is frequently an ongoing and messy situation. This response is frequently unsatisfactory. The French judge, with advice from the youth and others, is willing to try many alternatives.

Although I was originally sceptical about the effectiveness of judges under such circumstances, I soon learned that juveniles spoke of 'my judge.' Judges were responsible for specific geographical areas, thus enabling the juvenile to establish a relationship with a single judge. In one case, a juvenile appeared at court asking to see 'his' judge because he had left the residence where he was staying. However, as the judge was away for a few days, the boy talked with social workers, prosecutors, and others, but he wanted to tell *his* story to *his* judge and to no one else. In North America, it is unlikely that the system would respond to a runaway in such a tolerant manner, but in this situation, arrangements were made for the boy to stay in another facility until the judge returned.

Even though I use some aspects of the French system to provide ideas for change, I am also aware of weaknesses. For example, while many French deliquents are of Arab background, I saw no magistrates from that culture. By contrast, in Oakland, California, the two judges were black, and blacks were well represented among prosecutors, probation officers, and so on. In other words, minority-group offenders in Oakland have more successful role models than do the French minority group offenders. But this chapter is not designed to provide a balanced view of French juvenile justice or French society. The point is that, in French society, one with faults like ours and people with frailties like ours, a structure has been created that serves young people more effectively. I believe it is possible to capture some of the advantages of the French system through the creation of the role of 'social-service judge.'

The Social-Service Judge

In a formal court room, judges are restricted in the amount of problem-solving they can do. There are constraints on the information they can utilize prior to deciding on guilt. Once guilt has been determined, there are also other limitations in terms of exploring helpful alternatives. A social-service judge would be one operating in a non-punitive setting. Referrals could come from prosecutors, police, welfare, probation, school, and so on. For example, a prosecutor might prefer to avoid formal processing but, because of other potential problems facing the youth, have someone explore the situation further. While direct referrals to other agencies are possible, someone like a judge may be in a position to consider a wider range of possibilities.

Instead of demanding an appearance at a set time, the judge might talk with the youth by phone first. Should the meeting be with parents or not? Should the parents and youth talk to the judge separately? The judge would make it clear that he or she has no punitive powers while acting as a social-service judge. In addition, the judge might be disqualified from hearing any future case involving the youth. Without punitive powers, a judge could even permit the youth to talk about actual crimes or anything of relevant concern.

The goal would be to see if there were any services that would be helpful. For example, if the family were temporarily in disarray, a child might stay in a group home. Public or private agencies, or volunteer services, could be considered. Note that all participation would be voluntary. Failure to take part would not be an offence. While judges might be persuasive, they could not require compliance.

Naturally, the judge would need help from others to provide the actual services and thus would have people in social services, probation, the police, or volunteer agencies who could respond. Again, these services might normally be available, but a judge might be effective in seeing that a young person is not overlooked.

These services could become expensive, although probably less expensive than services committed to youths who become wards of the province. While a pilot project might be done through informal co-operation, eventually legislation might be needed to authorize the judge to guarantee payment for these services. In one sense, could we provide all of the help that is at present available to a child without having to make the young person a ward of the province? Instead of requiring that a juvenile be treated after being found guilty of an offence or found to be neglected, can we offer help under conditions where the youth can have more of a say? There is some evidence that having a voice in decisions makes people more willing participants. The goal would be to involve the youth in the process. The extent of involvement of the parents may depend on circumstances and the assessment of the judge.

There are two principles that would be central to this endeavour. First, the youth would be able to turn to someone who has a certain amount of clout. Parents and youths can be sloughed off; agencies might discourage a client, but it would be more difficult for them to slough off a determined judge. Second, agency personnel change from time to time, creating the possibility of discontinuity for the youth or family. Under a system where we were not stuck with formal lines of jurisdiction, the person actively helping the youth might be able to stay in contact for a longer period of time. Whether that person was a probation officer, social worker, or policeman would not matter, because no one has any formal power – only persuasion, with a judge as expediter. Obviously, a pilot project would lead to a variety of efforts that would change over time as the judges experimented with different situations.

Conclusion

This chapter has argued that Canada has permitted a clumsy and insensitive juvenile-justice system to evolve. Well-meaning people have attempted to correct many weaknesses with detailed legislation, but these efforts have failed. At the same time, we see illustrations of ingenuity at different levels in the system in attempting to adapt the bureaucracy to the child. Those efforts can be rewarded by modifying minor aspects of the system. The types of adaptations will varying from place to place, and one must always be alert to abuses.

A specific recommendation for change would be a public defender in juvenile justice. Such a role might advantageously alternate from time to time with the role of prosecutor. A second recommendation would be the creation of a social-service judge. In a helping role, this person would have all of the power available to the judge in the court room without the power to punish or restrict the liberty of young people. At present we have good people doing dirty work in a clumsy system. It is possible to utilize the talent and goodwill of these people more effectively.

Acknowledgment

The author would like to acknowledge support from the Ministry of the Solicitor General of Canada through their Contributions Grant; the Social Science and Humanities Research Council of Canada; and the Exchange of Researchers Program, National Research Council and the Government of France.

References

Blumberg, A.S. 1967. 'The practice of law as a confidence game: Organization cooptation of a profession,' *Law and Society Review* 1: 15–39

Brantingham, P., and P. Burns. 1981. *The Burnaby, B.C. Experimental Public Defender Project: An Evaluation Report*. Ottawa: Department of Justice Canada

Casper, J. 1971. 'Did you have a lawyer when you went to court? No, I had a public defender,' *Yale Review of Law and Social Action* 1: 4–9

Christie, N. 1977. 'Conflicts as property,' *British Journal of Criminology* 17: 1–26

Feeley, M. 1979. *The Process Is the Punishment: Handling Cases in a Lower Criminal Court*. New York: Russel Sage

Gallas, J. 1976. 'The conventional wisdom of state court administration: A critical assessment of an alternative approach,' *The Justice System Journal* 2: 35–55

Greenspan, E. 1982. 'The role of the defence lawyer in sentencing,' in C.L. Boydell and I.A. Connidis, eds, *The Canadian Criminal Justice System*, 200–10. Toronto. Holt, Rinehart and Winston

Hackler, J. 1983–4. 'Interpreting meaning in juvenile court: The use of local wisdom,' *Juvenile and Family Court Journal* 34: 71–82

– 1984. 'Canada,' in M. Klein, ed, *Western Systems of Juvenile Justice*, 39–69. Beverly Hills: Sage

– 1987. 'Stealing conflicts in juvenile justice: Contrasting France and Canada,' *Canadian Journal of Law and Society* 2: 141–51

– 1988. 'Practicing in France what Americans have preached: The response of French judges to juveniles,' *Crime and Delinquency* 34: 467–85.

Hackler, J., J. Brockman, and E. Luczynska. 1977. 'The comparison of role inter-relationships in the juvenile courts: Vienna and Boston,' *International Journal of Criminology and Penology*, 5: 367–97

Hackler, J., Garapon, C. Fringon, and K. Knight. 1987. 'Locking up juveniles in Canada: Some comparisons with France,' *Canadian Public Policy* 13: 477–89

Hagan, J. 1983. *Victims before the Law*. Toronto: Butterworths

Hagan, J., D. Alwin, and J. Hewitt. 1979. 'Ceremonial justice: Crime and punishment in a loosely coupled system,' *Social Forces* 58: 506–27

Hagan, J., I. Nagel, and C. Albonetti. 1980. 'The differential sentencing of white collar offenders in ten federal district courts,' *American Sociological Review* 45: 802–20

Havemann, P. 1986. 'From child saving to child blaming: The political economy of the Young Offenders Act, 1908–1984,' in S. Brickey and E. Comack, eds, *The Social Basis of Law*. Toronto: Garamond Press

Hughes, E. 1964. 'Good people and dirty work,' in H. Becker, ed, *The Other Side*. New York: Free Press

Lawrence, R. 1983–4. 'The role of legal counsel in juveniles' understanding of their rights,' *Juvenile and Family Court Journal* 34: 49–58

Lebel, B. 1981. 'Expertise et déontologie,' *Canadian Journal of Criminology* 23: 203–5

Los, M. 1987. 'La loi sur les jeunes contrevenants et les masse-media,' *Criminologie* 20: 7–33

McIntyre, L. 1987. *The Public Defender*. Chicago: University of Chicago Press

Reiss, A. 1971. 'Systematic observation of natural social phenomenon,' in H. Costner, ed, *Sociological Methodology*, 3–33. San Francisco: Jossey Bass

Smith, T. 1985. 'Law talk: Juveniles' understanding of legal language,' *Journal of Criminal Justice* 13: 339–53

Solomon, P. 1983. *Criminal Justice Policy; from Research to Reform*. Toronto: Butterworths

Wilks, C., L. Birnie, and C. Chamberlain. 1979. 'The Expectations of Children and Their Families Regarding Juvenile Court,' Family Court Clinic, Toronto (mimeo)

PART TWO

The Act and Its Implications

Bala and Kirvan begin this section by exploring the fundamental principles of the Young Offenders Act within the legal perspective. Six years have passed since the proclamation of the YOA, and a number of major court decisions have shaped the direction the legislation has taken. While there is little doubt of the importance of due process within the act, this aspect of the law has not gone unchallenged. Pearson and Beaulieau look at this aspect from the legal perspective in addressing, respectively, the impact of the YOA on legal representation of the accused, and on the role of judges. Schwartz follows this up with an overview of the current American system of juvenile justice. Much of Canada's Young Offenders Act is dependent on revisions to the U.S. youth law developed in the mid-1970s. Schwartz warns that, within the new system of American juvenile justice, youth can anticipate higher rates of detention as one outcome of a deterrent, civil rights–oriented youth law. Validating Schwartz's forecast, Leschied and Jaffe demonstrate, with supporting empirical evidence, that custody dispositons have increased alarmingly since the YOA was proclaimed.

4 The statute: Its principles and provisions and their interpretation by the courts

Nicholas Bala and Mary-Anne Kirvan

Historical Overview

From the beginning of legal history, there have been special rules for dealing with young persons who violated the law. Under English common law, the *doli incapax* (Latin for 'incapacity to do wrong') defence developed. A child under the age of seven was deemed incapable of committing a criminal act. For children between the ages of seven and thirteen inclusive, there was a presumption of incapacity, but this could be rebutted if there was evidence to establish that the child had sufficient intelligence and experience to 'know the nature and consequences of the conduct and to appreciate that it was wrong.'[1] While the *doli incapax* defence afforded certain protections to children, those children who were convicted faced the same penalties as did adult offenders, including hanging and incarceration in such places as the old Kingston Penitentiary.

In the latter part of the nineteenth century, social movements that sought to promote better treatment of children developed in Britain, the United States, and Canada. These movements led to such reforms as the establishment of child-welfare agencies and the creation of juvenile-justice systems, which had distinct philosophies and provided facilities separate from those of adult systems. The reformers of this time considered their paramount objective to be saving destitute and wayward children from a life of poverty and crime. Thus they did not draw a clear distinction between neglected and criminal children. One of the principal drafters of Canada's early delinquency legislation stated that 'there should be no hard and fast distinction between neglected and delinquent children, but ... all should be ... dealt with with a view to serving the best interests of the child' (W.L. Scott, quoted in Archambault 1983: 2). The efforts of these early reformers culminated with the enactment of the Juvenile Delinquents Act in 1908. This federal legislation provided that children were to be dealt with by a court and corrections system separate from the adult system. The JDA clearly had a child-welfare (or *parens patriae*[2]) philosophy, which was reflected in section 38: 'the care and custody and discipline of a juvenile delinquent shall approximate as nearly as may be that which should be given by his parents, and ... as far as practicable every juvenile delinquent shall be treated, not as a criminal, but as a misguided and misdirected child ... needing aid, encouragement, help and assistance.'

The Juvenile Delinquents Act created a highly discretionary system, which gave enormous power to police, judges, and probation officers, to do whatever they considered in a child's 'best interests.' There were no legislative guide-lines governing judicial sentencing, and youths who were sent to training school (reformatory) were generally subject to indeterminate committals. Release from reformatory occurred when correctional officials felt that rehabilitation had been effected. Under the JDA, youths could be subject to sanction for the status offence of 'sexual immorality or any similar form of vice.' While this was not an offence for adults, it was felt that the welfare of children could be promoted if they could be convicted of this offence and thus subjected to appropriate 'treatment.'

While the system created by the JDA in 1908 marked an enormous improvement in the treatment of children and adolescents over earlier times, many serious, interrelated problems still existed. By the 1960s, juvenile justice in Canada was subject to criticism from different sources.

One major criticism of the JDA was that it created a system that tended to ignore the legal rights of children. This was true to such an extent that there were occasions when guilt seemed to be presumed so that 'treatment' would not be delayed by 'unnecessary formalities.' In many parts of Canada, lawyers rarely represented youths charged in juvenile court, and until relatively recently many of the judges in juvenile court lacked legal training. Thus, some critics charged that the juvenile-justice system was unfair and unduly harsh with some youths. Other critics pointed out that certain judges exercised their discretionary powers to promote their perceptions of the best interests of children in such a way that sentences were too lenient and failed to adequately protect society.

The substantial discretion that the JDA gave to juvenile judges and correctional officers was not the only reason for criticism. Very significant control over the system was also vested with provincial directors by the act. As a consequence, there were enormous disparities across Canada in how juveniles were treated (Bala and Corrado 1985). The JDA allowed for the maximum age of juvenile jurisdiction to vary from province to province, ranging from the sixteenth to the eighteenth birthday. Provincial policies and legislation resulted in the minimum age varying from seven to fourteen; children under the minimum age in each province were dealt with exclusively by the child-welfare system. There were also great disparities in respect of diversion from the formal juvenile-justice system, access to legal representation, and use of community-based sentencing options.

The 1965 release of a report on juvenile delinquency in Canada (Department of Justice 1965) began a lengthy period of debate and gradual reform. Some provinces, most notably Quebec, took steps to change their juvenile-justice system by, for example, ensuring that young persons had access to lawyers and establishing a formal system of juvenile diversion. Other provinces lagged behind. On a federal level, discussion papers and draft legislation were released and commented upon, but it was only in February 1981 that the bill that would finally be enacted as the Young Offenders Act was tabled in Parliament. The constitutional entrenchment of the Canadian Charter of Rights and Freedoms in 1982 provided a strong impetus to federal reform efforts. Many of the provisions of the JDA appeared to ignore the legal rights guaranteed in the Charter. Further, the provincial disparities invited challenge under section 15 of the Charter of Rights , which guarantees equality rights. Thus, in 1982, with the support of all political parties, the Young Offenders Act (SC 1980–81–82–83, c.110) received parliamentary approval. The YOA came into force on 2 April 1984, except for the uniform maximum-age provisions.

The most controversial issue among politicians at the time of enactment of the YOA concerned the maximum age for youth-court jurisdiction. There was opposition to establishing a maximum-age jurisdiction running to the eighteenth birthday. Some of the provinces required to raise their age jurisdiction were concerned about costs and administrative difficulties associated with this change. There was also a widespread view that sixteen- and seventeen-year-olds should be held more fully accountable and dealt with in the adult system; this view is still expressed by some observers. The proclamation of the uniform maximum-age provision of the YOA was delayed until 1 April 1985, to allow all jurisdictions sufficient time to adapt.

Since the enactment of the YOA, controversy has also arisen over the minimum age of youth-court jurisdiction. Children under the age of twelve who commit criminal offences can be dealt with only under provincial child-welfare legislation. A few provinces are of the view that the minimum age of twelve is too high. The discussion over minimum age continues, and some individuals argue it should be lowered to ten, or perhaps even back to seven.

In 1986, several relatively minor amendments were enacted to respond to some issues connected with implementation of the act. Matters such as record-keeping, breach of probation orders, and publication of identifying information about dangerous young persons at large were dealt with in the 1986 amendments. These did not alter the philosophy or basic provisions of the act, but did facilitate implementation.[3]

In late 1980s, the YOA became the focus of considerable public criticism and political concern. Most of the attention was directed at the perceived inadequacy of a maximum three-year sentence for dealing with violent offenders, especially those convicted of murder, and at the difficulty in transferring youths into the adult system, where they may face much larger sentences. This criticism reflects broader public perceptions of increased violence among young persons.

In the summer of 1989, the federal government announced that it was considering a range of options for further amendment of the Young Offenders Act, and issued its Consultation Document, which reviewed a number of areas of concern. On 20 December 1989, the government introduced Bill C-58, containing proposals for the reform of the transfer provisions and sentencing for murder in youth court.

Principles of the Young Offenders Act

The YOA constitutes a clear departure from the JDA. There is a uniform national age jurisdiction of twelve through seventeen, as of the date of the offence, and the YOA is unmistakably criminal law, not child-welfare legislation. The discretion of police, judges, and correctional staff is clearly circumscribed by the YOA. The only justification for state intervention under the YOA is the violation of criminal legislation, and this must be established by due process of law. Society is entitled to protection from young offenders, and young offenders are to be held accountable for their acts. However, the YOA is not simply a 'Kiddies' Criminal Code.' Rather, the act establishes a youth-justice system separate from the adult criminal-justice system and distinctive in several critical respects. First, while it recognizes that young persons must be held accountable for criminal acts, they need not always be held accountable in the same manner or to the same extent as adults. Second, the YOA extends rights and safeguards to youth that go beyond those enjoyed by adults. Most important, the act recognizes that youths, by virtue of their adolescence, have special needs and circumstances that must be considered when any decision is made pursuant to the YOA.

The policy that is to govern where young persons come into conflict with the criminal law is set out in the act's Declaration of Principle, found in section 3. These principles are to guide the interpretation and implementation of the act:

3(1) It is hereby recognized and declared that

(a) while young persons should not in all instances be held accountable in the same manner or suffer the same consequences for their behaviour as adults, young persons who commit offences should nonetheless bear responsibility for their contraventions;

(b) society must, although it has the responsibility to take reasonable measures to prevent criminal conduct by young persons, be afforded the necessary protection from illegal behaviour;

(c) young persons who commit offences require supervision, discipline and control, but, because of their state of dependency and level of development and maturity, they also have special needs and require guidance and assistance;

(d) where it is not inconsistent with the protection of society, taking no measures or taking measures other than judicial proceedings under this Act should be considered for dealing with young persons who have committed offences;

(e) young persons have rights and freedoms in their own right, including those stated in the *Canadian Charter of Rights and Freedoms* or in the *Canadian Bill of Rights*, and in particular a right to be heard in the course of, and to participate in, the processes that lead to decisions that affect them, and young persons should have special guarantees of their rights and freedoms;

(f) in the application of this Act, the rights and freedoms of young persons include a right to the least possible interference with freedom that is consistent with the protection of society, having regard to the needs of young persons and the interests of their families;

(g) young persons have the right, in every instance where they have rights or freedoms that may be affected by this Act, to be informed as to what those rights and freedoms are; and

(h) parents have responsibility for the care and supervision of their children, and, for that reason, young persons should be removed from parental supervision either partly or entirely only when measures that provide for continuing parental supervision are inappropriate.

Accountability – Subsection 3(1)(a)

The principle of accountability should be viewed in its fullest sense. Underlying it is the assumption that adolescents are capable of independent thought and proper judgment. Accordingly, where a youth accepts responsibility for an offence or is found guilty of it, the youth is expected to be accountable to society generally and, where possible, to the victim.

This principle is, however, tempered by the concept of limited accountability, which holds that young persons should not, generally speaking, be held accountable in the same manner and to the same extent as would adults. The concept is most clearly reflected in the maximum disposition under the YOA, which is three years in custody, compared to life imprisonment, which an adult may face. The concept of limited accountability is especially important when sentencing youth or when deciding whether to divert a young person from the formal juvenile-justice system to alternative measures.

The transfer provisions (s. 16 of the YOA) allow for a marked departure from the principle of limited accountability. A transferred youth is dealt with in the adult justice system and is subject to the same sentences as an adult, up to and including life imprisonment.

For the majority of youths between the ages of twelve and seventeen years, the existence of a difficulty or condition, such as a mental or physical illness or a learning disability, may assist in explaining behaviour, but does not excuse it. However, sometimes such a young person should not be dealt with in the juvenile system at all, but rather under child-welfare, education, or mental-health legislation. Where the illegal behaviour is of secondary importance relative to the other difficulties facing the youth, and protection of the public is not at issue or is being adequately addressed outside the juvenile-justice system, use of the YOA may not be necessary or appropriate. The use of measures other than the YOA, in appropriate cases, is also specifically endorsed in subsection 3(1)(d) of the Declaration of Principle.

Another exception to a youth being made to assume responsibility for illegal acts arises if the youth is found to be not guilty by reason of insanity. If a youth is found to be not guilty by reason of insanity, he or she will be committed to a mental-health facility until it is determined that the mental illness has been cured.

Protection of Society – Subsection 3(1)(b)

A second major principle of the YOA is that society must be afforded the necessary protection from the illegal behaviour of young persons. Protection should not, however, be viewed in a narrow sense. It is submitted that this principle speaks to the responsibility of the juvenile-justice system to meet Canadian society's long-term interests in the reduction of crime by youth and the rehabilitation of young offenders, as well as communities' more immediate needs for protection from crime.

Special Needs of Youth – Subsection 3(1)(c)

While the YOA is clearly criminal legislation, it distinguishes itself from the law applicable to adults by its recognition that adolescents have special needs. The Declaration of Principle requires that the limited maturity and dependency of youth be taken into account, and that decisions made about youth reflect their 'special needs.'

The phrase 'special needs' warrants closer examination. Canada's juvenile-justice system is premised on a fundamental assumption that young persons have special needs by virtue of their adolescence. These needs will vary, depending on a youth's level of biological, psychological, and social development. The term 'special needs' therefore encompasses the needs of youth to form positive peer relationships. to develop appropriate self-esteem, and to establish an independent identity; it also extends to their health, educational, and spiritual needs. Over and above the needs of and developmental challenges facing all adolescents, the act recognizes the importance of identifying the additional needs of youth who may be suffering from such problems as a 'physical or mental illness or disorder, a psychological disorder, an emotional disturbance, a learning disability or mental retardation' (s. 13[1][e]).

For many youths appearing before the youth courts, their criminal behaviour constitutes an isolated and often not very serious act. For these youth such safeguards in the act as limits on dispositions (s. 20), involvement of parents (ss. 9, 10, 20), bans on publication of identity (s. 38), and restrictions on use of records (ss. 40–6) are adequate to promote their needs. For some youths, however, their criminal behaviour is part of a pattern of more serious difficulties. It is essential to understand the special needs of these youths if their interests, and the long-term interests of society, are to be met. A pre-disposition report (s. 14) or a medical or psychological assessment (s. 13) may be ordered by a youth court to better learn of the needs of an individual youth.

There are situations where the special needs of a young person require that provincial child-protection, education, or mental-health legislation be used rather than, or concurrently with, the YOA. It must be recognized that the needs of some troubled youths will be ongoing and fall outside the mandate of the criminal-justice system. The concept of 'special needs' should not be used to justify intervention under the YOA that is not commensurate with the offence. Thus, if a youth commits a relatively minor offence, this should not be used as a justification for a very severe disposition, even if this would afford 'treatment.' The principle of least possible interference (s. 3[1][f]) requires that other means, less intrusive than the criminal law and more appropriate, given the minor nature of the offence, be used to gain access to the needed treatment.

The making of various decisions about the young person, in particular in regard to sentencing, requires a careful balancing of the principles of accountability and protection of society against the special needs of youth. Sometimes, such a decision is not difficult to make, and it is possible to impose a disposition that recognizes 'treatment' needs. For example, it may be best for the youth and society to have a probation term imposed, with a condition that the youth attend substance-abuse counselling. In some situations, a residential or custodial disposition may be made that also involves treatment.

Other decisions are much more difficult to make. Perhaps the clearest choice between the protection of society and the needs of a young person occurs when consideration is being given to transfer to adult court, pursuant to section 16 of the YOA. Conflicting views on the appropriate balance in transfer cases are discussed more fully later in this chapter.

Alternative Measures and No Measures – Subsection 3(1)(d)

The YOA allows for young offenders to be dealt with outside the formal court system through the means of 'alternative measures.' Alternative measures are governed by section 4 of the YOA. Use of such a program is generally restricted to relatively minor, first offences. These programs have the advantage of being expeditious and informal, and they tend to minimize the stigmatizing affects of an appearance in youth court.

Subsection 3(1)(d) is intended to provide guidance to police and crown attorneys who are considering whether to lay charges. It indicates that, in the case of less-serious offences, there may be situations where it is appropriate to 'take no measures,' that is, to lay no charges. This serves as a formal endorsement of a traditionally exercised discretion not to commence criminal proceedings.

In *R. v. David L.*,[4] a thirteen-year-old boy who had been placed in a group home under child-welfare legislation was charged with an assault as a result of an altercation in which the boy punched a staff member. The youth court dismissed the charge, relying, in part, on subsection 3(1)(d) of the YOA, and stated that staff who occupy a 'parent-like' role should not look to the courts to deal with relatively minor disciplinary matters.

Rights of Young Persons – Subsections 3(1)(e) and (g)

The Declaration of Principle recognizes that young persons have 'rights and freedoms in their own right' and, additionally, 'that they should have special guarantees of these rights and freedoms.' One of the special rights of young persons is to have counsel provided by the state if they are unable to obtain or afford a lawyer (s. 11). Adults have the right to retain counsel, but if they cannot afford to do so they are forced to rely on the discretion of the legal-aid authorities. Another important special protection for young persons is found in section 56 of the YOA, which excludes from a trial any statement made by a youth unless special warnings are provided, most notably a warning of the right to remain silent and of the right to have a parent or lawyer present when a statement is made to the police. It was felt by Parliament that these types of special protections are essential because young persons may not fully understand their rights and may not be able to fully exercise them without special assistance.

Some have argued that those special rights unduly restrict police and crown attorneys. The justification for these rights for young persons has been questioned by some who believe that they are inconsistent with the principles of protection of the public and responsibility for criminal behaviour. This debate is not new to criminal justice, and certainly is not restricted to juvenile justice. However, in the context of youth-court proceedings, the debate takes on an added poignancy as it is sometimes argued that the exercise of legal rights may serve to defeat the needs of a young person.

Minimal Interference – Subsection 3(1)(f)

The principle of least possible interference requires that decision makers take the least intrusive measures, consistent with the protection of society and the needs of young persons and their families. In some situations, this means alternative measures, or no measures, will be appropriate. This principle will also affect decisions about pre-trial detention, disposition, and disposition review. The principle also requires that the YOA not be used as a vehicle for imposing a disposition on a youth that is more severe than warranted by the offence but perhaps justifiable on the grounds of treatment.

Parental Involvement – Subsection 3(1)(h)

The YOA recognizes that parents have an important responsibility for their children, and that young persons can often be best helped in a familial context. Subsection 3(1)(h) requires that decisions about pre-trial detention and disposition be made, taking into consideration the desirability of parental supervision. The YOA requires that parents be notified of the arrest of their child (s. 8) and of youth-court proceedings (s. 9). In certain cases, parents may be ordered to attend court (s. 10).

Parents also have the right to make submissions before a decision is made about disposition or transfer. It is important, however, to appreciate that parents are not parties to a YOA proceeding. It is only the young person who can retain and instruct counsel; parents are sometimes confused about this matter and want to be involved in directing a case.

The old Juvenile Delinquents Act provided that parents could be fined if their children committed criminal acts. The YOA eliminated this provision. The YOA requires that young persons alone should be responsible for their illegal acts, but recognizes that parents may have an important role in their rehabilitation. In some situations, parents may also have a role in the protection of the legal rights of their children.

The Principles of the YOA: An Assessment

Some commentators have suggested that the principles articulated in section 3 are inconsistent and hence offer no real guidance for the implementation of the YOA. Others have been critical of the apparent lack of prioritization among the principles articulated. One youth-court judge commented that section 3 reflects, 'if not inconsistency, then at least ambivalence about what approaches should be taken with young offenders' (Thomson 1982: 24).[5]

It is apparent that there is a level of societal ambivalence in Canada about the appropriate response to young offenders. On the one hand, there is a feeling that adolescents who violate the criminal law need help to enable them to grow into productive, law-abiding citizens; this view is frequently reflected in media stories about inadequate facilities for treating young offenders. On the other hand, there is a widespread public concern about the need to control youthful criminality and protect society. This view is reflected in media stories and editorials commenting on the alleged inadequacy of the three-year maximum disposition that can be applied to young offenders, a particular public concern in regard to those youths who commit very serious, violent offences.

While it may not be inaccurate to suggest that the Declaration of Principle reflects a certain societal ambivalence about young offenders, it is also important to appreciate that it represents an honest attempt to achieve an appropriate balance for dealing with a very complex social problem. The YOA does not have a single, simple underlying philosophy, for there is no single, simple philosophy that can deal with all situations in which young persons violate the criminal law. While the declaration as a whole defines the parameters for juvenile justice in Canada, each principle is not necessarily relevant to every situation. The weight to be attached to a particular principle will be determined in large measure by the nature of the decision being made and the specific provisions of the YOA that govern the situation. There are situations in which there is a need to balance competing principles, but this is a challenge in cases in the adult as well as the juvenile system.

When contrasted with the child welfare–oriented philosophy of the JDA, the YOA emphasizes the accountability of young offenders, due process, the protection of society, and limited discretion. In comparison with the adult Criminal Code, however, the YOA emphasizes special needs and the limited accountability of young persons. There is a fundamental tension in the YOA between such competing ideals as due process and treatment; in some situations, the act gives precedence to due process, though in exceptional circumstances treatment may be emphasized at the expense of due process. The underlying philosophical tensions in the YOA reflect the very complex nature of youthful criminality. There is no single, simple philosophy and no single type of program that will 'solve' the problem of youthful criminality. Judges and the other professionals who work with young persons who violate the criminal law require a complex and balanced set of principles like those found in the YOA.

The balance of this chapter will be devoted to a consideration of the substantive provisions of the Young Offenders Act, with a discussion of how they reflect the principles found in section 3 of the act and of how the courts have interpreted these principles in different contexts.

Arrest and Police Questioning

In addition to those rights guaranteed to all under the Charter of Rights, the YOA affords special rights and protections to young persons who are arrested. Some of these provisions are premised on the notion that many young persons lack the maturity and sophistication to fully appreciate their situation, and hence require special legal rights; other provisions are intended to involve parents in the process, both to protect the rights of their children and to recognize their supportive role.

The Charter of Rights provides that 'everyone has the right to be secure against unreasonable search or seizure' (s. 8); 'everyone has the right not to be arbitrarily detained or imprisoned' (s. 9); and

> Everyone has the right on arrest or detention
> (a) to be informed promptly of the reason therefor;
> (b) to retain and instruct counsel without delay and to be informed of that right; and
> (c) to have the validity of the detention determined ... and to be released if the detention is not lawful (s. 10).

The rights that are guaranteed to all under the Charter may be of special significance to young persons, as they are particularly vulnerable to police supervision.

In *R. v. Ina Christina V.*[6] a police officer observed a fifteen-year-old girl chatting quietly on a street corner in a place known by the officer to have an 'almost magnetic appeal for children who have run from home, some of whom have become the so-called "street kids" and acts as a focal point for may persons involved in prostitution and drug trafficking.' The officer concluded she was either 'loitering' (not a criminal offence) 'or possibly a runaway,' and purported to arrest her under provincial child-welfare legislation. A struggle ensued and the girl was charged with assaulting the police officer. In acquitting the girl of this charge, the judge observed:

> the evidence presented ... is more than sufficient to find that Christina V.'s rights were infringed under ss ... 8 and 9 of the Charter and denied under para. 10(b) of the Charter. In regard to the latter, although she was advised of her right to retain and instruct counsel without delay, there is no evidence that she was provided with the opportunity and means to do so. In advance of that, she was deprived of her liberty, the security of her person was invaded, her property was unjustly seized and searched and she was arbitrarily detained

and imprisoned. These gross violations of her fundamental rights were totally out of proportion with the situation and prescribed nowhere by law. Even if the law had provided for such interference, it would be unreasonable to find that such was demonstrably justified in a free and democratic society ...

The phenomenon of the runaway child is, in the first instance, a social problem. Left unaddressed, it too often escalates into a legal issue involving either or both child welfare authorities and law enforcement officers. The magnitude of the problem as it relates to downtown Toronto ... requires an urgent response. Undoubtedly, as a result of pressure from concerned parents, politicians and business people in the area, the Metropolitan Toronto Police Department has felt obliged to provide that response. Unfortunately, the standard law enforcement approach to the problem is woefully inadequate as well as improper.

As was exhibited in this case, good faith and a sense of duty on the part of the police falls far short of adequately addressing the situation. The runaway child who has been reported missing but has not committed any criminal offence *may* indeed be a child at risk. That is the issue which must be addressed first and it can only be accomplished in a competent and caring fashion by trained child care workers.

In addition to the protections afforded under the Charter of Rights, special provisions found in section 56 of the YOA are intended to ensure that there is no improper questioning of young persons by police and other persons in authority:

56 (2) No oral or written statement given by a young person to a peace officer or other person who is, in law, a person in authority is admissible against the young person unless
(a) the statement was voluntary;
(b) the person to whom the statement was given has, before the statement was made, clearly explained to the young person, in language appropriate to his age and understanding, that
(i) the young person is under no obligation to give a statement,
(ii) any statement given by him may be used as evidence in proceedings against him,
(iii) the young person has the right to consult another person in accordance with paragraph (c), and
(iv) any statement made by the young person is required to be made in the presence of the person consulted, unless the young person desires otherwise;

(c) the young person has, before the statement was made, been given a reasonable opportunity to consult with counsel or a parent, or in the absence of a parent, an adult relative, or in the absence of a parent and an adult relative, any other appropriate adult chosen by the young person; and

(d) where the young person consults any person pursuant to paragraph (c), the young person has been given a reasonable opportunity to make the statement in the presence of that person.

Section 56 is based on the recognition that young persons may lack the sophistication and maturity to fully appreciate the legal consequences of making a statement, and so require special protections when being questioned by police. It is also premised on the notion that some youths are easily intimidated by adult authority figures, and may make statements that they believe those authority figures expect to hear, even if the statements are false. It is hoped that consultation with a parent or lawyer will preclude the making of such false statements.

Section 56 has been invoked in a number of cases by the courts to exclude statements made by young persons. In *R. v. M.A.M.*, a sixteen-year-old youth with a learning disability was charged with gross indecency. The police officer who arrested the youth purported to inform him of his rights by reading from a form that reiterated the words used in section 56. The young person then waived his right to have a lawyer or parent present. In ruling the statements inadmissible, the British Columbia Court of Appeal wrote:

it appears ... that the learned trial judge was confronted with the requirements of s. 56 and concluded that having the contents of the two forms read to him, the young person did not know what to do in the circumstances and did not know why a lawyer would be necessary ... In my opinion, the course followed by the police officer in the present case did not meet the requirements of s. 56 of the *Young Offenders Act*. The forms themselves appear to be clear, but Parliament indicated the requirements that before the statement was made there must be a clear explanation to the young person. I am not persuaded that reading the contents of those two forms met the requirements imposed by Parliament before the statement could be taken from the young person ...

Parliament has paid special attention to the needs of young people for protective advice and has called on the police to provide it. There should be a genuine endeavour by the person in authority to describe the function of the lawyer and the benefits to the young person of having a lawyer, or parents, or relatives, or an adult friend present. That endeavour should be designed to lead to an appreciation on the part of the young person of the consequences of the choices that he makes.

Even had this young person been a person without any learning disability, the mere reading over of these two statements and then asking the young person to sign them, without any explanation to him whatsoever, would not, in my opinion, have been compliance with ss. (2) (b) and (c) of s. 56 of the *Young Offenders Act*.[7]

An interesting and difficult issue that has arisen in some cases is the extent to which individuals such as schoolteachers, principals, or social workers may be 'agents of the state' and hence should be expected to comply with the requirements of the Charter of Rights and section 56 of the YOA. In *R. v. H*,[8] a thirteen-year-old boy was charged with theft, and the prosecutor sought to have the court hear statements made by the youth to his teacher and the school principal. Prior to the statements being made, the teacher promised that, if the money was returned, nothing further would happen. Not surprisingly, neither the teacher nor the principal complied with the Charter or section 56 of the YOA. The court ruled the statements inadmissible because of the violation of the YOA and section 10 of the Charter of Rights. *R. v. H.* does not require school personnel to afford young persons the right to counsel in all situations, but it does indicate that, if this right is not afforded a youth prior to questioning, statements that are made may later be ruled inadmissible in youth court proceedings.

A somewhat different approach was taken in *R. v. J.M.G.*,[9] where a fourteen-year-old boy was charged with possession of a small amount of marijuana that had been discovered by his school principal after a search of the youth. The Ontario Court of Appeal emphasized that the search was carried out in the context of the principal's normal duties of maintaining discipline in the school, and hence did not constitute a violation of the Charter of Rights. The court recognized that, while the relationship between student and principal was not like that of policeman and citizen, 'there may come a time when such [significant legal] consequences are inevitable and the principal becomes an agent of the police in detecting crime.' In such a situation, a school principal or teacher might be expected to strictly comply with the warning requirements of the Charter. *R. v. H.* and *R. v. J.M.G.* illustrate that the courts will closely scrutinize each situation to determine the extent to which a principal or other person should be treated as an agent of the state. It may also be significant that *R. v. J.M.G.* involved the seizure of physical evidence, which was clearly indicative of the fact that the crime in question had been committed, while

R. v. H. involved only a statement, and the YOA has special provisions in regard to statements.

Section 9 of the YOA provides that, if a young person is arrested or detained, a parent must be notified 'as soon as possible.' A parent must also be notified in writing of any youth court hearings. If a parent is not available, notice may be given to an adult relative or other appropriate adult. The act also allows a youth court to order that a parent attend any proceedings if such attendance is considered 'necessary or in the best interests of the young person.' While parents are not parties to youth-court proceedings, they have a statutory right to address the court prior to disposition, disposition review, or possible transfer to adult court.

The Declaration of Principle, subsection 3(1)(h), recognizes the role of parents in the lives of their children, and sections 9 and 56 ensure that parents have notice of arrest, detention, and youth-court proceedings. These provisions are premised on the notion that parents will normally provide emotional support and ensure that a youth's legal rights are protected. It should be emphasized that, under subsection 56(2), it is the youth who has the right to decide whether or not a parent will be present during police questioning. Some youths may be unwilling to have parental involvement, and there may be cases where such involvement is clearly not appropriate. Parents will normally not be considered 'persons in authority,' and statements made to them by their children will usually be admissible, despite the absence of any form of caution.[10]

There may, however, be cases in which parental questioning will amount to duress, and a statement in such circumstances could be ruled inadmissible. In *R. v. S.L.*,[11] the judge felt that a father who became actively involved with the police in the questioning of his son about a suspected homicide became a 'member of the investigation team.' The court ruled the youth's confession inadmissible, saying:

> There is no doubt that most well-thinking parents in a situation involving the death of a youngster would be anxious to co-operate in finding the truth, but when that involves co-operating with the police and obtaining some incriminating evidence against their own child, and without being made aware of all the information that the police had against the child, it is, I feel, not a rightful situation and can constitute an abuse of the very special relationship of authority and influence that a parent has on his child.

Youths who are arrested for relatively minor charges are normally released, pending a hearing, but those charged with more serious offences, or who have long records of prior convictions, or who might not appear for trial, may be detained pursuant to the order of a youth-court judge or a justice of the peace. The law governing pre-trial detention of young persons is generally the same as that applicable for adults, but section 7 of the YOA specifies that such detention will normally be separate from adults. The YOA allows for detention with adults only if a court is satisfied that this is necessary for the safety of the youth or others, or if the youth is in a remote location and no youth-detention facilities are available within a reasonable distance. While pre-trial detention is normally separate from adults, youths who are waiting are often kept in the same facilities as young offenders who are serving sentences in custody.

Pre-trial detention has the potential of being extremely disruptive to a young person, as it may result in sudden removal from familiar surroundings and placement in an often intimidating, institutional environment. Such detention will usually interfere with schooling or employment, and with familial and peer relationships. To minimize such disruptions, subsection 7(1) of the YOA allows a youth-court judge or a justice of the peace to order that a young person who would otherwise be detained be placed under the care and control of a 'responsible person'; a 'responsible person' would normally be a parent or other adult who is trusted by the youth. This will only be done if the 'responsible person' undertakes in writing to exercise control over the youth and satisfy such other conditions as may be imposed, for example, ensuring that the youth refrain from consuming alcohol pending trial. A 'responsible person' who 'wilfully fails' to comply with the undertaking may be charged with an offence under subsection 7(2) of the YOA.

The YOA provides, in section 13, that, if there is a question about a young person's mental capacity to stand trial or if there is an application for transfer of the case to adult court, the youth court may order a medical, psychological, or psychiatric assessment prior to trial. In other situations, there is no jurisdiction for a mandatory pre-trial assessment. Assessments and transfer applications are discussed more fully below.

Alternative Measures

Paragraph 3(1)(d) of the Declaration of Principle recognizes the value of 'taking measures other than judicial proceedings' under the YOA. Section 4 of the YOA creates a legislative framework for 'alternative measures,' that is to say, for dealing with young persons outside the formal youth-court process.

Alternative measures are a form of diversion from the court process and are typically used for first-time offenders charged with relatively minor offences. An alternative-measures program allows a youth to be dealt with in a relatively expeditious, informal fashion and enables a youth to avoid a formal record of conviction. It is felt that some youths may be unnecessarily harmed by being 'labelled' as 'young offenders' through the formal court process, and that they may benefit from relatively informal treatment. Use of alternative measures is also consistent with the principle of 'least possible interference,' which is articulated in subsection 3(1)(f) of the YOA. Further, alternative-measures programs may increase the scope for involvement of parents, victims, and the community. Such programs may also be less expensive to operate than the formal youth-court system.

In most provinces, responsibility for alternative measures is given to a community agency with a paid staff or volunteers, though in some provinces government social workers or juvenile-probation staff are responsible (Rabinovitch 1986). Referrals of cases must initially be made by the police or crown attorney, who must be satisfied that alternative measures would be 'appropriate, having regard to the needs of the young person and the interests of society.' Further, the crown must be satisfied that sufficient evidence exists to take the case to court. The program administrator then meets with the young person and proposes some form of 'alternative measures,' which might involve, for example, an apology, restitution, some form of volunteer work, or a charitable donation.

Youths must 'fully and freely consent' to participating. The young person always has the option of having the charge dealt with in youth court. The youth must 'accept responsibility' for the offence alleged to have been committed; if the young person denies responsibility, the matter must go to court for a judicial finding of guilt or innocence. The young person must be advised of the right to consultation with a lawyer prior to participation.

If a young person agrees to participate and successfully completes the alternative measures agreed to, the charges must be dropped. Whether or not there is successful completion, no statement made by a youth in the process of consideration of whether alternative measures should be imposed may be used in later court proceedings. If there is only partial completion of alternative measures, there is a discretion as to whether the matter can be brought back to court.

While there is some controversy over the efficacy of alternative measures as opposed to court in terms of reducing future offences (see, e.g., Moyer 1980), every province except Ontario implemented section 4 of the YOA soon after it came into force in 1984. It was generally felt that alternative measures represented a socially useful experiment for dealing with first-time offenders in a humane, inexpensive fashion, and most of the provinces were prepared to participate.

The failure of Ontario to implement section 4 of the YOA was challenged as a violation of the equality rights guaranteed by section 15 of the Charter of Rights. In *R. v. Sheldon S.*[12] the Ontario Court of Appeal held that the absence of such programs in Ontario constituted a 'denial of equal benefit and protection of the law' on the basis of place of residence, and hence was in violation of section 15 of the Charter. The decision was under appeal to the Supreme Court of Canada; the government of Ontario established alternative-measures programs across the province on an 'interim basis.'[13] The Supreme Court of Canada reversed the decision of the lower courts, ruling that, in a federal state such as Canada, certain types of differences in treatment based on geography are constitutionally acceptable. Despite the Supreme Court judgment, the recently elected New Democratic government decided to continue alternative measures in Ontario, while reviewing their utility. Some of the pressure to maintain these programs results from the recognition that they divest cases from the already overcrowded court system.

Youth-Court Proceedings

Proceedings under the YOA are conducted in a specially designated 'youth court.' In a number of provinces, the family court, which is responsible for such matters as child protection and adoption, has been selected to be the youth court. In other jurisdictions, it is the provincial court, which deals with most adult criminal charges, that has been designated as the youth court, although the proceedings must be held at a separate time from those involving adults.

Ontario and Nova Scotia adopted a 'two-tier' youth-court model. As was the practice under the Juvenile Delinquents Act, twelve- to fifteen-year-olds are dealt with in family court, while sixteen- and seventeen-year-olds are proceeded with in the adult provincial court, albeit with adult-court judges nominally sitting as youth-court judges. Critics argued that Ontario and Nova Scotia simply acted in an expedient fashion and have failed to implement the spirit of the YOA by maintaining the court jurisdiction in effect under the JDA (Bala 1987; Stuart 1987). However, the courts have held that the two-tier implementation model is permitted under the YOA and does not violate the Charter of Rights.[14] In 1990, the Ontario government announced that all cases would be dealt with by the family court, which is gradually gaining responsibility for all ages of youths in the province; however, responsibility for service provision will remain divided between the social-service ministry (for ages twelve to fifteen years) and corrections (for ages sixteen to seventeen years).

In section 52, the YOA stipulates that proceedings in youth court are to be similar to those governing 'summary-conviction offences' in adult court. This means that the proceedings are less complex and more expeditious than those applicable to the more serious adult 'indictable offences.' More specifically, this means that there are no preliminary inquiries, and all trials are conducted by a judge alone; there are no jury trials in youth court. It is felt that it is particularly important for young persons to have the more expeditious resolution of their cases available through summary procedures. The courts have held that the failure to afford young persons an opportunity for trial by jury does not violate the provisions of the Charter of Rights, which guarantee equality and the right to a jury trial to persons facing imprisonment of five years or more. In *R. v. Robbie L.*, the Ontario Court of Appeal emphasized that the maximum penalty under the YOA is three years, rather than the life sentence an adult may face for certain serious offences. Justice Morden wrote:

> the *Young Offenders Act* is intended to provide a comprehensive system for deal-ing with young persons who are alleged to be in conflict with the law which is separate and distinct from the adult criminal justice system. While the new sys-tem is more like the adult system than was that under the *Juvenile Delinquents Act* it nonetheless is a different system. As far as the aftermath of a finding of guilt is concerned, the general thrust of the *Young Offenders Act* is to provide less severe consequences than those relating to an adult offender ... the estab-lishment of the legal regime ... for dealing with young persons, which is sepa-rate and distinct from the adult criminal justice system, is of sufficient importance to warrant the overriding of the equality right alleged to be in-fringed in this proceeding.[15]

While a young person being tried in youth court is denied the opportu-nity to a preliminary inquiry and a jury, a youth is afforded all of the procedural protections given to an adult who faces a summary charge. There is a constitutionally based presumption of innocence (s. 11[d] of the Charter of Rights), with the onus upon the prosecution to prove its case. If a not-guilty plea is entered, the crown will call witnesses to establish its case, and each witness will be subject to cross-examination. The youth is entitled to call witnesses and to testify, subject to the crown's right of cross-examination, but there is no obligation upon the accused to adduce any evidence or testify. After all the witnesses are called, there may be submis-sions (or arguments), and the judge then renders a verdict. If the judge is satisfied, beyond a reasonable doubt, that the offence charged has occurred, a conviction is entered, and the case proceeds to disposition under the YOA. Otherwise, an acquittal is entered, and this ends the YOA proceeding, though in appropriate cases the youth might still be dealt with under provincial child-welfare or mental-health legislation.

Most cases under the YOA do not, in fact, result in trials, but rather in guilty pleas. Frequently the youth recognizes that an offence has occurred and wishes to plead guilty. If a guilty plea is entered, the crown attorney will read a summary of the evidence against the youth. Section 19 of the YOA has a special provision requiring a judge in youth court to be satisfied that the facts read by the crown support the charge. If they do not, the judge must enter a plea of not guilty and conduct a trial. This provision recognizes that a youth may not appreciate the significance of a guilty plea as fully as would an adult.

It is not uncommon for a guilty plea in youth court to be the product of a 'plea bargain.' A 'plea bargain' is typically the result of informal discussions between the crown attorney and the lawyer representing the youth. There is an agreement to plead guilty to certain charges in exchange for dropping of other charges or a request by the crown to the court for a particular disposition. Though considered controversial by some, 'plea bargaining' is not regarded as unethical or illegal. It should be noted that, if there is plea bargaining, the judge is not bound to impose the disposition requested by the accused.

The YOA affords very important rights in regard to the provision of legal representation. Section 11 requires that, as soon as a young person is arrested or appears in youth court, the youth is to be advised of the right to counsel. If the young person is 'unable' to obtain counsel, the youth-court judge shall 'direct' that legal representation be provided. While adults have the right to retain counsel, if they are unable to afford a lawyer, they must rely on legal aid, which has fairly stringent criteria for deciding whether to provide representation. The YOA guarantees that, whenever a youth is 'unable' to obtain counsel, it will be provided. It has been held that, when assessing financial ability to retain counsel, the court should not consider parental resources in their decision.[16] Since the few young people have significant financial resources, in practice this means that most youths are represented by lawyers who are paid by the state.

While a youth is not obliged to be represented by a lawyer and may choose to appear unrepresented or assisted by some other adult, such as a parent, the effect of the YOA has been to ensure that most youths are represented by counsel. This has proven controversial to some observers, who have argued that securing legal representation often results in unnecessary delays and that lawyers often fail to promote the 'best interests' of adolescent clients (Leschied and Jaffe 1987: 428). However, the YOA is clearly criminal law, and it is understandable that those subject to potential punishment by the state are entitled to full legal representation; young persons without lawyers are rarely in a position to appreciate the significance of their involvement in the legal system or to protect their rights. It is apparent that, in some localities, administrative difficulties have resulted in delays in obtaining legal counsel, and that some lawyers involved in the representation of young persons lack the training or sensitivity to provide truly adequate legal services. However, denial of access to counsel does not seem an appropriate strategy for dealing with these problems; rather administrative changes and increased training would be desirable.

The YOA has a number of provisions intended to protect the privacy of young persons involved in the youth-court process and to minimize the stigmatization they may face. Section 38 provides that the media cannot publish identifying information about a young person, though in 1986 a special exception was added to the YOA, at the request of the police.[17] If a youth is at large, the police may seek an order from a youth-court judge allowing publication of identifying information; the judge must be satisfied that the youth is 'dangerous to others' and that publication is necessary to assist in the youth's apprehension.

Section 39 stipulates that, while youth-court proceedings are generally open to the public, the judge may make an order excluding some or all members of the public if their presence 'would be seriously injurious or seriously prejudicial' to the young person.

Sections 40 to 46 govern records; access to records of youths involved with the court system is generally restricted. While police may fingerprint and photograph youths charged with indictable offences, the central records of the Royal Canadian Mounted Police must be destroyed five years after the completion of any sentence for an indictable offence, provided the youth commits no further offences in that five-year period. Local police forces and others who have records related to young offenders are not obliged to destroy their records, but their use is severely restricted after the five years have passed. Section 36 of the YOA prohibits employers governed by federal law from asking whether a potential employee has ever been convicted of an offence under the YOA. These provisions recognize the 'limited accountability' of young persons and are intended to afford a 'second chance' to those who are convicted under the YOA and do not commit further crimes for a specified period.

Disposition and Disposition Review

Young persons convicted of offences pursuant to the YOA receive a 'disposition,' or 'sentence,' pursuant to section 20 of the act. Dispositions range through: an absolute discharge; a fine of up to $1000; an order for restitution or compensation; an order for up to 240 hours of community service; an order for up to two years' probation; an order for treatment for up to two years; an order for custody for up to three years.[18]

For less serious offences, a court may make a disposition immediately after a finding of guilt. For more serious offences, however, the court will normally adjourn to allow preparation of a report to assist the court. Most commonly, the youth court will request a 'pre-disposition' report, sometimes called a 'social history,' which is prepared by a youth-court worker. The worker will interview the youth, the youth's parents, the victim, and any other significant individuals, and will summarize the youth's background and provide information about the offence. Frequently the report will include a recommendation about disposition. Although not binding on the court, these recommendations are usually influential. The youth, of course, has the right to challenge the report, and may introduce independent evidence about disposition. Parents also have the right to make submissions prior to disposition.

In more serious cases, or cases where there is particular concern about a young person, the court may make an order under section 13 of the YOA for a psychiatric, medical, or psychological assessment to assist in arriving at an appropriate disposition.

Following the enactment of the YOA, appellate courts in different Canadian provinces have gradually articulated a dispositional philosophy for young offenders. In *R. v. Richard I.*,[19] the Ontario Court of Appeal acknowledged that, in comparison with sentencing adults, 'the task of arriving at the "right" disposition may be a considerably more difficult and complex one, given the special needs of young persons and the kind of guidance and assistance they may require.' In *R. v. Joseph F.*, Justice Morden of the Ontario Court of Appeal wrote:

> While undoubtedly the protection of society is a central principle of the Act ...
> it is one that has to be reconciled with other considerations, such as the needs
> of young persons and, in any event, it is not a principle which must inevitably
> be reflected in a severe disposition. In many cases, unless the degree of seri-
> ousness of the offence and the circumstances in which it was committed mil-
> itate otherwise, it is best given effect to by a disposition which gives emphasis

to the factors of individual deterrence and rehabilitation. We do not agree that it puts the matter correctly to say the whole purpose of the Act is to give a degree of paramountcy to the protection of society – with the implication that this is to overbear the needs and interests of the young person and must result in a severe disposition.[20]

One controversial issue is the extent to which courts making dispositions under the YOA should take into account the principle of general deterrence. In *R. v. G.K.*, the Alberta Court of Appeal declined to impose a custodial disposition on a youth without a prior record who was convicted of armed robbery, emphasizing that a psychiatric report indicated that there was no likelihood of a recurrence of delinquent acts. Justice Stevenson wrote:

> We ... reject the suggestion that the young offender's sentence should be modelled on the sentence that would be imposed on an adult offender. If a custodial sentence is warranted then it ought not to be lengthier than that which would be imposed on an adult ... In any event, deterrence to others does not, in my view, have any place in the sentencing of young offenders. It is not one of the principles enumerated ... in s.3 of the Act which declares the policy for young offenders in Canada.[21]

However, most other appellate courts have held that general deterrence may play a role in the sentencing of young offenders. The Ontario Court of Appeal specifically rejected the approach of the Alberta Court of Appeal in *R. v. G.K.*:

> The principles under s.3 of the *Young Offenders Act* do not sweep away the principle of general deterrence. The principles under that section enshrine the principle of the protection of society and this subsumes general and specific deterrence. It is perhaps sufficient to say that ... the principles of general deterrence must be considered but it has diminished importance in determining the appropriate disposition in the case of a youthful offender.[22]

Another controversial issue is the extent to which courts should consider the promotion of the welfare of a youth as a basis for imposing a custodial sentence. In *R.R. v. R.*, the Nova Scotia Court of Appeal upheld a sentence of five months' open custody imposed on a fourteen-year-old youth without a prior record who was convicted of the theft of a skateboard. The court felt the youth 'desperately requires strict controls and constant supervision.'[23] The commission of the offence was considered a justification for imposing needed care, even though the sentence was grossly is proportionate to the offence and far in excess of what an adult would have received for the same offence.

A more common approach, however, has been to reject the use of the YOA simply as a route for providing treatment. In *R. v. Michael B.*[24] the Ontario Court of Appeal overturned an order for five months' open custody imposed upon a youth who committed a relatively minor assault and had no prior record. The trial judge had been concerned that the boy was suicidal, and neither his family nor the mental-health facility he had been staying in wanted to accept him. Justice Brooke concluded that incarceration under the YOA 'was not responsive to the offence, but in reality was what seemed at the time a sensible way of dealing with a youth who had a personality problem and needed a place to go.' The Court of Appeal suggested that involuntary commitment to a mental-health facility under provincial incompetency law was the appropriate route to follow; in fact, this had occurred by the time the case came before that court.

As a result of the YOA's distinctive dispositional philosophy, and reflecting the fact that many youths involved in the criminal-justice system have not committed serious offences, the majority of convicted young offenders receive dispositions that keep them in their communities. The YOA allows the imposition of an absolute discharge if the court considers 'it to be in the best interests of the young person and not contrary to the public interest.' This disposition is usually reserved for minor first offenders and results in no real sanction being imposed, other than the fact of conviction. Restitution, community service, and fines allow the court to impose a real penalty on the youth, without unduly restricting freedom. In appropriate cases, victims may be compensated by restitution.

The most frequently imposed disposition under the YOA is probation.[25] The nature of a probation order depends on the circumstances, and various conditions may be imposed. Typical conditions might be that a youth maintain a curfew, attend school, or reside with parents. Probation may also entail regular reporting to a probation officer, and might even be used to require a youth to live in a foster home or with a suitable adult person.[26]

One of the most controversial dispositional provisions of the YOA deals with 'treatment orders,' which allow a youth to be 'detained for treatment' in a psychiatric hospital or other 'treatment facility,' instead of in custody. Such orders may be made only on the recommendation of a medical, psychiatric, or psychological report, prepared pursuant to section 13 of the YOA, and only if the youth and the facility consent; normally parents must also consent to such an order being made, though there is provision for dispensing with parental consent.

The statutory requirement that the youth consent to a treatment order, found in section 22, has been criticized, in particular by some mental-health professionals. Very few treatment orders have been made, and it has been argued that few youths are prepared to admit that they need treatment, even if they are highly disturbed. Some critics have advocated removal of the requirement for a youth's consent to such a treatment order, although they acknowledge that 'the efficacy of compulsory treatment for young offenders is an area laden with considerable debate' (Leschied and Jaffe 1987: 427).

In considering the issue of 'treatment orders,' it should be noted that rehabilitative services can be provided in custody facilities without a court order for 'treatment.' The YOA requires only that a youth consent to being '*detained* for treatment,' where such an order is made *instead* of placing a youth in custody, though it should be noted that provincial laws may require that young persons in custody, like adults, give informed consent to the provision of mental-health services. Further, without their consent, young offenders may be placed on probation, with a requirement that they attend counselling or participate in a special program (for example, for drug or alcohol abuse or for adolescent sexual offenders).

In cases involving severely disturbed youths, the insanity provisions of the Criminal Code or provincial mental legislation may be invoked to require that a youth be involuntarily confined in a mental-health facility. Some youths who commit relatively minor offences are diverted in order to receive assistance for their 'special needs' through the mental-health education or child-protection systems. It would seem that, in many situations, the failure of young offenders to receive appropriate treatment and rehabilitation is not a result of inadequacies in the law, but rather reflects a lack of resources or suitable facilities.

The 1989 federal Consultation Document on possible legislative reforms suggested various options intended to ensure that young offenders receive appropriate 'treatment' for their 'special needs.' This is a complex issue since it involves an interaction of provincial mental-health laws and young-offenders legislation, as well as the relationship of mental-health and young-offenders facilities. In view of the complexity and lack of consensus about these issues, it is not surprising that the federal government decided to postpone action in this area.

There may be a good argument that there is a need to clarify the YOA to ensure that young offenders in custody can receive counselling and therapy, even if they do not technically 'consent' to this. However, it must be appreciated that most forms of therapy require the co-operation of a young person to be effective. The most effective means of successfully engaging a young offender in therapy or counselling will usually involve offering early review and release from custody as an incentive to participation; it also makes some sense to offer early release to a youth who has successfully undergone treatment. It may also be necessary to consider amending the YOA to ensure that involvement in treatment is appropriately taken into account in making review decisions.[27] It may also be helpful to consider having legislative provisions to ensure that young offenders are not subjected to such intrusive procedures as drug treatment or electro-shock therapy without their consent. The availability of involuntary drug treatment might result in simply sedating young offenders rather than dealing with their real problems.

The most serious disposition that can be ordered under section 20 of the YOA is placement in a custodial facility. For most offences, the maximum custodial disposition is two years, but for offences for which an adult may receive life imprisonment the maximum is three years.[28] The YOA requires a judge who is placing a youth in custody to specify whether the sentence will be served in 'open custody' or 'secure custody,' with subsection 24.1 stipulating that secure custody is to be used only for more serious offences, or where there is a history of prior offences.

Subsection 24.1 of the YOA specifies that an open-custody facility is a 'community residential centre, group home, child care institution, or forest or wilderness camp, or any other like place of facility' designated as 'open' by the provincial government, while a 'secure custody' facility is a place 'for the secure containment or restraint' of young persons that is designated as secure by the provincial government. The intention of the act is that judges should have a degree of control over the level of restraint imposed on a youth.

Provincial governments also retain significant control over custody placements because they are able to designate the level of specific facilities. The courts have indicated, however, that they will cautiously review provincial designations. In one case, a Prince Edward Island court held that one floor of a building that had formerly served as an adult jail and was then serving as a secure-custody facility could not simply be designated a place of 'open custody.' The judge stated:

Undoubtedly the physical characteristics are not the only things to be looked at. Other factors which make a place suitable for open custody would include the security that is in place, the number of staff, the qualifications of the staff, bearing in mind that one of their primary functions is to teach young offenders how to better achieve in society. Additionally, a place of open custody will have a program set up for the benefit of the offenders.[29]

Since the YOA has come into force, in most provinces there has been an increase in the use of custodial placements for young persons who have violated the criminal law (Markwart and Corrado 1989: 13). This trend may, in part, be attributed to the attitudes of some youth-court judges, who appear to have emphasized the protection of society and the youth's responsibility over the recognition of special needs and limited accountability. Although the case has yet to be convincingly made, it may be that some of the increased use of custody may be attributed to changing patterns of criminality, and, in particular, to an increase in violent crime by young persons.[30]

It may also be that in those provinces where the age jurisdiction was raised, older youths who had been appearing in adult court as 'first-time offenders' (their juvenile records being ignored) were appearing in youth court with long records of prior offences.

Further, it seems that some youth-court judges have been making extensive use of open custody as a 'middle option' for youths who have not committed serious offences, but who 'need some help.' Prior to the enactment of the YOA, many of these youths were placed in residential facilities under child-welfare legislation. At least in some jurisdictions, the enactment of the YOA has apparently been accompanied by a shift in resources from the child-welfare and mental-health systems towards the juvenile-justice system. Professionals who work with young persons might want to use other types of resources, but they may feel that the only available facilities are young-offender custody facilities, and hence become involved in recommending their use for troubled young persons who have committed offences.

It must be appreciated that use of custody has not increased in all provinces since the enactment of the YOA. Most notably in Quebec, the rate of custodial dispositions has not changed appreciably since the YOA came into force, though that province has a more extensive child-welfare system for dealing with troubled adolescents than do most other Canadian jurisdictions. It is apparent that there are very significant differences in sentencing patterns in different jurisdictions under the YOA.

It remains to be seen whether this trend to increased use of custody will continue. In most provinces, the appellate courts have rendered decisions that reduce the length of custodial dispositions for young offenders, and emphasize limited accountability and the recognition of special needs of young persons. As originally enacted, the YOA placed certain restrictions on the use of custody, requiring a pre-disposition report before any custodial disposition was made, and restricting the use of secure custody to cases where a more serious offence occurred or where there was a record of prior offences. In amending subsection 24(1) of the YOA in 1986, Parliament provided that a youth court should not place a young offender in open *or* secure custody unless this was considered 'necessary for the protection of society ... having regard to the seriousness of the offence and ... the needs and circumstances of the young person.' Under the original legislation, this consideration applied only to secure custody.

In addition to these signals from the appellate courts and Parliament on the use of custody, the 1989 federal Consultation Document suggested various options to further amend some of the sentencing provisions of the YOA with the objective of ensuring that custody is not used inappropriately. One option was to eliminate the statutory distinction between open and secure custody, in the belief that some judges may be inappropriately using open custody in situations where they would not make an order just for 'custody.' Another option in the federal paper is to add specific offence criteria that must be satisfied before an order is made for open custody, similar to those found in subsections 24.1(3) and (4), which now restrict use of secure custody.

There are other possible reforms that might be considered, though they did not find their way into the federal document. Should there be an amendment to the Declaration of Principle, for example, to provide that the long-term interest and protection of society would be best served by the rehabilitation of young offenders (Canadian Council on Children and Youth 1990)? Would such a charge have any effect on the actual sentencing practices of the courts? Or should there be more explicit sentencing guide-lines for youth courts, as have been proposed for adult offenders by the Canadian Sentencing Commission (Brodeur 1989)?

Given the critical importance of sentencing to the young-offenders system and the apparent increase in the use of custody, there is clearly a need for careful study and appropriate action to ensure that custody is being used only to the extent necessary to protect society. Restricting use of custodial dispositions may ultimately require amendments to the YOA; there will almost certainly need to be changes to provincial policies and programs as well.

Disposition Review

When a youth is ordered into custody, provincial correctional officials have significant control over the youth's placement. While the youth court specifies a level of custody, correctional officials select the specific facility a youth will reside in and can move the offender from one facility in that level to another. Provincial officials may also permit the temporary release of the youth from custody, either to engage in employment, education, or other activities or to return home for a specified period of time. Additionally, correctional officials have the authority under the YOA to transfer a youth from an open- to a secure-custody facility for up to fifteen days, if there has been an escape or attempted escape, or if, in their opinion, this is 'necessary for the safety' of the young person or others in the open-custody facility. Subsection 24.5 of the YOA allows correctional officials to apply to a youth-court judge to transfer a young offender who has reached age eighteen into a provincial adult correctional facility for the remainder of the youth's custodial sentence. Such a transfer shall be allowed only if the youth court, after a hearing, is satisfied that it is 'in the best interests of the young person or in the public interest.'

The YOA provides that, once a disposition has been imposed on a young offender, the youth court retains the authority to conduct a review hearing to ensure that the disposition remains current and appropriate to the needs of the youth. For youths placed in custody, there is a mandatory review hearing by the court after one year, with the possibility of an earlier review, but there is no parole for young offenders. Correctional officials may release a youth from custody into probation or may transfer a youth from secure to open custody, but these decisions are subject to the approval of a youth-court judge; normally these processes can be carried out without a hearing, though sometimes one is required. There continues to be controversy over the effectiveness of the review process. In certain localities, there are delays in conducting review hearings and some judges seem reluctant to reduce originally imposed dispositions (Ontario Social Development Council 1988: 39).

At a review hearing, the youth court cannot increase the level of security specified in the original disposition. However, if there has been a wilful failure to comply with a disposition, for example, a breach of probation or an escape from custody, this would constitute an offence for which a new disposition may be imposed.

The 1989 federal Consultation Document contained proposals intended to facilitate the review process and ensure that young offenders are transferred to less-secure settings as early as possible. Legislative action concerning disposition reviews will doubtless have to await amendments to the legislative provisions dealing with disposition.

Transfer to the Adult System

The most serious decision to be made regarding a young person charged with an offence is transfer to the adult system. Such a transfer can occur only after a youth-court hearing, which must be held prior to an adjudication of guilt or innocence. If a youth-court judge orders transfer, there will be a trial in adult court. If there is a conviction in an adult court, sentencing will be in accordance with the principles applicable to adults. If a transfer order is made, adult laws relating to disclosure of records and trial publicity will also apply.

Although it is theoretically possible for a youth to seek transfer, for example in order to have the benefit of a jury trial, it is usually the crown that seeks transfer in order to subject the young person to the much more severe maximum penalties that can be imposed in adult court. Transfer applications are generally made if the crown considers the three years' maximum custodial disposition under the YOA inadequate for the protection of the public or in terms of social accountability, or because the security afforded by youth-custody facilities is considered inadequate.

Under section 16 of the YOA an application for transfer can be made in regard to any serious indictable offence alleged to have been committed by a young person fourteen years or older at the time of the alleged offence. Transfer is to be ordered only if the youth court 'is of the opinion that, in the interest of society and having regard to the needs of the young person' it is appropriate. In deciding whether to transfer a case, subsection 16(2) instructs the courts to consider: the seriousness of the alleged offence; the age, character, and prior record of the youth; the adequacy of the YOA as opposed to the Criminal Code, for dealing with the case; the availability of treatment or correctional resources; and any other relevant factors.

Transfer hearings are adversarial in nature, but they are not formal criminal trials. The rules of evidence are greatly relaxed, and the court can receive hearsay evidence about the youth's background and the circumstances of the alleged offence. The court need not be satisfied beyond a reasonable doubt that an offence occurred, but rather decides what is the appropriate forum for the trial and disposition of the charge in question.[31] Witnesses are often called to describe the differences between the likely fate of the youth if placed in custody under the YOA or incarcerated pursuant to the Criminal Code. A pre-disposition report must be presented at a transfer hearing, and there is often a section-13 psychiatric report prepared as well. Generally, the central issues in a transfer hearing are the amenability of the youth to rehabilitation within the three-year period prescribed as the maximum YOA disposition, and the availability of resources appropriate for achieving this goal.

There has been substantial disagreement between provincial appellate courts in Canada about the appropriate interpretation of the standard for transfer set out in subsection 16(1) of the YOA 'the interest of society ... having regard to the needs of the young person.' The courts compared this to the standard articulated under section 9 of the Juvenile Delinquents Act – that transfer was to occur only if 'the good of the child and the interest of the community demand it.'

Justice Monnin of the Manitoba Court of Appeal wrote: 'the test under this Act [the YOA] is different than [sic] that under the old *Juvenile Delinquents Act* ... In the new test there is at least a slight emphasis on the interest of society having regard to the needs of the young person.'[32] Another Manitoba decision commented:

> With the advent of the *Young Offenders Act* the transfer provisions ensure a
> more realistic approach to transfer. The fact that transfer exists in certain
> cases for those over the age of fourteen, by implication, considers that in some
> instances those youths will face a period of adult incarceration. While the pri-
> mary concern has now shifted so that the interests of society would appear to
> be of primary importance, the needs of the young person are still to be ad-
> dressed and these needs might well be so addressed with the treatment avail-
> able in an adult institution.[33]

This emphasis on the protection of society is most apparent in Manitoba and Alberta, and has led to a relatively high transfer rate in those jurisdictions, especially for murder and attempted murder. While some of the variation in transfer rates may reflect differences in judicial perceptions of the adequacy and security of the youth corrections system in different provinces, it is also apparent that there is significant disagreement as to the appropriate interpretation of section 16.

The approach of the Manitoba and Alberta courts can be contrasted with the more restrictive approach to transfer taken in Quebec, Ontario, and Saskatchewan courts. In *R. v. Mark Andrew Z.*, the Ontario Court of Appeal refused to transfer a youth who, at the age of fifteen, shot and killed his mother and sister. Justice MacKinnon observed that 'a charge of murder does not automatically remove a youth from the youth court.' The judge stressed the amenability of this youth to treatment and wrote: 'In light of s. 3 [of the YOA] I do not think that the interests of society or the needs and interests of the young person are to be given greater importance one over the other. They are to be weighed against each other having regard to the matters directed to be considered in subs. 16(2).'[34]

In September 1989, the Supreme Court of Canada rendered judgments on two transfer appeals from Alberta, *R. v. S.H.M.* and *R. v. J.E.L.* The Supreme Court affirmed the decision of the Alberta Court of Appeal to transfer the youths to the adult system; the youths were seventeen at the time of the alleged offence and charged with the brutal murder of an unconscious man. The majority of the Court stated that it was inappropriate to say that the crown faced a 'heavy onus' or had to demonstrate that the circumstances were 'exceptional,' though the Supreme Court recognized the 'seriousness of the decision.'[35]

At first glance, it might appear that the effect of these decisions will be to make it easier for the crown to succeed in having youths transferred to adult court, especially for murder charges, since the Supreme Court stated that the crown did *not* face a heavy onus, and upheld decisions of an appellate court, which has tended to transfer cases and has taken a relatively broad interpretation of section 16. However, there remains some doubt about the ultimate effect of the Supreme Court of Canada decisions. The majority judgments failed to directly address the fact that different appellate courts have taken different approaches to the interpretation of section 16. The Supreme Court also emphasized that its role was limited to correcting an 'error of principle,' while the legislation gave the trial courts and provincial appeal courts a 'discretion' to decide cases. Madam Justice McLachlin wrote: 'It is inevitable that in the course of the review, some factors will assume greater importance than others, depending on the nature of the case and the *viewpoint of the tribunal in question*. The Act does not require that all factors be given equal weight, but only that each be considered.'[36]

It may be that the Supreme Court decisions will not give the lower courts much direction as to the proper interpretation of section 16, and that different courts will continue to have different interpretations of this critical legislative provision.

The lack of direction provided by the Supreme Court of Canada was remarked upon by Locke J. of the British Columbia Court of Appeal in *R. v. E.T. et al.*[37] He quoted the passage from the judgment of McLachlin J., set out above, and stated: 'This provides little specific guidance. It appears to leave an almost completely free hand.'

If it is true that little guidance has been provided by the Supreme Court of Canada, there will continue to be injustice, as youths in different jurisdictions will receive very different treatment. This may heighten the need for legislative reform, though it remains to be seen whether the reforms proposed in Bill C-58 will produce greater uniformity.

Amendment of the Transfer and Murder Provisions: Bill C-58

Judges and correctional experts have recognized the inadequacies of the present provisions governing transfer, especially in regard to murder. In a case involving first-degree murder, a judge is faced with a choice between the three-year maximum disposition under the YOA and the possibility of life imprisonment with no opportunity for parole for at least twenty-five years.[38] In some cases, neither extreme may be appropriate; one is too short and the other too long. In *R. v. Mark Andrew Z.*, the Ontario Court of Appeal refused to transfer a youth facing a first-degree murder charge, with Justice MacKinnon stating: 'Put bluntly, three years for murder appears totally inadequate to express society's revulsion for and repudiation of this most heinous of crimes ... This is obviously an area for consideration and possible amendment by those responsible for the Act.[39]

A leading juvenile forensic psychiatrist, Dr Clive Chamberlain, supported the view that, for homicides, judges acting under the YOA should be able to impose sentences of longer than three years, noting that, for a few highly disturbed youths, it may be necessary to have up to ten years of treatment in a secure setting. Dr Chamberlain commented on the problem with the YOA's three-year maximum disposition, saying that it

> puts pressure on the Crown to move these kids into the adult court, where a 25 year murder sentence is available. As a result some of them will wind up in the adult prison population, where there is no treatment for them and where they just get worse ... Society would be better served, I believe, if the three-year maximum term of the youth system – of which the greater part involves counselling – were extended in the rare cases where kids kill somebody. (Quoted in Bagley 1987: 61).

There has also been considerable public and media concern expressed about the inadequacy of the provisions of the YOA for dealing with violent offences, particularly with murder. Much of this is directed towards the judicial reluctance, at least in such provinces as Ontario, Saskatchewan, and Quebec, to transfer youths, and the perceived inadequacy of a three-year sentence for certain offences, most notably murder. As discussed above, some of the judicial reluctance to transfer, even in murder cases, reflects the enormity of the consequences of transfer, in terms of both length of sentence and the place where the sentence will be served.

In Bill C-58 (2nd Session, 34th Parliament [1989]), which received first reading in Parliament on 20 December 1989, the federal government set out its proposals for the amendment of the transfer and murder-sentencing provisions of the YOA. This bill was studied by a parliamentary committee in autumn 1990, but must still be approved by Parliament as a whole. At the time of writing (January 1991), there is some uncertainty as to whether and when Parliament will enact Bill C-58 into law.

The features of the bill that have received the most public attention deal with first- and second-degree murder. For young persons convicted in youth court of these offences, the maximum disposition is altered from three years in custody to five years less a day,[40] which shall consist of not more than three years in custody plus a period of 'conditional supervision.' At the time scheduled for release under conditional supervision, the youth court may order that a young offender not be released 'if it is satisfied that there are reasonable grounds to believe that the young person is likely to commit an offence causing the death or serious harm to another person prior to the expiration' of the period of the total disposition that the youth is serving. Otherwise, a youth-court judge will set conditions prior to the release, establishing the terms on which the youth will reside in the community. The released youth may be apprehended for a breach of a condition and, following a hearing, may be required to remain in custody for part or all of the original disposition. The decision to cancel the conditional supervision is subject to further court 'review.'

For young persons who are charged with first- or second-degree murder and have been transferred to adult court and convicted, Bill C-58 provides that the sentence shall be life imprisonment, just as for an adult. However, unlike at present, where transferred youths must serve ten to twenty-five years, as adults must, before being eligible for parole, the sentencing judge in adult court will set a parole-eligibility date of five to ten years. In establishing the parole-eligibility date, the sentencing judge shall have 'regard to the age and character of the offender, the nature of the offence and the circumstances surrounding its commission,' and to any recommendation of the jury.

For all offences where a youth court is considering transfer, not just murder, Bill C-58 proposes a change in the test for transfer. The new subsection 16(1.1) stipulates that, 'in making the determination' whether to transfer a case,

> the youth court shall consider the interest of society, which includes the objectives of affording protection to the public and rehabilitation of the young person, and determine whether those objectives can be reconciled by the youth remaining under the jurisdiction of the youth court, and if the court is of the opinion that those objectives cannot be so reconciled, protection of the public shall be paramount and the court shall order that the young person be proceeded against in ordinary court in accordance with the law ordinarily applicable to an adult charged with the offence.

Assessment of Bill C-58

Bill C-58 provides significantly more flexibility for dealing with youths who commit murder. In particular, for first-degree murder, judges will no longer be forced to choose between three years, which may often seem too short, and life imprisonment with no parole for twenty-five years, which may seem too harsh. The increased flexibility is desirable, for it will allow the courts to impose a sentence more appropriate to the circumstances of the offence and offender. Further, the increased flexibility should go some way to reducing the enormous interprovincial disparities that have arisen under the present legislation. At least in part, these disparities reflect a situation where judges are forced to choose between two extreme positions. While there may continue to be differences in how the new provisions are interpreted and applied, the consequences of these differences in approach will be reduced.

Reducing the parole-eligibility date for youths convicted of murder in adult court reflects the principle of limited accountability of young offenders, as well as the fact that many of them are amenable to rehabilitation, even those who commit homicide. The introduction of the concept of 'conditional supervision' for young offenders who stay in the youth system has considerable value, and recognizes that youths often require supervision and support after their release from custody. It remains to be seen how conditional supervision will operate in practice. It is important that these provisions not simply result in two more years being added to custodial sentences, and that adequate resources are provided to ensure meaningful supervision after release.

Some critics have expressed concerns about Bill C-58. For example, the Canadian Council on Children and Youth wrote:

A major omission in Bill C-58 is the failure to allow the sentencing judge to order that a youth who has been transferred be placed in a youth custody facility, at least until reaching the age of 18. The place where young persons serve their sentences may be more important than the length of the sentence. Youths placed in adult facilities are unlikely to receive appropriate educational or rehabilitative services, and are at high risk of physical or sexual exploitation by adult inmates ... The concerns are especially pronounced for youths who are not close to their eighteenth birthday and may spend a significant portion of their adolescence within the social and physical confines of a federal prison, surrounded by adult offenders. (1990:20).

At present, section 733 of the Criminal Code allows youths who have been transferred into adult court to be 'transferred back' into a youth-custody facility until age twenty, but this can occur only if both the adult correctional officials and the youth correctional officials agree.[41] In practice, correctional officials have rarely, if ever, invoked section 733 to 'transfer back.'[42] The lack of use of subsection 733(1) appears to reflect concerns about space, security, and programming in youth facilities for this type of youth, as well as resource and jurisdictional concerns.

The overall impact of the new legislation will, to a large extent, depend on how it is interpreted and applied by the courts. The possibility of longer sentences in youth court may cause some judges to keep some youths charged with murder in the youth system. However, it seems that it was the prospect of a very long period of incarceration that made many judges reluctant to transfer. A period of five to ten years before parole eligibility may seem more appropriate, and even though the life sentence remains, this may tend to diminish the reluctance some judges have demonstrated in deciding to transfer.

At present the YOA stipulates that the court should be of 'the opinion that the interests of society and having regard to the needs of the young person' provide the basis for transfer hearings. The test proposed in Bill C-58 requires the court to consider 'the interest of society, which includes the objectives of affording protection to the public and serving the needs of the young person and determine whether those objectives can be reconciled' in the youth system, and only if these objectives cannot be reconciled in the youth system, 'protection of the public shall be paramount and the court shall order' that the youth be transferred.

It seems likely that there will again be a period of uncertainty, as the courts begin to interpret the new transfer provision. While the enumerated factors set out in subsection 16(2) of the YOA will continue to be relevant, it seems that with the change in wording in the primary test the pre–Bill C-58 transfer jurisprudence will be of limited relevance. It seems probable that the question of the interpretation of section 16 will ultimately have to be brought back to the Supreme Court of Canada.

From a legal realist perspective, one can ask whether judges actually place significant emphasis on the exact verbal test for transfer. The test under the old Juvenile Delinquents Act seemed almost impossible to satisfy; the crown had to establish that both the 'good of the child and the interest of the community demand[ed] transfer,' yet, in practice, there were more cases transferred under the JDA than under the YOA. It seems that, in reality, judges are more heavily influenced by their own biases and by the consequences of transferring a youth, or not doing so, than by merely considering the verbal test.

It remains to be seen what the effect of altering the verbal formula will be. If it results in more transfers, this may be most apparent in regard to offences other than murder, for in regard to murder, the change in the sentencing and parole provisions may make it difficult to ascertain the effect of the change in the verbal test in subsection 16(1.1). It would be regrettable if there is a significant increase in the extent to which non-murder cases are transferred, since, for the vast majority of youths, a maximum three-year sentence in a youth facility is more than adequate for either rehabilitation or punishment, and the consequences of transfer to the youth may be quite detrimental, especially if the youth is placed in an adult facility. To the extent that there is an increase in transfers, for murders or other cases, it will be important that adult correctional authorities develop appropriate programs and services for young persons.

Conclusion

The Juvenile Delinquents Act came into force close to the start of the twentieth century, and, by the 1980s, major reforms were inevitable. The Young Offenders Act created a relatively uniform, national scheme for dealing with adolescents who violate the criminal law. While these youths are not afforded a child-welfare approach, neither are they subject to the full rigours of the adult criminal-justice system.

The Young Offenders Act was passed by Parliament in 1982, just months after the Canadian Charter of Rights and Freedoms became part of our Constitution and, indeed, part of the Canadian way of life. Albeit a more circumscribed piece of legislation, the YOA has also marked a fundamental reform. The act has achieved certain objectives, most notably recognizing the legal rights of young persons and their capacity to accept responsibility for their acts, but also recognizing their special needs. The act is premised on the right of Canadian society to be protected from the criminal behaviour of youth, but also recognizes society's duty to help its youth overcome their criminal behaviour.

The Young Offenders Act is still a relatively new piece of legislation. A process of adjustment and implementation is continuing. Some involved in the juvenile-justice system continue to view the new legislation with a degree of scepticism. Some are reluctant to accept change and continue to hope for a return to the child-welfare approach of the old Juvenile Delinquents Act. Some fail to see the possibility for meeting the special needs of youth without abandoning their legal rights. But, for many, an initial period of frustration that accompanies any major change is giving way to growing acceptance of the new legislation. Concerns continue to be expressed by many observers about the adequacy of facilities, programs, and resources devoted to dealing with young persons in conflict with the law.

While individual provisions of the YOA require scrutiny and perhaps reform, it is submitted that the act's Declaration of Principle reflects a societal consensus concerning young offenders, though these principles may be difficult to apply in individual cases. Though some sections of the act may be modified in coming years, it seems unlikely that, in the foreseeable future, Parliament will engage in a major revision of the YOA or change its fundamental principles. It is worth noting that the YOA's Declaration of Principle has been the subject of considerable international attention and is being held up as a model at the United Nations.

Acknowledgment

Some portions of this chapter appeared in J. Hornick, J. Hudson, and B. Burrows, *Justice and the Young Offender in Canada* (Toronto: Wall and Thompson, 1988). This material is reproduced with permission. The views expressed in this chapter are those of the authors; in particular, they are not intended to reflect the policies of the Department of Justice of Canada.

Notes

1 Criminal Code, section 13; repealed as of 1 April 1985 by the Young Offenders Act, section 72.
2 The Latin term *Parens patriae* literally means 'father (or parent) of the country,' but has come to mean a philosophy of state intervention based on the assessment of a child's best interests.
3 Bill C-106, sc 1984–85–86, C. c.32, in force 1 September and 1 November 1986
4 *R. v. David L.* (1985), *Young Offenders Service* 85–033, at 3103 (BC Prov. Ct)
5 See also *R. v. S.H.M.* (1987), 35 CCC (3d) 515 (Alta CA), where the court stated (at 524–5): 'Section 3 contains some statements which directly conflict with other declarations of principle in the same section. The balance between these conflicting principles is, in the individual case, not easy.'
6 *R. v. Ina Christina V.* (1985), *Young Offenders Service* 85–106, at 7212 (Ont. Prov. Ct–Fam. Div.), per Main Prov. J.
7 *R. v. M.A.M.* (1986), 32 CCC (3d) 567, at 571 and 573 (BC CA)
8 *R. v. H.* (1985) *Young Offenders Service* 85–029, at 4140 (Alta Prov. Ct–Yth Div.)
9 *R. v. J.M.G.* (1986), 56 OR (2d) 705 (Ont. CA)
10 *R. v. A.B.* (1986), 50 CR (3d) 247 (Ont. CA), leave to appeal to SCC refused 26 May 1986; see also YOA, subsection 56(6).
11 *R. v. S.L.* (1984), *Young Offenders Service* 84–020, at 4085 (Ont. Prov. Ct–Fam. Div.)
12 *R. v. Sheldon S.* (1986), *Young Offenders Service* 86–131, at 7375 (Ont. Prov. Ct–Fam. Div.); upheld (1988), 16 OAC 285, 63 CR (3d) 64 (Ont. CA), revd (1990) 57 CCC (3d) 115 (SCC)
13 Ontario's 'interim' alternative-measures program was challenged under the Charter of Rights. The Ontario criteria for eligibility for the program are considered narrower than the guide-lines in other provinces. Some Ontario youth-court judges ruled that this violated sections 7 and 15 of the Charter. See *R. v. G.S.* [1988] WDFL 1781, *Young Offenders Service* 88–117, per King Prov. J. However, in *R. v. G.S.* (1988), 46 CCC (3d) 332 (Ont. CA), the Ontario Court of Appeal ruled that Ontario's interim alternative-measures scheme was justified by the need to protect society, and was constitutionally valid. The court noted that, otherwise, all provinces would have to adopt the eligibility criteria of the most liberal province.

The Ontario 'interim' scheme is probably the most procedurally complex in Canada, since it requires at least one court appearance by the young person before the case is referred to alternative measures. Some critics contend that this defeats many of the purposes of the alternative measures, since the youth may feel stigmatized by the court appearance, and needlessly utilizes scarce judicial resources.

14 *R. v. R.C.* (1987), 53 CR (3d) 185, *Young Offenders Service* 87–052, at 7353 (Ont. CA). See, however, *R. v. Richard B.* (1986), *Young Offenders Service* 86–134, at 7353–6 (Ont. Yth Ct), which invoked section 15 of the Charter to place a sixteen-year-old youth in a local open-custody facility designated for twelve- to fifteen-year-olds. The failure to have an open-custody facility near the youth's home was held to violate the Charter. It may be that individual youths who can establish detrimental treatment because of the two tiers may still successfully invoke the Charter.

15 *R. v. Robbie L.* (1986), 52 CR (3d) 209, at 219 and 25 (Ont. CA); for a similar result, see *R. v. S.B.* (1989), 50 CCC (3d) 34 (Sask. CA).

16 *R. v. Ronald H.* (1984), *Young Offenders Service* 3319 (Alta Prov. Ct); *R. v. M.* (1985), *Young Offenders Service* 3322 (Ont. Prov. Ct–Fam. Div.)

17 Bill C-106, SC 1984–85–86, C. c-32. See subsection 38(1.2) of the YOA.

18 As discussed below, under Bill C-58 it is proposed that the maximum sentence for young offenders convicted, in youth court, of murder will be five years less a day.

19 *R. v. Richard I.* (1985), 17 CCC (3d) 523 (Ont. CA)

20 *R. v. Joseph F.* (1985), 11 OAC 302, at 304

21 *R. v. G.K.* (1985), 21 CCC (3d) 558, at 560 (Alta CA)

22 *R. v. Frank O.* (1986), 27 CCC (3d) 376, at 3277 (Ont. CA)

23 *R.R. v. R.* (1986), *Young Offenders Service*, 3461–34

24 *R. v. Michael B.* (1987), 36 CCC (3d) 572, at 574 (Ont. CA)

25 In 1988–9, Statistics Canada reported that there were 41,130 young offenders' cases with findings of guilt, for which the most serious dispositions were: absolute discharge, 3 per cent; fine, 14 per cent; community service and restitution, 8 per cent; probation, 48 per cent; open custody, 13 per cent; secure custody, 12 per cent; other, 2 per cent (includes thirty-six treatment orders).

26 *R. v. W.G.* (1985), 23 CCC (3d) 93 (BC CA)

27 At present, subsection 28(4)(c) specifies that a ground for review is that 'the young person has made sufficient progress to justify a change in disposition.' While this arguably should make progress in treatment relevant to a review decision, some judges apparently do not interpret it this way.

28 If more than one disposition is being made regarding a youth who has been convicted of more than one offence, subsection 20(4) provides that the combined dispositions may not exceed three years. However, subsection 20(4.1) governs when a youth who is already in custody commits a further offence; in this situation, no new dispositions may exceed three years, though the effect of

the new disposition may result in a total sentence of more than three years.

29 *Re L.H.F.* (1985), 57 Nfld & PEI R44, at 46 (PEI SC). It should be noted that the facility that was the subject of the judgment was being used only on an 'interim basis' while a new facility was being prepared. For a case illustrating the reluctance of courts to overrule provincial designations, see *R. v. Christopher F.* [1985] 2 WWR 379 (Man CA).

30 It would require an analysis of offence and disposition patterns to establish whether the increased use of custody reflects an increase in criminal activity. Presumably, it would also be necessary to compare changes over time in provinces where there has been an increase in use of custody and provinces where there has not been an increase. Comparisons with pre-YOA data are difficult to make because of changes in age, jurisdiction, and methods of collecting data. Further, it must be appreciated that official statistics represent police charges and not actual offences, and may be affected by charging policies.

It is, however, significant to note that, between 1986 and 1989, Statistics Canada reported a 10 per cent increase in violent-crime charges in youth court for all provinces except Ontario, while that province reported a 26 per cent increase in such charges from 1985 to 1988 ('Violent crimes by youths rise 10% in 3 years,' *Toronto Star*, 21 April 1990; see Statistics Canada 1990). This would suggest that there has been an increase in violent crime by young persons, and the increase in the use of custody may partially be a response to this.

31 *R. v. J.H.* (1986), 76 *Nova Scotia Reports* (2d) 163 (NS SC)

32 *R. v. C.J.M.* (1985), 49 CR (3d) 226, at 229 (Man CA)

33 *R. v. J.T.J.* (1986), *Young Offenders Service* 3409–31, at 3409–32 (Man. Prov. Ct–Fam. Div.)

34 *R. v. Mark Andrew Z.* (1987), 35 CCC (3d) 144, at 162. To a similar effect, see also *R. v. N.B.* (1985), 21 CCC (3d) 374 (Que. CA), and *R. v. E.E.H.* (1987), 35 CCC (3d) 67 (Sask. CA).

35 *R. v. S.H.M.; R. v. J.E.L.* (1989), 71 CR (3d) 259 and 301 (SCC). See also accompanying critical annotation by N. Bala (71 CR [3d] 320).

36 *R. v. S.H.M.; R. v. J.E.L.* (1989), 301, at 305; emphasis added

37 *R. v. E.T. et al* (1989), 9 WCB (2d) 43 (BC CA). The BC Court of Appeal refused to transfer three youths charged with first-degree murder.

38 Under section 742 of the Criminal Code, for a second-degree murder the parole-eligibility date is set at the time of sentencing from ten to twenty-five years. Section 745 of the Criminal Code allows for an inmate serving a sentence for first- or second-degree murder to seek a jury review after fifteen years for 'early' parole eligibility. To date, such reviews have rarely resulted in parole eligibility before the date set at the time of sentencing.

39 *R. v. Mark Andrew Z.* (1987), 162

40 The maximum total disposition that a youth court may impose is five years less a day. Thus, young persons tried in youth court are *not* entitled to a jury trial under subsection 11(f) of the Charter of Rights.

41 It should be noted that subsection 24.5 of the YOA allows a young offender who is in custody and who is over the age of eighteen to be transferred to a provincial correctional facility for adults if a youth-court judge, after conducting a hearing, 'considers it to be in the best interests of the young person or in the public interest.' *Provincial* adult correctional facilities have inmates serving sentences of less than two years, i.e., those who have committed less serious offences, unlike the *federal* adult facilities that a youth is placed in after a section-16 order.

42 In *R. v. Timothy V.*, as yet unreported 20 April 1990 (Ont. HC), Then J. refused to transfer a fifteen-year-old youth charged with attempted murder and several other offences. At the transfer hearing, an official of the Correctional Services of Canada testified that he was not aware of any cases in which section 733 had been utilized. Justice Then stated that it would be 'highly speculative' and hence not appropriate to take account of section 733, in the absence of clear evidence that this provision would be invoked for this particular youth.

References

Archambault, O. 1983. 'Young Offenders Act: Philosophy and principles,' *Provincial Judges Journal* 7 (2): 1–7

Bagley, G. 1987. 'Oh, what a good boy am I: Killer angels chose when friends die,' *The Medical Post*, 8 December 1987: 9, 51

Bala, N. 1987. Annotation to *R. v. Robert C. Young Offenders Service* 7353–3 to 7353–6

Bala, N., and R. Corrado. 1985. *Juvenile Justice in Canada: A Comparative Study*. Ottawa: Ministry of the Solicitor General of Canada

Brodeur, J. 1989. 'Some comments on sentencing guidelines,' in L.A. Beaulieu, ed, *Young Offenders Dispositions*, 107–17. Toronto: Wall & Thompson

Canada, Department of Justice, Special Committee on Juvenile Delinquency. 1965. *Juvenile Delinquency in Canada*

Canadian Council on Children and Youth. 1990. *Brief in Response to Federal Consultation Document on Young Offenders Act Amendments*. Ottawa.

Leschied, A., and P. Jaffe. 1987. 'Impact of the *Young Offenders Act* on court dispositions: A comparative analysis,' *Canadian Journal of Criminology* 30: 421–30

Markwart, A., and R. Corrado. 1989. 'Is the Young Offenders Act more punitive?' in L.A. Beaulieu, ed, *Young Offenders Dispositions*, 7–23. Toronto: Wall & Thompson

Statistics Canada. 1990. *Canada Yearbook*. Ottawa: John Deyell

5 Legal representation under the Young Offenders Act[1]

John C. Pearson

Every person accused of a crime is entitled to satisfactory legal representation. This principle was considered a basic tenet of our criminal-justice system long before section 10 of the Canadian Charter of Rights and Freedoms (the Charter[2] gave constitutional status to the right to retain and instruct counsel.[3] Yet legal representation of non-adults accused of criminal behaviour has traditionally rested on unsure footing. Legally incapable of contracting for legal services and lacking independent financial resources, minors have been dependent on the willingness and ability of their parents to engage legal representation on their behalf.[4]

Those responsible for the Juvenile Delinquents Act (JDA)[5] actually considered eliminating lawyers from the juvenile-court process altogether.[6] In their view, the juvenile did not need legal representation. There was nothing in the process that the juvenile had to be protected from. While the JDA was enacted pursuant to the federal criminal-law power,[7] in spirit the act was decidedly non-criminal. A juvenile delinquent was to be treated not as a criminal but rather as a misguided child[8] in need of the assistance of a judge who would assume the role of a wise and caring parent.[9] It was thought that, under such a regime, due-process protections were simply not required. Indeed, they would stand in the way of the juvenile court doing its job.

Concern over public reaction to an explicit statutory prohibition against lawyers weakened the resolve of the framers of the JDA.[10] The legislation that eventually emerged contained no reference whatsoever to lawyers. The original intention was, however, implicitly evident in the act. The interests of the juvenile were 'represented' in court by a probation officer.[11] Proceedings were 'informal'[12] and appeals discouraged.[13] No legal error was allowed to vitiate a decision that was in the best interests of the juvenile.[14]

Eventually, the flaws in this approach to juvenile criminality became obvious.[15] In the *Gault*[16] and *Kent*[17] decisions, the U.S. Supreme Court pointed out that, because a juvenile could be found 'delinquent' and subjected to a loss of liberty, the juvenile-court process was comparable in seriousness to a felony prosecution. In such circumstances, good intentions and a benevolent judge were no substitute for due process and a defence lawyer. As the court noted: 'the juvenile needs the assistance of counsel to cope with problems of law, to make skilled inquiry into the facts, to insist upon regularity of the proceedings, and to ascertain whether he has a defence and to prepare and submit it.'[18]

In Canada, the 1965 federal report entitled *Juvenile Delinquency in Canada*[19] decried the paradox that existed between the notion, 'basic to our system of law,' that, in any proceedings where a person's liberty may be affected, the person is entitled to counsel and the reality that the 'great majority' of children who appeared in juvenile court were not represented by counsel. The report was unable to determine whether this discrepancy between principle and reality was attributable to a lack of appreciation on the part of parents that their children were entitled to counsel, a financial inability to retain counsel, or a belief that children did not need or want legal assistance.[20]

The importance of legal representation in criminal proceedings was further emphasized in 1972 with the adoption of the Canadian Bill of Rights[21] and its declaration that no law of Canada was to be construed or applied so as to deprive an arrested or detained person of the right to retain and instruct counsel without delay.[22] In the waning years of the JDA legal representation of juveniles became more prevalent, especially after legal-aid assistance was established.

In 1984, the right to retain and instruct counsel achieved constitutional status with the proclamation of the Charter. The drafters of the Young Offenders Act (YOA)[23] were not, however, content to rely solely on the right to counsel declared in the Charter. They were determined to give even more vitality to the right of accused young persons to legal representation. Section 11 of the YOA not only provides that a young person has the right to retain and instruct counsel without delay, at any stage of proceedings against him or her, but also requires arresting police officers and judicial officers at every stage of the process to advise the young person of his or her right to be represented by counsel and to give the young person a reasonable opportunity to exercise that right. The act goes well beyond the constitutional minimum mandated by the Charter and seeks to attach special significance to legal representation in YOA proceedings.

Shortly after the YOA was enacted, an old problem reared its head. In a series of decisions,[24] the Manitoba Court of Appeal held that section 11 of the act had not altered the legal incapacity of minors to retain counsel. Accordingly, a lawyer could represent a minor only through the minor's guardian or guardian *ad litem* or through the public trustee. These rather startling decisions produced a quick legislative response.[25] Subsection 11(1) was amended to read: 'A young person has the right to retain and instruct counsel without delay, *and to exercise the right personally*, at any stage of proceedings' (emphasis added). This amendment would appear to overcome the legal disability arising from the common-law position that children (like the insane) are incapable of instructing counsel.[26]

Recognition by the law that the accused is entitled to obtain the services of a lawyer is only the first step in providing satisfactory legal representation. The law must also supply an environment in which the lawyer can operate effectively. The juvenile-court process gave the lawyer very little to work with. Disclosure mechanisms were non-existent, the rules of evidence relaxed, and legal errors considered inconsequential. The YOA, however, attempts to breathe life into the right to retain counsel. It replaces the informality of the juvenile-court process with the same procedural framework that applies to adults charged with summary-conviction offences.[27] In addition, no longer can a juvenile be labelled 'delinquent' because of vague allegations that he or she engaged in 'sexual immorality or any similar form of vice.'[28] Only if a young person is found guilty of a specific offence created by an act of Parliament can a disposition be imposed. The limbo of *sine die* adjournments [29] and 'yo-yo clauses'.[30] has been superseded by a specific dispositions of fixed duration.[31] To ensure that its mandates are complied with, the YOA provides young persons with the same appeal routes available to adults.[32] In short, the defence lawyer has available to him or her most of the due-process tools of the trade.

Subsection 3(1)(g) of the YOA declares the fundamental principle that 'young persons have the right, in every instance where they have rights or freedoms that may be affected by this Act, to be informed as to what those rights and freedoms are.' This principle finds concrete expression in the requirement in section 56 of the act that, before the police take a statement from a young person, they must 'clearly explain' to the young person 'in language appropriate to his age and understanding' that he has the right to consult with counsel or a parent. The young person must also be given a reasonable opportunity to exercise this right and, unless the young person desires otherwise, any statement made to the police must be made in the presence of the person consulted. Failure on the part of the police to comply with these requirements will render inadmissible any statement taken from the young person, unless the young person expressly, in writing, waives these rights.

These provisions seek to ensure that the young person makes an informed choice about legal representation; they do not guarantee that he or she will be legally represented during police interrogation. The young person may elect to consult with a parent or another adult rather than a lawyer, or may execute a written waiver of his or her rights. To derive real benefit from section 56, the young person must have the experience and understanding to meaningfully decide whether the assistance of counsel would be helpful.

There is reason to question whether the majority of young persons possess the sophisticated reasoning ability required to make this important decision. American research indicates that one-third of juveniles sixteen years of age and under who have had few or no prior significant contacts with the police believe that defence attorneys defend the interests of the innocent but not the guilty.[33] A Canadian study[34] involving twenty-two juveniles legally represented in delinquency hearings showed that many of the juveniles did not really understand the function of defence counsel. Only seven juveniles felt that the defence lawyer was 'on their side.' These findings suggest that merely informing young persons of their right to counsel and providing them with an opportunity to exercise that right may not be sufficient. For the right to counsel to be truly meaningful, young persons who lack the necessary experience, education, or intelligence ought to be provided with a clear explanation of the services that a lawyer can provide.

The concept of waiver is also problematic in the context of police interrogation. The YOA insists on written waiver in the hope that it will force the young person to reflect upon the significance of deciding to proceed without the assistance of a lawyer or parent. Are young persons able to understand, without assistance from an adult, the consequences of waiving legal representation? A number of empirical studies suggest not.[35]

Alternative Measures

The YOA contains a vehicle for undoing much of the good that has been done in securing more effective legal representation for young persons. The tendency of the professional participants in the juvenile-justice system to chafe under formalized procedures has been noted by an American observer:

> as soon as we proceduralize the informal system, a third parallel system may emerge again to divert children away from the proceduralized system and to process them in a discretionary manner. It seems as if persons who work with troubled children actually refuse to give up their discretionary power. If these people are denied overt exercise of that power in one direction, they will simply find another dimension in which to act.[36]

The YOA provides just such a 'parallel system' in section 4 of the act, which states that 'alternative measures may be used to deal with a young person alleged to have committed an offence instead of judicial proceedings under this Act.' Alternative measures are, in essence, pre-trial diversion. They establish an 'informal' procedure for dealing with young persons accused of crime. Section 4 does specifically provide for the right to legal representation but, once again, there is no guarantee that the young person will, in fact, have legal representation. If parents and young persons have difficulty appreciating the need for counsel when they are going through the court system, how likely is it that they will recognize the need when a 'non-judicial' resolution is being proposed? Once alternative measures are invoked, the young person is dealt with by a system that has none of the mechanisms required in order for legal representation to be effective. A well-meaning diversion committee, from which there is no appeal, determines society's response to the young person's criminal conduct. The philosophy behind the juvenile-court movement is played out on another stage.

Disclosure

Access to information is another crucial component of effective legal representation. As noted above, the YOA seeks to facilitate access of the lawyer to a primary source of information: the client. By adopting the provisions of the Criminal Code relating to summary-conviction proceedings, the act also ensures that the defence has available to it at least the minimum disclosure requirements of valid information and the ability to demand particulars.[37] In addition, the act requires disclosure to the defence of any medical or psychological[38] or pre-disposition[39] report received by the youth court and makes available to the defence the young person's court and government records.[40]

In order to make full answer and defence at trial, defence counsel must know, before trial, the case against his or her client. This raises the issue of crown disclosure, a topic on which the YOA is silent. Disclosure remains, at least until trial, a matter within the sole discretion of the prosecutor.[41] Recently, the Supreme Court of Canada finally recognized and gave legitimacy to the role of the preliminary inquiry in the disclosure process.[42] Preliminary inquiries, however, are not available under the YOA.[43] The best assurance of adequate disclosure in youth-court proceedings rests with crown representation by a qualified crown attorney who is either subject to ministerial disclosure guide-lines or alive to the duty of fairness that must be borne by those who represent the crown. In some cases, inadequate disclosure, arising from prosecutorial intransigence and the lack of a formal disclosure mechanism, may constitute a violation of the young person's right, guaranteed by section 7 of the Charter, not to be deprived of life, liberty, and security of the person, except in accordance with the principles of fundamental justice.[44]

Legal Aid and the YOA

Legislation that accommodates and encourages legal representation will be of little value unless the accused is actually able to obtain the services of a lawyer. Prior to the advent of legal aid, legal services were not available to most juveniles. While the children of the affluent might find the family lawyer 'representing their interests' in juvenile court, and the occasional notorious case would attract a lawyer who was willing to represent a juvenile client on a *pro bono* basis, for most juveniles legal representation was financially out of reach.

The legal-aid revolution produced provincial legislation that provided for duty counsel, or private counsel retained through legal aid, to represent juveniles in delinquency proceedings. This legislation is now available to young persons charged with criminal offences.[45] The YOA also contains a statutory 'safety net.' Subsection 11(4) provides that, where a young person wishes to obtain counsel but is unable to do so, the youth-court judge shall refer the young person to the provincial legal-aid, or -assistance program. If no such program is available or the young person is unable to obtain counsel through an available program, the youth-court judge may, and on the request of the young person shall, direct that the young person be represented by counsel. Where such a direction is made, the attorney general of the province in which the direction is made is required by the act to provide for the appointment of counsel. It appears that the various provincial legal-aid plans are prepared to provide legal assistance to young persons in cases where subsection 11(4) directions have been made and the constitutional validity of the provision has not yet been challenged.[46]

The Role of Counsel

In order to establish a satisfactory solicitor/client relationship, the lawyer must be able to receive instructions from his or her client. For the client to be satisfied with the relationship, the lawyer must be prepared to carry out the client's instructions. In most cases, the lawyer has little difficulty either receiving or carrying out the instructions of his or her adult clients. When the client is a young person, special problems can emerge.

Most fundamentally, the young person may not be able to communicate with counsel. While solicitor/client communication need not produce a specific statement from the client as to a preferred outcome, it should at least take the form of a general expression of the client's attitudes or feelings with respect to the major issues in the proceedings.[47] The young person must also possess the ability to make decisions that will have significant future consequences. As one commentator has pointed out, the young person may possess the ability to reach a decision, yet not want to reach one, not want to express one, or not want to have the decision presented in court.[48]

The YOA provides the lawyer with little help in coming to grips with these problems, Section 13 of the act does permit the youth court to order the young person examined by a qualified person where there are reasonable grounds to believe that the young person may be suffering from a physical or mental illness or disorder, a psychological disorder, an emotional disturbance, a learning disability, or mental retardation, and a report by the qualified person might be helpful in making a decision under the act, but this provision will be of assistance in only a limited number of cases. When immaturity or lack of education give rise to questions regarding the young person's capacity to give instructions, the lawyer must make what is essentially a subjective assessment. In making this assessment, the lawyer will, almost inevitably, bring to bear his or her own perspective and opinion. There is a real danger that the lawyer will consider the client 'incapable' of giving instructions because he or she insists on pursuing a course of action that the lawyer considers contrary to the client's best interests.

When the client is an adult, it is clear that it is not part of the role of counsel to make the client's decision for him or her. The lawyer is under a professional and ethical obligation to provide the client with the best possible advice with respect to the client's legal rights. It is up to the client to make the fundamental decisions: whether to plead guilty or not guilty, whether or not to testify, and what position to advance at sentencing.

The juvenile-court process was not conducive to the functioning of the traditional role of defence counsel. Resistance to court-initiated interference with the liberty of the juvenile was viewed as inappropriate obstruction, contrary to the best interests of the child. A prevalent judicial attitude was that counsel for the juvenile should take advantage 'of all the potential powers of the court to promote the best interests of the child'[49] rather than seek to free the client from the jurisdiction of the court. This type of judicial attitude resulted in some lawyers 'conceding the adjudicatory phase and resolving to somehow effect the disposition.'[50] Often, defence counsel saw their role as that of an *amicus curiae* who assisted the court by securing the co-operation of the juvenile and by providing the court with information to be used in determining what should be done in the best interests of the child. Other lawyers asserted that 'the role of counsellor to the child is the primary and most important role which a lawyer can play in the juvenile court process. This role is demanding and time consuming. It calls not only for legal expertise but a thorough knowledge of the diagnostic and therapeutic techniques developed and used by the social sciences.'[51]

In 1981, a subcommittee of the Law Society of Upper Canada[52] released a devastating critique of these attitudes. The subcommittee expressed the view that, even where the child lacked the capacity to properly instruct counsel, there was no place in criminal proceedings for 'counsel representing a child to argue what is in his opinion in the best interests of the child. Counsel should not be deciding whether training school would be 'good' for the child.'[53]

The subcommittee had little sympathy for the lawyer who was not sure whether his client could competently give instructions. If counsel did not believe he could accept the instructions of the child, then he should withdraw from the matter. He should 'in all events' conduct himself 'as if he was acting for an adult.' As a consequence, it was inappropriate, 'under any circumstances,' for counsel to provide information to the court if to do so breached solicitor/client privilege. If the lawyer was the juvenile's legal representative, then 'it is advice with respect to the legal rights of the child which is being provided, and that advice is being provided to the child, not to the parents, not to the court, and not to the society, but only to the child.[54]

The YOA contains a number of provisions that illuminate the role intended for defence counsel in the youth-court process. The act makes it clear that counsel for the young person is expected to vigorously advance the position of the young person over those of other interested parties. Where it appears to the youth court that the interests of the young person and his or her parents are in conflict, or that it would be in best interest of the young person to be represented by his or her own counsel, subsection 11(8) of the act requires the court to ensure that the young person is represented by counsel independent of his or her parents.

The Declaration of Principle in section 3 of the act also helps in defining the role of defence counsel by articulating the policy of Canada with respect to young offenders. Fundamental to this policy is a recognition that young persons who commit offences should bear responsibility for their contraventions. The youth-court process, like the adult-court process, is concerned initially with determining responsibility for criminal conduct. When the question of responsibility has been resolve,d the focus shifts to a consideration of how society can best be protected from the illegal behaviour. In such a framework, the role of counsel is clear. The lawyer must use all his or her skills to restrict state interference with the liberty of his or her client. This is the traditional role of the defence lawyer. It rests at the very heart of the notion of the right to counsel. The YOA endorses this role by declaring in subsection 3(1)(g) that young persons have a right to the least possible interference with their freedom that is consistent with the protection of society. It is the job of the defence lawyer to see to it that this principle is respected throughout the youth-court process. All state interference is to be resisted, unless the client otherwise directs.

In one area, however, the YOA handicaps counsel in performing this role. Where a medical or psychological report has been ordered, subsection 13(6) permits the youth court to withhold the whole or any part of the report from the young person, where the person who made the report states in writing that disclosure of the report would likely be detrimental to the treatment or recovery of the young person or would be likely to result in bodily harm to, or be detrimental to the mental condition of, a third party. This provision flies in the face of the principle, declared in subsection 3(1)(3), that young persons have the right to participate in decisions that affect them. How can participation take place when the young person is denied access to information that must be considered in reaching the decision? The provision also allows consideration of the welfare of others to take precedence over the integrity of the youth-court process. It places counsel for the young person in the impossible position of having access to information that cannot be divulged to the client. It is a provision that has no place in criminal legislation.

Legal Education

For the legal representation to be truly satisfactory, the lawyer must possess the legal knowledge necessary to competently advise the client and the advocacy skills required to carry out his or her instructions. The enactment of the YOA presented the legal profession with a formidable challenge. Not only did the contents of a lengthy and complex new statute have to be absorbed, but also the profession had to adjust to a new juvenile-justice ethos.

For the most part, the counsel who appeared in juvenile court were 'family law' specialists. With the coming of the YOA, the criminal defence bar had to take an interest in the representation of non-adults charged with criminal offences. In Ontario, for instance, sixteen- and seventeen-year-olds, who had previously constituted a significant percentage of the clientele of the criminal-law practitioner, were now being proceeded against in a new court,[55] under a new law.

The task of preparing the profession for its new role has fallen mainly upon the law schools,[56] the departments of education of provincial law societies,[57] and the continuing legal-education committees of the Canadian Bar Association.[58] Convincing the profession to reject the *amicus curiae* and 'guardian' roles often assumed under the JDA has not proved difficult. These roles were largely discredited before the YOA was enacted.[59] For reasons that are largely economic, young persons are primarily represented by young counsel who were not schooled in the philosophy of the juvenile court. The fact is that the profession was never really comfortable with the role forced upon it by the juvenile-court movement. It was a role easily rejected.

While the law-school juvenile-justice courses are delving into the historical and philosophical underpinnings of the YOA bar-admission and continuing legal-education programs have tended to concentrate on the fundamentals. What does the act say? How are its provisions being interpreted by the courts? How can the young offender system be 'worked' to the client's benefit? These are the questions that the practising bar apparently wants to have answered. They are the questions that the defence bar should be asking. They suggest that counsel want to be able to defend young persons charged with crimes in the same way they do adults. They suggest that the role of counsel intended by the YOA is being assumed.

Conclusion

Throughout the YOA emphasis is given to: 1 / establishing the right of counsel for the young person to be present during proceedings; 2 / ensuring that the young person is advised of this right; and 3 / providing the young person with a reasonable opportunity to exercise the right. At no time is the young person compelled to have legal representation. While the act recognizes[60] that, because of their 'state of dependency and level of development and maturity,' young persons have 'special needs and require guidance and assistance,' it is not prepared to thrust counsel upon them. Indeed, the act provides alternatives to legal representation. It permits parents or other 'suitable adults' to take the place of counsel at every stage of the proceedings.[61]

To insist that all accused young persons be represented by counsel would be to deny young persons freedom of choice. Such an approach would be inconsistent with the act's view of young persons as free and independent legal actors. But, for freedom of choice to be of value, the consequences of choosing one path over another must be clear. It would appear that, for many young persons, the consequences of declining legal representation are far from clear.

The YOA has had a significant impact on the legal representation of non-adults. It has extinguished any lingering doubts as the legitimacy of the place of defence counsel in the juvenile-justice system and has installed a legal environment in which lawyers can exercise their traditional role on behalf of young persons. While the act has not solved many of the problems associated with assuring young persons access to counsel, it has improved the situation. Thanks to the YOA, the right to retain and instruct counsel is now a much healthier and more meaningful right in Canada.

Notes

1 The opinions expressed in this chapter are those of the author and do not necessarily represent policy of the Department of the Attorney General for the Province of Nova Scotia.
2 Part I of the Constitution Act, 1982

3 *Re R. and Speid* (1983), 8 CCC (3d) 18 (Ont. CA), *R. v. Robbillard* (1987), 23 CRR
364 (Ont. CA). The right to retain counsel in felony cases was first granted in
English law by the Trials for Felony Act, 1836.

4 As Bernard M. Dickens has pointed out: 'Decisions of utterly fundamental
lifelong and at times life-shortening effect upon children have traditionally
been made by courts before which they have not been represented': 'Representing the child in the courts,' in J.F.G. Baxter and M. Eberts, eds, *The Child
and the Courts* (Toronto: Carswell, 1978), 273–98

5 SC 1908, C-40

6 Jeffrey S. Leon, 'The development of Canadian juvenile justice – a background
for reform, '*Osgoode Hall Law Journal* 15 (1977): 71, at 102

7 *A.G. [B.C.] v. Smith* (1969) 1 CCC 244(SCC); 'Constitutional justice – Juvenile
Delinquents Act characterized as criminal law legislation,' *Canadian Bar
Review* 46 (1968): 473

8 R.S., C. 160, s. 38

9 R.S., C. 160, s. 3

10 R.S., C. 160, S. 3, n. 5

11 R.S., C. 160, s. 31

12 R.S., C. 160, s. 17

13 An appeal was available only 'on special grounds,' with 'special leave' of a
Supreme Court judge; R.S., C. 160, s. 37

14 R.S., C. 160, s. 17

15 To some observers, the flaws were obvious much earlier. See, for example, J.H.
Wigmore, 'Juvenile court v. criminal court,' *Illinois Law Review* 21 (1926): 375.

16 *In re Gault* 387 U.S. 1(1967)

17 *Kent v. United States* 383 U.S. 541 (1966)

18 *In re Gault* 387 U.S., at 36

19 Department of Justice Committee on Juvenile Delinquency, *Report: Juvenile Delinquency in Canada* (Ottawa: Queen's Printer, 1965)

20 *Juvenile Delinquency in Canada*, p. 143

21 8–9 Elizabeth II, C. 44 (Canada)

22 8–9 Elizabeth II, C. 44 (Canada), s. 2(c)(ii)

23 1980–81–82–83, C. 110, proclaimed in force 2 April 1984

24 *R. v. W.W.W.* (1985), 20 CCC (3d) 214 (Man. CA); *R. v. Wayne W.*, [1984] 6 WWR
447, 29 Man. R (2d) 77; *R. v. R.J.M.H.* (1985), 36 Man. R. (2d) 202 (CA)

25 1986, c. 32, s. 9

26 For a detailed discussion of the question of capacity of a minor, see F. Maczko,
'Some problems with acting for children, '*Canadian Journal of Family Law* 2
(1979): 267

27 YOA, s. 52

28 JDA, s. 2(1)

29 JDA, s. 20(i)(b)

30 Subsection 20(3) of the JDA provided that, where a child had been adjudged to be a juvenile delinquent, he or she could be brought back before the court, at any time prior to reaching the age of twenty-one years, and the court could take additional action against the child.

31 YOA, 2. 20(3)

32 YOA, s. 27

33 Thomas Grisso, *Juveniles' Waiver of Rights: Legal and Psychological Competence* (New York: Plenum Press, 1981)

34 K. Catton and P. Erickson, 'The Juvenile's Perception of the Role of Defence Counsel in Juvenile Court,' Unpublished Master's thesis, Centre of Criminology, University of Toronto, 1972

35 T. Grisso and C. Pomicter, 'Interrogation of juveniles: An empirical study of procedures, safeguards, and rights waiver,' *Law and Human Behavior* 1 (1977): 321–42

36 Victor L. Streib, 'The informal juvenile justice system – a need for procedural fairness and reduced discretion,' *John Marshall Journal of Practice and Procedure* 10 (1976): 41, at 65

37 Criminal Code, s. 731

38 YOA, s. 13(4)(a)(i) and (iii)

39 YOA, s. 14(5)(a)(i) and (iii)

40 YOA, s. 44.1

41 *Lemay v. The Queen*, [1952] 1 SCR 232. But, see *R. v. Demeter* (1975), 25 CCC (2d) 417 (Ont. CA) and *Savion v. The Queen* (1980), 52 CCC (2d) 276 (Ont. CA)

42 *Re Skogman and The Queen* (1984), 13 CCC (3d) 161 (SCC)

43 The absence of jury trials in YOA proceedings was held not to violate section 15 of the Charter in *R. v. L.(R.)* (1986), 52 CR (3d) 209 (Ont. CA). Presumably, the same principles would apply with respect to preliminary hearings.

44 See *Re Regina v. Arviv* (1985), 19 CCC (3d) 395 (Ont. CA).

45 The Legal Aid Act, RSO, 1980, C. 234

46 Christopher Bentley, 'Initial contact with the client and developing a case strategy,' in J. Arnap and J.C. Pearson, eds, *Representing Young Offenders: Selected Practice Issues*, B1–B14 (Toronto: Law Society of Upper Canada, Department of Education, 1988)

47 Jeffrey S. Leon, 'Recent developments in legal representation of children: A growing concern with the concept of capacity,' *Canadian Journal of Family Law* 1 (1978): 375, at 379

48 Leon, 'Recent developments,' 375, at 379

49 William T. Little, 'The need for reform in the juvenile courts,' *Osgoode Hall Law Journal* 10 (1972): 225, at 227

50 S.J. Cohen, 'A lawyer looks at juvenile justice,' *Criminal Law Bulletin* 7 (1971): 513, at 521

51 G. Johnston, 'The function of counsel in juvenile court,' *Osgoode Hall Law Journal* 7 (1969–70): 199, at 205

52 *Law Society of Upper Canada Subcommittee Report on the Legal Representation of Children* (Toronto, May 1981)

53 *Subcommittee Report*

54 *Subcommittee Report*

55 More accurately, sixteen- and seventeen-year-olds in Ontario are proceeded against in the old court with a new name. The Provincial Court (Criminal Division) has been designated a youth court and, by administrative directives, sixteen- and seventeen-year-olds are dealt with in this court. See *R. v. R.C.* (1987), 56 CR (3d) 185 (Ont. CA)

56 For an example of the type of excellent material that is now available for law-school juvenile-justice courses, see N. Bala, H. Lilles, and G. Thomson, *Canadian Children's Law* (Toronto: Butterworths, 1982).

57 In Ontario, the Law Society of Upper Canada Department of Education has organized a number of programs relating to the YOA. For example, a program presented on 20 February 1988 covered a wide range of topics, including pursuing information, developing a case strategy, the role of counsel representing the mentally ill young offender, and advocacy at the dispositional stage.

58 For an example of the type of material covered in continuing-education programs, see 'Young Offenders Act: An Update.' a program presented on 10 May 1986 by the Continuing Legal Education Committee of the Canadian Bar Association – Ontario. Topics covered included arrest and release of young offenders, statements, transfer applications, the public and the press, and records.

59 See, for example, S. Wizner, 'Juvenile justice and the rehabilitative ideal: A response to Mr Stapleton,' *Yale Review of Law and Social Action* 1 (1970): 85; and Patricia Erickson and Richard G. Fox, 'Defence counsel in juvenile court: A variety of roles,' *Canadian Journal of Criminology and Corrections* 14 (1972): 1323.

60 YOA, s. 3(1)(c)

61 YOA, s. 11(7)

6 A comparison of judicial roles under the JDA and YOA

Judge Lucien A. Beaulieu

The role of the youth-court judge in juvenile-justice matters has, since the proclamation of the Juvenile Delinquents Act, been a sometimes confusing one. By virtue of court processing of young offenders, there has been a determination by the Parliament of Canada that such offences by young persons of specified age need to have access to a court where a presiding judge can make determinations, not only on matters of guilt, but also on the substantive matter of what to do with the young person once the finding of guilt has been determined. The tension between the degree of emphasis placed by youth-court judges on the criminal aspects of the proceedings as opposed to the welfare nature of the proceedings has occasioned the way for considerable debate around the role of the presiding judge in youth-court matters. Despite reviews of the Young Offenders Act as being a more criminal justice–oriented act, there continues to be a demand for the youth-court judge to consider, in certain cases, the special needs of the young persons. The declaration with respect to special needs continues, therefore, to underscore the 'protective' role that the youth-court judge carries.

This protective attitude also pervaded the juvenile-justice system under the Juvenile Delinquents Act, or, at least, it was supposed to. The juvenile-court judge was intended to be a social physician charged with diagnosing the individual needs of, and issuing the prescription for, the delinquent child, rather than to sit as an impartial adjudicator of a dispute between the crown and the accused. This ideal, however, was never realized. For one thing, the view that delinquency and deviant behaviour were maladies capable of 'treatment' was severely flawed. Even if there were some validity to it, there were too many aspects of the 'treatment' that were simply beyond the control of the judge. One American law professor described this impotence thus: 'Community conditions and pressures cannot be altered by a court. A juvenile court judge cannot order the creation of 50,000 new jobs for inner-city youth. He cannot create better housing. He cannot re-juvenate the schools.'[1]

On 2 April 1984, the new Young Offenders Act came into force.[2] Its expectations are less ambitious, and it allows youth-court judges to assume the roles of impartial arbiters between the crown and the accused youth, although it does not overlook the youth's needs and interests. It does, however, arm the youth with a variety of rights previously unavailable, or conferred on a discretionary basis. It does not abandon the ideal of rehabilitation and reformation of the young person, although it does introduce other components into the sentencing calculus. Under this act, the youth court still retains a distinctive identity. It is not just another criminal court.

This chapter will measure the actual or perceived differences in the role of the juvenile-court judge under the Young Offenders Act and the Juvenile Delinquents Act in the context of this changed perception surrounding the principles of juvenile justice.

In order to understand the recent evolution in the role of the juvenile-court judge, one has to compare the two pieces of legislation that provide judges with guidance in their judicial determinations.

For the purpose of comparing the Juvenile Delinquents Act with the Young Offenders Act, I have found it personally useful to borrow the analytical approach of Charles Reason to the character of legislation.[3] Reason suggested that any legislation has both an 'expressive character' and an 'instrumental character.' If the former represents the values that society aims to protect and the latter represents the manner in which society prosecutes or implements the protection of those values, then it may be assumed that a judge's role will be affected by both. It is my hope that this examination of the expressive and instrumental characters of the Juvenile Delinquents Act and the Young Offenders Act may provide a useful backdrop against which to measure the role of the juvenile-court judge against the youth-court judge.

The Expressive Character of the Juvenile Delinquents Act

The Criminal Aspect

Crucial to the understanding of the Juvenile Delinquents Act and to its successor, the Young Offenders Act, is the observation that both were promulgated under Parliament's authority to legislate in respect of criminal law and criminal procedure. Both are, at their heart, criminal statues. This feature was not the result of some perverse design by federal legislators, but was necessitated by the division of legislative powers between the Dominion and the provinces under Canada's constitution.

In the United States, criminal-law making is a power largely vested in the state legislatures, which also have jurisdiction over civil matters, such as child protection. A state legislature can dictate what shall and what shall not be a crime. In its juvenile-delinquency law, a state legislature can say (as it has, indeed, said) that an act or omission that would be an offence at the hands of an adult shall not be an offence if committed by a young person, but shall instead be an act of 'delinquency.' Because delinquency is not a crime but a civil act, it is handled by civil courts called juvenile courts. And because a state legislature has jurisdiction over civil matters,it can vest the juvenile courts with the powers to try to dispose of these young persons in a civil context, including a child-welfare context, as usually happens.

In 1908, the Canadian Parliament's first Juvenile Delinquents Act was patterned on American models, but Canada's constitutional structure did not lend itself to the importation of the civil format. Certainly, Parliament could have declared that 'delinquencies' shall not be crimes, but had it done so, it would have been powerless to deal with delinquency in civil context, for that was within the legislative sphere of the provinces. In 1908, either the provinces were unwilling or unprepared to assume control over young offenders under their child-protection laws or Parliament felt that the provincial child-welfare statutes were inadequate. As a result, section 3 of the original *Juvenile Deliquents Act* pronounced: 'The commission by a child of any of the acts enumerated in paragraph (c) of section 2 of this Act, shall constitute *an offence to be known as a delinquency*.'

This is the source and origin of the characteristic that would eventually lead to the discomfort of those espousing the 'child-saving' paternalism that would generate the tension between the 'treatment' and 'due process' schools of thought. This single feature is the ultimate cause of the 'criminalization' of the juvenile-court process that treatment professionals have come to lament. Whether this is a necessary feature will be explored later.

What made the tension between the treatment and due-process philosophies worse was that 'delinquency,' although defined as an 'offence,' swept in a wide range of activities. Any offence created by a federal statute or regulation could be a delinquency; so could any violation of provincial law or municipal by-law or ordinance. But it went farther than that. The 'omnibus' offence of delinquency could include acts that were not criminal for adults – acts of 'sexual immorality or any similar form of vice' or any act that rendered the child liable to committal to an industrial school or a juvenile reformatory under any provincial or federal law.

Procedural Paternalism

Although Parliament could not adopt the civil aspects of American delinquency statutes, it did decide to import some of the procedural features of these laws. It was the reception of these ingredients that, for a long time, fuelled the belief that the juvenile court was a rehabilitative tribunal dispensing *ad hoc* dispositions for the greater good of the young offender. This clinical façade facilitated the behavioural professions and the child-savers, and openly discouraged intervention by criminal-law lawyers or civil libertarians.

Among these items of procedural paternalism was the requirement that trials in the juvenile court were to be held *in camera*, closed to public view. There was a ban on publication of any facts that could identify the child or his or her family. Children who were arrested and were awaiting trial were to be kept in special facilities in which there were to be no accused adults or convicted adults. Parental involvement in the court process was encouraged by the requirement that the child's parents had to be served with written notice of the proceedings. And the trial of the child was to be summary in nature, almost as if the alleged offence was trivial. Section 14 of the original 1908 act stated: 'On the trial of a child, the proceeding may, in the discretion of the judge, be as informal as the circumstances will permit, consistently with a due regard for a proper administration of justice.' A later amendment to the act added this protection: 'No adjudication or other action of a juvenile court with respect to a child shall be quashed or set aside because of any informality or irregularity where it appears that the disposition of the case was in the best interests of the child.'

A more controversial inclusion was the provision for transfer to adult court. In the United States, this was an awesome power, for by it, the civil juvenile court waived or surrendered its jurisdiction over the child into the hands of the ordinary criminal courts. This act of abdication signalled the juvenile court's opinion that the child in question was beyond the rehabilitative skills of the juvenile-justice system and that the forsaken child should be treated just like any other accused coming before the criminal courts. In Canada, however, the juvenile court *was* already a criminal tribunal, but for a variety of motives (not all of which are clear), perhaps including the preservation of the clinical image of the juvenile court, this transfer provision was adopted in 1908 and has survived into the new Young Offenders Act. The extent of its use has, in my estimation, always been a barometer of the level of confidence in the youth-justice system.

Dispositional Paternalism

If a child had been found 'guilty' of a delinquency, the Juvenile Delinquents Act offered a very special set of sentencing powers, including committal into the care of a local children's aid society or committal to an industrial school. The act specified that 'The action taken shall, in every case be that which the court is of opinion in the child's own good and the best interests the community requires.' The preamble to the 1908 act contained the following direction to the sentencing judge: 'WHEREAS it is inexpedient that youthful offenders should be classed or dealt with as ordinary criminals, the welfare of the community demanding that they should on the contrary be guarded against association with crime and criminals, and should be subjected to such wise care, treatment and control as will check their evil tendencies and to strengthen their better instincts.' This paternalistic slant was repeated in section 31 of the 1908 act, which stated:

> This Act shall be liberally construed to the end that its purpose may be carried out, to wit: That the care and custody and discipline of a juvenile delinquent shall approximate as nearly as may be that which should be given by its parents, and that as far as practicable, every juvenile delinquent shall be treated not as a criminal but as a misdirected and misguided child, and one needing aid, encouragement, help and assistance.

Here was an open invitation to 'treatment' and to a range of expertise far beyond the experience of most court-room lawyers. The judge's discretion to order sanctions that reflected the 'purpose' of the act knew few, if any, limits.

Subsequent changes to the Juvenile Delinquents Act introduced restrictions on the right to appeal. Appeal was possible within very severe time limits and even then only with the 'special leave' of a supreme-court judge 'on special grounds.'

Noticeably absent from the text of the Juvenile Delinquents Act was any mention of the child's rights. The provision even closest to suggesting any right to representation was, in all places, the one itemizing the duties of a probation officer, one of which was the duty 'to be present in court in order to represent the interests of the child when the case is heard.' The not so subtle message here was: 'Lawyers not welcome.'

Instrumental Character of the Juvenile Delinquents Act

In the first fifty years of the existence of the juvenile courts in Canada, there is little doubt that judges acted as 'wise' and caring parents, with little regard to the formalities of the law of evidence, criminal procedure, or even natural justice. I am personally aware of cases where a child was convicted not so much because he or she was guilty beyond a reasonable doubt, but because the conviction automatically guaranteed the child a priority admission to a certain facility or treatment centre that, in the opinion of the judge, offered a program that could 'straighten out' the child. Lawyers saw the juvenile court as a 'welfare committee or a bureau of investigation'[4] and the Manitoba Court of Appeal described it as an 'experimental' court.[5]

Judges had little patience for legal technicalities. In one trial, a juvenile-court judge reacted thus to a technical defence raised by a lawyer:

> I certainly feel that Mr. MacKinnon has good argument and I think I can see a possibility that the accused could be innocent. Something, quite frankly, that troubles me in this type of a case and in cases in juvenile court – I don't know the exact quote but I think of the – what has been said about if one is not certain, that it is better to err on the side of mercy than otherwise and in juvenile court I am inclined to think that erring on the side of mercy would be to not let juvenile offenders think that they can get away with these offences, on offences – on matters that perhaps are good at adult level but would deny a young person the help of the workers in the juvenile court and perhaps leave them with the idea that it fairly easy to get away with these offences.'[6]

Lawyers were simply not being part of the helping 'team' when they came in to impede and obstruct the process of the court with legalistic arguments. Writing as late as 1974, one veteran juvenile-court judge was still able to say:

> I would, however, like to qualify the statement that the presence of lawyers in juvenile courts will provide better justice by adding the rider that these lawyers should be lawyers who understand what the juvenile court is trying to do, who

are in harmony with its basic philosophy, who take a socio-legal, and not a strict legal, approach to the problems of children.

When a lawyer comes into a juvenile court, throws his brief case down on the counsel table and announces to the court: 'I represent this accused. He is pleading guilty,' the presiding judge knows at once that the lawyer thinks that he is in a criminal court for children, that he does not know what it is all about, that he has never understood, if indeed, he has read, section 3 of the Juvenile Delinquents Act.'[7]

Appellate courts were well aware of the reputation that juvenile courts had acquired for 'informal justice.' On appeals from orders to transfer the trials of young persons from the juvenile court to an ordinary adult criminal court, appellate courts often would suggest that truly serious offences were beyond the competence of the juvenile courts, who lacked the technical procedures to handle such matters.[8]

By 1960, it was becoming apparent that something was wrong with the existing juvenile-justice system. Its philosophy was being recognized as a failure. Perhaps its original expectations were overly optimistic and ill founded. Certainly, the provinces failed to invest meaningful resources into the system. The juvenile courts never achieved any respectful stature as courts of law, often operating out of basements of court-houses, presided over by judges who were poorly paid and often not legally trained. The treatment philosophy was also coming under attack. Events and ideas were reshaping public attitudes. The controversy surrounding the trial of Steven Truscott, a young boy of fourteen years, charged with murder, raised the public consciousness on some of these issues in the early 1960s. In the United States, civil-rights movements were gathering strength and achieving successes in the court rooms and in the political arena. In Canada, the government of John Diefenbaker announced in 1961 the appointment of a committee within the federal Department of Justice to make recommendations on the juvenile-justice system, the first step in a long process that ultimately led to the passage of the Young Offenders Act. In 1965, Parliament passed Diefenbaker's cherished Canadian Bill of Rights. A few provincial governments quietly began to improve the level of appointment to the juvenile-court bench, choosing as candidates lawyers who brought with them an increased awareness of the requirements of the laws of evidence, of criminal procedure, and of due process.

The text of the Juvenile Delinquents Act had not yet changed, but the new group of judges were beginning to interpret it from a different perspective. Discretionary powers given by the act were exercised fairly.

Technical defences were actually being accepted as grounds for acquittal. Crown attorneys were 'invited' or otherwise encouraged to prosecute cases, and defence lawyers were made welcome. In one case, for example, a juvenile-court judge remarked: 'I might add that it makes no difference whether the accused before the court is an adult or a juvenile. The procedure to be followed in a trial prior to plea and a finding of delinquency should be the same. The right of an accused who has pleaded not guilty must be respected regardless of the fact that he is in law still a juvenile.'[9] Where the Juvenile Delinquents Act was silent on a matter, it seemed sensible to follow the traditions of the ordinary criminal courts in which the accused is often given the benefit of any doubt. It was a matter of 'fundamental rights: rights which we provide the sorriest scoundrel tried in our criminal courts and should accord with double-handed generosity to an immature lad.[10] Some of these rights were enumerated in a dissenting judgment of the Manitoba Court of Appeal (soon thereafter vindicated by the Supreme Court of Canada):

> It is an important Court and should not only observe the principles of criminal law but should be conducted with decorum.
>
> The Juvenile Delinquents Act is intended to protect children. Section 17 of the Act ... does not deprive an accused of any of the safeguards which are fundamental to our criminal jurisprudence:
> 1. It does not take away the right to full answer and defence;
> 2. Accused children should not be questioned without being warned or in the absence of parent or counsel;
> 3. An alleged statement or confession should not be used without it being established that it was voluntary;
> 4. An accused child cannot be required to give evidence against himself;
> 5. Witnesses who understand the meaning of an oath must be sworn;
> 6. The Act does not do away with open and fair trials.[11]

A sure mark of confidence in the juvenile court was the increasing number of cases during the 1970s in which appellate courts dismissed appeals from the refusal of a juvenile court to order a transfer to adult court on charges as serious as murder. The appellate courts were becoming convinced that the young accused would receive equally adequate and fair treatment, if not better, at the hands of a juvenile court as at the hands of an adult court, with or without a jury.

To be sure, the Juvenile Delinquents Act was still full of inequalities and biases over which judges were powerless to interfere. The Canadian Bill of Rights of 1965 was not a sufficiently powerful tool to upset these discriminatory provisions, such as restricted rights of appeal or different age limits on the juvenile court's jurisdiction in different parts of the country. It was not until the coming into force of the constitutionally enshrined Canadian Charter of Rights and Freedoms in 1982 that these discriminations could be seriously attacked, but, by then, the Juvenile Delinquents Act was in its dying days.

The only area where the juvenile-court judge (and the successor youth-court judge) went with little challenge was the sentencing stage. Both crown attorneys and defence lawyers appear to be reluctant to maintain any sort of control over this very significant stage of the proceedings. His Honour Judge Nasmith described the timidity in this way: 'That finishes my part. I will now gladly turn the whole matter of disposition over to you, judge, and your wonderful network of social workers.'[12] In this vaccuum, the judge is almost forced to assume carriage of the sentencing hearing. Nothing in the new Young Offenders Act encourages greater activism from the lawyers, and judges have few sources of leverage to compel lawyers to more meaningful participation. Thus, judges are often left to their own devices, ordering pre-disposition reports or requiring psychological examinations or other evidence that counsel choose not to submit to the court.[13]

In many respects, therefore, juvenile-court judges in certain provinces were already working within the spirit of the Young Offenders Act before its proclamation into force. For this judge, the transition from the old statute to the new case was smooth and passed almost without a ripple. In other places, however, the change may have come much more abruptly partly out of second-guessing that the Young Offenders Act would not actually be proclaimed.

The Expressive Character of the Young Offenders Act

The Criminal Aspect

The Young Offenders Act, like the Juvenile Delinquents Act, is still criminal law, but is more a procedural statute. It has abandoned the concept of the all-embracing offence of 'delinquency' in favour of charging the young person directly under the Criminal Code or other statute. Parliament has also abdicated its former control over provincial and municipal offences and the old 'status' offences and has confined the authority of the youth court to violations of federal law only. This change should be a signal that Parliament's concern is no longer with protection of children's welfare but with the criminal conduct of young persons.

Minimum Age of Criminal Liability

With the passage of the Young Offenders Act, the lower age limit of criminal immunity was raised from seven years to twelve years. Children under twelve years of age who engage in criminal activities are supposed to be swept up by the provincial child-protection laws, which, of course, vary from one part of the country to another. In the Northwest Territories, for example, section 14 of the Child Welfare Act provides in part that:

> For the purposes of this Part, a child is deemed to be in need of protection when, ...
> (i) he is or, in the absence of evidence to the contrary, appears to be under the age of twelve years and behaves in a way which, in the case of any other person, would be an offence created by an Act of Parliament or by any regulation, rule, order, by-law or ordinance made thereunder or an enactment or municipal by-law.[14]

There is no case law, either in the Northwest Territories or elsewhere, to indicate how such protection matters are processed. Do the normal civil standards of proof apply, or must the alleged criminal act be proved beyond a reasonable doubt? In any event, the point is that child-protection laws have assumed a measure of jurisdiction that previously had been exercised as criminal-law jurisdiction by the juvenile courts.

Procedural Due Process

One of the most noticeable features of the Young Offenders Act is its emphasis on the rights of the young person who is charged with an offence. The youth has not only the right to legal representation, but the right to have a court-appointed lawyer to represent him or her. The youth has the same rights to bail as do adults accused of an identical offence. The general rules of evidence concerning the admissibility or suppression of an accused's statements to police or to other persons in authority apply to young persons, with a few extra protections included.

But the old paternalism has not entirely disappeared. The mere fact that there is a separate youth-corrections system testifies to Parliament's desire to accord deferrence to young persons. There is still the prohibition on publishing any information that could identify the young person or his or her family. There is a restricted access to youth-court and police records. There is still a provision for parental notice of the proceedings and for parental involvement. Subsections 13(6) and 14(7) of the new act codify an old unwritten practice of allowing the judge to withhold certain reports from the young person that, in the judge's opinion, could prove harmful to the youth's well-being.

Section 16 of the new act preserves the power to have the young person transferred to an ordinary criminal court. The transfer hearings under the previous act could be initiated by the court. That is no longer possible, and the application must be brought by either the prosecution or the defence. With the increased recognition of procedural due process in the new act generally, the transfer hearings now appear to focus more on the dispositional aspects that might obtain in the youth or adult courts. The forum in which the adjudication of guilt or innocence is determined should not be markedly different. What remains in this special hearing is a somewhat troublesome and almost schizophrenic 'presumed innocent but assumed guilty' approach. What is essentially a disposition hearing is held prior to a finding of guilt. The evidence to be considered, including pre-disposition, medical, and psychological reports, is presented and seen in a rather artificial fashion. There are no facts 'so-found.' The needs of the youth and the interest of society must be assessed on alleged facts and information that may be incomplete because such issues as the youth's feelings towards the alleged offence or the victim cannot be explored. It is a process that is difficult to reconcile with the traditional principles of due process and judicial responsibility.

Section 4 codifies the most unusual aspect of the old paternalism. Under the previous act, there arose in several centres throughout the Dominion juvenile-diversion programs. They appeared without any statutory authority but operated with the blessing of one or more provincial government departments and sometimes with the tacit approval of the juvenile court. Their appearance coincided curiously with the adoption of due-process safeguards by the juvenile court, and it has been suggested by a few writers that when due process began to infect the juvenile-justice system, the old child-savers did not disappear but resurfaced in another form, that of the juvenile-diversion committees. Section 4 of the Young Offenders Act is an apparent attempt to legitimate those alternatives to the judicial process.

The most potent tool in the youth's favour, one that did not exist for most of the duration of the old Juvenile Delinquents Act, is the Canadian

Charter of Rights and Freedoms. Its application to the youth-court process is openly proclaimed in subsection 3(1)(e) of the Young Offenders Act. With its invocation, the youth-court judge has the power to exclude or to suppress evidence that was obtained by methods that infringed or denied rights or freedoms guaranteed by the Charter.

Dispositional Reform

The range of dispositional powers conferred under the Young Offenders Act has generated some criticism from certain quarters of the behaviourial professions.[15] Whereas, under the old Juvenile Delinquents Act, the juvenile-court judge had no power to impose temporal limits on certain dispositions, the corresponding provisions in the Young Offenders Act are no longer open-ended. Custodial terms cannot exceed an absolute duration of three years for the most serious of offences; probation orders may not exceed two years; and community-service orders must not extend beyond 240 hours. Residential treatment orders can only be made with the consent of the young person, his or her parents, and the treatment facility.

These limitations have distressed certain treatment professionals. Time-limited custodial orders, in their view, run the risk of expiring before any significant treatment program can be completed, or before the needed range of services can be delivered for the rehabilitation of the youth. Parliament, however, did not have rehabilitation as its sole motive for these dispositions. A close reading of the act discloses that the protection of society is a concern as important as that of reformation. Equally disquieting to these professionals is the requirement of the youth's consent to any treatment. What is overlooked in this criticism is that, even in the golden days of paternalism under the Juvenile Delinquents Act, there was no authority at all in the juvenile court to order residential treatment of a juvenile delinquent. The fact that it was done as a matter of practice should not obscure the hard reality that it was almost certainly done illegally. There was no power in the juvenile court, either under the Juvenile Delinquents Act or under any other federal statute, to issue an order directing a juvenile offender to submit himself or herself to a treatment program. Probation orders, it is true, sometimes carry as a condition the requirement that the probationer 'seek out and be amenable to' some program or another, but such a term hardly qualifies as a treatment order. The fact that the Young Offenders Act finally offers a legitimate means of ordering treatment should, it seems, be the occasion for rejoicing rather than criticism.

Another interesting feature of the new act is the great control that the youth court has over the disposition after it is made. Under the Juvenile Delinquents Act, there was often no such control, and the juvenile correctional authorities had a free hand to do what they pleased, even to release the juvenile from custody the day after the juvenile court had ordered him or her to be committed into custody. The review provisions of the new act require the prior approval of the youth court to most proposed alterations in the youth's disposition.

Appeal rights have been greatly reformed. The crown and the young person have the same rights of appeal as would an adult who had been found guilty of an identical offence.

The Instrumental Character of the Young Offenders Act

Since the philosophy of the Young Offenders Act is not entirely coherent and since the majority of the judges presiding over the youth court used to preside over the old juvenile court, one can expect certain inconsistencies in the manner in which the act is administered. Only a few examples can be offered in this limited space to illustrate the ideology of some of the judges.

Police officers have the power under the child-protection laws of several provinces to apprehend children whom they have reasonable and probable grounds to believe to be in need of protection. This power of civil apprehension is occasionally open to abuse, allowing the police to intervene legitimately to obtain evidence that then forms the basis of a criminal charge. For example, in one Alberta case,[16] a police officer noticed a girl in a video arcade in the company of other girls whom he knew to be involved in narcotics. He approached the girl as a possible 'runaway' child and asked her to open her purse, in which, it turn out, were credit cards and identification stolen from another person. In the course of the girl's trial for possession of stolen property, the legality of the policeman's search of the purse was called into question. The judge ruled that the search, which began under the province's child-protection laws, was proper even though the fruits of the search were used to support a criminal charge. Two Ontario cases reached the opposite conclusion. In the first of these,[17] police officers located a girl reported to be missing by her mother. She was not arrested, but was being driven to the police station prior to being taken home when one of the officers opened her purse and found some marijuana. The judge excluded the evidence, finding that the police station was not a place of safety to which a child apparently in need of protection is to be brought and there was no lawful reason to have the girl in the cruiser at all. This was an unlawful detention of the child and the resultant search of the purse was equally unlawful, as was the seizure of the marijuana. The exclusion was ordered under the Canadian Charter of Rights and Freedoms. In the second case,[18] a police officer spotted a girl quietly sitting in a downtown shopping mall known to be a hang-out for 'street kids.' Suspecting her to be loitering or a runaway, he asked the girl for identification. When a computer check disclosed that she was reported missing from her parents' home, she was allegedly 'arrested' under the Child Welfare Act and 'read her rights.' When she resisted a search through her shopping bags, a scuffle broke out in which she was charged with assaulting an officer. The judge found that there are no 'arrest' powers under the Child Welfare Act. Instead, all that the act permitted was

> an apprehension of the child for reasons completely devoid of any criminal connotation and related solely to the protection of the child. In a situation where no criminal act has been or is likely to be committed, the formal arrest of a child constitutes such a traumatic intrusion that it is liable to lead to considerable emotional upset, fear and panic. That is precisely what resulted in this case. Even if the purported arrest constituted a lawful apprehension of Christina within the context of [the Child Welfare Act], there was a statutory obligation on the officers to have removed her to a place of safety. Fifty-two Division has no such designation.
>
> These gross violations of her fundamental rights were totally out of proportion with the situation and are prescribed nowhere by law.

This divorce between the Young Offenders Act and provincial child-welfare laws is reflected elsewhere in the jurisprudence. The highest appellate courts in several provinces have maintained that the dispositional powers of the act are not intended to be a substitute for child-protection laws. Where one youth-court judge imposed a lengthy open-custody order on a youth, justifying it by his concern for the youth's welfare, the Alberta Court of Appeal reduced it, saying that a custodial disposition of a youth court is not a make-shift state-wardship order.[19] In Manitoba, a youth-court judge imposed one year of secure custody, nine months of open custody, and one year of probation on a youth who participated in a theft of a truck. The lad had a prior record and was involved in drugs and alcohol. The Manitoba Court of Appeal found the sentence excessive for the offence committed, and concluded that it was the trial judge's way of imposing a wardship order on the youth. The appellate court reduced the sentence, saying that the child-protection authorities can intervene any time that they please, but that the Young Offenders Act must not be regarded as a substitute for child-welfare laws.[20] In an Ontario case,[21] a young person with a personality disorder was charged with minor assault; the youth-court judge ordered five months of open custody, to be followed by probation. The Ontario Court of Appeal said that it was wrong for the judge to have imposed a sentence not warranted by the fact merely because of the youth's mental problems. The court added:

> the appellant is now hospitalized. His mental health and his care are in the hands of the medical authorities. This is as it should be, rather than attempting to deal with such things under the criminal justice system ... There is obviously an urgency that those persons who have authority in relation to the mental health act in some way come to the assistance of this youth, but resorting, to the *Young Offenders Act* is not the appropriate vehicle to do this.

A rather dramatic further example was provided in a case where a young girl pleaded guilty to breaching a probation order that required her to reside with her mother. She was out of control and periodically supported herself by prostitution. The trial judge found that, ordinarily, such an offence would attract thirty days of custody, but to protect this girl from her own folly and to ensure that she got the care and treatment that she was obviously not receiving from the provincial child-protection authorities, the judge ordered six months of secure custody. The girl appealed, and the appellate court reduced the custody to thirty days, remarking:

> It is a rule, long settled, that the processes of the criminal law cannot be used to order confinement solely for the purposes of treatment of a physical or mental disorder or to save an offender from his own vices ...
>
> I am of the view that the learned sentencing judge was not entitled to impose a sentence of six months closed custody upon the appellant notwithstanding his lofty motives ...
>
> He should have left it up to the child welfare authorities to intervene and to take proceedings for wardship if they felt that the appellant was in need of protection. His concern that the relevant provincial legislation may not be adequate to enable a judge hearing that application to make a wardship order should not affect what would otherwise be the proper sentence for this offence. The lack of enabling legislation is something that should be addressed to the provincial legislature in order to ensure that all young persons in this

situation are adequately protected, rather than to use the process of the criminal courts which are not intended for that purpose.[22]

Judges are an inventive lot and have found a variety of means to make the Young Offenders Act work in ways that the legislators had never intended. At least two youth-court judges created a 'conditional discharge' disposition out of a rather interesting fusion of subsections 20(1)(a) and 20(1)(1) of the act.[23] Lengthy custodial orders may be achieved by attaching to the maximum custody order a probation order with a term that the youth reside in a particular facility. Neither of these decisions has yet been challenged in the appellate courts.

Conclusion

The role of the youth-court judge is indeed a complex one. The Young Offenders Act has articulated a new belief in the expectations of the role of the youth-court judge as responding to the needs of due process and emphasizing the accountability and responsibility of the young offender. There continues to be a demand for the youth-court judge also to acknowledge the special needs of the young person. Some judges have suggested that these goals for the legislation, and hence the demands for the youth-court judge, may within themselves be incompatible. Whether, indeed, this is so, the fact is that there exists the requirement of the youth-court judge to manage not only the needs and civil rights of the young person, but also the concerns for protection of the community. The foregoing discussion has attempted to describe the complexity of legislation and the role of the judge. It has been stated as well that the concerns of the justice system do not end with the court proceeding but, in many respects, really begin a process of addressing the concerns of young people and a protection of society. These goals are not incompatible within themselves. The attempt to achieve the desired balance between those different interests a formidable challenge to the youth-court judge. The exercise of judicial discretion throughout the process has been reined in expressly. This need not, however, prevent the youth-court judge from exhibiting and exercising the sensitivity and other human values associated with the juvenile-court judge. Those same human qualities can and should remain evident within the context of the more traditional judicial role that is suggested and encouraged in the new act.

The new act challenges our collective appreciation of values regarding youth crime in our society. Whether those values are accurately reflected in the legislation, and whether we are successful in enforcing them in the exercise of our respective responsibilities, are questions whose answers must await time and experience.

In the final analysis, the youth-court judge will play but one important role within the entire evolution of developing an appropriate response to youth crime in Canada.

Notes

1 Douglas J. Besharov, 'A proposal to reorient the juvenile process,' *Family Law Quarterly* 19 (1984): 243

2 sc 1980–81–82–83, c 110; now rsc 1985, c Y-1

3 C. Goff and C. Reason, *Corporate Crime in Canada: A Critical Analysis of Anti-combines Legislation* (Scarborough: Prentice-Hall, 1978)

4 A.C.L. Morrison, 'Juvenile courts,' *Canadian Bar Review* 20 (1942): 516, at 524

5 *Re L.Y.*, (1944) 2 wwr 36 to 38, (1944) 3 dlr 796, 82 ccc 105 (Man. ca)

6 *The Queen v. Moore* (1972), 22 ccc (2d) 189 at 191 bc sc), quoting from the transcript of the juvenile-court proceedings

7 Roy St George Stubbs, 'The role of the lawyer in juvenile court,' *Manitoba Law Journal* 6 (1974): 65, at 70

8 *Re L.Y.*, n 7; *The Queen v. Truscott* (1959), own 320, 125 ccc 100 (Ont. ca)

9 Unreported decision of Main, Prov. J., in *The Queen v. D.J.D.*, 15 December 1975, Ont. Prov. Ct (Fam. Div.) of the Jud. Dist. of York. See also closing paragraphs of *The Queen v. Kroh* (1975), *Chitty's Law Journal* 345, at 346 (Ont. Prov. Ct–Fam. Div) and *The Queen v. B.C.* (1977), 39 ccc (2d) 469, at 471 (Ont. Prov. Ct–Fam. Div.).

10 *The Queen v. Tillitson*, (1947) 2 wwr 232, 89 ccc 389 (bc sc)

11 *Queen v. Gerald X.* (1958), 25 wwr 97, at 113, 121 ccc 103, at 119, 28 cr 100, at 115 (Man. ca) *per* Chief Justice Adamson, dissenting. It was this dissenting opinion that was vindicated by the Supreme Court of Canada at (1959) scr 638, 22 dlr (2d) 129, 124 ccc 71, 30 cr 230, 5 rfl Rep. 374.

12 A. Peter Nasmith, 'Paternalism circumscribed,' *Provincial Judicial Journal* 7 (4; 1983): 16, at 17

13 See generally Sheena J. MacAskill and H.T.G. Andrews, 'The role of the youth court judge at the dispositional hearing,' *Provincial Judicial Journal* 47 (1985): esp. 67–71.

14 R.S. nwt 1974, c. C-3, as amended by 1984, c. 2 (1st Sess.)

15 See, for example, Alan D.W. Leschied, 'Balancing rights and needs: Addressing the dilemma in Canadian juvenile justice policy,' *Canadian Journal of Family Law* 6 (1981): 369; Alan Leschied and Paul Gendreau, 'The declining role

of rehabilitation in Canadian juvenile justice: Implications of underlying theory in the Young Offenders At,' *Canadian Journal of Criminology* 28 (1986): 315.

16 *The Queen v. L.M.L.*, unreported decision of Brownlee, Prov. J., 15 November 1985, Alta Prov. Ct (Yth Div.), digested at 15 WCB 270, 1985 AWLD 005.

17 *The Queen v. D.E.M.*, unreported decision of Nasmith, Prov. J., 26 April 1984, Ont. Prov. Ct (Fam. Div.), digested at 13 WCB 397, 3 & 4 OLWCD 66 (305–009)

18 *The Queen v. Ina Christina V.*, unreported decision of Main, Prov. J., 25 September 1985, Ont. Prov. Ct (Fam. Div.), digested at 15 WCB 19, (1985) WDFL 2088, 5 OLWCD 395 (525–028)

19 *The Queen v. E.B.* (1987), 78 AR 280 (Alta CA)

20 *The Queen v. Dallas A.* (1986), 44 Man. R. (2d) 104, 30 CCC (3d) 564

21 *The Queen v. Michael B.* (1987), 22 OAC 100, 36 CCC (3d) 573 (Ont. CA)

22 *Teresa C. v. The Queen*, unreported decision of Slahany, D.C. J, 14 January 1988, Ont. Dist Ct, digested at 4 WCB (2d) 203, (1988) WDFL 723, 7 LWCD 832 (741–050)

23 *The Queen v. Robert C.H. and James D.H.*, unreported decision of Caney, Prov. J., 22 January 1987, Ont. Prov. Ct (Fam. Div.), digested at 1 WCB (2d) 475, (1987) WDFL 1113; and *Re Michael M.*, unreported decision of Lilles, Terr. J., 13 August 1987, Yuk. Terr. Ct, digested at 2 WCB (2d) 459

7 The death of the *parens patriae* model

Ira M. Schwartz

Juvenile-justice policy in the United States grew out of the social reforms that took place in America around the turn of the century. The 'child-savers,' the reformers of that period who were concerned with the plight of children, deplored the fact that delinquent, dependent, and wayward youth were treated the same as adults. For example, delinquent children were handled in the adult criminal courts and often incarcerated in adult jails and prisons. When confined, they were subjected to inhumane and degrading conditions and sometimes housed side-by-side with hard-core adult offenders (Schlossman 1977: 59).

The 'child-savers' advocated for and helped to create a separate system for the handling of children. The system was based on the premise that children were not responsible for their actions and that they should be treated and rehabilitated rather than punished. It was a system rooted in the belief that the emerging social and behavioural sciences would be able to provide the knowledge and expertise needed to diagnose problems and that appropriate and effective treatment would occur at the hands of trained professionals (e.g., probation officers, social workers, child-development specialists, psychiatrists, and psychologists) (Schlossman 1977: 57–9). The 'child-savers' also felt that children should be worked with and treated in their own homes, to the extent that such was possible. If that was not possible, they felt that children should be housed and treated within facilities that were designed especially for them.

One of the most important elements of this new system consisted of a separate court for children. The first such court was created in Chicago, Illinois, in 1899. The concept proved to be very popular and, within a few decades, juvenile courts had sprung up all around the country.

The philosophy of the juvenile court was based on the *parens patriae* model. 'As originally conceived in the late nineteenth century, juvenile courts were to be social welfare institutions designed to help rather than to punish children who have committed crimes. Instead of subjecting children to the rigors of formal criminal trials, the juvenile court dealt with them informally. In exchange for this informality, the juvenile offender gave up procedural safeguards commonly afforded criminal defendants' (Piersma et al 1977: 13). The *parens patriae* model of the juvenile court remained intact for nearly three-quarters of a century. Beginning in the 1960s the model has been under attack, and there is considerable evidence that it has been gradually eroding since that time. For example, the process and procedures for handling delinquents in the juvenile courts have become similar to those to which adults are exposed in the criminal courts. There has also been a decreased emphasis on treatment and rehabilitation in favour of policies emphasizing public protection and punishment. Moreover, the best available evidence suggests that these trends are likely to continue in the foreseeable future.

Judicial Intervention in the Juvenile Courts

U.S. Supreme Court

Decisions by the u.s. Supreme Court in the mid-1960s and early 1970s had a profound impact on the restructuring of the juvenile court. These decisions were triggered by cases regarding violations of civil rights and abuses of juvenile-court discretion and power. When confronted with these issues, 'the Court has held that juveniles are entitled to a broad range of procedural protections previously denied them' (Piersma et al 1977: 13).

For example, in 1966, the court addressed the important issue of the requirements for waiving juveniles to the adult courts. After sifting through the arguments, the court held in *Kent v. United States* (1966) that juveniles were entitled to a hearing before they could be transferred from the juvenile courts to the adult criminal courts for prosecution (Piersma et al 1977: 13).

In 1967, the court handed down the landmark *Gault* decision. This case posed a direct challenge to the informality of juvenile-court proceedings because the court was asked to consider the due-process needs for youth, particularly when they were confronted with the prospect of being incarcerated in a correctional facility. After carefully reviewing the facts, the court

imposed the following requirements on the delinquency determinations:
(1) the child and his [or her] parents must be given adequate and timely notice of charges against the child so that they will have a reasonable opportunity to prepare for the hearing; (2) the child and his [or her] parents must be
advised of the child's right to be represented by counsel and if they are unable to afford counsel, that counsel will be appointed; (3) the privilege
against self-incrimination is applicable to juvenile proceedings; and (4) the
child has the right to confront and cross-examine witnesses against him' [or
her]. (ibid: 14)

A few years later, the court was confronted with the issue of the standard
of proof required for an adjudication of delinquency. This was an important issue because large numbers of young people were found guilty of
crimes, or determined to be in need of coercive treatment and services that
in some way restricted their liberty, based upon limited evidence and
hearsay. In keeping with earlier decisions that essentially gave juveniles
some of the same due-process and procedural safeguards accorded adults,
the court required that the standard of proof be 'beyond a reasonable
doubt' for adjudication in delinquency matters (Piersma et al 1977: 14)

State Supreme Court

Litigation over the rights of juveniles and the role of the juvenile court
shifted to the states in the 1980s. Drawing upon the groundwork laid by the
U.S. Supreme Court, various state supreme courts handed down decisions
that placed even further restrictions on the juvenile court. Although state
supreme-court decisions apply only to the jurisdictions in which they are
decided, it is clear that they are following the general trend towards
making the juvenile court more formal and ensuring that the rights of
young people are protected.

For example, in 1987, the Supreme Court of Arkansas ruled that 'the
exercise of exclusive jurisdiction over juveniles is not a permissible function
of the county courts under the Arkansas Constitution' (*Walker v. Arkansas*
1987: 1). The net effect of this decision was to declare the juvenile courts
in Arkansas unconstitutional. The decision, which was authored by the
Chief Justice of the Arkansas State Supreme Court, referred to the fact that
'the [U.S.] Supreme Court held that juvenile court delinquency hearings
must encompass the essentials of due process and fair treatment given to
adults' and noted that the county courts did not meet this standard (ibid: 7).

In a concurring opinion, one of the associate justices wrote that the

Arkansas juvenile code authorizes 'a system of juvenile referees to act for the county judges as juvenile judges' (*Walker*, 2). The justice commented that 'referees and masters are simply substitutes for the judge, and there is no place in our judicial system for permanent substitutes for judges. Such referees mean only one thing to the people that have to appear before them: their problem does not deserve the attention of a real judge' (ibid: 3). To perpetuate this system, the justice concluded that it 'would be a disservice to the people ... it would mean to continue to treat juvenile matters as a second-rate legal problem' (ibid).

In 1988, a dispute between the family court and the attorney general's office in Delaware resulted in an important decision in that state's supreme court. The primary focus of the decision centred on the role of the attorney general with respect to the prosecution of delinquency cases. However, the Delaware State Supreme Court also addressed the issue of the appropriateness of family court-appointed masters to hear minor delinquency matters.

The case involved a twelve-year-old boy who was charged with an assault. The attorney general's office filed a delinquency petition against the youth but declined to appear at a fact-finding hearing before a family court–appointed master. The youth's attorney, a public defender, filed a motion to dismiss the case because the prosecutor, the attorney general, failed to appear (*Delaware v. Wilson* 1988: 3–4). The attorney general's office also filed a motion and requested that the case not be dismissed. The attorney general argued in a brief filed in the Delaware State Supreme Court that 'the Family Court rule which purports to require the Attorney General to participate in proceedings before masters is in conflict with statutory law and, in addition, encroaches upon the constitutional authority of the Attorney General to determine the manner and method of prosecution' (ibid: 2–3). As a result, the attorney general claimed that his office 'has the option to decline to participate in such proceedings' (ibid: 5).

The Delaware State Supreme Court ruled that the attorney general was obligated to prosecute this case, particularly since the attorney general's office filed the delinquency petition against the youth (Wilson, 3, 11). More important, however, the court felt that the policy issue raised by the attorney general regarding the appropriateness of using family court–appointed masters to hear delinquency cases needed to be addressed.

The Delaware State Supreme Court acknowledged that 'the use of masters in the Family Court is authorized by statute' (Wilson, 12). The justices also indicated that the court was sensitive to the fact that the use of masters was an effective way to help the family court manage its large and complex caseload (ibid: 17). Despite this, the court held that masters 'are not judges but are instead ministerial officers who are appointed by, and hold office at the pleasure of the Chief Judge of the Family Court [10 *Del. c.* s 913]. The exercise of judicial authority under the Delaware Constitution, whether in courts created by the constitution or by the statute, is limited to those persons who have been appointed by the Governor and confirmed by the Senate' (ibid: 12). Accordingly, the court ruled that 'the use of masters to perform duties which are essentially judicial' was unconstitutional (ibid: 17–18).

Getting Tough with Juveniles

The restructuring of the juvenile-justice system in the United States has not been limited to changes in the role of the juvenile court and in the due-process and procedural protections given to children. These changes have also been accompanied by a dramatic shift in youth-detention and correctional policies. In particular, there has been a de-emphasis upon treatment and rehabilitation as the primary focus of youth correctional interventions in favour of policies and programs that promote punishment and public protection.

Prosecuting Juveniles in the Adult Courts

One of the clearest examples of the shift in youth-correctional policies has been the movement to handle like adults greater numbers of juvenile law violators. Since 1978, lawmakers in more than half the states have enacted legislation regarding the handling of juveniles in the adult courts (Hamparian et al 1982: 78). In general, these statutory changes lowered the age at which juveniles could be waived to the adult courts, removed certain offences from the jurisdiction of the juvenile courts, and granted prosecutors more discretion in choosing where to prosecute juvenile offenders (ibid: 5–6).

These statutory changes have had a significant impact on juvenile-sentencing policies, particularly for juveniles who committed violent crimes or who were chronic repeaters. In 1981, there were 1445 persons eighteen years of age or younger confined in adult prisons in the United States (Bureau of Justice Statistics 1987). By 1984, the number mushroomed to 3996 (National Council on Crime and Delinquency 1988). Slightly more than 1000 of these youths were incarcerated in prisons in

Florida, a state where prosecutors have been given the most discretion in terms of deciding whether juveniles should be tried in the adult courts.

Get-Tough Policies in Youth Corrections

State lawmakers and juvenile-justice professionals also advocated for 'get-tough' policies and approaches for those juveniles who remained under the jurisdiction of the juvenile courts as well as for those youths who were committed to state and local youth-detention and correctional systems. For example, 'a number of states have attempted to stiffen juvenile court penalties for serious juvenile offenders through (1) mandating minimum terms of incarceration (Colorado, New York, and Idaho) or (2) enacting a comprehensive system of sentencing guidelines (Washington)' (Krisberg et al 1986: 9).

Also, the practice of committing youth to serve time in pre-adjudication detention facilities – a practice more commonly referred to as the 'short, sharp, shock' – gained in popularity and became more formalized (Schwartz, Jackson-Beeck, and Anderson 1984: 231).

The period from the mid-1970s to the mid-1980s was characterized by a declining youth population and relatively stable or slightly declining rates of serious juvenile crime. These trends, coupled with the enactment of the federal Juvenile Justice and Delinquency Prevention Act of 1974, led juvenile-justice reformers and child advocates in the United States to predict that the rates of juvenile incarceration would decline. Unfortunately, largely because of the impact of the punitive policies that were implemented, their predictions did not materialize.

As can be seen in table 1, the incarceration rates of juveniles in training schools on any one given day declined slightly between 1974 and 1979 and then increased significantly between 1979 and 1985.

TABLE 1*
U.S. public training schools, one-day counts and rates 1974–85

	1974	1979	1982	1985
One-day count	25,397	23,200	25,071	25,003
Rate per 100 000	86	81	91	96

*Rates calculated based upon youth age ten to the upper age of juvenile-court jurisdiction in all fifty states and the District of Columbia
SOURCE: U.S. Census Bureau, Children in Custody

The data for youth confined in detention centres reveal a somewhat similar pattern. As indicated in table 2, the incarceration rates of juveniles in detention facilities remained unchanged between 1974 and 1979. After that time they increased sharply.

TABLE 2
u.s. public detention centres, one-day counts and rates 1974–85

	1974	1979	1982	1985
One-day counts	11,010	10,683	13,048	13,843
Rate per 100,000	37	37	47	53

SOURCE: u.s. Census Bureau, Children in Custody

Juveniles in Adult Jails

Approximately fifteen years has passed since the enactment of the federal Juvenile Justice and Delinquency Prevention Act of 1974. One of the main thrusts of this legislation when it was first signed into law by President Ford was to discourage the practice of placing juveniles in adult jails. In 1980, the legislation was amended to call for an outright ban on the jailing of children within a five-year period of time (u.s. Congress, Subcommittee on Human Resources of the Committee on Education and Labor House of Representatives 1980: 20). This deadline was subsequently extended by Congress for another two years.

The best available evidence indicates that there has been virtually no progress towards this important goal. Data from the Bureau of Justice Statistics of the u.s. Department of Justice reveal that the number of juveniles incarcerated in adult jails on a given day has remained relatively stable between 1978 and 1986 (Bureau of Justice Statistics 1987).

State and local elected public officials and juvenile-justice professionals maintain that the lack of available community-based alternatives and inadequate fiscal resources are the most common obstacles to removing children from adult jails. While there is little doubt about the merit of these arguments, there is also evidence that children are confined in adult jails because some juvenile-justice professionals and elected public officials feel that it is an appropriate sanction and that it has a deterrent value (Schwartz, Harris, and Levi 1988: 145). The implications of this are that the 'get-tough' policies and practices that contributed to the growth in the numbers of juveniles committed to adult prisons, the continued high rates of incarceration in training schools, and the increase of youth committed to serve time in detention centres are also evident with respect to the incarceration of children in adult jails.

Discussion

The juvenile-justice system in the United States is in the process of being restructured. Judicial, legislative, and administrative changes over the past two and a half decades have resulted in a gradual and significant erosion of the *parens patriae* model.

In the judicial arena, decisions of the u.s. Supreme Court and various state supreme courts have essentially declared that children are entitled to some of the same fundamental due-process and procedural protections accorded adults. While there are some who maintain that these decisions have had no significant impact, 'the new reality of the juvenile and criminal justice systems is a virtual convergence in procedure and substance' (Feld 1981: 242). These developments, as observed by Feld, lead one to conclude that 'in light of the many real similarities, not the nominal differences, there is scant reason to persist in the fiction of a separate, and ultimately second-class, juvenile adjudicative process' (ibid: 242).

The assaults on the *parens patriae* model and concerns about the quality of justice for children will, in all likelihood, continue in years ahead. There is mounting evidence that large numbers of juveniles who appear in the juvenile courts for both status (e.g., running away from home, school truancy, and being beyond the control of one's parents) and delinquency offences are not represented by counsel (Feld 1987: 30). This alarming situation even includes youths who have been committed to training schools and those who have been removed from their homes and 'placed' in residential treatment centres (ibid: 30). There is also evidence that, even when youths have access to counsel, the quality of their representation is suspect, a problem that raises the overarching concern that, despite what advances have been made, children continue to receive second-rate justice (Knitzer and Sobie 1984: 3; Feld 1987: 33).

In addition, there has been increasing concern in the United States over the large and growing numbers of young people being hospitalized for psychiatric and substance-abuse treatment. While more needs to be known about this phenomenon, it is apparent that a substantial proportion of these admissions are inappropriate and could be treated just as effectively, or more so, on an out-patient basis (Jackson-Beeck, Schwartz, and Rutherford 1987: 155–64). Also, although these youth are considered 'voluntary' admissions, it is clear that many of them are coerced into treatment and housed under lock and key. This has prompted a number of juvenile-justice scholars and child advocates to call for due-process and procedural safeguards in this area as well (Weithorn 1988: 834–5; Balos and Schwartz 1988: 645–6).

The legislative and administrative changes in juvenile justice have generally been characterized by policies and practices aimed at cracking down on juvenile law violators. These developments have largely manifested themselves by increased rates of incarceration of young people in adult prisons and in youth-detention and correctional systems. What evidence there is suggests that these trends are showing some signs of waning, although there is significant variability between the states. For example, lawmakers in Michigan recently enacted a number of juvenile-crime control bills (DeRose 1988: 1). In general, the legislation is expected to result in greater numbers of juveniles being sentenced to Michigan's prison system and longer sentences for those youths committed to state youth correctional facilities. The estimated cost, both capital and operational, to house these youth in Michigan's prisons and training schools over the next few years is in excess of $250 million (ibid: 1; Michigan Association of Children's Alliances *News Bulletin* 1988: 4). In California, plans have been developed to construct four new 600-bed institutions to relieve severe overcrowding in California Youth Authority (CYA) facilities (DeMuro and DeMuro 1988: 1–2). Also, Arizona youth corrections officials are in the process of increasing the number of training-school beds in the state and have begun the construction of a new large institution for girls.

In contrast, there are a growing number of states where policy makers and juvenile-justice professionals have recently taken steps to reduce their reliance on institutional care. For example, training schools have been closed or the populations substantially reduced in Utah, Oklahoma, Maryland, Oregon, Colorado, Louisiana, Delaware, Kentucky, North Dakota, South Carolina, Georgia, and Florida. In the case of Utah, an independent evaluation of the youth corrections reforms in that state by the National Council on Crime and Delinquency indicated they were successful from both a public protection and an economic perspective (Van Vleet, Rutherford, and Schwartz, 1987: 28). Moreover, policy makers and juvenile-justice officials in such other states as Maine, Nevada, Wyoming, Montana, Mississippi, and Ohio are in the process of re-examining their juvenile crime-control policies with an eye towards possibly cutting down on their rates of incarceration and expanding the availability and diversity of community-based programs.

Conclusion

There are some observers of the juvenile-justice system in the United States who maintain that the *parens patriae* model is dead. This is not quite the case. The *parens patriae* model is alive, but not well. However, if the judicial, legislative, and administrative assaults on the juvenile court that date back to the mid-1960s continue, then the one-hundredth birthday of the juvenile court will prove to be a bitter-sweet event. It will come at a time when the juvenile court will have been abolished in some jurisdictions and will be well on the way to being eliminated in others.

Undoubtedly there will be some who will vehemently disagree with the prediction that the juvenile court will be put to rest. Be that as it may, the one principle that must guide whatever public-policy options are pursued in this area is that the juvenile court or, for that matter, any court that handles delinquency matters must above all other things administer justice (Schwartz: in press).

In addition, it must be pointed out that some of the strongest proponents of the 'get tough' policies that swept through the country in the mid-1970s and early 1980s were juvenile-justice officials, particularly law-enforcement personnel, prosecutors, juvenile-court judges, and probation and parole workers. These officials must recognize that they cannot have it both ways. They cannot, on the one hand, advocate for placing more juvenile law violators in the criminal courts and for more adult-like sanctions while, on the other hand, advocating for the maintaining of the existing juvenile-justice system where young people are essentially treated as if they are incompetent and less than full citizens.

While the recent developments in some states to reduce their reliance on the incarceration of juveniles in training schools is encouraging, the long-term juvenile-incarceration picture is alarming. Given the fact that the youth population is projected to increase in the United States, particularly the numbers of black and Hispanic youths – the youths who are the most vulnerable – experts are predicting that the rates of juvenile incarceration will increase significantly in the decades ahead. Unfortunately, the statistics revealing the enormous growth in child poverty in recent years, the continued high rates of school drop-outs, the widespread availability of drugs, and the decline in meaningful employment and career opportunities in many of the large industrialized cities – all of which impact on minorities more adversely than on others – give credence to these predictions.

Finally, it must be pointed out that the erosion of the *parens patriae* model does not necessarily have to lead to 'get-tough' policies and punitive approaches. For example, the juvenile court in Utah has been more formal and has incorporated all of the due-process and procedural protections mandated by the U.S. Supreme Court. At the same time, policy makers and juvenile-justice officials in Utah have closed their one large 450-bed training school. In its place, they developed a youth corrections system that has two 30-bed high-security treatment units for violent offenders and chronic repeaters, and a diverse network of community-based programs for all other delinquent youth committed to the state. The high-security treatment units are largely staffed with child-care workers and teachers. The youths have individualized treatment plans. Moreover, the transformation of Utah's youth corrections system to a deinstitutionalized model has not been accompanied by an increase in the use of adult courts and of youth being sentenced to the adult-prisons system.

References

Balos, B., and I.M. Schwartz. 1988. 'Psychiatric and chemical dependency treatment of minors: The myth of voluntary treatment and the capacity to consent,' *Dickinson Law Review*, 92 (3, Spring): 631–47

Bureau of Justice Statistics. 1987. *Jail Inmates 1986*. Washington, DC: U.S. Department of Justice

Delaware v. Wilson 202 Del. (1988)

DeMuro, P., and A. DeMuro. 1988. 'Mortgaging the Future: *A Critique of CYA's Current Plans to Relieve Overcrowding.*' Unpublished report

DeRose, C. 1988. Memorandum to Solomon, 12 April

Feld, B.C. 1981. 'Juvenile court legislative reform and the serious young offender: Dismantling the "rehabilitative ideal,"' *Minnesota Law Review*, 65 (2, Jan.): 167–242

– 1987. '*In re Gault* Revisited: A Cross-state Comparison of the Right to Counsel in Juvenile Court.' Unpublished manuscript

Hamparian, D.M., L.K. Esetep, S.M. Muntan, R.R. Priestino, R.G. Swisher, P.L. Wallace, and J.L. White. 1982. *Major Issues in Juvenile Justice Information and Training: Youth in Adult Courts: Between Two Worlds*. Washington, DC: U.S. Government Printing Office

Jackson-Beeck, M. I.M. Schwartz, and A. Rutherford. 1987. 'Trends and issues in juvenile confinement for psychiatric and chemical dependency treatment,' *International Journal of Law and Psychiatry* 10: 153–65

Kent v. United States, 383 U.S. 541 (1966)

Knitzer, J., and M. Sobie. 1984. *Law Guardians in New York State: A Study of the Legal*

Representation of Children. New York: Executive Committee of the New York State American Bar Association

Krisberg, B., I.M. Schwartz, P. Litsky, and J. Austin. 1986. 'The watershed of juvenile justice reform,' *Crime and Delinquency* 32 (1, Jan.): 5–38

Michigan Association of Children's Alliances *News Bulletin*. 1988.

National Council on Crime and Delinquency. 1988. 'Youth Confinement in Adult and Juvenile Facilities.' Unpublished data.

Piersma, P., J. Ganousis, A.E. Volenik, H.F. Swanger, and P. Connell. 1977. *Law and Tactics in Juvenile Cases*. Philadelphia: American Law Institute–American Bar Association

Schlossman, S.L. 1977. *Love and the American Delinquent*. Chicago: University of Chicago Press

Schwartz, I.M. In press. *(In)justice for Juveniles: Rethinking the Best Interests of the Child*. Lexington, MA: Lexington Books

Schwartz, I.M., L. Harris, and L. Levi. 1988. 'The jailing of juveniles in Minnesota: A case study,' *Crime and Delinquency* 34 (2, Apr.): 133–49

Schwartz, I.M., M. Jackson-Beeck, and R. Anderson. 1984. 'The "hidden" system of juvenile control,' *Crime and Delinquency* 30 (3, July): 371–85

U.S. Congress Subcommittee on Human Resources of the Committee on Education and Labor House of Representatives. 1980. *Juvenile Justice Amendments of 1980*. 96th Cong., hearing, 19 March

Van Vleet, R., A. Rutherford, and I.M. Schwartz. 1987. *Reinvesting Youth Corrections Resources: A Tale of Three States*. Ann Arbor, MI: Center for the Study of Youth Policy

Walker v. Arkansas, 1, 86–184 Ark. (1987).

Weithorn, L.A. 1988. 'Mental hospitalization of troublesome youth: An analysis of skyrocketing admission rates,' *Stanford Law Review* 40 (3, Feb.): 773–838

8 Dispositions as indicators of conflicting social purposes under the JDA and YOA

Alan W. Leschied and Peter G. Jaffe

Much has been made of the transgressions of civil rights encountered by youths and their families under the Juvenile Delinquents Act (JDA). It is important, therefore, in the context of rather negative reviews of the JDA, to remember that the original theoretical underpinning of the act was not so much to mete out justice to young persons as it was to 'heal' the sufferings that young persons had experienced leading to their committal of an offence and judgment of being delinquent. The original 'child-savers' wanted to do nothing less than rescue young persons from the families and social conditions that promoted the evils that had befallen Canada's young people of the day. The assumption was that young persons became delinquent as a response to poor parenting or economic and social disadvantages. Therefore, the sole purpose of the JDA was to take delinquents 'in a state of need' and provide for those needs through some form of state-mandated intervention. Hence, as is well known to the general readership in juvenile justice in Canada, judges held a free hand in placing young persons in a range of facilities, with the intent of correcting past wrongs. Hence, the focus for disposition was not so much the offence as it was the offender. Young persons presenting to the court with a rather minor offence could potentially be placed in training school if the court felt that such intervention was justified, based on the young person's being judged in need of specific guidance and direction. The judge was allowed an extremely liberal interpretation of the best-interests ethic (s. 20[5]) under this statute regarding disposition, and was not weighted down by complexities of civil-rights and court-room procedure.

A considerable amount of attention has been focused on the abridgment of civil rights within this ethic of social purpose under the direction of the juvenile court (Bala and Clarke 1981; Leon 1977). Little attention was paid to proportionate sentencing based on the offence, and even less emphasis was placed on standardization of sentencing across jurisdictions. The statute gave considerable liberties to individual judges, providing for individual interpretations of the 'best interest' ethic.

Few people today would argue in favour of the extent of intrusiveness allowed under the JDA. Recent authors (Leon 1977; Grant 1984) are correct in their estimation that society was well overdue for a revamping of the social purpose and obligation to provide state care for young persons under the JDA. Society simply could not support a system that produced results from training-schools stays that could reduce reoffending by only one-third (Lambert and Birkenmeyer 1972).

Civil libertarians railed against the JDA specifically because of the lack of proportionality in sentencing based on the nature of the offence. As well, they objected to the court's power to order committal to training school indefinitely – or to retain some authority over the offender until his or her twenty-first birthday. The extent of discretion used by non-judicial officials in recommitting young persons to training school was considered abusive. The lack of determinacy specifying length of time in training schools or group homes also opened the way for abuses to occur. Essentially, except for province-wide monitoring by such systems as training-school advisory boards, non-judicial officials governing the JDA-based juvenile-justice system were largely unmonitored and unevaluated. While one article suggested that the JDA-based system was not working well in keeping young people out of trouble (Lambert and Birkenmeyer 1972), there is only minimal evidence of the impact of the JDA in keeping young persons out of difficulty. Though there are specific cases frequently cited to underscore the abuse of legal rights for young persons under the *parens patriae* system (Bala and Clarke 1981), there is not a great deal of information that would lead to empirical findings regarding the extent of the abuse. Rather, the fact of potential abuse in individual case studies was sufficient to raise concerns with civil libertarians and others.

There is some evidence to suggest that, prior to the proclamation of the YOA, some provincial jurisdictions had attempted to restrict the use of training schools under dispositions through amending provincial law, while establishing policies that provided a clear message to the court with guide-lines respecting sentencing. For example, in Ontario, in 1977, there was a repeal of section 8 of the Ontario Training Schools Act, which meant that young persons could no longer be committed to training school for offences that could not be prosecuted through the court had they been committed by an adult (Grant 1984). This section spoke directly to the concerns regarding the placement of young persons charged with truancy, and specifically females who had come to court at the behest of parents who were concerned about their inability to manage their child. Data indicate that, in 1973, committals to training school under section 8 of the Ontario Training Schools Act accounted for almost half (42.5 per cent) of all committals made. By 1975, the provincial policy had directed courts to consider alternatives to dispositions regarding training school with this delinquent group, and the relative percentage dropped to 16.1 per cent (Birkenmeyer and Polonski 1976). Notably, committals to training school for females following the repeal of section 8 in 1977 were reduced from 30 per cent in the early 1970s to 14 per cent in 1981–2 (Ontario Ministry of Community and Social Services 1977). During the 1970s and early 1980s, Ontario also reduced the total number of training schools from thirteen to seven, and the bed capacity by two-thirds. In Ontario, the closure of training schools and shifts in policy from institutionalization to community-based programming encouraged the development of a specialized group of foster homes as well as specialized treatment programs in children's mental-health centres (Leschied and Thomas 1985). There is little doubt that these policy shifts from Ontario, dating from the mid-1970s, were in part the result of anticipation of the more rights-oriented YOA. It is also evident that other provinces were showing signs of parallel development in provincial legislation through the reduction of institutionalized care to community-based care for juvenile delinquents, as was reflected, for example, in Quebec's Youth Protection Act.

The Young Offenders Act, as has been well established in both numerous reviews and case law, is not child-welfare legislation (Bala 1986). Whereas, the JDA based its social purpose on the provision of guidance and direction for youths judged to be out of control in both their families and their communities, the YOA emphasizes young persons' responsibility and accountability within a legal framework.

Specific to dispositions, this shift in emphasis allowed for four important developments: 1 / the standardization of dispositions across jurisdictions; 2 / provisions for determinant sentencing; 3 / the prohibition of committals to child-welfare agencies; and 4 / the prohibition of committal to treatment centres without the consent of the parents, young persons, and the facility to which the referral was being made.

Table 1 summarizes the dispositions made available under the JDA and the YOA.

It has been argued (see e.g., Leschied and Jaffe 1986, 1987) that the basis for the YOA's emphasis in dispositions is partly a recognition of the

TABLE 1
Dispositions made available under Juvenile Delinquents Act and Young Offenders Act

	Juvenile Delinquents Act	Young Offenders Act
Discharge	Suspend final disposition (s. 20[1][a])	Allows for absolute discharge following finding of guilt (s. 20[1][a])
Delays in proceedings	Adjournment allowed for occasional court reappearance (s. 20[1][b])	Judge must dispose of matter at hand; cannot arbitrarily delay proceedings
Fines	Imposition of fines to a maximum of $25 (s. 20[1][c]); judge may also order that parent/guardian pay fine if considered contributor directly or indirectly in the commission of the offence (s. 2.22[1])	Imposition of fines to a maximum of $1000 to be levied directly against the young person (s. 20[1][b])
Probation	Young person placed in custody of a probation officer or designate (s. 20[1][d])	Young person placed on probation for a period not to exceed two years (s. 20[1][j])
Committal to child-welfare authority	Youth committed to the charge of any children's aid society as designated under provincial legislation (s. 20[1][b])	No provision allowed for child-welfare commital
Institutionalized care	Youth committed to a training school or unspecified length of time; when released can be recommitted at the discretion of the probation officer and superintendent of the industrial school	Young person committed to custody to be served continuously or intermittently for a specified period to a maximum of three years (s. 20[k][i][ii]); judge to determine if custody to be served in secure or open facility (s. 24[2]
Treatment	Treatment placements not specified in act but typically made a a term of probation not requiring consent of the young person	Under (s. 20[1][i]), judge may order youth to be detained for treatment for specified length of time with conditions set forth under s 22(1), which requires consent of the parents, youth, and treatment facility
Restitution	Not specified under the act; could be made a a term of probation	Section 20(1)(d)(e)(f) allows the court to order that youths make personal or financial restitution to victims
Community service order	Not specified under the act; could be made as a term of probation	Allows for judge to order under (s. 20(1)(g) the youth to provide community service with the restriction that, under s 21(8) such service can be completed in 240 hours

need to protect the civil rights of young persons (Bala and McConville 1985); partly a response to the pessimism expressed in reviews of the literature reflecting the ineffectiveness of treatment programs for juveniles (Shamsie 1981); and partly a belief that dispositions under the JDA were 'too soft.' In many respects, the liberal agenda of encouraging state intervention on behalf of children and youths has been discouraged, and, offsetting this, an increasing emphasis on the conservative agenda of 'getting tough' with youth crime, balanced by the protection of civil liberties, has been given pre-eminence (Leschied and Gendreau 1986).

The disposition summary in section 20 of the YOA outlines the possible courses of action the youth-court judge can take in consequencing youth crime. These range from less serious interventions, such as restitution, a community-service order, or a fine to the more onerous dispositions of open and secure custody. All dispositions are determinant in their length and specific in their nature. For example, the type of custody – open or secure – and length is specified by a youth-court judge, though the specific location of custody is left to the provincial director.

It would appear that the disposition section of the YOA manifests the belief expressed in the first principle (s. 3 [1]), which indicates that youths will be held accountable and responsible. The sanctions outlined in section 20 are made in the context of proportionate sentencing based on the seriousness of the charge and are meant to have a specific deterrent effect on subsequent behaviour of the young offender. Though there have been attempts by judges to use young-offender dispositions as a general deterrence, these expressions have been overturned by higher courts. Specific deterrence has been considered the more appropriate sentencing policy.

The specific nature of what constitutes the disposition is left to the individual provinces to determine. For example, what might constitute open custody in one province may not correspond to open custody in another province. Hence, the nature of programming and the degree of intrusiveness of programming are not determined by the federal statute. In some respects, the lack of specificity has left open the exact nature and intent of the sanctions outlined in section 20. For example, since section 22 requires the youth to consent to treatment, many jurisdictions have noted this exclusion from treatment by the consent section as dictating the need for an absence of treatment in custodial dispositions where the youth does not have the option of withholding consent. In other words, if treatment were to be allowed in open- or secure-custody facilities, then there would not have been the exclusion under section 22 to allow young persons to exempt themselves from treatment by withholding or withdrawing their consent. Therefore, the nature of custody is left to each provincial jurisdiction to determine on its own, though there have been cases where the definition of 'open custody' has been considered too intrusive to fit the definition of what constitutes an open facility.

There are some data to suggest that individual youth-court judges have interpreted the declaration of principle pertinent to sentencing as encouraging incarceration. Data from a study by Hanscomb (1988) suggest that three-quarters of family-court judges in Ontario who responded to a survey on dispositions felt there was greater emphasis on punishment/accountability; one in five judges noted the shift to increasing incapacitation; and almost half (42 per cent) felt this reflected a trend towards general deterrence. Two notable quotes from judges, who maintained anonymity in this study, share beliefs that one hears routinely in the YOA system. The first judge noted: 'I hope that I haven't changed; the system is forcing more punishment! I predicted that more kids would be jailed under the YOA rather than less as promised. I was right! Incarceration has been up an astounding amount.' The second judge commented: 'I don't like to but I must give rehabilitation less emphasis under the YOA.'

Additional data from Manitoba suggest that there has been an increasing emphasis on open custody (Manitoba Community Services 1986). Alberta judges are reportedly concerned that, with a de-emphasis on treatment, custodial facilities are becoming nothing more than 'warehouses' (Gabor, Greene, and McCormick 1986). These findings seem to have been met with some surprise by YOA scholars who felt that one of the encouraging aspects of the YOA was the move towards deinstitutionalization. It is therefore ironic that data from Ontario with respect to committals to training schools under the JDA suggest that, prior to the YOA, there was a decrease in the number of youths placed in training school, only to have a consequent increase in committal rates once the YOA was proclaimed (Ontario Ministry of Community and Social Services 1983; Leschied and Jaffe 1987).

Tables 2 and 3 summarize disposition data from a JDA year (1981–2) and YOA year (1986–7). The provincial data illustrated are extracted from figures compiled through the Canadian Centre for Justice Statistics. Notably, under the YOA, approximately 31 per cent of dispositions have been for custody, whereas training school committals were only 13 per cent under the JDA. Some judges have suggested that open custody is used in may cases where, were the child-welfare option still available, youths would be placed in group or foster homes. One could debate the different

TABLE 2
Dispositions under the Juvenile Delinquents Act, 1981–2

Type of disposition	Percentage
Suspended/Adjourned	13.1
Reprimand	3.4
Fine/Restitution	28.7
Probation	32.2
Child-Welfare Order	5.1
Training School	12.6
Other	4.9

NOTE: Includes provinces of Alberta, Saskatchewan, Manitoba, Quebec, New Brunswick, Nova Scotia, and Newfoundland; N = 72,818 delinquencies.
SOURCE: Canadian Centre for Justice Statistics

TABLE 3
Dispositions under the Young Offenders Act, 1986–7

Type of disposition	Percentage
Absolute discharge	3.2
Fine/Restitution	12.9
Community service order	6.5
Probation supervision	45.1
Open custody	14.9
Secure custody	16.2
Treatment order	0.1
Other	1.0

NOTE: Includes periods of reporting data to Statistics Canada by provinces of Alberta, Saskatchewan, Manitoba, Quebec, New Brunswick, Nova Scotia, and Newfoundland; N = 73,866 delinquencies.
SOURCE: Canadian Centre for Justice Statistics

environments and mandates of foster homes relative to those of the average YOA open-custody placement. Even so, if child-welfare committals are combined with the training-school committals in the JDA data, committals to custody under the YOA are still almost twice as frequent. Another datum of note is the extremely low rate of treatment orders made. Table 4 summarizes committals under subsection 20 (1) (i) for 1984–7. During that period, the number of treatment orders made across seven provinces was slightly more than 75.

TABLE 4
Treatment orders made under section 20(1)(i) of the Young Offenders Act, 1984–5

Year	Number of orders made
1984/5	89
1985/6	58
1986/7	80

NOTE: Includes provinces of Alberta, Saskatchewan, Manitoba, Quebec, New Brunswick, Nova Scotia, and Newfoundland; N = 73,866 delinquencies.
SOURCE: Canadian Centre for Justice Statistics

It has been reported (see e.g., Leschied and Jaffe 1986, 1987) that judges have utilized the community-service-order option and probation frequently, and have encouraged the use of custody. As previously reported, section-20 dispositions with respect to treatment has been largely ignored.

Two reasons would seem to account for the low rates of use of the treatment disposition. The first relates to the interpretation by judges of the YOA as being largely criminal-justice legislation and, indeed, as others have commented, not child-welfare legislation. Second, the fact that the civil-rights aspects of the legislation require consent by the young person excludes many young persons who, though perhaps in need of treatment intervention, may not have the insight and foresight to make a decision allowing for placement in a treatment centre (Leschied and Jaffe 1986). An elaboration of reasons for the low rates of consent for committals under section 20 (2) is found elsewhere (Leschied and Hyatt 1986).

Once again, a comparison of tables 2 and 3 makes it apparent that the wishes of the legislators in revising juvenile-justice law, making penalties more harsh, have been actualized. Committals to custody have been far greater than speculated. Committals to treatment have been few in number. As commented upon by Reid and Reitsma-Street (1984), it is quite apparent, as expressed through the disposition section, that the YOA is emphasizing crime control to the exclusion of child-welfare and treatment concerns.

Summary

Juvenile-justice legislation expresses the state's belief that crime by young persons needs to be controlled: the dispositions available under this legislation express the philosophy and intent of the legislation. The YOA

has marked a significant shift away from child-welfare/treatment intervention to accountability and responsibility with specific deterrence to individual crime. The obvious question at this point, posed not only by
legislators, but more importantly by the public, is whether or not the
sanctions allowed under the YOA are sufficient and of the nature that will
have the desired effect of controlling youth crime.

The debate with respect to effectiveness in controlling crime has a long
history. Martinson (1974) focused this debate by stating, in a rather
inflammatory article, that nothing worked when it came to intervention,
and the least we can do as a society is to sanction those who break laws and
hope that sufficient punishment will provide a deterrence to subsequent
crime. This rather scathing review by Martinson has been rebuked by
many, most notably Palmer (1978 and Gendreau and Ross (1979, 1987).
The debate rages on. The recent review of the rehabilitative literature by
Gendreau and Ross (1987) suggests, from a positive view, that human
behaviour can be changed. This review would seem to give sufficient
encouragement to those who want to see a more liberalized view of the
nature of interventions specific under sentencing/dispositional practices.
However encouraging the literature is, actual practices in sentencing and
policies within justice seem not to follow it. Specific to the YOA, recent data
produced through the Centre for Criminal Justice Statistics would suggest
that offence rates by persons of young-offender age have shown a steady
increase since 1984. This has occurred at a time when Canada, except for
the province of Quebec, has seen a coincidental decrease in the adolescent population. Does this suggest that the policies specific to the YOA have
failed? It is difficult to conclude at this point that an increased crime rate
in young persons can be tied to any specific policy. More controlled studies
need to be carried out in order to address this very important issue. One
such study that has been carried out by the authors has examined the
recidivism rates of a more disturbed group of young offenders who
appeared in youth court in southwestern Ontario. These data suggest that
the deterrence-focused dispositions of the YOA seem not to have the same
effect of reducing crime as did the treatment disposition within the JDA
(Leschied, Austin, and Jaffe 1988). Further research needs to be reported
to examine this very critical issue. What can be stated thus far with respect
to dispositions under the YOA is that, in their nature and practice, YOA
dispositions seem to be following the legislation's intent, as evidenced in
the increased rates of custody and emphasis on more accountability
provisions with respect to sentencing, and individual-restitution programs,
as evidenced in community-service orders. The decrease in emphasis on

rehabilitation/treatment is also evidenced in the extremely low numbers of youths committed under subsection 20 (2) pursuant to treatment disposition. Hence, the principles of due process and accountability in the act seem to be expressed in the current available data. Data reflecting on implementation of child-welfare and special-needs principles appear invisible.

There is some recent evidence to suggest that some judges are becoming frustrated at the inflexibility of the YOA sentencing process. A recent, as yet unreported case of one judge in an urban southwest Ontario jurisdiction committed a thirteen-year-old female to a period of secure custody not in response to the serious nature of the crime she committed – a 'breach of probation' – but out of concern for the fact that the girl had been involved in street prostitution and her history included many serious risk factors for subsequent disturbance, such as sexual abuse.

The court, in passing disposition, noted the reality that teenage prostitution was not a criminal issue but rather a 'life-style' concern. The court was quite conscious of contravening the YOA concept of having the limitation to intrusiveness commensurate with the nature of the offence. The judge in question invited the defence to appeal his decision, which indeed occurred, and the disposition was overturned.

It is difficult at this point to estimate the degree of discordance between what people view as the desired social purpose in young-offender policy and the realities manifest in YOA practice.

Social purpose in the JDA reflected the intense belief that the state played a vital role in recognizing and assisting young persons who were see as committing crimes not out of a sense of 'badness' but largely out of social mistreatment. This belief has given way to a young-offender system that views young persons as needing court advocates to mitigate largely against the uninvited intrusion of the state (Bala and McConville 1985) and to see behaviour and motivation rectified through punishment rather than treatment. In the United States, Shireman and Reamer (1986) have noted this evolution reflected in the following cogent passage:

> The perceptible move away from the forgiving views of the child savers is not entirely inappropriate. Today we are far less naive about the nature of juvenile crime and ways of responding to it than we were at the turn of the century. Solicitous care, nurturance, and affection are not enough to alter the ways of many contemporary offenders. Sophisticated treatment, trained professionals, adequate facilities, and an emphasis on due process are essential ingredients in any reasoned effort to confront the modern-day variety of juvenile crime.

The relative simplicity and paternalism of the child saving days are now obsolete.

Yet, in our pursuit of updated measures to handle today's offenders, we seem to have lost a particular virtue of the child savers. No matter what one believes about the motives of the principals of that movement – whether or not one accepts the cynical assessments of that era – the optimism and faith in youths that moved the child savers now has largely evaporated. (pp. 170–1)

Have Canadians let their 'optimism and faith in youth ... evaporate'? It is clear that a review of JDA and YOA dispositions marks a significant shift in how Canadians are dealing with youthful crime. However, this shift suggests a dramatic paradox. In an effort to provide civil rights and due process for young offenders and save them from the unfettered paternalism of JDA judges, a worse consequence may have resulted. The increase in custodial sentences and decreased access to rehabilitative services may suggest more process but less meaningful outcomes for young offenders. One hopes that a new generation of child-savers and civil libertarians can become stronger allies in creating a balance in the Canadian juvenile-justice system.

References

Bala, N.M. 1986. 'The Young Offenders Act: A new era in juvenile justice,' in B. Landau, ed, *Children's Rights in the Practice of Family Law*, 238–54. Toronto: Carswell

Bala, N.M., and K.L. Clarke. 1981. *The Child and the Law*. Toronto: McGraw-Hill Ryerson

Bala, N.M., and B.J. McConville. 1985. 'Children's rights: For us against treatment,' *Canada's Mental Health* 33 (4): 2–5

Birkenmeyer, A.C., and M. Polonski. *Trends in Training School Admissions: 1967–1975*. Toronto: Ministry of Correctional Services

Gabor, P., and P. McCormick. 1986. 'The Young Offenders Act: The Alberta court experience in the first year,' *Canadian Journal of Family Law* 5 (2): 301–19

Gendreau, P.G., and R.R. Ross. 1979. 'Effective correctional treatment: Bibliotherapy for cynics,' *Crime and Delinquency* 25 (4): 463–89

– 1987. 'Revivification of rehabilitation: Evidence from the 1980's,' *Justice Quarterly* 4 (3): 349–408

Grant, T. 1984. 'The "incorrigible" juvenile: History and prerequisites of reform in Ontario,' *Canadian Journal of Family Law* 4 (3): 293–318

Hanscomb, D.K. 1988. 'The Dynamics of Disposition in Youth Court.' Unpublished Research Report, University of Toronto

Lambert, L.R. and A.C. Birkenmeyer. *An Assessment of the Classification System for Placement of Wards in Training Schools: Factors Related to Classification and Community Adjustment*. Ministry of Correctional Services Research Report. Toronto: Ontario Ministry of Correctional Services

Leon, J.S. 1977. 'The development of Canadian juvenile justice: A background for reform,' *Osgoode Hall Law Journal* 15 (1): 71–106

Leschied, A.W., and P. Gendreau. 1986. 'The declining role of rehabilitation in Canadian juvenile justice: Implications of underlying theory in the Young Offenders Act,' *Canadian Journal of Criminology* 28 (3): 315–22

Leschied, A.W., and C.H. Hyatt. 1986. 'Perspective: Section 22(1), Consent to treatment order under the Young Offenders Act,' *Canadian Journal of Criminology* 28 (1): 69–78

Leschied, A.W., and P.G. Jaffe. 1986. 'Implications of the consent to treatment section of the Younger Offenders Act: A case study,' *Canadian Psychology* 27 (3): 312–13

– 1987. 'Impact of the Young Offenders Act on court dispositions: A comparative analysis,' *Canadian Journal of Criminology* 29 (4): 421–30

Leschied, A.W., and K.E. Thomas. 1985. 'Effective residential programming for "hard-to-serve" delinquent youth,' *Canadian Journal of Criminology* 27: 161–77

Leschied, A.W., G.A. Austin, and P.G. Jaffe. 1988. 'Impact of the Young Offenders Act on recidivism of special needs youth: Clinical and policy implications,' *Canadian Journal of Behavioural Science* 20 (3): 322–31

Manitoba Community Services. 1986. *Young Offenders Act: The Second Year*. Winnipeg

Martinson, R. 1974. 'What works! Questions and answers about prison reform,' *The Public Interest* 35: 22–54

Ontario Ministry of Community and Social Services. 1977. *Operational Review of Observation and Detention Homes. Report One: Where We Are*. Toronto

Palmer, T. 1978. *Correctional Intervention and Research: Current Issues and Future Prospects*. Lexington, MA: Heath

R. v. Theresa C. Judgement unreported. (Ont. Prov. Ct–Fam. Div. County of Waterloo), His Honour Judge G. Campbell.

Reid, S.A., and M. Reitsma-Street. 1984. 'Assumptions and implications of new Canadian legislation for young offenders,' *Canadian Criminology Forum* 7: 1–9

Shamsie, S.J. 1981. 'Anti-social youth: Our treatments do not work – where do we go from here?' *Canadian Journal of Psychiatry* 26: 357–64

Shireman, C.H., and F.G. Reamer. 1986. *Rehabilitating Juvenile Justice*. New York: Columbia University Press

PART THREE

Mental-Health Perspectives

Issues related to young offenders have, in Canada, never been solely the concern of the legal community. There has been a high level of integration of non-legal professional involvement in both the administration of the juvenile-justice system and the expression of how to address the causes of youth crime. The three chapters in this section provide perspectives on how mental-health practitioners can address issues related to youth crime. Awad addresses the assessment issues as they relate to understanding the needs and causes of youth crime. Patterson suggests that there is wisdom in attempting to meet the developmental needs of adolescents who find themselves in conflict with their communities by virtue of their behaviour. Webster, Rogers, Cochrane, and Stylianos talk about the particular dilemma arising out of the treatment and assessment issues regarding mentally disordered young offenders – a highly volatile group of adolescents that not only commit crimes resulting in court actions but are subject to serious mental-health disorders that the youth-court process is ill-equipped to handle.

9 Assessing the needs of young offenders

George A. Awad

The passage of the Young Offenders Act in Canada on 2 April 1984 introduced a new philosophy in dealing with youthful crime. A reading of the act clearly shows its legalistic nature and indicates that the needs of young offenders form a minor portion of the principles and dispositions sections. Only three of the more than one hundred pages of the act address the assessment of the needs of a young offender.

However, these three pages, section 13 (Medical and Psychological Reports), are an important feature of the YOA. Section 13 gives a youth-court judge power to order a young person to be examined by a 'qualified person' and for a written report to be submitted to the court. This section clarifies the different aspects of this order: the purpose of the assessment; when and what type of an assessment to order; who is qualified to do an assessment; the length of time allowed for the assessment when the young person is in custody; to whom the report may be disclosed; when a report may be withheld from those who usually get it; the right to cross-examine the qualified person; the fact that the report will be part of the record; and the limits of confidentiality in a time of danger. What follows is an elaboration of this section.

Purpose: There are three reasons for ordering medical and psychological reports: (a) to consider an application under section 16 for a hearing whose purpose is to decide whether a young person, usually one who is accused of committing a serious crime, should be transferred to the adult courts; (b) to determine whether a young person is, on account of insanity, unfit to stand trial; and (c) to make or review a disposition under this act. The last named is by far the most common reason for making this order.

When and What: The report may be ordered at any time during the proceedings. The report may be ordered with the consent of the young person and the prosecution, on a judge's motion, or on the application of either party. The report may be ordered when the court has reasonable grounds to believe that the young person may be suffering from a physical or mental illness or disorder, a psychological disorder, an emotional disturbance, a learning disability, or mental retardation. However, the act does not define any of these terms or the differences between them, such as distinguishing a mental illness or disorder from an emotional disturbance. In addition, the medical and psychological reports may be ordered when the court believes that a medical, psychological, or psychiatric report may be helpful in making any decision pursuant to this act. Again, there is no clarification as to what these types of reports are, how they differ, and whether the type of report is ordered in response to a particular type of illness or disorder – that is, it is not specified whether psychological disorder or emotional disturbance requires a medical, psychiatric, or psychological report. It seems that the purpose of this section was to cast the net as wide as possible with regard to when to order such a report. In addition, this section gives the judge wide discretion with regard to the reasons for ordering a report. However, one wonders whether a single condition, such as 'the presence of clinical concerns' on the part of the judge and/or crown and defence counsel, is sufficient for such a wide casting of the net. The judge and the lawyers are not trained to suspect medical, emotional, or learning disorders. Subsequently, they do not know when to order a medical, psychiatric, or psychological assessment. While judges and lawyers are sensitive enough to recognize clinical concerns about a young person, such as bizarre behaviour, depression, or unusual offences, to order a clinical assessment, it is more reasonable to let the 'qualified person' decide what type of assessment is needed to answer the questions asked.

Who Does It? Other than for the purpose of determining insanity or fitness to stand trial (s. 13[1][b]), when a qualified medical practitioner is needed, a 'qualified person' may perform the assessments. Subsection 13(11) defines the qualified person as one duly qualified by provincial law to be a practising physician, a psychiatrist, or a registered psychologist. In addition, a qualified person may be one who is qualified in the opinion of the youth court or a person or persons designated by the lieutenant governor in council of a province or his or her delegate. Although social work is not named as a profession in subsection 13(11), the youth court may qualify experienced social workers to perform such an assessment. In addition, the qualified person doing a report may be cross-examined by the young person, his or her counsel, or an adult assisting the young person, and by the prosecution.

Length of Time: There is no time limit for submission of the report when the young offender is not in custody. It is the experience of clinicians that section-16 and dispositional reports may take from four to six weeks to complete. However, insanity assessments may be done in a shorter period of time, except in complex cases. When a young person is remanded for the purpose of an examination, a report has to be submitted within eight days. However, if a qualified person satisfies the court, in writing, that more time is needed to complete the assessment, the young offender may stay in custody for a longer period, but not exceeding thirty days.

The Report: The youth court shall distribute the report to the young person, his or her counsel and parents, and the prosecution. However, when a qualified person thinks that a young person in custody is likely to endanger his or her life or the life of others, then the assessor can notify the person in charge. This provision adds another person to whom the contents of the report may be disclosed. In addition, the report may be withheld from the private prosecutor when the disclosure of the report is not necessary to the prosecution of the case and may be prejudicial to the young person. Also, a report may be withheld from any party when the qualified person can convince the court that such disclosure may be detrimental to the treatment or recovery of the young person, or may result in bodily harm, or may be detrimental to the mental condition of a third party. Finally, a report shall be part of the record.

It is clear that these reports are not confidential and are accessible to all the parties involved. In addition, once a report is in the hands of the people mentioned, its further distribution is almost inevitable. A clinician writing such a report should assume that it is public and may be read by more people than those who get copies of it. Withholding the report from any party is rarely requested.

An important aspect of this section is the absence of any guide-lines regarding the content of the report. Unlike the section on pre-disposition reports (section 14), section 13 offers no guide-lines as to who should be interviewed (aside from the young offender) or what the report should contain or how it should be structured. Presumably, the intent is to protect the clinicians' professional independence by allowing them to decide what to do and how to write their reports. With such responsibility, the clinician should always aim to write high-quality clinical reports. The contents should be brief and concise, but include all relevant data that would help the parties understand why a particular young person did what he or she did and what may be the best disposition for that person.

In general, section 13 is progressive and clear and makes it possible for the clinical needs of the young person to be addressed while protecting him or her from secret and potentially harmful reports whose contents are unknown to their subject. In addition, it guarantees professional independence while exercising quality control by making a clinician subject to cross-examination. It also provides for a legally sanctioned protection in potentially harmful situations.

Results of Implementation

The immediate results of the correctional thrust of the act are increased and longer custody orders (Leschied and Gendreau 1986; Leschied and Jaffe 1986). The de-emphasis on the needs has made reflected in a decrease in the number of section-13 orders being made, particularly in Ontario. Even though there have been some minor increases since 1986, the numbers of such orders continue to be lower than the referrals for assessment made under the Juvenile Delinquency Act, which did not have a comparable section.

There are several possible explanations for this change. The first is that this section can be understood only within the context of the act. As suggested previously, the Declaration of Principle section (section 3) focuses on the legal rights of young people, their responsibilities for their actions, and protection of society (Awad 1987). The principles that focus on the needs of the young person are ambivalently presented, and there are always legal qualifications and disqualifications. In general, this act represents the official move in handling youthful crime from a therapeutic state, with its focus on needs and best interests, to a legalistic state, with its emphasis on responsibilities, rights, and due process. The rest of the act clearly focuses on these legalistic guide-lines. Section 13 is one of the few instances where the focus is on the needs of the children. However, such a focus may get lost within the general thrust of the act.

This change in philosophy, as well as the procedural and structural changes initiated by this act, was highlighted in the choice topics by various workshops held in conjunction with recent conferences on the YOA. One topic was that the only goal of the YOA is to administer justice;

second, that the less a judge knows about the young person the better – or, as a crown attorney once suggested, the best medical and psychological reports are those that are one page in length. Even though these topics were conceivably presented this way in order to be provocative, they do point in the direction the act has taken.

One may assume that this change in philosophy has affected judges, the crown, defence lawyers, and clinicians. Judges now see themselves more as arbitrators of justice, whose goal is to find out whether a young person is guilty or not and to administer the disposition that fits the crime. Most judges may see themselves as having no *parens patriae* role to play under this act, and do not think that their role is to look out for the best interests of the young person. This attitude is reinforced by the fact that it is common for young offenders to have legal representation, and, thus, the best interests of the young offender is the responsibility of the defence counsel. Judges are less likely to order an assessment on their own than to elect to wait for the defence or the crown to request it. Both the defence and the crown may have their own reasons for avoiding or not considering a request for such assessments. Crown attorneys see it as their job to convict the offender and protect society. Thus, they do not see the needs of the young person as their responsibility. They may not want to have a clinical report that presents a sympathetic view of the offender and offers clinical reasons for his or her behaviour. However, the main goal of the defence counsel is to find his or her client not guilty and follow the dictum that the less the judge knows the better. Defence counsel may worry about information or clinical assessments that give a negative impression about the client. Some defence counsel have publicly stated that they never agree to have such an assessment done. In addition, there are practical reasons why defence counsel do not consider requesting such an assessment, including their lack of involvement in such cases. A high proportion of young offenders come from lower socio-economic classes and often are represented by duty-counsel or legal-aid lawyers. There are so many restrictions on such lawyers that they may not have the necessary time to delve into their cases. The result is that none of the three parties involved has an interest in requesting an assessment order. Such a result was highlighted in a recent study (Lewis et al 1988) of fourteen juveniles condemned to death. Most of these juveniles exhibited major neurological impairment, organic dysfunction, low IQ, and psychotic disorder and had histories of physical and sexual abuse. Yet, no court assessments were made, despite the fact that such findings could have mitigated the sentence they received.

In addition, two practical changes may also have contributed to the decrease in assessments ordered under this legislation. One change is that juveniles under age twelve no longer are considered to have criminal responsibility. However, the decrease is minor; even prior to the act, referrals of juveniles under age twelve for assessment counted for only 2 per cent of the referents (Leschied and Wilson 1986). In some jurisdictions, the age limit was increased to eighteen. However, in Ontario, the sixteen-to eighteen-year-old offenders are handled by criminal-court judges sitting as youth-court judges. There, the judicial philosophy discussed above has a long history and tradition, and few assessment orders are made. The second reason may be that the 'qualified person' section excludes social workers, as a group, from doing those assessments. This exclusion may have removed some people who traditionally have done assessments of juvenile delinquents from the pool of potential assessors. It is a well-known observation that the absence of providers will diminish the requests for services.

The Effect of the Act on Clinicians

The clinicians doing these assessments are also affected by the legalistic atmosphere. Most clinicians find working under this act to be quite different from doing so under the JDA and from their other clinical work. Previously, most clinicians saw themselves as part of a team that included the judge, probation officer, and personnel of other agencies who were concerned about the welfare of the young person. Now it is clear that there are no such teams. The clinician is more likely to be seen as an adversary by one or more parties and is now more likely than ever before to be cross-examined. This likelihood has affected the quality of the assessment and the type of report written. In addition, this adversarial role is quite different from what clinicians see as their role, namely, to act as healers and therapists of troubled youngsters and their families. Unfortunately, some clinicians have been engulfed by this atmosphere and have adjusted their assessments and reports accordingly. A clinician is a clinician in any situation, and his or her role, particularly in dispositional reports, is to assess the needs of the young person and to help such youngsters.

It is also clear that the focus of this section is to assess the needs of the young person; thus, any assessment that does not fully address those needs is not only outside the role of clinicians, but also not asked for under this act. A good clinical assessment is what is required here. Even though there are no guide-lines for the assessment and the report, the pressure is on the clinician to do a quick, short assessment and to provide a short report that addresses specific concerns. This pressure has affected the way reports are written. Thus, instead of doing a thorough assessment of all the systems involved with the young offender, one is more likely to write a shorter report. One change in the letters prepared by the Toronto Family Court Clinic has been documented in a study by Melville (1987). There has been a decrease in the number of third-party references since the act came into effect. While this finding reflects the caution of clinicians, it does not indicate a decrease in the quality of the reports.

Perhaps the most important effect of this atmosphere on the clinician is a sense of futility about the relevance of a thorough clinical assessments since there is no correlation between the clinical findings and disposition. In other words, the YOA is a legalistic act that brought back the concept of punishment or disposition that fit the crime. Once a young person is found guilty of a crime, there are limits to what can be done, and these limits are set in sentencing guide-lines that have their roots in the criminal-justice system. Even if a judge is concerned about the clinical condition of the offender, there is not much he or she can do to respond to those emotional and behavioural disorders. For example, a young person was caught shoplifting four times in a row and was referred for an assessment. The assessment revealed a seriously disturbed young man with major problems in functioning and in ability to test reality. He presented as an anxious person who was struggling with impulses he could not control. The assessment pointed out the need for major clinical intervention, perhaps including long-term hospitalization. However, this disposition was not possible because the offence was a relatively minor one, calling for a minor disposition. Thus, the intensive assessment of this young person served no purpose since there was no connection between the clinical findings and what could be recommended.

As discussed previously, the Declaration of Principle focuses on the needs of young people ambivalently. The same ambivalence is clearly seen in the dispositional sections. Section 20 clearly states that a judge may direct (20[1][a]), impose (20[1][b]), and order (20[1][c] and [d]), without any conditions being placed on his or her power and without any necessity for the consent of the young person or his or her family. The only clinical disposition mentioned in this section is secure treatment (20[1][i]), which is a major form of clinical intervention. Although this subsection is called an order, it is not really one, because it can be made only with the consent of the young person and his or her family (22[1]). This illustrates the ambivalence about responding to the clinical needs of a young person, for why else can a judge order anything, including incarceration, but not hospitalization? One may argue that this particular disposition is different from others because it involves attempts to change the young offender and his or her family against their will. To me, this reflects primitive anxieties about clinical work and is a regression to primitive society's belief in shamanism and sorcery. Clinicians do not have the power, skills, or ability to change people against their will. The goal of involuntary hospitalization is to create a milieu with boundaries to control a young person who is unable to control himself or herself. Once such control is in place, a young person and his or her family are often calm enough to make individual, group, or family therapy possible. A second argument against this disposition is that the period of hospitalization may be longer than a custody sentence that is appropriate to an offence. I argue that involuntary hospitalization is not incarceration, and that longer hospitalization is not equivalent to a similar time in jail. However, a compromise may be to have an order for hospitalization for the same length of time as an incarceration order appropriate for the offence. However, it should be possible for the treatment team to be able to give the young offenders some community privileges, including visits home or work outside, according to the young person's progress, instead of keeping him or her totally locked up for the period of time specified by the order.

The Needs of Young Persons

I will end this chapter on assessing the needs of young offenders by posing and trying to answer some questions about the needs of young persons. Do young persons have special needs? Are such needs different from their rights? Is it possible to respond to the needs of young offenders without losing their legal rights?

I will start by presenting a case vignette that illustrates the difficulties clinicians face in working with young offenders.

Joanne was a fourteen-year-old adopted girl, referred for assessment following a series of minor thefts. The assessment revealed that Joanne was removed from her biological parental home at age six months because of major neglect by her parents. Following foster care for one year, she was adopted. She had a relatively uneventful childhood, then began getting into trouble in early adolescence. The trouble was arguments with her family about the issue of control and her sexual behaviour. The family reacted strongly to her challenge of their authority, her misbehaviour at home, her running away, and the company of street people that she kept while on the run. The problems escalated and resulted in mutual rejection, culminating in a breakdown of the adoption. This event was followed by a couple of foster-home placements before she was placed with a family who cared for her and were willing to stick it out with her on a long-term basis. This was when the problems escalated again.

Following a clinical assessment, it was formulated that Joanne was an extremely anxious child who was very sensitive to feelings of rejection and fear of abandonment. It was felt that she tested the limits of her adoptive family's commitment to her by acting out. Unfortunately, they responded by rejecting her. At the time of the referral, it was felt that she was again anxious and testing the commitment of her current foster family. However, because of her acting-out tendencies, she responded to her anxieties by running away and misbehaving. It was felt that the best disposition was to put her on probation for a relatively long period, with an order to reside at home and attend a special day-school program. There was also a curfew order and an order to avoid certain company. Very soon, Joanne tested the order to attend school and observe the curfew, and was taken to court immediately and placed in detention for three days. She responded to that by attending school and observing curfew, although she continued to be a behavioural problem at school and to be uncooperative in individual and family therapy. However, within four to five months, she calmed down and started to deal with issues of abandonment and separation and her anxiety about whether she was being accepted by her foster family. They responded by being patient and sticking with her. There was some testing behaviour at home and of the curfew, but both were responded to with firmness and kindness. Unfortunately, the probation order was only for six months and, when it was over, there was a major increase in her behavioural problems, and she started again to miss her individual and family sessions. She started staying out late, hanging around groups of street kids, and indulging in alcohol and drug abuse. However, she was not caught committing any criminal offence and, thus, could not be charged or put back on probation. Soon, she stopped attending the individual and family sessions. It was felt that her behaviour was again caused by anxiety about separation that was contained by the probation order, but had intensified when the probation order was terminated.

What does this case vignette illustrate? It illustrates that there are adolescents who are unable to control themselves and, acting on impulse, expose themselves to dangerous behaviour. Once external controls are imposed on them, some of them get enough control that therapeutic work can result in behavioural and intrapsychic changes. However, the length of time needed for such control may be longer than what can be imposed according to criteria set by the seriousness of the offence, rather than the clinical needs of the offender. Once these controls are removed, there is a sudden and predictable deterioration that erases most of the progress they have made.

With this case vignette in mind, I will now address the needs of young persons. Young people need an environment that will give them the best opportunities for growth and development. One may even say that this is the right of young people. In fact, I would suggest that, in an ideal situation, the needs of young people and their psychological rights may be the same. Providing such an atmosphere for development is a complex, and at times, poorly understood process. However, it is clear that, at some time in their life, particularly in early adolescence, there is a need to establish autonomy and, later, identity, through a process that includes projections, testing, and controlling behaviour. Very often, the family can handle such behaviour through various measures until the adolescent works through the issues of autonomy and identity, and settles down. In some situations, the family is unable to provide such controls, and the adolescent may escalate the conflict and become unable to control himself or herself. It is in these cases that external controls need to be imposed to protect the adolescent. However, the controversy is over whether such controls should be imposed only when the young person commits criminal offences or when the young person commits an 'uncriminal offence,' such as running away, abusing alcohol, and endangering himself or herself. A strict libertarian, legalistic approach would consider criminal-code offences only, holding the offender responsible for his or her offences, and giving a disposition that fits the crime. The system is logical and internally coherent. However, it loses sight of the adolescents and their developmental needs and ultimately makes no psychological sense.

Can anything be done to respond to the needs of the young offenders without sacrificing their legal rights? It seems unlikely that there are going to be any major changes in the act that would alter its thrust. However, one should not abandon hope and should, instead, be ready with some specific recommendations for changes. If major changes were possible, I would recommend the following two to enhance the focus on the needs of the children.

First, the Declaration of Principle section should be changed to unequivocally focus on the needs of young persons and give them status equal to their legal rights. There should also be a clear mandate for the judge to balance the needs of the young person with his or her rights and with the protection of society. I assume that this focus on needs is possible under this act because the recognition of the need of young persons is its *raison d'être*. Otherwise, why do we have the YOA? If there are no special needs, then why not simply extend the Criminal Code and the criminal-court procedures to this age group? This change may mean that, at times, a disposition may fit the offender as well as the offence.

A second major change is required in the disposition section. A range of clinical dispositions may be useful. These vary from attendance for out-patient treatment in mild cases to involuntary hospitalization for extended periods of time for severely disturbed cases.

However, these changes are unlikely to occur in the foreseeable future. What is more likely and useful is a thorough knowledge of the act on the part of clinicians and attempts to use the act as it is, to provide for the needs of young offenders. With that in mind, there are two areas where the clinical needs of young offenders may be addressed. However, before discussing them, the whole issue of ordering people into treatment needs some analysis.

There is not enough space here to delve into the issue of involuntary treatment thoroughly. However, I would like to suggest that there should be a place for court-ordered treatment in dealing with young offenders. Some young offenders and their families deny the problem (as in sexual offenders and sexual abuse) or defend against getting treatment. Thus, these families and young people are unreachable without a court order. In addition, one should be clear about what a court-ordered treatment means. Court-ordered treatment simply helps the clinician to overcome the family's or the individual's resistance to attending. Once young people and their families start attending, it is up to the clinician to engage them in the therapeutic process. Court-ordered treatment does not force the family to change and does not involve any mind-altering drugs or methods. In my experience, families and antisocial youths belong to three groups. Two groups, both in the minority, are those who want help and those who are adamantly opposed to any intervention. The third group, the vast majority of these people, are ambivalent and anxious about seeking help. Thus, the role of the court-ordered treatment is to facilitate their seeing a clinician in order to determine whether a therapeutic alliance can evolve. Other-wise, the method of treatment is the same as with voluntary patients, namely, discussion, negotiation, and change (Awad and Perillo 1988).

With that in mind, I suggest that there are sections in the act that could be used to respond to the needs of young offenders.

1 / Probation orders (s. 23) may include 'attending school or such other

place of learning' (23[2][d]) and 'resid[ing] with a parent or such other adult as the court considers appropriate' (23[2][e]) or 'in such a place as the provincial director or his delegate may specify' (23[2][f]). In addition, section 23(2)(g) specifies that 'the young person comply with such other reasonable conditions set out in the order as the court considers desirable, including conditions for securing the good conduct of the young person and for preventing the commission by the young person of other offences.' This section may indicate clinical intervention to secure the good conduct of the young person and prevent the commission of further offences. Thus, more co-ordination between clinicians and probation officers is the best way to ensure out-patient treatment.

2 / Orders for secure custody may be the only way to respond to the needs of serious offenders. Thus, attempts should be made to make secure custody a place where treatment could occur. There is no encouragement or prohibition of such rehabilitative philosophy in secure custody. However, introducing treatment into secure custody may be challenged in court. In addition, it is only the serious offenders, those who may not be clinically disturbed, who get there, even though they might not need the clinical help offered. Accordingly, the more disturbed adolescents will still be outside the realm of being helped.

Finally, a thorough review of the act may discourage clinicians because of the act's unclinical and anti-clinical attitude. There seems to be an underlying tone suggestive of the need to protect offenders from clinicians. Such an atmosphere should only provoke clinicians to be more astute and scientific in their thinking and be very clear about what the needs of young people are and how to respond to them.

References

Awad, George. 1987. 'A critique of the principles of the Young Offenders Act,' *Canadian Journal of Psychiatry* 32 (August): 440–3

Awad, George, and Carmen Perillo. 1988. 'The court as a catalyst in the treatment process,' *American Journal of Psychotherapy* 42 (April): 290–6

Leschied, Alan, and Paul Gendreau. 1986. 'The declining role of rehabilitation in Canadian juvenile justice: Implications of underlying theory in the Young Offenders Act,' *Canadian Journal of Criminology* 28: 315–22

Leschied, Alan, and Peter Jaffe. 1986. 'Implications of the Young Offenders Act in modifying the juvenile justice system: Some early trends,' in N. Bala and H. Lilly, eds, *Young Offenders Service*, 7525–32, Toronto: Butterworths

Leschied, Alan, and Susan Wilson. 1986. 'Criminal liability of children under twelve: A problem for child welfare, juvenile justice or both,' *Canadian Journal of Criminology* 30: 17–29

Lewis, Dorothy, Jonathan Pincus, Barbara Bard, Ellis Richardson, Leslie Prichep, Marilyn Feldman, and Catherine Yeager. 1988. 'Neuropsychiatric, psychoeducational, and family characteristics of 14 juveniles condemned to death in the United States,' *American Journal of Psychiatry* 145 (5): 584–9

Melville, Tom. 1987. 'An issue of confidentiality: Widened disclosure in the clinical context,' *Faculty of Law Review* (University of Toronto) 43 (1): 179–86

10 A developmental perspective on antisocial adolescents

P.G.R. Patterson

The Juvenile Delinquents Act (1908) presented a number of difficulties, which can perhaps best be summarized by the feeling that its child-welfare/rehabilitation/needs/treatment orientation allowed too wide a flexibility in potential disposition, thereby permitting a wide variety of possible sentences for similar offences and exposing young offenders to possible infringements of their civil rights and the 'benevolent tyranny' of judges as they attempted to use their broad discretionary powers in the 'best interests of the child' (Leschied and Gendreau 1986). This flexibility led, at times, to a perceived inequity in the handling of cases, some young delinquents seeming to get off 'too lightly,' while others (for similar offences) seemed to have had their liberty restricted for an unconscionable length of time by an 'indeterminate' treatment order. In their attempt to correct these difficulties, the authors of the new Young Offenders Act chose to apply a simple and obvious device – that of standardization. In practice, this meant applying many of the standards of the adult court ('due process') to juvenile courts, applying the standards of the Canadian Charter of Rights and Freedoms and the Canadian Bill of Rights (devised with adults in mind, but necessarily applied to juveniles so as to be 'without discrimination by virtue of age'), introducing determinate sentencing, and vastly curtailing (and, therefore, standardizing) the number of possible disposition options available to judges. Whether intentional or otherwise, the emphasis has had to shift from the offender and his or her needs (where the almost infinite variety of permutations and combinations would make standardization impossible) to the offence itself (where the limited number of possibilities, which can be both counted and measured, make codification and standardization quite feasible) – a 'needs to deeds' shift that has been commented on at length by Awad (1987) and by Leschied and his colleagues (Leschied and Gendreau 1986; Leschied and Thomas 1985). Indeed, orders for treatment (commonplace under the benevolent 'child welfare' orientation of the Juvenile Delinquency Act) have become a rare event under the Young Offenders Act because of the necessity of their receiving the consent of the young offender (Leschied and Hyatt 1986).

'Fair for one, fair for all' must be one of the earliest, most basic, and most obvious ways of establishing even-handedness and impartiality, and it has given rise to the long-cherished precept that 'all men should be treated equally under the law.' This principle has much merit, but in its most concrete and literal form it provides a rough and primitive justice indeed – the simplest version of which would be 'Hang them *all*!' This conclusion is based upon the entirely unwarranted assumption that 'all men are created equal' and that every person and every situation is the same – an assumption so patently untrue and so against the basic laws of nature (which depends upon diversity for all progress) that to have continued to cling to it would have resulted in far more injustice than justice and would have given an entirely new meaning to the old adage 'justice is blind.' Indeed, the evolution of our system of justice may be said to have paralleled our ability to differentiate between categories and groups of people and situations. This differentiation provides for a more sophisticated principle that might be termed 'equality among equals.' The development of such concepts as *mens rea*, diminished responsibility, and the McNaghten Rule (to name only a few) has enabled our system of justice – for all its faults – to become one of the best, most humane, and most fundamentally 'just' in the history of the world.

In this light, the Juvenile Delinquents Act, when it was proclaimed in 1908, represented a tremendous advance in the evolution of justice in so far as it recognized and made provision for the fact that young people were different, not only from adults, but also from each other – and even from what they themselves might become if their personal development were to be fostered and nourished. Thus, despite the difficulties noted at the beginning, it allowed for considerable differences in motives, development, and needs of young offenders and made provision for a considerable range of possible interventions and consequences.

Viewed from this perspective, the Young Offenders Act would seem to be a remarkably regressive piece of legislation. The principle of standardization noted above to be the backbone of the new act's attempt to rectify the deficiencies of the Juvenile Delinquency Act is diametrically opposed to the principle of differentiation that has just been identified as being responsible for much of the positive evolution of our system of justice over the centuries. True, the Young Offenders Act pays lip-service in its Declaration of Principle to the fact that younger persons are not the same as adults, but there is no acknowledgment of potential differences *between* offenders, and the focus upon accountability, rights, freedom, offences, determinate sentencing, and consent for treatment appears to have seriously restricted any ability or tendency to distinguish in practice between various groups, categories, and needs of young persons (Leschied and Jaffe 1986; Leschied and Gendreau 1986; Leschied and Thomas 1985). Even the differences of young offenders from adults seem to be minimized, a process Awad (1987) refers to as 'adultomorphization.' And, in addition to being regressive from a philosophical point of view, preliminary results would seem to indicate that recidivism under the new act has increased (Leschied, Austin, and Jaffe 1988) and that therefore even the deterrent impact of the provisions in the new act are not working as its authors had hoped.

Indeed, from a developmental psychiatrist's point of view, it is hard to see how the Young Offenders Act *could* work very well for many of the target population, since so many of its underlying assumptions about many of this group are likely to be wrong. For instance, the emphasis on standardizing the principle of accountability depends on the assumption that most young offenders are capable of being accountable or responsible for their actions. *Chronologically* perhaps they should be, but *developmentally* many of them are still struggling with issues from the pre-school level – an age when only very limited accountability can or should be expected. It is one thing to expect a person who is capable of seeing things from another person's point of view to act in accordance with that knowledge; it is quite another to expect similar standards of behaviour from someone who is still totally preoccupied with egocentric issues and who hasn't even begun the process of 'decentration' yet. Similarly with rights and freedoms – most parents know that you do not provide children with rights and freedoms on the basis of chronological age alone. You wait until the child demonstrates some developmental capacity to handle the responsibility that goes with it. Even the law recognizes that children should not be automatically granted the right to pilot a motor vehicle on the basis of chronological age alone, but acknowledges that some sort of test of knowledge and ability is necessary first.

Similar issues arise with the right to consent, withhold consent, or withdraw consent for treatment, and it is interesting to note that the legal philosophy that recognizes the developmental limitations of children's ability to assess the future implications of non-school attendance and protects them from jeopardizing their entire future by withholding their freedom of choice on this issue until the age of sixteen is the *same* legal philosophy that allows them the right to refuse to attend for treatment of major psychosocial disabilities, which, untreated, can result in far more damage to their future than a deficit in education (which can, potentially, be made up at any time). These issues have been exceptionally well explored by Leschied and Hyatt (1986) and Leschied and Jaffe (1986), and need no further elaboration here. Suffice it to say that this is the single most puzzling – one is tempted to say 'stupid,' but politeness and humility prevail – provision in the new act. Defensive exclusion, avoidance, and denial being the primitive defence mechanisms that they are, surely the only adolescents with the courage and maturity to be able to recognize and acknowledge their need for help of this nature are the ones who, in fact, need it the least. Who can seriously imagine a sullen, rebellious, antisocial thirteen-year-old saying to a judge: 'Please, Your Honour, I find myself sorely afflicted with anxiety about my self-esteem and basic security; torn with ambivalence about the need to grow up and assume adult responsibilities; tempted to lie, cheat, and steal at every opportunity; and truculent in the face of authority. On this basis, I consent to trustingly put myself in the hands of further unknown authority figures who will confront me at every opportunity; read my innermost thoughts; subject me to positive and negative reinforcement contingencies and possibly to legal (Heaven forbid!) mind-altering drugs; force me to experience and deal with my sadness and depression and anger at an uncaring world; put me to bed at ten o'clock every night for an indefinite period; and otherwise persuade, coerce, and cajole me into acting in what they consider to be my own best interests. Too long I have tarried in a failed attempt to assert my autonomy and independence. Let them take me away, deprive me of my power and control, and help me explore the terrors of the vulnerability and dependency of my childhood.'

But of all the efforts to standardize an approach and ignore differences, the insistence upon viewing most offences as a uniform group of meaningless pieces of behaviour that can all be effectively responded to – and discouraged or deterred in the future – with a single consequence varying only in duration (restriction of freedom through probation or custody) is the most naive and the most likely to fail. The assumption seems to be that a book may be understood, judged and responded to by its cover – surely a tenuous hypothesis at best. This chapter is not the place to outline a full developmental theory of behaviour, but perhaps a few examples would suffice to illustrate the potential perils of such an assumption.

Let us, for the purposes of illustration, make a few assumptions of our own. Let us accept, for the moment, that each individual has two strong inborn tendencies that ultimately help to shape his or her method of coping with the world. The first of these is a drive towards *homonomy*, that is, towards interpersonal connections with supportive and friendly people. The first expression of this is the drive towards attachment to one's parents and preserving that attachment, at least through the early dependent years. This is followed by the development of peer relationships, meaningful participation in society, marital relationships, and ultimately the relationships with one's own children. The second drive is the drive towards *autonomy*, first expressed as a drive for exploration as a toddler, then as the 'terrible two's,' and later as a drive for independence, self-sufficiency, self-expression, productive work, and other personal freedoms. As a very general rule-of-thumb, the 'normal' individual will have achieved a comfortable balance and integration of both these drives, whereas the 'disturbed' individual will have had a relative surfeit or deficiency of one or both thrust upon him or her and hence will be in a constant state of uncomfortable tension. Both the nature of, and the developmental timing of, the factors that have led to such an imbalance are of considerable importance (Thompson and Patterson 1980, 1986), but are beyond the scope of this chapter.

With this briefest of backgrounds, let us now take 'oppositional behaviour' as an example of behaviour that might bring a young person into conflict with the law – perhaps through a single act of aggression or through the defiance of a specific person or regulation. To be more specific, let us suppose that a burly fifteen-year-old boy has assaulted a teacher. What set of circumstances might lead up to this, and what would be the predictable response to a given form of intervention? Developmentally, the earliest difficulty that might lead to such an assault would be an absence (or complete suppression) of the homonomous drive for meaningful interpersonal relationships secondary to the failure to form any kind of adequate attachment since birth. Such circumstances are most likely to arise when an infant is grossly neglected (at least emotionally – and often physically, as well) and is subsequently transferred from hand to hand through a multiple succession of placements (Steinhauer 1980). Such individuals appear to have very little feeling for their fellow human beings – very little capacity for caring or empathy – and appear to be almost entirely preoccupied with their own interests. They appear to have little anxiety about their interpersonal relationships, and many of the normal social controls such as 'What would people think?' or 'People would be hurt or wouldn't like you if ...', are of little or no relevance to these individuals, even though they are often capable of being quite charming and appearing to be quite likeable. This group is often referred to as 'psychopaths' or 'sociopaths,' and the only societal controls that appear to be effective with them are the fear of clear and noxious consequences. Unfortunately, these are likely to be effective only if applied with great consistency (the occasional ability to 'get away with it' breeds eternal hope for the future) and if the individual believes that he or she is likely to get caught (necessitating fairly constant observation and monitoring). Ordinary psychotherapy or other forms of 'treatment' are not normally effective with this group and, although some people believe that they *can* be treated (by being forced into an attachment relationship through a prolonged period of intense and closed treatment), society does not normally have sufficient resources for this and has to fall back on behavioural controls instead. This would seem to be the group for whom the Young Offenders Act was designed, but fortunately they are relatively few in number. Even the Young Offenders Act, however, would need to be *very* strictly applied and its potential loopholes carefully guarded against. In our case sample, the attack on the teacher might have been relatively unprovoked and resulted from some minor frustration or, alternatively, might have been part of attempted robbery. Rapid application of the Young Offenders Act at full strength would be an appropriate response, although no guarantee against future episodes if the young offender saw an opportunity for avoiding consequences.

Developmentally, the next group who might perpetuate such an offence consists of those who have formed an attachment, but an unreliable one that is constantly being jerked from under their feet. Conditions at home may vary from great indulgence and overgratification to unpredictable rage-filled attacks. These poor children are desperately confused and basically very mistrustful of all relationships, though they are constantly seeking them out in the hope of finding a fulfilling one. Indeed, they are so concentrated upon the achievement of a satisfying, homonomous, interpersonal relationship and the development of an adequate security base that they tend to neglect the development of their autonomous functioning; and their school performance, their peer relationships, and their ability to look after themselves or act in their own best interests tend to fall apart in the process. These individuals can be quite explosive when betrayed, although they often portray a profound anxiety to please in between explosions, making inumerable promises of good behaviour in the future. However, having so much reason to be mistrustful, they are constantly testing out their relationships, frequently by covert misbehaviour and failure to meet expectations, thereby both providing a test and acting out their anger about past betrayals by committing their own betrayals in the present.

In our case example, an offender at this developmental level would likely have developed an apparently very positive relationship with the teacher, then betrayed the teacher in accordance with the dynamics outlined above, would then have been confronted by the teacher and threatened with withdrawal of support, and reacted explosively. Shortly after the episode, however, the child would likely appear very remorseful and make numerous promises of good behaviour in the future, and the cycle would repeat. These children are very difficult to treat in an out-patient setting because they tend to relate extremely well to their therapist initially in an almost ingratiating fashion, while denying their anger and acting it out in the face of even small frustrations by failing to keep their appointments. Consequently, the need to be treated on an in-patient, residential basis – frequently over a long period of time – where they can be helped to develop healing relationships and learn to trust these. The Young Offenders Act, as constructed at present, will have little impact on these individuals as, without the capacity to order them into long-term residential treatment, it cannot hang on to them long enough. Consequences have little impact because the feelings behind the behaviour simply overwhelm reality-testing and the ability to appreciate future consequences of present behaviour. This is a group who might initially consent to treatment in their desire to please and ingratiate themselves after an impulsive act. However, if so empowered, they will withdraw their consent when faced with the first frustrations in a treatment setting.

A third group of children would include those who have developed a positive attachment and connection to their early caretakers, but one that has been inadequate in providing a sufficient degree of nurture and protection, so that the child has been forced too early to fall back on his or her own autonomous functioning in order to survive. In many of these cases, there is a frank parent-child role reversal on many occasions, where the child actually has had to look after the parent. For these children, their autonomy is clearly of paramount importance, as their very survival depends on it. Any encroachment on or infringement of their autonomy will thus be seen as a life-threatening assault, and they will fight back with all their strength. Underlying this most obvious characteristic is often a so-called masked depression secondary to the insufficiency of age-appropriate nurturing and protection that they have received. These children do not do well in the face of arbitrarily imposed authority, and particularly do not do well in a coercive environment, because they have had little reason to believe in benevolent and adequate caretaking relationships and believe that their own independent exercise of their autonomy is their only means of survival. If the latter is threatened or removed from them, they become extremely anxious and urgently seek out methods of regaining control, the theme on which they concentrate exclusively. In our case example, the assault on the teacher would very likely have been provoked by the teacher having threatened the boy's survival by, in some way, threatening his autonomous functioning – for instance, by humiliating him or degrading him in front of his peers. If they are in touch with their underlying depression, these individuals may be treated on an out-patient basis by developing a relationship with a benevolent, non-authoritarian, reliable individual. In more severe cases, where the depression is so painful that it has to be avoided by denial and by the exercise of pseudo-autonomous (and often unrealistic) displays of 'macho' independence, treatment becomes much more difficult. Any consequences applied by the Young Offenders Act or other means that limit freedom and autonomy have to be vigorously resisted and defied, and these individuals are almost forced by these dynamics to run from open-custody settings. If caught and subjected to further coercion (especially if punitive or arbitrary), their need and efforts to escape will be redoubled, and a vicious circle (sometimes of extremely dangerous proportions) can then ensue; the paradoxical situation arises where those trying to protect the child are, in fact, responsible for driving him or her to greater excesses of potentially self-destructive behaviour. By virtue of their dynamics, these individuals literally cannot consent voluntarily to treatment, and simple custody will not only not be effective, because of their tendency to run or psychologically divorce themselves from relationships, but will also frequently make them even *more* determined to prove their independence – often by repeating the offence – as soon as they are released. For the more extreme cases, the only intervention that can be effective is placement in a secure treatment setting where they can be contained, while, over time, they can gradually be desensitized to their 'phobia' of loss of autonomy, a benevolent and trustworthy relationship can be established, and slowly they can be helped to work through their painful feelings of depression. Unfortunately, this is currently impossible under the Young Offenders Act, and, before the Mental Health Act can be invoked, extremely dangerous behaviour has to be displayed. Prior to the age of sixteen, they can sometimes be placed in hospital for a short period of time under the authority of parents or guardians, but there are many restrictions on this action and many courses of appeal – the latter process being an exercise of autonomous functioning that colludes with their defences and precludes treatment while it is in process. 'Determinate sentencing,' of course, would be a particular anathema in the attempt to treat these severely disturbed youngsters. A short sentence would entirely preclude treatment, and with a moderate or longer sentence there would always be the danger that one had just finally begun to get under the defences when the sentence would end, autonomy would be restored, and the whole process would have become an exercise in futility. Worse, such a failed effort would likely lead the youngster to be even more phobic of treatment in the future. A particularly dangerous turn of events could occur if the sentence happened to be up just at the time when the child was experiencing the fullest and most painful of the depressive feelings and release was experienced as an abandonment. A serious suicidal gesture could easily result.

A final group of youngsters who might, under certain circumstances, have assaulted their teacher would be those with normal personalities and no background of psychopathology but whose normal ego-functioning was temporarily overwhelmed. Apart from all the organic conditions that might cause this, a number of psychological events might also be responsible, including acute grief reactions occasioned by the loss by death or separation or divorce of a loved one (especially a sibling or parent) or an acute traumatic event, such as a rape or an assault. Such an incident would likely be an isolated event – perhaps precipitated by an untactful or incautious remark or an unsympathetic attitude – and might well be followed shortly by feelings of acute remorse. (Remorse would not be a *necessary* criterion, however – especially if the teacher were the subject of a temporary displacement of feelings.) Under these circumstances, behavioural consequences would not be helpful, and might even be destructive. The Young Offenders Act would seem to have little role to play other than to assuage the outraged feelings of the victim. Repetition of the act would seem to be unlikely in any event.

It is hoped that these four vignettes will have served to illustrate the complexities involved in interpreting and appropriately responding to what, at first glance, might seem to be a 'simple' piece of behaviour. It is even more particularly hoped that they will have served to illustrate how responses to the 'offence rather than the offender' and attempts at 'standardization' or to 'make the punishment fit the crime' will often, without further consideration, be ineffective or – worse – actively exacerbate the situation and provoke recidivism.

Clearly our legislation cannot long remain so 'offence' focused that we, as a society, are not permitted to respond differently to two young men who both have stolen knives – one for the purposes of committing armed robbery and one for the purposes of committing suicide. An appropriate response to one could be extremely inappropriate for the other, and our legislation needs the flexibility to be able to recognize and respond to their differences. Equally clearly, however, the rights of the individual (for *both* liberty and treatment) need to be respected, and the principles of 'personal responsibility' (up to developmental capacity) and 'least intrusive and restrictive alternative' (capable of addressing the needs of the individual) are eminently sensible. These principles *do* need to be universal and 'standardized' across situations, and are too important to be allowed to be 'flexible.' The problem seems to be one of developing the capacity to respond to the *whole* person and not just focusing exclusively on one aspect – whether that aspect be behaviour, rights, or developmental needs. Viewed from this perspective, the Young Offenders Act may well have been an important and necessary step in our evolution, refocusing our attention, as it does, on the issue of individual rights and freedoms and personal responsibility. However, as outlined above, the price has been high, and the baby has gone down the drain with the bath water. We need now to move on and combine that which is good from both the Juvenile Delinquency Act and the Young Offenders Act. One hopes that the resultant combination will standardize and entrench the important principles, addressed in the Young Offenders Act, while still allowing for adequate recognition of differences between offenders and providing for a wider flexibility and range of possible dispositions and varying *combinations* of custody and treatment, in accordance with the needs of the whole person who has signalled his or her distress by means of the offence that has summoned society's attention.

References

Awad, G. 1987. A Critique of the principles of the Young Offenders Act,' *Canadian Journal of Psychiatry* 32: 440–3

Leschied, A.W., G.A. Austin, and P.G. Jaffe. 1988. 'Recidivism rates of special needs youth: Clinical and policy implications,' *Canadian Journal of Behavioural Science* 20 (3): 322–31

Leschied, A.W., and P.G. Gendreau. 1986. 'The declining role of rehabilitation in Canadian juvenile justice: Implications of underlying theory in the Young Offenders Act,' *Canadian Journal of Criminology* 28 (3): 315–22

Leschied, A.W., and C. Hyatt. 1986. 'Perspective Section 22(1): Consent to treatment order under the Young Offenders Act,' *Canadian Journal of Criminology* 28 (1): 69–78

Leschied, A.W., and P.G. Jaffe. 1986. 'Implications of the consent to treatment section of the Young Offenders Act: A case study, *Canadian Psychology* 27 3): 312–13

Leschied, A.W., and K.E. Thomas. 1985. 'Effective residential programming for hard-to-serve delinquent youth: A description of the Craigwood program,' *Canadian Journal of Criminology* 27: 161–77

Steinhauer, P.D. 1980. *How to Succeed in the Business of Creating Psychopaths Without Even Trying*. Vol. 2 and 4: *Training Resources in Understanding, Supporting and Treating Abused Children*; Foster Parents Training Program for Children's Aid Societies. Toronto: Ministry of Community and Social Services, Children's Services Division, Section 9, 239–328, December 1980.

Thompson, M.G.G., and P.G.R. Patterson. 1980. 'Children and adolescents,' in H. Merskey, ed, *Psychiatric Illness*, 3rd ed, 182–238. London: Balliere-Tindell

– 1986. 'The Thompson-Patterson scale of psychosocial development: I: Theoretical basis,' *Canadian Journal of Psychiatry* 31: 387–97

11 Assessment and treatment of mentally disordered young offenders

Christopher D. Webster, Joy M. Rogers, Jeanette J. Cochrane, and Stanley Stylianos

Despite the lack of demonstrable success in prevention and treatment programs to date, society remains reluctant to fall back on purely retributive sanctions for juvenile offenders. Treatment efforts continue, and research on prediction and primary prevention of delinquency indicates that there may be cause for qualified optimism. (Widom 1986: 278)

There is general agreement that juvenile social deviance is a complex phenomenon, having multiple determinants, manifestations, and sequelae (Barker 1982). Likely this diversity contributes strongly to what Davidson and colleagues (1986) have referred to as a 'legacy of frustration' in developing effective treatment solutions for youthful deviance. The view adopted by some in the past that all young offenders are suffering from emotional or psychiatric disturbances requiring treatment is now, sensibly enough, being discounted. Yet, there is broad agreement that a subgroup of individuals exists whose antisocial behaviour is directly linked to psychological problems (Steinhauer 1978). There is also another target population whose emotional pathology may be brought to light for the first time during the assessment process or custodial period that follows the delinquent act, but whose disorder may not be clearly associated with the need to commit such acts (Geismar and Wood 1986). These two groups of mentally disordered young offenders are the focus of this chapter.

Our aim is to offer those involved with planning, delivering, and evaluating services for young offenders a 'window' on the current wisdom regarding assessment and treatment of young persons in trouble with the law and for whom there are questions about mental competence or stability. Because our emphasis is on providing information of the greatest practical value, we will draw selectively from related fields of knowledge rather than conduct an exhaustive critical review. The following issues are addressed from the perspective of the published literature: 1 / general characteristics of the mentally disordered young offender; 2 / approaches to, and issues arising from, the assessment of the young offender for fitness to stand trial, dangerousness, and treatability; 3 / types of interventions and settings now being employed for the treatment and management of emotionally disturbed young offenders; and 4 / systems-level perspective on the provision of clinical services to these youth.

The Mentally Disordered Young Offender: Clinical Profile

What is a 'young offender'? How does a young offender differ from a 'delinquent'? What is a mental disorder? Legal meanings of such terms differ from psychiatric and psychological understandings (Webster 1984). It is tempting to limit our discussion solely to 'young offenders' as they are legally defined by the Young Offenders Act and its various sections (Solicitor General Canada 1982). Yet it would be remiss not to point out that many circumstances dictate whether individual youthful offenders are brought within the ambit of the new law. A considerable number of young persons who have committed illegal acts are being dealt with under municipal care and safety statutes. Whether or not a young person is charged depends on the particular jurisdiction in which the alleged offence was committed, the amount of discretion used by attending police officers, the public mood, and no doubt many other factors (Binder 1988).

'Delinquency' is a term that is ubiquitous in the scientific literature as a generic descriptor for those youths who are in conflict with either the law or society. Delinquent behaviours range from those associated with clear violation of the law, such as violence against people or property; offences that contravene accepted values and health or social standards (for example, drug and alcohol abuse or sexual misconduct); and acts that would not necessarily be illegal if committed by an adult, but that are deemed inappropriate for those having the status of child or adolescent. However, with the introduction of the Young Offenders Act in Canada, the terms 'young offender' and 'delinquent' have come to be associated with radically different legal and philosophic stands regarding youth in trouble with the law. Throughout this chapter, both terms will appear but they are not meant to be interpreted in a legal sense. It would be misleading, however, to rely solely on concepts of delinquent behaviour as a basis for discussing the characteristics of either young offenders in general or the smallest group of those who are mentally disturbed. Such a framework fails to capture the heterogeneity representative of this population.

Considerations of Prevalence

Although adolescence can be an intense and tumultuous time, characterized by mood swings, testing behaviours, poor judgment, and problematic relationships, only a small number of young persons manifest delinquent or markedly socially deviant behaviours. Similarly, an even smaller proportion of all adolescents are diagnosed as suffering from a major psychiatric disorder such as schizophrenia. However, the numbers of young persons in the general population who are reported as being emotionally disturbed in a clinical sense are considerably larger. Moreover, research studies usually find that almost all children and adolescents who are diagnosed as psychotic receive treatment, but that the majority of those who are categorized as clinically maladjusted are not receiving treatment (Dohrenwend et al 1980).

Accurate statistics on the prevalence of mental disorders and emotional disturbances in Canadian young offenders are not available. To our knowledge, a proper epidemiological survey of young offenders has not yet been conducted in Canada. Such figures as may be reported by various jurisdictions are bound to be seriously flawed as they necessarily represent only those young offenders who have come to the attention of mental-health professionals because of the seriousness of their condition or the fact that they have sought help.

To further complicate this issue, studies of the prevalence of psychiatric disorders in the general population of adolescents have yielded a wide range of estimates, depending on the population and age range studied, as well as the methodology and approaches to classification and measurement adopted by the researchers. There are markedly different views expressed in the psychiatric literature regarding the prevalence of various diagnostic categories, and the definitions and causes of childhood disorders. Reported prevalence figures range from 7 to 25 per cent (Sas and Jaffe 1986). As a diagnostic entity, depression effectively illustrates the heterogeneity found among mentally disordered delinquents. Estimates of the prevalence of moderate to severe depression have ranged from 23 to 50 per cent (Sas and Jaffe 1986).

Based on the findings of twenty-five U.S. studies, Dohrenwend and colleagues (1980) estimated the prevalence of 'clinical maladaptation' in schoolchildren to be at least 12 per cent and the rate of psychosis in adolescence at over 1 per 1000. Using a community sample and internationally accepted criteria, Kashani and colleagues (1987) found the prevalence of conduct disorder needing psychiatric intervention to be 8.7 per cent. The Ontario Child Health Study (1986), which is one of the best Canadian studies of the prevalence of emotional disturbance among children and youth aged four to sixteen years, reported that 18 per cent of all subjects had one disorder or more. The prevalence of neurosis in youths twelve to sixteen years of age (indicated by dysphoric mood, compulsive or obsessive symptoms, and/or strong feelings of tension, nervousness, or anxiety) was 5 per cent for boys and 12 per cent for girls. Conduct disorder was found to be more common as children became older, and more prevalent in boys (almost 11 per cent) than girls (just over 3 per cent). Hyperactivity was reportedly just over 7 per cent for adolescent boys and 3 per cent for girls in the same age group. Environmental factors found to be most strongly associated with psychiatric disorder were a poorly functioning family, being on welfare, and living in subsidized housing.

Characteristics of Mentally Disordered Youth Offenders

Any attempt to fit young offenders into discrete categories according to the types of emotional disturbances and disorders that affect them is an exercise doomed to failure. The complexity and the sheer numbers of these problems prohibit neat classification or brief discussion. Some conditions (for example, anorexia nervosa) are reported so infrequently by young offenders that they are better dealt with elsewhere. Also, the causes and manifestations of a few psychiatric disorders still represent so great a challenge to researchers and clinicians that efficacious approaches to assessment and treatment have not yet been developed. Nevertheless, the responsibility remains to care for those affected by severe psychopathology while attempts to advance the state of knowledge continue. For this reason, the best that can be done here is to present some arbitrary groupings based loosely on type and severity of psychopathology. For illustrative purposes, examples of the kinds of problems that would be included under each category are also provided, together with the treatment responses that are most frequently required.

Broadly, mentally disordered young offenders can be expected to include the following subgroups:

Youths suffering from neurotic disorders or emotional disturbances specific to childhood and adolescence. Some of these young persons may be previously fairly well-adjusted individuals whose antisocial behaviour derives from a reactive process related to one or more recently experienced life situations such as the death of a parent or severe family disharmony. Clinical descriptors used for their conditions may include 'situational adjustment reaction' or 'reactive depression.' Others may be found to have had a fairly long history of unresolved personal and/or family conflicts that have culminated in delinquent behaviour.

Many young offenders whose emotional problems fall into this general category can be treated by skilled mental-health professionals in out-patient or community-based crisis-intervention services especially developed to serve adolescents. Therapeutic approaches frequently used for this population include individual or family counselling, group therapy, and self-help or support groups. These various treatment ventures are apt to be situated in a range of non-institutional settings. However, sometimes adolescents in emotional crisis experience such severe reactions that they present a danger to themselves or others. A short period of residential admission or hospitalization may be needed to conduct a proper assessment, deal with suicide risk, or stabilize those who have experienced acute emotional decompensation. The acting-out behaviour of youths subsequently found to be severely depressed has been termed 'masking behaviour,' or 'depressive equivalents' by Sas and Jaffe (1986). These authors note that some young offenders present as anxious, impulsive, resentful of authority, socially introverted, and having paranoid ideation. Their clinical picture, often characterized by a pattern of violence against others and refractoriness to treatment, is similar to Agee's description of what she termed the 'aversive treatment evader' (1979). Such youths, who are said to constitute approximately 20 per cent of depressed delinquents, are thought to be best managed in secure settings (Sas and Jaffe, 1986).

Those with severe psychopathology. We refer here to those suffering from major mental illnesses such as affective disorders, psychoses, or eating disorders, and those with marked neuropsychological impairments. While symptoms of psychosis and organicity have been infrequently reported in studies of young offenders (Werry 1979), there is some research evidence that violent young offenders display more psychotic and organic symptoms than do relatively non-violent delinquents (Lewis and Shanok 1979). In one American study, delinquents referred by the court for psychiatric hospitalization and voluntarily admitted non-delinquents were found to manifest equally severe psychopathology, with nearly identical levels of psychotic and organic symptoms (Shanok et al 1983). As the onset of schizophrenia often occurs in adolescence, initial diagnosis and early treatment of this disorder may have particular relevance to the population of young persons considered in this chapter.

Some young persons experiencing acute episodes of major psychiatric disorders can pose a serious suicide risk (Miller, Chiles and Barnes 1982; Sas and Jaffe 1986). Many will need close monitoring and, at least, short-term treatment and stabilization, usually in a hospital setting. Most require intensive and prolonged management, together with continuity of care in settings appropriate to their changing condition.

Young persons exhibiting either equivocal signs or more conclusive evidence of neurological impairment characteristic of minimal brain dysfunction or hyperkinetic syndrome constitute another group believed to be at increased risk for antisocial behaviours or conduct problems (Werry 1979). As noted by Sargent (1988), new developments in neuro-psychiatry highlight the importance of the role of such factors as individual biochemical differences, temporal-lobe dysfunction, and attention-deficit disorders in deviant behaviour. Unfortunately, in many instances the neurological problems of young offenders are not identified before they have become known to the justice system.

Although mental retardation is not considered by the general public and service-delivery structures to be a psychiatric disorder, nevertheless it is included as a category in the most recently internationally adopted psychiatric classification system, DSM-IIIR (American Psychiatric Association 1987). Mildly and moderately retarded adolescent offenders are being identified by juvenile-justice systems with increased regularity (Denkowski and Denkowski 1983). Some of these youths are functionally illiterate, aggressive, and deficient in social skills. Thus, assessment and intervention programs for young offenders must be equipped to deal with the possible influence of organic contributors.

Those with conduct disorders and learning disorders. These problematic conditions are listed on Axis II in the American Psychiatric Association's DSM-IIIR (1987). While some writers have long argued that psychiatry should relinquish its role in the management of these disorders (Szasz 1963), most experts agree that learning and conduct disorders are 'co-owned' by a variety of disciplines. Psychiatry, psychology, education, social work, and corrections must work together to address the multiple assessment and treatment demands of learning- and conduct-disordered youth. For example, some adolescents diagnosed as 'borderline,' who typically have difficulty maintaining important relationships, show considerable overlap with conduct-disordered youth (Green 1983); these individuals apparently benefit most from psychiatric and psychological management approaches. Other conduct-disordered youth are perhaps more effectively treated in correctional settings.

Substance abusers. The association between crime and the excessive use of alcohol and drugs across Canada is well documented. There are certainly strong indications that drug and alcohol dependence play a major part in the initiation and maintenance of delinquent behaviours. For example, in the province of Alberta in 1978, about 9 per cent of juvenile offences (committed by those under sixteen years) were alcohol- or drug-related (Clarke Institute of Psychiatry 1983). There are indications that underlying psychiatric disorders are associated with early age of onset (under age fifteen) of substance abuse (Czechowicz 1988). However, while most psychiatric classification systems include categories for disorders conno-ting substance-related dependency, the assessment and treatment of this population is usually not the prime responsibility of the field of psychiatry. Most provinces have developed separate service systems that deal with addiction research, education, and treatment.

Addiction is considered by many to be a chronic health problem. Although a variety of approaches to treatment have been developed over many years, there is evidence that treatment in general is unsuccessful more often than not (success rates are estimated at between 30 and 40 per cent according to Cox et al (1983). Self-help programs specially developed for youth, and long-term residential programs that emphasize behaviour-modification techniques, confrontation, and peer pressure, seem to offer the greatest chance of success in dealing with seriously addicted adoles-cents. The importance of early identification of the existence of substance-abuse problems, along with individual contributors, cannot be overem-phasized. In some instances, family problems may be implicated; in other cases, a young person may be using alcohol or drugs in a vain attempt to defend against clinical depression.

The 'impossible' or 'hard-to-serve' youth. Most mental-health professionals agree about the existence of a small subgroup of youths who are unusually refractory to usual interventions. Terms used to designate this subgroup include the 'impossible' or 'hard-to-serve' youth. These labels have been used to describe youths with a variety of conditions, including sociopathic personality, conduct disorder, and multiple diagnoses (e.g., psychiatric disorder and mild retardation), as well as substance abusers and sexual offenders. Rather than contributing to an improved understanding of the etiology and management of specific disorders, terms like 'hard to serve' have come to have pejorative meanings and point to gaps in our current knowledge of effective service delivery. It is clear that such youths are not members of a homogeneous group, and do not lend themselves readily to subclassification.

As a means of promoting greater understanding of 'impossible' youth, Rae-Grant coined the term 'Ovinnik syndrome' (1978). This does not currently represent an established clinical syndrome, but was developed as a means of operationalizing what precisely is meant by 'hard to serve.' According to Rae-Grant, the syndrome spans a complex of symptoms, including impaired relationships with peers and adults; antisocial behaviour, such as aggressive or assaultive conduct, temper tantrums, fire setting, or stealing; school problems, such as truancy or underachievement; and self-destructive behaviour, as, for example, substance abuse, suicide attempts, or frequent running-away. Those diagnosed as 'Ovinniks' would typically display eight to ten of these symptoms.

No matter how these 'hard-to-serve' youths are defined, all who write about them agree that some agency must deal with them. The important elements in providing treatment for this subpopulation are: planning and implementing co-ordinated intervention and follow-up services; relatively long-term residential treatment in specialized facilities (preferably in rural settings); the employment of sufficient numbers of specially trained, motivated staff supplied with sufficient support and back-up consultation; and balancing the mixture and controlling the numbers of these youngsters in a given treatment centre.

No matter how painstaking and expensive the treatment effort, its effect is often nullified in the absence of careful planning and decision making with regard to subsequent placement. While it may be true that some conduct disorders abate with the passage of time, an active strategy for planning and implementing follow-up is essential to the success of any treatment program. It is widely understood that discord follows when young persons are abruptly returned to the disordered social worlds from which they came.

Approaches to Assessment

Psychiatric and psychological assessments provide ways of identifying and understanding an individual's relative social adjustment or maladjustment. The kind of assessment conducted depends on the questions that need to be addressed. The focus of such evaluations may be on isolated dimensions of behaviour or on more global aspects (O'Leary and Johnson 1979). Although clinical assessment is a general process of gathering behavioural information, it frequently entails the more specific task of classifying abnormality, namely, diagnosis.

There is no single instrument or approach that is considered totally satisfactory for the assessment of children (O'Leary and Johnson 1979). Approaches to assessment include a variety of methods and tools, such as projective devices, dimensional rating scales, observational methods, and interviewing techniques. In order to be clinically useful, an assessment instrument or tool must be both reliable and valid. Simply stated: an instrument is considered reliable if it yields similar scores for a given individual on at least two separate test occasions and if it yields similar results in the hands of at least two different investigators. In order to be valid, an assessment tool should actually measure what it purports to measure. Many assessment instruments and methods do, though, create conflicting results in regard to their clinical usefulness and, in particular, reliability and validity. Therefore, in conducting assessments it is most appropriate to consider information drawn from a variety of sources, specifically noting points of agreement and disagreement. Woe to clinicians in court attempting to defend their clinical testing practices largely on the basis of unsubstantiated beliefs in the efficiency of the instruments selected for use (Jeffrey 1964; Faust and Ziskin 1988).

In some instances, assessments are conducted too readily and with too little consideration of their actual, rather than intended, effects on the individual being assessed. A large part of the difficulty is that young offenders tend to be remanded by the courts for assessment without it ever being specified with precision what the evaluation is expected to accomplish. The mental-health worker, in the absence of instruction, is obliged to guess the court's motive in making the remand. Information later supplied to the court may be off target and may lead to the consideration of material that is extraneous to the matter at hand. It may even be that the mental-health response yields information inappropriate to the particular stage of the hearing or trial (e.g., the report may bring forward at trial information about previous record or even guilt in the matter before the court).

In some instances, it is felt that assessment may entrap the offender and so provide a serious infringement of legal rights. This view deviates from a *parens patriae* (state-protection) doctrine. Rights-centred advocates argue that if clinical evaluation might compromise an individual's rights and worsen his or her situation, it may be more just to circumvent the assessment process. Clinical evaluation may sometimes infringe individual rights by: 1 / promoting a denial of bail, which would be available under ordinary circumstances; 2 / adding additional time to a term of incarceration; and 3 / ascribing undue importance to minor psychological or behavioural anomalies, which when recorded result in a designation that serves as an 'admission ticket' to the mental hospital on subsequent occasions.

Assessment of Fitness to Stand Trial

A single case involving a New Brunswick juvenile can be cited to indicate the vital importance of a mental-health opinion about fitness when rendered to the court. Emerson Bonnar, age sixteen at the time, was held on a Warrant of the Lieutenant Governor as unfit for some sixteen years on the basis of a single incident of purse snatching (Griffiths, Klein, and Verdun-Jones 1980). Of the various issues that mental-health workers address on behalf of the court, fitness to stand trial is probably the easiest to tackle. Yet it should be recalled that it is the courts themselves that make or do not make the remands for assessment. Some judges are prone to remand, others not (Webster, Menzies, and Jackson 1982). This being the case, fitness is a concept hard to pin down and to standardize.

Since the Canadian Criminal Code does not define fitness, it has been left to the mental-health professionals to devise means of evaluating the construct. Efforts to proceed beyond the clinical and intuitive towards the development of reliable and valid scales to assess competency have been limited and sporadic. Robey's (1965) early checklist is replete with difficulties. The Competency Screening Test (CST) of McGarry and colleagues (1974) has also been subjected to strong criticism. Since patients themselves provide the information directly on the form, it has limited use for patients who are either substantially mentally handicapped or experiencing major psychoses.

To date, the most successful device, one apparently worth further development and exploration, has been the Competency Assessment Instrument (CAI) of McGarry and colleagues (1974). This is a thirteen-item semi-structured interview schedule. Most items are legally centred. There is a full manual for the instrument, and a good deal is known about its psychometric properties. In recent years, the CAI has been extended to include psychiatric items and has been made suitable for use by Canadian evaluators (Roesch, Webster, and Eaves 1984). It appears that the device can be used effectively by mental-health workers from various disciplines. Though not standardized as yet on mentally disordered young offender populations, the so-called Fitness Interview Test (FIT) is available to help clinicians reach sound and reliable conclusions about fitness within thirty minutes or so. Roesch and Golding (1987) point out the difficulties that can arise for patients when evaluators do not understand the full implications of their work, do not assemble in advance the necessary background information, and do not keep the fitness issue separate from insanity defence and other issues.

Assessment of Dangerousness

Much has been written on the topic of dangerousness in the past twenty years. Steadman and Cocozza's (1974) follow-up study of some 1000 New York mental patients helped focus attention on the 'false positive' problem. This large cohort was released outright or transferred to conditions of reduced security as a result of a legal ruling involving Johnny Baxstrom. The essential finding, since replicated (Thornberry and Jacoby 1979), was that few of these supposedly 'dangerous' patients committed violent acts upon their release.

These findings have raised the question of how well clinicians are able to predict the violent conduct of their patients. In a general way, the answer seems to be, not very well. Some influential commentators have argued that mental-health workers should abandon the attempt (e.g., Stone 1985) while others like Greenland (1985) have argued that predictions could be made more accurate were clinicians to attempt the task with more care and attention to detail. A single, useful rule of thumb seems to be that those persons who have been violent in the past are likely to continue their actions into the future. This observation is reinforced partly by the results of long-term follow-up studies of delinquent children, and partly by attempts to predict the behaviour of young offenders upon release from custody (West 1985).

One difficulty is that no psychometric tests have been shown unequivocally to have predictive power with respect to dangerousness. Various attempts have been made to check the predictive acumen of standard psychological tests like the Minnesota Multiphasic Personality Inventory (MMPI), but with limited success (Megargee 1988). The major difficulty appears to be that usual psychometric instruments do not and cannot place sufficient emphasis on situational factors (Monahan 1981). One recent attempt to devise a predictive instrument, the Dangerous Behaviour Rating Scheme (DBRS), ended in failure (Menzies, Webster, and Sepejuk 1985). Yet the authors continue to receive requests for the manual upon which the test is based – probably because the courts have a strong appetite for mental-health opinion about 'dangerousness.' It helps to solve the court's seemingly intractable dispositional problems, and there is more than a suggestion that the courts incorporate or dismiss mental-health opinion according to the specific nature of the case at hand (Applebaum 1984). Some have argued that perhaps the most compelling scientific question is how mental-health workers go about the task of ascribing dangerousness (Ptohl 1978). Certainly it would seem to be the case that evaluators form their judgments to some extent on the basis of seemingly extraneous factors like physical attractiveness (Esses and Webster 1988).

That mental-health workers are frequently not as competent or expert as they would wish to seem has recently been argued with considerable force (Faust and Ziskin 1988). These authors point specifically to the ascription of dangerousness. Yet it remains the case that, likely, 'mental health professionals, by using specialized assessment techniques, may be able to discover evidence relevant to assessments of dangerousness that is not readily ascertainable by lay persons' and may be 'uniquely aware of and able to perceive syndromes of attitudes, affects, and behaviour that are indicative of potential violence' (Litwack and Schlesinger 1987: 249; see also Pollock, McBain, and Webster: In press).

Litwack and Schlesinger (1987) offer for the mental-health worker a tentative means of classification for use in predicting dangerousness. According to this scheme, which can only be sketched here, there are five categories of offences to be considered: 1 / environmental or sociogenic (i.e., potential for future violence depends upon value systems, maturity, and the strength of associations to which offenders will return); 2 / situational (e.g., relatively low potential for future violence once the situational difficulties are resolved, as in some domestic disputes); 3 / impulsive (i.e., diffuse, poorly structured crimes as a result of a lack of personality integration); 4 / catathymic (i.e., one-shot incidents as a result of brief failure of ego function); and 5 / compulsive (i.e., the risk of further violence for strongly compulsive individuals tends to be relatively high). Litwack and Schlesinger (1987) provide a valuable service in drawing attention to the fact that, with many different types of offender and violent patients combined in statistical analyses, we may indeed know little about the predictors of violent behaviour. Careful subtyping along the lines these authors suggest may eventuate in clinical procedures more scientifically robust than those currently available. Certainly we would refer readers to this thoughtful contribution and also to Mulvey and Lidz (1984).

Assessment for Pre-disposition Report and Treatment Planning

The preparation of pre-disposition reports is, it would seem, less contentious than the making of projections about dangerousness (though, in fact, the latter issue is often incorporated into the former task). Individuals have been judged guilty by the time these reports are prepared. In calling for a report, the court has an opportunity to seek mental-health opinion about whether or not the individual can be helped through the provision of specific services. The issue boils down to 'treatability.' Yet, recent literature shows that clinicians can differ markedly as to the kinds of treatment they would consider beneficial in specific cases (Quinsey and MacGuire 1983; Quinsey 1988).

Psychometric Assessments

The psychometric classification of young offenders has been advocated as a means of understanding the varieties of delinquent behaviour and their causes (Warren 1978) and to plan effective intervention strategies (Quay 1979). Classification systems have been developed for the purpose of differential assignment to treatment. Consideration of these efforts would merit an entire chapter, but a few may be mentioned as examples: 1 / the Behaviour Problem Categories (BPC); 2 / the MMPI typology developed by Megargee (Veneziano and Veneziano 1986); 3 / the Interpersonal Maturity Level scheme (I-Level) (Warren 1978); and 4 / the Conceptual Level Matching Model (CLMM) (Reitsma-Street 1984).

The Behaviour Problem Categories (BPC) comprises four dimensions: conduct problem or unsocialized aggressive; personality problem or neurosis; inadequate or immature; and socialized aggression or subcultural. Youths are scored on each dimension and subsequently classified on the basis of case history, observer checklist, and self-rating questionnaires (Pauker and Hood 1979; Quay 1979).

Megargee's MMPI-based typology is used to classify juveniles as: normal; neurotic, with acting-out as a consequence of unresolved emotional conflict; disturbed, demonstrating pre-psychotic symptoms; and characterological, having an antisocial personality disorder (Veneziano and Veneziano 1986).

The I-Level system is a well-known classification system for young offenders, based on a general theory of personality development. In this system, psychological development is described in terms of a hierarchical scheme of interpersonal maturity. Assessment is carried out to determine the way in which a young person perceives himself or herself and others. Seven different theoretical levels of maturity have been defined. In addition, nine empirically derived, mutually exclusive I-Level subtypes have been developed to classify individuals on the basis of their typical response styles (Warren 1983). Youths are classified within this system using either a semi-structured clinical interview, which may be assisted by the Interview Rating Questionnaire (Warren 1986), or the Jesness Inventory, a self-report personality questionnaire (Jesness 1975). A highly structured interview has been developed by M.A. Fréchette of the University of Montreal for use with francophone delinquents.

Evidence for the utility of I-Level classification as an effective approach to treatment planning has been provided by the extensive studies of the California Youth Authority (Jesness 1975, 1988). Youths classified as conflicted or neurotic, and subsequently assigned to treatment regimens tailored to meet their specific needs, performed significantly better on outcome measures than did control-group youths receiving conventional placement in a training school. Recidivism rates were greatly lowered for test-group youths; at four-year follow-up after discharge, control-group youths had 81 per cent greater arrest rates and 63 per cent greater conviction rates than did test-group youths (Harris 1988; Reitsma-Street 1984).

The Conceptual Level Matching Model (CLMM) is similar to the I-Level system. The CLMM evaluates the cognitive complexity and interpersonal maturity, focusing on individual differences in the ability to cope with conflict, authority, and ambiguity in the social environment (Reitsma-Street 1984; Reitsma-Street and Leschied 1988). The Conceptual Level (CL) of delinquents is usually determined using the Paragraph Completion Method (Hunt et al 1971). Measures of CL have been studied extensively and shown to be both reliable (Gariner and Schroder 1972; Miller 1978) and valid (Hunt 1977–8).

There is evidence to support the use of the CLMM as a means of effectively matching client to intervention strategy. Brill (1978) and Leschied, Jaffe, and Stone (1985) have shown that youths matched to program structure on the basis of CL had fewer days out of program, acting-out incidents, and offences at follow-up than did youths who were not. Similarly, CL matching of hard-to-serve youths to program structure has demonstrated recidivism rates significantly lower than those found in the published literature for a similar population (Bosse and Leblanc 1981; Leschied and Thomas 1985).

Psychological Assessments

Providing comprehensive assessments and recommending suitable intervention for the courts, to assist them in making appropriate dispositions, involves more than simply a psychometric or psychiatric evaluation. The medical model neglects environmental influences that have been related to involvement in antisocial activities. 'An underlying premise of the assessment process is that a child's difficulties cannot be assessed in isolation. The emphasis therefore is on determining the interaction effect of the child's individual characteristics and the environment' (Jaffe et al 1985: 55). It is necessary to take a psychosocial approach when providing assessments and recommending treatments.

Most of the research into the etiology and dynamics of juvenile delinquency suggests the importance of contextual or situational variables such as early developmental history, family functioning, educational problems, and peer relationships. In particular, the social functioning of families is considered to be an important determinant in the socialization or resocialization of the young offender (Geismar and Wood 1986). Assessment of family functioning is important both for insight into the current functioning of the child and in order to determine the willingness and ability of the family to be involved in the court-ordered treatment of the young offender. Scales such as the Family Environment Scale (Moos and Moos 1981) or the St Paul Scale of Family Functioning (Geismar 1980) have been used effectively for carrying out this type of assessment.

The treatment plans and recommendations must also take into consideration the availability of services in the community and their ability to provide effective treatment for the mentally disordered young offender. Thus a comprehensive assessment must involve a multidisciplinary team approach in which psychiatrist, psychologist, social worker, and other mental-health professionals consult together and with agencies and schools that have been, or are currently, providing services to the adolescent.

Approaches to Treatment

There is now a large literature surrounding the so-called nothing works controversy (see Gendreau 1985; West 1985, Gendreau and Ross 1987). For well over a decade, academic and clinical authors have been arguing for and against Martinson's (1974) gloomy assertion about the ineffectiveness of correctional treatment. As Gendreau notes, 'nothing works' suggests that there is no evidence to show that rehabilitation attempts of various kinds produce demonstrable positive changes. He and his colleagues have written persuasively and consistently from the other point of view.

It now seems that the whole debate is inane, the issue being ill-defined and methodologically muddled. Most knowledgeable contemporary commentators who have examined the effectiveness of various programming approaches (Bosse and Leblanc 1981; Leschied and Thomas 1985; Reitsma-Street 1984) stress that the most important issue to be addressed is 'What works and with whom?' Appreciable gains certainly seem to have been made in some programs where young offenders are properly assessed and classified and are then matched to intervention strategies appropriate to their needs. As noted by Reitsma-Street (1984) and West (1985), programs are frequently implemented ineffectually and so cannot be assessed properly. Other evaluations have relied solely on recidivism rates in assessing outcome rather than examining other possible indices of improvement such as social interactions and school performance (Fishman 1977; Roesch and Corrado 1979).

Gendreau and Ross (1979, 1987), in two major reviews of offender rehabilitation literature, provide 'bibliotherapy' for cynical opponents to treatment of correctional populations. Their critical appraisals cover programs providing family and community interventions, and various approaches to counselling, behaviour management, and biomedical treatment. They conclude that many treatment-program failures can be attributed to: 1 / using a unitary approach for a complex set of problems; 2 / relying on an outcome measure, such as recidivism, to the exclusion of equally important outcome dimensions; 3 / failing to account for individual differences in responsiveness to treatment; 4 / failing to supply adequate amounts of treatment over time; and 5 / failing to ensure interagency communication.

The intervention approaches discussed by Gendreau and Ross are used in the following brief review. Their groupings represent a convenient way of organizing the literature. However, it must be recognized that although the mental-health and correctional fields have adopted the same terminology to describe various programming approaches, the meaning of these terms in an operational sense likely differs considerably from one individual or setting to another. This no doubt adds to the confusion that prevails. Several interrelated issues that are crucial to the effective delivery of mental-health services to young offenders must be addressed at the start. Specifically, what characterizes a program as therapeutic, as opposed to custodial? In addition, do the terms applied to particular settings automatically indicate the kind of care a youth requiring psychiatric care might receive in them? Are such terms as 'community-based residential centre' and 'group home' universally understood by field workers? Part of the problem is that every centre or home has its own particular culture that is continually changing and therefore hard to describe (Redl 1982; Waggoner 1983–4).

Perhaps the most useful way to respond to the questions raised above is to address the distinction between custody and treatment. It is important to note that designations per se are not necessarily particularly helpful. Similar, or even identical labels, when applied to settings, do not carry with them a clear indication or assurance of the kind of care offered. The term 'group home,' for example, does not have any universally understood meaning. One may envision a group home to be a community-based, and therefore a deinstitutionalized, treatment-oriented environment. In fact, it may be nothing more than a setting that offers enlightened residential services and containment. While some therapeutic benefit may derive from this kind of group home, it is not treatment directed by design.

In order for an environment to be considered therapeutic, or a treatment setting, it must satisfy certain requirements. It must be structured and offer intensive, theoretically driven intervention provided by sufficient numbers of properly trained staff. There are group homes that are specifically designed in this way and are rightfully designated treatment settings. These facilities do not have containment as their principal objective, but they may provide varying degrees of restriction and security. Similarly, the term 'specialized foster care' has recently come into use to distinguish ordinary foster care from specialized multidisciplinary programs for disturbed and/or delinquent youngsters. These have a strong therapeutic philosophy determined by agencies, and use carefully selected and trained paraprofessionals as foster parents (Webb 1988).

The program examples that follow are included because they satisfy the necessary criteria to be designated as treatment options. What is most noteworthy in these examples is the range of treatment options at least theoretically available to the mentally disordered offender population. The subheadings may be regarded as 'signposts' to facilitate exploration of these options; others reviewing this body of literature may have organized these programs under different headings.

Community-Based Programs

Individual and family therapies are directed at alleviating intrapersonal distress and modifying those interactions at home and at school that promote delinquent behaviour (Tharp and Wetzel 1969). Youths, alone or together with their family members, learn alternatives to socially malad-aptive behaviour through the development of added insights and appropriate role models provided by a therapist. Various forms of behavioural contracting are often included in these therapies. While family-based intervention is viewed by many as an important treatment strategy, it has not been found to be very useful in highly disorganized families, or in cases where youths are severely disruptive (Gendreau and Ross 1979). A comprehensive review of the literature on family treatments (Geismar and Wood 1986) concludes that, although studies with stronger designs and methods are needed, there is more evidence to date supporting the benefits of family interventions based on behaviour modification and social-learning techniques than those of non-behavioural forms of family therapy.

Diversion programs have been developed as a means of steering young offenders away from the process of formal adjudication by providing for such alternatives as restitution and the performance of community services (Rettig 1980; Kraus and Haselton 1982; Jaffe et al 1985–6). We include them in discussing approaches in helping youthful offenders who are emotionally disturbed because in the mental-health field such programming is viewed as important from the perspective of preventive intervention. The underlying principle here is that youths, by being labelled as 'delinquent,' may become more susceptible to continued involvement with the court system (Davidson et al 1986). In some instances, emotionally disturbed adolescents live in a milieu where being viewed as 'bad' is less anxiety-provoking and stigmatizing than being labelled as 'crazy' by their peer group. Thus they may resort to expressing their disturbance through deviant acts. Opponents to these programs have argued that diversion identifies individuals who would ordinarily not be processed through the juvenile-justice system.

Some diversion programs have reported beneficial results for young adolescents, and especially first offenders with minor infractions. For example, one program reported that, over a ten-month period, only 2.6 per cent of a total of 509 cases came into the juvenile-justice system as compared with 10.6 per cent of 216 processed through normal court intake (Rettig 1980). A fairly well-designed investigation of three types of diversion interventions that featured the use of well-trained paraprofessionals revealed reduced recidivism rates for offenders at one- and two-year follow-up, in comparison with attention-placebo, and usual treatment conditions of the justice system (Davidson et al 1986). However, another study examining young offenders in two cities in Ontario yielded similar recidivism rates for adjudicated and diverted youths (Jaffe et al 1985–6). Personal experience with Canadian diversion programming and our perusal of the literature lead us to support the Gendreau and Ross conclusion, i.e., that the results of such programs rest heavily on what is actually provided to which target group, for how long, and by whom. Too many programs are superficial and fragmented in content, short in duration, and delivered in a haphazard way by personnel who are insufficiently trained, lack committment to the approach, or are overburdened with myriad other responsibilities.

Programs featuring behaviour-modification techniques have been used widely with varying degrees of success in day programs and in community-based residential and institutional environments. The techniques are based on social-learning theory, which considers deviant behaviour to be the result of inadequate learning of socially endorsed behaviours. Therapy that relies on social-learning theory focuses on the development of life skills and effective strategies for interpersonal problem-solving. Programs attempt to foster greater conformity, self-esteem, and effectiveness in social interactions, while reducing egocentricity, alienation, and susceptibility to peer pressure.

Especially in group homes or specialized foster-care settings, a token economy based on a system of rewards for socially desirable behaviours is often at the heart of this treatment approach. Various group-home models that rely on such behavioural strategies have been described in the literature. Achievement Place is one example of a community-based, residential treatment setting that has reported considerable success in using trained 'teaching parents' (Leschied and Thomas 1985). Although Achievement Place and similar contingency-management models have reported significant in-program gains in the control of delinquent behaviour, questions have been raised as to the extent to which positive outcomes have a lasting effect and are generalizable to natural-home settings. In one study, a structured family-setting group home proved significantly more effective in reducing in-program delinquency than did conventional group homes (Kirigin et al 1982). Moreover, there was a significant inverse relationship between self-reported delinquent behaviour and the amount of time spent with group-home parents (Solnick et al 1981). However, treatment benefits were not sustained after discharge. On the basis of clinical evidence, another short-term behaviour-management program in a residential setting reported significant behaviour change for a heterogeneous group of young offenders (Beitel et al 1983).

There is some indication from the clinical and research reports that behaviour modification or 'conditioning' therapies may be useful approaches for treating adolescent substance abusers and sex offenders in both closed and open settings (Gendreau and Ross 1987; Becker, Kaplan, and Kavoussi 1988). Out-patient programs for this particular population frequently use a combination of therapeutic strategies within a structured group-therapy approach. A recently described rural program for male sex offenders (Smets and Cebula 1987) claims a high success rate over three years in preventing repeat offences and features joint male/female group leaders for role modelling; peer interaction, pressure, and competition; systematic progression through five therapeutic steps; cognitive restructuring through educational components; and guided client self-evaluation.

Special out-patient programs attached to hospitals with psychiatric units or children's residential mental-health treatment settings have also been found to be useful either as a means of providing follow-up support and rehabilitation after in-patient psychiatric treatment or in trying to avoid admission. In a report of one out-patient program, Shorts (1985) demonstrated that treatment failure, through attrition or dismissal for violent behaviour, could be attributed to: not being a member of a social club; having mainly delinquent friends; perceiving oneself as unhappy compared to others; and being truant. Another study, which compared two methods of treating substance-abusing young offenders, found that in-patient psychodynamically oriented psychotherapy was no more effective than out-patient treatment when relative measures of social functioning were compared (Amini et al 1982).

In-patient or Residential Treatment

Therapeutic programming in hospitals and secure residential or custody settings has received some consideration from researchers. One investigation found that emotionally disturbed female status offenders made significant gains in maturity of attitudes and perception following treatment that featured a highly structured behaviour-management program (Munson and Revers 1986). Another study found that a group of violent, mentally disordered young offenders did better than a comparison group on a variety of adjustment indices after long-term treatment in a secure and behaviourally oriented therapeutic milieu (Hartstone and Cocozza 1983). Other investigators have reported that, following a ninety-day program of residential treatment based on Carkhuff's Human Relations Training Model, a significant number of young offenders graduated successfully to less structured community settings (Dattilio 1981).

Hospital-based crisis service have also been viewed by experts as particularly relevant for the treatment of acutely disturbed adolescents. This type of program appears to reduce the need for in-patient admission and encourage engagement in therapy. With adolescents, as their symptoms diminish, motivation for treatment often declines quickly (Piersma and Van Wingen 1988).

Gendreau and Ross (1987) do not profess much enthusiasm for what they term 'biomedical methods' of treatment for delinquent behaviours. However, their comments reflect the fuzziness of the boundaries between the treatment of delinquency and psychiatric illness and could be misconstrued by those working with young offenders. A period of in-patient hospitalization may well be required to stabilize and begin intensive treatment of the comparatively small numbers of offenders with major psychiatric disorders – which may be causally connected to the delinquent behaviours. While Gendreau and Ross only briefly discuss examples of support for the effectiveness of pharmacological treatments for such diseases as schizophrenia, the children's mental-health literature contains a plethora of evidence favouring the use of drug therapies for particular conditions.

There are also strong indications that interventions that include several phased program components (some of which are residential) can be especially beneficial for troubled adolescents. The Craigwood-Bridgeway program in London, Ontario, is one such example. A preliminary evaluation of the program, which includes both high- and low-structured residential programming and a community-based component, provided encouraging results (Lescheid and Thomas 1985). At one-year follow-up, 86 per cent of residents were either working or attending school. While one-third of ex-residents continued to be involved with the law, the average number of charges per resident had dropped from 6.2 at admission to fewer than one charge. As Lescheid and Thomas point out, these data should be viewed with caution since a control group is absent. However, they offer support for the belief that intervention approaches developed to treat seriously emotionally disturbed children can be effective for 'hard-to-serve' youths.

Specialized in-patient programs aimed specifically at the 'impossible child' have been subjected to little evaluation. However, several descriptions exist of apparently beneficial program models developed in Europe and North America (Kirigin et al 1982). Reports usually emphasize the importance of location (use of a remote setting); admitting small numbers; selecting motivated, skilled staff who care about the youths entrusted to them and who are properly supported; developing structured activities (conducive to release of physical energy and tension, skills-building, education); and providing long-term treatment (of varied and flexible therapeutic modalities).

Therapeutic camping programs have also been reported as effective alternatives for 'hard-to-serve' and antisocial young offenders from urban environments (Jesness 1975). As noted by Gendreau and Ross (1987), a number of similar types of resources, also referred to as 'wilderness' and 'outward bound' programs, have been described as useful for rehabilitating this target group, but longer-term follow-up studies of participants are required to assess their effect.

In general, programs reporting success in treating troubled youth as measured by a variety of treatment outcomes appear to have several elements in common:

1 Program objectives and methods are carefully developed based on an established theoretical framework; these are articulated clearly to staff and clients so that all concerned fully understand their respective roles.
2 Most programs employ some forms of behaviour-modification techniques, social-learning education, and skills-building. Typically, they rely strongly on structure and a phasing-in of increased responsibilities and rights as a reward system. Daily routines approximate 'real life' as closely as possible. Inclusion of peer-appraisal mechanisms, support groups, activities-of-daily-living sessions, and group decision making is common.
3 Staff are assisted to develop the requisite skills and receive regular education on the job.
4 On-site client-centred and program-centred consultation provided by experts is available on a regular basis and when warranted by special situations.
5 Programs are designed to be flexible so as to be able to adapt to changing individual and community needs.
6 Interventions are adjusted to the needs of individuals in terms of nature and intensity (e.g., while individual therapy may be the modality of choice, one hour weekly may be enough for one young client and

insufficient for another; conversely, relatively minor problems may be exacerbated by misplaced and overzealous effort).

7 Individual programs are linked to a functional web of programs and specialists serving the same community.

8 Programs incorporate some means of attempting to evaluate their effectiveness and to follow up clients.

Systems-Level Issues in Service Delivery

Locus and Focus of Assessment and Treatment

The effective delivery of services to mentally disordered young offenders requires that attention be paid to the four key questions posed by Warren (1978), namely: 1 / What types of treatment are indicated? 2 / For whom are they needed? 3 / Under what conditions are they most effectively provided? and 4 / In what type of setting should they be delivered? The issue of where assessment and treatment are most appropriately provided is particularly salient for the mentally disordered young-offender population.

As Barker (1982) has noted, deinstitutionalization as espoused by Wolfensberger (1982) cannot be seen as a panacea. The management of young offenders in community-based as opposed to institutional settings will not necessarily result in positive outcomes. For some youths, there may be a concurrent need for both confinement and treatment in order to effect rehabilitation. The secure or locked unit may be the locus of choice for managing the aggressive, violent, or suicidal offender (Sas and Jaffe 1986). Such facilities may not be readily available outside institutional settings.

As Sas and Jaffe contend, juvenile-justice and children's mental-health systems face a dilemma that hinges on whether programs should be designed to control or treat problematic behaviour or to accomplish both aims. This is certainly a concern for staff dealing with depressed youths whose masking behaviours may be severely disruptive or dangerous. Psychiatric settings and mental-health centres accustomed to dealing with primary psychiatric illness may be ill-equipped to deal with individuals who are refractory to conventional interventions. Alternatively, while correctional settings may be well prepared to control disruptive and dangerous behaviour, treatment may be neglected. If mentally disordered young offenders are to be provided with the services they need, it is obvious that policy makers and planners need to develop mechanisms for increasing collaboration between personnel and programs in both systems. Thus far, the Young Offenders Act, with its emphasis on the client's right to refuse treatment and on the use of probation and custody, appears to contradict the approaches of prevention, treatment, and rehabilitation pursued by the mental-health system. It would seem that this is furthering fragmentation and separations within and between the two systems.

Whittaker (1979) has correctly noted that the issues regarding locus of service are also concerned with those of 'focus.' It is essential that 'powerful' treatment environments be developed, and these may include a variety of potential settings. Freeman's (1983) observation that a comprehensive system for the difficult-to-serve psychiatric patient should include hospital- and community-based 'cure' and 'care' facilities is no less apt for the mentally disordered young offender.

Program Evaluation

Improvement of treatment and rehabilitative programming rests heavily on advancement of knowledge through carefully designed and executed experimental research and program evaluation. Government bodies should encourage such research through their funding mechanisms and policies. And when particular intervention models are shown to be beneficial, it is crucial that program information is disseminated widely, that proven programs are assured of long-term funding, and that other programs based on the same model are mounted and evaluated elsewhere.

Continuity of Care

This long-standing corner-stone of health-service planning represents the *sine qua non* of what is considered 'good' care (Bachrach 1981) and as such is particularly relevant to service planning for the mentally disordered young offender. As explicated by Bachrach, continuity of care is a multidimensional concept defined as the process of unimpeded patient movement among the diverse elements of the service-delivery system. The patient should move freely through the system, receiving as much care over time as his or her particular situation demands.

In the field of mental health, one of the most interesting developments during the past decade aimed at improving continuity of care has been the proliferation of case-management programs based on the functional rehabilitation techniques of Anthony (1979). Case managers have the advantage of not being agents of a control system in the same way as are probation and parole officers. They carry out a number of functions, including social-skills training, based on functional needs, and the approach relies strongly on the client's own priorities and goals. The task involves advocacy, role-modelling, co-ordination, referral and linkage, and monitoring of client progress over time. It is important to recognize that some programs for youthful offenders that have been subjected to more stringent evaluation and found to be beneficial have used case-management approaches (e.g., the diversion program of Davidson et al 1986).

Ensuring continuity of care requires that certain conditions be met:

1 Services need to be *comprehensive*. Patient planning needs to be individual to avoid 'dumping,' that is, placement without regard to specific target problems.
2 Services must be both *available* and *accessible*. It does little good to have intervention and facilities that are available in theory only.
3 Services must be *co-ordinated* and *continuous*. One component of the patient-care system must 'know' what the other is doing. In a system made up of multiple agencies and facilities, communication must be ensured between those who plan services and those who provide them. Vigilance is needed to document patient movement through and between mental-health, court, and correctional systems. Care may otherwise become disjointed or discontinuous.

There are numerous potential impediments to continuity of care. These include; failure to clarify interagency roles or connections for patient care; inadequate staffing, resulting in an 'overloading' of the system; geographic barriers, especially in remote or rural regions; time delays in the movement of patients from one jurisdiction or program to another; inadequate after-care and monitoring of progress through the system; and monetary restrictions, in particular where agencies serving the same group are competing for funds.

The ultimate goal in the provision of psychiatric care for any age group is to provide an integrated, complete, and easily accessible range of services (McKelvey 1988). Both community-based and hospital-based options, equipped with an 'easily activated set of linkages' among the various service components, are essential (Whittaker 1979). For this reason, Whittaker and other experts have argued cogently that, where the 'continuum of care' is compromised, all intervention programs will have reduced efficacy. Gendreau and Ross (1979, 1987) provide considerable support for this widely held premise in their discussions of the benefits of services for young offenders.

Both community-based and hospital-based service components have relative merits. This view is supported by studies emphasizing the differential matching of treatment interventions to specific subgroups of young offenders (Bosse and Leblanc 1981; Lescheid and Thomas 1985; Reitsma-Street 1984). Mentally disordered young offenders are heterogeneous with respect to underlying pathology and treatment needs. Some may require intensive intervention at the level of secure or closed settings, some can be effectively treated in outpatient settings, and some will inevitably require both residential and home-based therapies at various times as their conditions and circumstances change.

Summary and Conclusions

This chapter has provided an overview of issues related to the assessment and treatment of mentally disordered young offenders. Members of this subgroup are extremely heterogeneous with respect to their differential classification and management. Most mentally disturbed youth have multiple and ever-changing needs not only because their problems are multifaceted but also because they are in a state of developmental transition. For this reason, rehabilitation rests heavily on determining and constantly reviewing which treatment is most appropriate, for whom, and under which conditions. It is essential to develop accessible and comprehensive cure and care components that are well-co-ordinated, flexible, and continuous. Programs must rest on a sound base of knowledge and be staffed by properly trained personnel. Both community-based and residential (hospital- or detention-based) services are necessary elements of a service-delivery system for these troubled youths, with choice of setting and treatment modalities being determined by the *nature* and *severity* of disorder and client needs.

References

Agee, V. 1979. *Treatment of the Violent Incorrigible Adolescent*. Lexington, MA: Lexington Books

American Psychiatric Association. 1987. *Diagnostic Statistical Manual of Mental Disorders (DSM-IIIR*, 3rd ed. Washington DC: American Psychiatric Association

Amini, F., N. Zilberg, E. Burke, and S. Salasnek. 1982. 'A controlled study of inpatient vs outpatient treatment of delinquent drug abusing adolescents: One year results,' *Comprehensive Psychiatry* 23: 36

Anthony, W.A. 1979. *The Principles of Psychiatric Rehabilitation*. Amherst, MA: Human Resources Press

Applebaum, P.S. 1984. 'The Supreme Court looks at psychiatry,' *American Journal of Psychiatry* 141: 827–35

Bachrach, L.L. 1981. 'Continuity of care for chronic mental patients: A conceptual analysis,' *American Journal of Psychiatry* 13: 1449–56

Barker, P. 1982. 'Residential treatment for disturbed children: Its place in the '80s,' *Canadian Journal of Psychiatry* 27: 634–9

Becker, J.V., M.S. Kaplan, and R. Kavoussi. 1988. 'Measuring the effectiveness of treatment for the aggressive adolescent sexual offender,' in R.A. Prentky and V.L. Quinsey, eds, *Human Sexual Aggression: Current Perspectives*, 215–34. Annals of the New York Academy of Sciences 528

Beitel, A., P. Everts, B. Boile, E. Nagel, C. Bragdon, and B. MacKesson. 1983. 'An innovative approach to group therapy in a short term inpatient adolescent unit,' *Adolescent* 18: 1

Binder, A. 1988. 'Juvenile delinquency,' *Annual Review of Psychology* 39: 252–82

Bosse, M., and M. Leblanc. 'Boscoville: Evaluation de son efficacité à traverse l'évolution psychologique de ses pensionnaires pendant et après le séjour,' *Canadian Journal of Criminology* 23: 27–41

Brill, R. 1978. 'Implications of the conceptual level matching model for treatment of delinquents,' *Journal of Research in Crime and Delinquency* 12: 212–46

Clarke Institute of Psychiatry. 1983. *Southern Alberta Study of Psychiatric Needs and Provisions*. Report to the Southern Alberta Psychiatric Services Committee. Toronto

Cox, T.C., M.R. Jacobs, A.E. Leblanc, and J.A. Marshman. 1983. *Drugs and Drug Abuse: A Reference Text*. Toronto: Addiction Research Foundation

Czechowicz, D. 1988. 'Adolescent alcohol and drug abuse and its consequences – An overview,' *American Journal of Drug and Alcohol Abuse* 14 (1): 189–97

Datillio, F. 1981. 'The Carkhuff systematic human relations training model in a short term treatment program for adolescent offenders,' *Adolescence* 16: 865–9

Davidson, W., R. Redner, C. Blakely, C. Mitchell, and J. Emshoff. 1986. 'Diversion of juvenile offenders: An experimental comparison,' *Journal of Consulting and Clinical Psychology* 55: 68

Denkowski, G., and K. Denkowski. 1983. 'Group home designs for initiating community-based treatment with mentally retarded adolescent offenders,' *Journal of Behavior Therapy and Experimental Psychiatry* 14: 141

Dohrenwend, B.P., B.S. Dohrenwend, M.S. Gould, B. Link, R. Neugebauer, and R. Wunsch-Hitzig. *Mental Illness in the United States: Epidemiological Estimates*. New York: Praeger

Esses, V.M., and C.D. Webster. 1988. 'Physical attractiveness, dangerousness, and the Canadian Criminal Code,' *Journal of Applied Social Psychology* 18: 1017–31

Evans, J., H. Clark, and S. Hinman. 1981. 'Community reaction to a treatment program for youthful offenders: Staff perceptions vs consumers evaluation ratings,' *Psychological Reports* 49: 994

Faust, D., and J. Ziskin. 1988. 'The expert witness in psychology and psychiatry,' *Science*, July: 31–5

Fishman, R. 1977. 'An evaluation of criminal recidivism in projects providing rehabilitation and diversion services in New York City,' *Journal of Criminal Law and Criminology* 68: 283–305

Freeman, S.J.J. 1983. 'The chronic psychiatric patient rediscovered: Ten propositions,' *Canada's Mental Health*, December: 15–19

Gariner, G.S., and H.M. Schroder. 1972. 'Reliability and validity of the paragraph completion method,' *Psychological Reports* 31: 951

Geismar, L.L. 1980. 'St Paul scale of family functioning,' in L.L. Geismer, ed, *Family and Community Functioning*, Metuchen, NJ: The Scarecrow Press

Geismar, L.L. and Katherine Wood. 1986. *Family and Delinquency: Resocializing the Young Offender*. New York: Human Sciences Press

Gendreau, P. 1985. 'Critical comments on the practise of clinical criminology,' in M.H. Ben-Aron, S.J. Jucker, and C.S. Webster, eds, *Clinical Criminology: The Assessment and Treatment of Criminal Behaviour*. Toronto: M and M Graphics

Gendreau, P., and R. Ross. 1979. 'Effective correctional treatment: Bibliotherapy for cynics,' *Crime and Delinquency* 21: 463–89

– 1987. 'Revivification: Evidence from the 1980s,' *Justice Quarterly* 4: 349–407

Green, M. 1983. 'Treatment of borderline adolescents,' *Adolescence* 18: 729

Greenland, C. 1985. 'Dangerousness, mental disorder, and politics,' in C.D. Webster, M.H. Ben-Aron, S.J. Hucker, eds, *Dangerousness: Probability and Prediction, Psychiatry and Public Policy*, 25–40. New York: Cambridge University Press

Griffiths, C.T., J.F. Klein, and S.M. Verdun-Jones. 1980. *Criminal Justice in Canada: An Introductory Text*. Toronto: Butterworths

Harris, P.W. 1988. 'The interpersonal maturity level classification system: I-Level,' *Criminal Justice and Behaviour* 15: 58–77

Hartstone, E., and J. Cocozza. 1983. 'Violent youth: The impact of mental health treatment,' *International Journal of Law and Psychiatry* 6: 207

Hunt, D.E., L.F. Butler, J.E. Noy, and M.E. Rosser. 1971. *Assessing Conceptual Level by the Paragraph Completion Method*. Toronto: Ontario Institute for Studies in Education

– 1977–8. 'A conceptual level matching model for coordinating learner characteristics with education approaches,' *Interchange* 8: 78–90

Jaffe, P., B. Kroeker, C. Hyatt, M. Miscevick, A. Telford, R. Chandler, C. Shanahan, and B. Sokoloff. 1985–6. 'Diversion in the Canadian juvenile justice system: A tale of two cities,' *Juvenile and Family Court Journal*, Winter: 59

Jaffe, P., A.W. Leschied, L. Sas, and G.W. Austin. 1985. 'A model for the provision of clinical assessment and service brokerage for young offenders: The London Family Court Clinic,' *Canadian Psychology* 26: 54–61

Jeffery, R. 1964. 'The psychologist as an expert witness on the issue of insanity,' *American Psychologist* 19: 838–43

Jesness, C.F. 1970. *Sequential I-Level Classification Manual*. Sacramento: Department of Youth Authority

– 1975. 'Comparative effectiveness of behaviour modification and transactional analysis programs for delinquents,' *Journal of Consulting and Clinical Psychology* 43: 758

– 1988. 'The Jesness inventory classification system,' *Criminal Justice and Behaviour* 15: 78–91

Kashani, J.H., A.E. Daniel, L.A. Sulzberger, T.K. Rosenberg, and J.C. Reid. 1987. 'Conduct disordered adolescents from a community sample,' *Canadian Journal of Psychiatry* 32 (9): 756–60

Kirigin, K., C. Braukmann, J. Atwater, and M. Wolf. 1982. 'An evaluation of teaching family (Achievement Place) group homes for juvenile offenders,' *Journal of Applied Behaviour Analysis* 15: 1–16

Kraus, J., and S. Haselton. 1982. 'Juvenile offenders diversion potential as a function of policy perceptions,' *American Journal of Community Psychology* 18: 171

Leschied, A.W., P.G. Jaffe, and G.L. Stone. 1985. 'Differential response of juvenile offenders to two detention environments as a function of conceptual level,' *Canadian Journal of Criminology* 27 (4): 467–76

Leschied, A., and A. Telford. 1985. 'Recidivism among young adult offenders: Implications for the Young Offenders Act,' *Canadian Mental Health*, March: 7

Leschied, A., and K. Thomas. 1985. 'Effective residential programming for "hard-to-serve" delinquent youth: A description of the Craigwood Program,' *Canadian Journal of Criminology* 161 (April): 161–77

Lewis, D., and S. Shanok. 1979. 'Medical histories of psychiatrically referred delinquent children: An epidemiologic study,' *American Journal of Psychiatry* 136: 231

Litwack, T.R., and L.B. Schilesinger. 1987. 'Assessing and predicting violence: Research, law, and applications,' in I.B. Weiner and A.K. Hess, eds, *Handbook of Forensic Psychology*, 205–57. New York: Wiley

Martinson, R. 1974. 'What works? Questions and answers about prison reform,' *The Public Interest* 35: 22–54

McGarry, A.L., et al. 1974. *Competency to Stand Trial and Mental Illness*. Hew Publication No. HSM 73–9105. Washington, DC: U.S. Government Printing Office

McKelvey, R.S. 1988. 'A continuum of mental health care for children and adolescents,' *Hospital and Community Psychiatry* 39 (8): 870–3

Megargee, E.I. 1988. 'Research on the prediction of criminal behaviour,' in H. Goppinger, ed, *Applied Criminology – International: XXXVIth International Course in Criminology*, 84–100. Bonn: Forum Verlag Godesberg

Menzies, R.J., C.D. Webster, and D.S. Sepejak. 1985. 'The dimensions of dangerousness: Evaluating the accuracy of psychometric predictions of violence among forensic patients,' *Law and Human Behaviour* 9: 49–70

Miller, A. 1978. 'Conceptual systems theory: A critical review,' *Genetic Psychology Monographs* 97: 77–126

Miller, M., J. Chiles, and V. Barnes. 1982. 'Suicide attempters within a delinquent population,' *Journal of Consulting and Clinical Psychology* 50: 491

Mobley, M.J. 1987. 'Psychotherapy with criminal offenders,' in I.B. Weiner and A.K. Hess, eds, *Handbook of Forensic Psychology*, 602–29. New York: Wiley

Monahan, J. 1981. *Predicting Violent Behaviour: An assessment of Clinical Techniques*. Beverly Hills: Sage

Moos, R., and B. Moos. 1981. *Family Environment Scale Manual*. Palo Alto, CA: Consulting Psychologists Press

Mulvey, E.P., and C.W. Lidz. 1984. 'Clinical considerations in the prediction of dangerousness in mental patients,' *Clinical Psychological Review* 4: 379–401

Munson, R., and M. Revers. 1986. 'Program effectiveness of a residential treatment centre for emotionally disturbed adolescent females as measured by exit personality tests,' *Adolescence* 21: 305

O'Leary, K.D., and S.B. Johnson. 1979. 'Psychological assessment,' in H.C. Quay and J.S. Werry, eds, *Psychological Disorders of Childhood*, 210–46. New York: Wiley

Ontario Child Health Study. 1986. *Summary of Initial Findings*. Toronto: Ontario Ministry of Community and Social Services, Queen's Printer

Pauker, J.D., and E. Hood. 1979. *A Review of Four Classification Systems for Classifying the 'Impossible' Child and Adolescent*. Toronto: Ministry of Community and Social Services

Piersma, H.L., and S. Van Wingen. 1988. 'A hospital-based crisis service for adolescents: A program description,' *Adolescence* 23 (90): 491–500

Pollock, N., I. McBain, and C.D. Webster. In press. 'Clinical decision making and the assessment of dangerousness,' in K. Howells and G. Hollin, eds, *Clinical Approaches to Aggression and Violence*. Chichester: Wiley

Ptohl, N. 1978. *Predicting Dangerousness: The Social Construction of Psychiatric Reality*. Lexington, MA: Lexington Books

Quay, H.C. 1979. 'Classification,' in H.C. Quay and J.S. Werry, eds, *Psychopathological Disorders of Childhood*, 1–42. New York: Wiley

Quinsey, V.L. 1988. 'Assessments of the treatability of forensic patients,' Behavioral Sciences and the Law 6: 443–53

Quinsey, V., and A. Maguire. 1983. 'Offenders remanded for a psychiatric examination: Perceived treatability and disposition,' *Journal of Law and Psychiatry* 6: 193–205

Rae-Grant, N. 1978. 'Arresting the vicious cycle: Care and treatment of adolescents displaying the "Ovinnik Syndrome," ' *Canadian Psychiatric Association Journal* 23 (Supplement): 22–40

Redl, F. 1982. 'Child care work,' *Journal of Child Care* 1: 3–9

Reitsma-Street, M. 1984. 'Differential treatment of young offenders: A review of the conceptual level matching model,' *Canadian Journal of Criminology* 26: 2

Reitsma-Street, M., and A.W. Leschied. 1988. 'The conceptual-level matching model in corrections,' *Criminal Justice and Behaviour* 15 (1): 92–108

Rettig, R. 1980. 'Considering the use and usefulness of juvenile detention: Operationalizing social theory,' *Adolescence* 15: 444

Robey, A. 1965. 'Criteria for competency to stand trial: A checklist for psychiatrists,' *American Journal of Psychiatry* 122: 616–23

Roesch, R., and R.R. Corrado. 1979. 'The policy implications of evaluation research: Some issues raised by the Fishman study of rehabilitation and diversion services,' *Journal of Criminal Law and Criminology* 70: 530–41

Roesch, R., and S.L. Golding. 1980. *Competency to Stand Trial*. Urbana: University of Illinois Press

– 1987. 'Defining and assessing competency to stand trial,' in I.B. Weiner and A.K. Hess, eds, *Handbook of Forensic Psychology*, 278–394. New York: Wiley

Roesch, R., C.D. Webster, and D. Eaves. 1984. *The Fitness Interview Test: A Method for Examining Fitness to Stand Trial*. Toronto: Centre of Criminology, University of Toronto

Sargent, J. 1988. 'New approaches to delinquency: Inclusive thinking and integrated interventions,' Book review, *Contemporary Psychology* 33 (4): 354

Sas, L., and P. Jaffe. 1986. 'Understanding depression in juvenile delinquency: Implications for institutional admission policies and treatment programs,' *Juvenile and Family Court Journal*, 37: 49

Sas, L., P. Jaffe, and J.R. Reddon. 1985. 'Unravelling the needs of dangerous young offenders: A clinical-rational and empirical approach to classification,' *Canadian Journal of Criminology* 27: 83–96

Schwitzgebel, R., and D.A. Kolb. 1964. 'Inducing behaviour change in adolescent delinquents,' *Behaviour Research and Therapy* 1: 297–304

Shanok, S., S. Malani, O. Ninan, P. Guggenheim, H. Weinstein, and D. Lewis. 1983. 'A comparison of delinquent and nondelinquent adolescent psychiatric inpatients,' *American Journal of Psychiatry* 140: 582

Shorts, I. 1985. 'The prediction of in-programme failure among delinquent youths in a non-residential community-based programme,' *British Journal of Clinical Psychology* 24: 301

Smets, A.C., and C.M. Cebula. 1987. 'A group treatment program for adolescent sex offenders: Five steps toward resolution,' *Child Abuse and Neglect* 11: 247–54

Solicitor General Canada. 1982. *The Young Offenders Act, 1982*. Ottawa: Department of the Solicitor General

Solnick, J.V., C.J. Braukmann, M.M. Bedlington, K.A. Kirigin, and M.M. Wolf. 1981. 'The relationship between parent-youth interaction and delinquency in group homes,' *Journal of Abnormal Child Psychology* 9: 107–19

Steadman, H.J., and J.J. Cocozza. 1974. *Careers of the Criminally Insane: Excessive Social Control of Deviance*. Lexington, MA: D.C. Heath

Steinhauer, P. 1978. 'The Laidlaw foundation workshop on "the impossible child," ' *Canadian Psychiatric Association Journal* 23 (Supplement): 61

Stone, A.A. 1985. 'The new legal standard of dangerousness: Fair in theory, unfair in practice,' in C.D. Webster, M.H. Ben-Aron, and S.J. Hucker, eds, *Dangerousness: Probability and Prediction, Psychiatry and Public Policy*, 1–11. New York: Cambridge University Press

Svec, H., and J. Bechard. 1988. 'An introduction to a metabehavioural model with implications for social skills training for aggressive adolescents,' *Psychological Reports* 62: 19–22

Szapocznik, J., A. Perez-Vidal, A.L. Brickman, F.H. Foote, D. Santisteban, O. Hervis, and W.M. Kurtines. 1988. 'Engaging adolescent drug abusers and their families in treatment: A strategic structural systems approach,' *Journal of Consulting and Clinical Psychology* 56 (4): 552–57

Szasz, T.S. 1963. *Law, Liberty and Psychiatry*. New York: Macmillan
– 1977. 'Psychiatric diversion in the criminal justice system: A critique,' in R.E. Barnett et al, eds, *Assessing the Criminal: Restitution, Retribution, and the Legal Process*, 99–120. Lexington, Mass: Ballinger

Tharp, R.G., and R.J. Wetzel. 1969. *Behaviour Modification in the Natural Environment*. New York: Academic Press

Thornberry, T.P., and J.E. Jacoby. 1979. *The Criminally Insane: A Community Follow-up of Mentally Ill Offenders*. Chicago: University of Chicago Press

Veneziano, C., and L. Veneziano. 1986. 'Classification of adolescent offenders with the MMPI: An extension and cross-validation of the Megargee typology,' *International Journal of Offender Therapy and Compensative Criminology* 30: 11

Waggoner, S.C. 1984. 'First Impressions,' *Child Care Quarterly*. 12: 247–55

Warren, M.Q. 1983-4. 'Interpersonal maturity level classification (juvenile): Diagnosis and treatment of low, middle and high maturity delinquents,' research report, California Youth Authority, Sacramento

– 1978. 'The impossible child, the difficult child and the other assorted delinquents: Etiology, characteristics and incidence,' *Canadian Psychiatric Association Journal* 23: 22-40

– 1983. 'Applications of interpersonal-maturity theory to offender populations,' in W.S. Laufer and J.M. Day, eds, *Personality Theory, Moral Development and Criminal Behaviour*, 23-50. Lexington, MA: Lexington

Webb, D.B. 1988. 'Specialized foster care as an alternative therapeutic out-of-home placement model,' *Journal of Clinical Child Psychology* 17 (1): 34-43

Webster, C.D. 1984. 'On gaining acceptance: Why the courts accept only reluctantly findings from experimental and social psychology,' *International Journal of Law and Psychiatry* 7: 407-14

Webster, C.D., R.J. Menzies, and M. A. Jackson. 1982. *Clinical Assessment before Trial: Legal Issues and Mental Disorders*. Toronto: Butterworths

Webster, C.D., D.S. Sepejak, R.J. Menzies, and F.A.S. Jensen. 1982. 'Preliminary observations on the outcome of clinical predictions of dangerousness,' in C.D. Webster, R.J. Menzies, and M.A. Jackson, eds, *Clinical Assessment before Trial*. Toronto: Butterworths

Werry, J. 1979. 'Organic chapters,' in H.C. Quay and J.S. Werry, eds, *Psychological Disorders of Childhood*, 90-133. New York: Wiley

West, D. 1985. 'Clinical criminology under attack,' in M.H. Ben-Aron, S.J. Hucker, and C.D. Webster, eds, *Clinical Criminology: The Assessment and Treatment of Criminal Behaviour*, 1-13. Toronto: M and M Graphics

Whittaker, J. 1979. *Caring for Troubled Children*. San Francisco: Jossey-Bass

Widom, C.S. 1986. 'Juvenile delinquency,' in W.J. Currant, A.L. McGarry, and S.A. Shah, eds, *Forensic Psychiatry and Psychology: Perspectives and Standards for Interdisciplinary Practice*, 263-83. Philadelphia: F.A. Davis

Wolfensberger, W. 1982. *Normalization*. Toronto: National Institute on Mental Retardation

Ziskin, J. 1957. *Coping with Psychiatric and Psychological Testimony*, 2nd ed. Marina Del Rey: Law and Psychiatry Press

PART FOUR
Impact of the Young Offenders Act on Special Groups

In Part III, Patterson and Webster made the point that there are many unique aspects to the offending behaviour of young people and it is necessary, if not sufficient for effective intervention, to take into account these individual differences. In an effort to place this issue in greater perspective, this part examines the impact of YOA principles on two specific groups that are receiving considerable attention in the entire area of social policy related to the care and control of young people. The argument put forth by Crealock with learning-disabled young offenders, and Reitsma-Street with female young offenders, suggests the necessity of considering the particular dilemma for each of these groups: the YOA principles tend to polarize debate in the direction of discounting the importance of individual differences. This fact has received considerable attention, as it would appear that the Declaration of Principle within the YOA is somewhat equivocal as to whether case law should, in whole, determine disposition, or whether the 'special needs' of young persons should receive recognition by the court. These two chapters make the argument that individual differences are necessary if a complete understanding is to be provided on the nature of offending within these two large constituent groups of youths who commit crimes and end up in the youth court. It is necessary to consider the condition under which these two groups commit crimes, as it will be the court's response to these youths that will determine the proclivity for reoffending and the potential for resolution of the particular dilemma in which these youths find themselves.

12 Characteristics and needs of the learning-disabled young offender

Carol M. Crealock

In the past two decades, the link between being learning disabled (LD) and being involved in delinquent behaviour has been examined and confirmed in both Canada and the United States (Crealock 1987a; Murray 1976). The issues that are most frequently discussed are the nature of the linkage, the identification of learning disabilities, their incidence, and remedial implications. This chapter will begin with a discussion of the nature of the linkage and then will look at definitions and characteristics that are currently used to identify young offenders (YO) with LD, report on the incidence figures found as a result of identification, and, finally, discuss the implications for remedial programs that address the links that are possible through the Young Offenders Act (YOA).

Models Related to the LD/YO Link

While most of the literature in the field to date has demonstrated that there is a correlational link between LD and YO (Crealock 1987b; Keilitz, Zaremba, and Broder 1979; Mauser 1974), there has also been some work that has suggested a more direct causal link (Zimmerman et al 1979; Keilitz and Dunivant 1987; Larson 1989). Out of this more recent work, three models (school failure, susceptibility, and differential treatment) have been developed to explain the LD/YO relationship.

The school-failure model suggests that the learning disability causes school failure, which, in turn, leads to dropping out and juvenile delinquency. The school-failure descriptors include negative labelling, greater likelihood of association with peers who might also be prone to delinquent behaviour, failure to bond with school as a meaningful place and/or teachers as significant adults, economic incentives of crime since school failure rules out more traditional means of vocational success, and external attributions of responsibility for behaviour. Partial validation for this model comes from an experimental study with 230 adjudicated delinquents (120 LD, 110 non-LD) who received up to sixty hours of remedial instruction over and above their regular school program during one academic year. While the overall academic gains were modest and attitude to school basically unchanged, there were significant reductions in self-report delinquent behaviours and in official delinquency (Keilitz and Dunivant 1986). The authors felt that the results were derived primarily from the establishment of a relationship with the learning-disabilities teacher.

The second model that links LD and delinquency is the susceptibility theory (Post 1981). This model suggests that a constellation of cognitive, social, and emotional characteristics (lack of impulse control, inability to predict consequences of action or to understand cause-effect relationships, poor perception of social cues, suggestibility, and a tendency to act out) make the learning-disabled student more susceptible to involvement in delinquent activities. This view has received support from both cross-sectional and longitudinal studies. Keilitz and Dunivant (1986) indicate support for this theory in findings that an inability to anticipate consequences and irritability contributed directly to delinquent behaviour.

The differential-treatment model (Broder et al 1981; Zimmerman et al 1979; Keilitz and Dunivant 1987) suggests that even if learning-disabled and non–learning disabled adolescents engage in comparable amounts of delinquent behaviour, the learning disabled are more likely to be picked up by police, to be adjudicated as delinquent, and to receive more severe dispositions. It is argued that this occurs because the learning-disabled youth is not as likely to plan an effective escape or excuse strategy and because he or she may behave inappropriately to police or court officials. In their *Guide to the Young Offenders Act*, Hardy and Dunn-Worndl (1983) recommend certain behaviours to the adolescent who comes before the courts. These include writing down everything you can remember prior to and during an arrest; remembering that you have rights and can use them; responding politely to officials; restraining tendencies to 'spill it all out'; and clearly communicating with the court officer about your wants, ambitions, and goals. Most learning-disabled adolescents have difficulties in all of those areas – their writing skills and sequential memory are poor, they tend to be impulsive rather than reflective, and only rarely can they organize their past, present, and future hopes in a coherent manner.

Support for the differential-treatment model comes from several sources. Zimmerman and associates (1979) and Broder and associates

(1981) looked at 1005 public school boys and 687 adjudicated delinquent males. They found no difference between learning-disabled and normal adolescents on actual number of delinquent acts as revealed through a self-report process. However, almost twice as many learning-disabled boys (33 per cent) were adjudicated as delinquent as were non–learning disabled boys (18 per cent). Crawford (1985) reported that the incidence of being taken into custody and being adjudicated as delinquent was 9 per cent in the learning-disabled population and 4 per cent in the non–learning disabled population. She noted that there were no differences among the two groups in terms of severity of disposition, but that for comparable offences, the learning-disabled youths were more likely to be arrested and adjudicated. Similar results are reported by Hackler and Paranjape (1984) in a study that compared judicial reactions to juvenile theft in Canadian provinces.

Of the three models presented, support is strongest for the susceptibility and differential-treatment models but somewhat weaker for the school-failure model.

Definition of Learning Disabilities

Learning disabilities have been defined by many persons concerned about the problem. While their specific wording may differ, most definitions refer to three essential aspects: a clause stating the specific areas in which the disability is manifested (this usually includes a clause that describes the disability in terms of a discrepancy between what the student would normally be expected to achieve, i.e., potential, and what he or she is currently achieving, i.e., actual performance); an exclusion clause stating that the disability is not primarily attributable to any other cause; and a clause attributing possible causation to a variety of events, usually of a psychoneurological or biochemical nature (Canadian Association for Children with Learning Disabilities 1981).

While the definition implies a multifaceted approach to identifying and assessing learning disabilities, the operational definition in the field usually focuses on the exclusion of mental retardation as a cause of the learning problem and a statement of degree of academic retardation in the langauge and/or mathematics areas. These are usually assessed through an intelligence test and several achievement measures, which results in a working definition of an LD student as one with at least average intellectual potential and academic retardation of two or more years in one or more basic subjects. Additional testing and observation in cognitive and behavioural areas may be carried out to confirm a diagnosis of learning disabilities, but they are usually secondary to the intelligence and achievement aspects of assessment.

After academic retardation, the characteristics of LD that are found most frequently in the adolescent are impulsivity, restlessness, short attention span, immaturity, poor organizational skills, poor social skills, and production of incomplete assignments and poor written work. The three areas that seem to be most pervasive and that have been found to overlap most frequently with delinquent behaviour are problems in the academic achievement, cognitive, and social areas (Parker and Asher 1987; Crealock 1987a; Larson and Gerber 1987; Milich and Widiger 1987).

The most overwhelming shared characteristic between learning-disabled youths and young offenders is academic problems, usually involving retardation in one or more subject areas and attendance issues. Because, under the Young Offenders Act, attendance problems as a result of truancy are no longer considered delinquent acts, the degree of overlap between the young offender and the learning-disabled populations may be reduced. However, a large number of both populations have been shown to have serious academic problems with lags of two or more years, so this problem will continue to constitute a major area of overlap. Specific manifestations of the problem have been identified in terms of inability to meet school standards; communication problems between principals, teachers, and students; repeated grades; academic problems beginning in the primary grades; lack of motivation; failure to see relevance of school success to their future; classroom behavioural difficulties; and serious academic retardation of two to five years in basic subject areas for as many as 50 per cent of the delinquent population studied.

Reading and writing are two basic skill areas that are required in all subject areas at the high-school level. They are also skills that many LD students have continuing difficulties with. The specific problems they have in reading include: reading slowly; reading less frequently, if at all; skipping hard words; being unaware of miscues; hating to read aloud; being easily distracted; showing signs of anxiety when reading; and reading word-for-word rather than by phrases (Lipsett 1985). Given the increasing volume of reading required at the secondary level, these difficulties make the learning experience very frustrating. Another serious problem for the LD student comes in presenting complex ideas in written form. While some can cope relatively well with reading demands, most have difficulty in many aspects of writing. These include production aspects, such as spelling and handwriting, and organization and composition aspects that demand a well-thought-through logical presentation of the issue, argument, or topic being explored. Scardamalia and Bereiter (1985) argue that the older student who must use writing to solve problems must be able to read the assignment for key identifiers of the task, convert these into memory probes, retrieve the needed content from memory, test the content to see if it fits the task demand, and translate that content into appropriate written language. Many LD students have problems with these tasks. The following example of writing illustrates them:

> The Who is coming to Toronto Dec. 11⁵. This concert will be vidoe tape because this is The Who last concert ever.
> The concert will be held in the maple leafs Gordens. The tickets will be around $22.50. The tickets are not On sole yet.

This writing sample is the response of a sixteen-year-old LD boy of above-average intelligence to a request that he write about some activity he enjoys. In addition to having problems with handwriting and spelling, he was very concerned about 'face saving' and avoided topics and courses that required him to write lengthy pieces. He also tried not to use words he couldn't spell, which further compounded his problems in expressing complex ideas and thoughts on paper.

In addition to specific reading and writing problems, LD adolescents have other problems coping with secondary school. Zigmond and associates (1984) have identified the following ten survival skills for the special-needs high-school student: meets due dates, completes assignments, arrives at school on time, follows written directions, doesn't back-talk teachers, attends class every day, exhibits interest in academic work, accepts consequences of behaviour, doesn't fall asleep in class, and behaves appropriately while in class. Because of problems with time awareness, distractibility, emotional liability, and reading and writing, LD students often have difficulty at the secondary-school level and so are very much 'at risk' in the system for early-leaving, truancy, and adjustment difficulties.

The second major category of overlapping characteristics is in the cognitive area. Here authors have reported a tendency to be impulsive rather than reflective in decision making (Murray 1976; Koopman 1983; Douglas 1972). Murray has found an overlap between both populations on this characteristic, while Koopman reports it in the adult criminal and Douglas in the learning-disabled student. Murray and Koopman also report on an inability to learn from experience that is characteristic of the learning-disabled offender. Other characteristics mentioned include poor understanding of cause and effect and confused verbalization (Koopman 1983), poor organizational skills (Douglas 1972), and poor problem-solving skills (Schumaker et al 1982). These cognitive deficits occur in spite of average intellectual skills.

Additional problems include short attention span, difficulty following instructions, literal concrete thinking as opposed to abstract thinking, inconsistency of performance, inflexibility, spatial problems, greater occurrence of minimal brain damage, and faulty time concepts involving an inability to project themselves into the future or to defer gratification. These have been reported for learning-disabled young offenders by several investigators (Koopman 1983; Yeudall 1979; Murray 1976). In each case, the learning-disabled and young-offender populations studied showed more of these characteristics than would be expected from incidence among the general population.

The third category of characteristics that show significant overlap between learning-disabled and juvenile-delinquent populations is adequate social skills (Murray 1976; Koopman 1983; Schumaker et al 1982; Phil 1984; Leschied, Coolman, and Williams 1983; Kronick 1983). The specific characteristics mentioned here are poor understanding of social cues, poor social conversation skills, propensity to say irrelevant or inappropriate things, inability to give or receive positive and negative feedback or to negotiate with peers, peer acting out, socially isolated behaviours, generally poor peer relations, and immaturity that often translates into egocentricity and an inability to understand the other's point of view.

In summarizing the above, the typical profile of a learning disabled young offender would be: a male youth who has experienced serious academic failure beginning in the early grades, which has resulted in two or more years' academic retardation in the core subjects of reading, writing, and mathematics; who shows cognitive deficits in his ability to solve problems and appreciate cause-and-effect relationships; who shows problems in attending to relevant stimuli and tends to be impulsive; who has a poor understanding of social situations, which results in poor peer interactions; who has a history of emotional and aggressive response to frustration; and who frequently comes from a lower-class family that has experienced considerable stress and breakdown.

Incidence

One of the more important reasons for the growing interest in the LD/YO connection has been the reports on incidence. While researchers in the learning-disabilities field itself have generally agreed on incidence rates of 2 to 3 per cent in the general population (Hallahan and Kauffman 1982; Hewitt and Forness 1984; Hammill and Bartel 1981), they have also noted a range from 1 to 30 per cent, with a sharp increase noted in the figures (Will 1986). In the delinquency literature, incidence rates have ranged from lows of 1 to 40 per cent (Sawicki and Schaeffer 1979; Spreen 1981; Murray 1976; Keilitz, Zaremba, and Broder 1979; Zimmerman et al 1979; Ireland 1987) to highs of 60 to 90 per cent (Murray 1976; Podboy and Mallory 1978; Reiter 1982; Swanstrom, Randle, and Offord 1981; Dalby, Schneider, and Arboleda-Florez 1982; Wilgosh and Paitich 1982; Berman 1978). A crude average across these studies is approximately 30 to 40 per cent, which is far in excess of what would be expected in the general population.

Again, however, one has to look at the operational definition used in various studies to account for the high incidence rates. Basically the assessment consists of a battery of intellectual and academic tests. Two of the more moderate estimates (Zimmerman and associates, and Sawicki and Schaeffer) found 37 and 33 per cent of the adjudicated delinquent populations looked at had learning disabilities. In both cases, large numbers of adolescents were initially screened according to school records, and then those who showed high risk for learning disability were further assessed with psychological and education instruments plus full developmental and medical case histories and investigations of family functioning. Other investigators, such as Wilgosh and Paitich (1982) in a recent Canadian study, used a conservative criterion for learning disabilities of two years or more below grade level on achievement tests and found 61 per cent of males and 63 per cent of females, all of whom were at or above average on the intelligence measures used, to be learning disabled.

Ireland (1987), using both a discrepancy factor and specific evidence of cognitive deficit, however, found only 12 per cent of an incarcerated young-offender population to have learning disabilities. What is probably most important in these incidence figures is not the absolute percentage reported, but the percentage relative to the one the authors cite as typical in the general population. If one views incidence in this way, it would appear that there are two to three times as many learning-disabled adolescents in the young-offender population as there are in the overall adolescent population.

Remedial Implications

The passing of Bill C-61 (1982), and its concern about the most appropriate ways both to protect society and to meet the needs of the young offender, have led to a growing appreciation of the incidence of learning disabilities among this population and of the need to develop more specific programs to meet their needs. This is especially relevant, given the lack of evidence that many of the current approaches have been able either to prevent further criminal involvement or to rehabilitate many young offenders (Shamsie 1980; Crealock 1978). This remains so even though there is increasing demand for support such as that indicated in the recommendations of *Child at Risk* (1980), a report of the standing senate committee on Health, Welfare and Science, which states, 'we recommend that the Federal, Provincial and Territorial governments encourage the development of needed community resources and services to deal with young offenders a) before they appear in court, to make a court appearance unnecessary; and b) when a court appearance is unavoidable, to provide viable alternatives in their disposition' (p. 56). Trends at the provincial level also indicate a desire to find effective ways of providing appropriate alternatives for delinquent adolescents at the community level (*Three Decades of Change* 1983) and these too have prompted government at all levels to look to increased alternatives for young offenders, reflected in the Young Offenders Act in the list of alternative dispositions that may be given in youth court. These include absolute discharge; fine; compensation to the victims in goods, money, or personal service; a community-service order; treatment in a hospital or other appropriate facility; probation; or committal to intermittent or continuous custody.

There are several problems that mitigate against specific programming for the LD/YO adolescent. One of them involves the dearth of pre-disposition information that would help the courts appreciate the individual needs of each young offender and thus recommend a program more specifically tailored to these needs. This problem may be overcome with the full implementation of the Young Offenders Act since it does provide for the preparation of very full disposition reports that include general information about the young person's current behaviour, maturity, and plans for the future; history of previous delinquencies, familial relationships, and school and employment records; alternative measures; and availability of community service.

A second problem involves the paucity of programs that have clearly demonstrated that treating the LD/YO as a specific subgroup does result in decreases in recidivism and increases in academic and vocational achievement. A review of the literature (Ross and Gendreau 1979; Crealock 1987a) suggests that no single program thrust is as useful as a many-faceted thrust that involves several of the program elements listed below:

1 a behaviour-modification program that draws the students' attention to appropriate social and academic behaviours;
2 a nutritionally well-balanced diet;
3 the involvement of the community through liaison with school personnel, through the use of volunteers in the institutional program, and through parent training in effective interaction with adolescents;
4 remedial instruction in language and mathematics that is meaningful to the adolescent;
5 problem-solving training of a general cognitive nature that is directed towards life-skills and coping strategies;
6 the development of an active recreation program that involves students positively with their peers and staff; and
7 implementation by sensitive, caring individuals who value the young offender and see his or her potential for growth and who are well trained in their subject and in their ability to match the individual needs of students to appropriate curriculum and instruction

There have been programs that have incorporated several of these elements effectively. The Step-Up program and the LD-JD Project sponsored by the Association of Children with Learning Disabilities have focused on remediation in academic areas, while the programs developed by Larson and Gerber (1987) and Ross and Fabiano (1983) have focused on social cognitive areas.

The subjects involved in a follow-up evaluation of the Step-Up program in Vancouver (Thompson et al 1983) were 253 adjudicated delinquents who had an average of 4.7 adjudicated offences prior to attending Step-Up. Eighty-eight per cent had a learning disability as defined by the Canadian Association for Children with Learning Disabilities, and as indicated by a checklist that covered movement skills, visual skills, auditory skills, concept formation, and behaviour symptoms. Fifty-three per cent of them had attended special education classes in their communities prior to Step-Up and 60 per cent had failed at least one grade; their mean age was fifteen years, ten months. The program offered individualized remedial training for two 2-hour sessions, five days a week. The teaching methods were eclectic and included a modified token economy plus any instructional technique that would help the individual learn. Students were tested daily in math, spelling, reference, and oral reading, with a view to improving previous scores on a regular basis. The goals of the program were as follows:

1 To improve basic academic skills for youth referred by Probation Officers.
2 To reduce the number of times that the participants are adjudicated delinquent on further offences.
3 To encourage appropriate social development.
4 To demonstrate that, even at adolescence, a remedial school program can successfully rehabilitate students.
5 To provide a positive learning experience for a wide variety of university students whose careers involve working with youth. (Thompson et al 1983: 28)

Evaluation of the program has found that each of the goals has been met. Questionnaire data were positive from students, parents, teachers, and the community at large. In terms of what they were actually doing, 106 were working, 50 were at school, 22 were homemaking, 25 were unemployed but not in trouble with the law, 4 were hospitalized, 2 were deceased, 20 couldn't be traced, and 18 were in custody. The 18 who were in custody represent 7.1 per cent of the total group, while those who were actually pursuing jobs or schooling represent 70.4 per cent of the population. These data represent a significant improvement over recidivism rates (approximately 33 per cent) more frequently reported in the literature.

The LD-JD project sponsored by ACLD (Keilitz and Dunivant 1987) involved 973 teenagers who had not been adjudicated delinquent and 970 youths who had been adjudicated delinquent by the courts. Extensive testing in ability, achievement, and behavioural areas was conducted with each student, and information was also obtained from his or her school files. On a self-report questionnaire, those students who were identified as LD reported that they had committed an average of 266 delinquent acts in their lifetime, while those who were not identified as LD reported that they had committed 185 delinquent acts. This difference was supported by data on official delinquency. Nine per cent of the LD boys had been officially adjudicated as delinquent while only 4 per cent of their non-LD peers had been so adjudicated. Fifty-seven LD adolescents from the non-JD group were followed over a two-year period. At the end of the time, they were found to have had more official contacts with the juvenile-justice system and greater increases in delinquent behaviour than did their non-LD peers.

A second phase of this project involved 400 officially adjudicated delinquent boys and girls. They were randomly assigned to control or remediation groups. The focus of the remedial program involved individual instruction in the academic area of greatest deficiency. It had been intended that the students would receive four 50-minute sessions per week for one school year. In fact, the average participant received 32 hours of remediation over a six-month period. The results indicated improvements in all achievement measures for the treatment group. However, a minimum of 55 to 65 hours of instruction time was required before the positive effects were statistically significant. In terms of level of self-reported delinquent behaviour and change in recidivism rates, there were positive effects but these were largely at a non-significant level. Again, however, for adolescents who had received a minimum of 40 to 50 hours of instruction, the treatment was significantly effective in reducing future delinquency. While the remedial focus was on academic achievement, the authors concluded that the major factor contributing to the successes of the program was not academic-skill improvement per se, but social bonding through the development of close interpersonal relationships between the adolescent and the teacher. However, they support the academic focus and conclude that 'remediation may have been precisely the kind of situation that was needed to facilitate socialization and attachment: one in which motivation was aroused, concern demonstrated, traits and values modeled, and hard effort expended' (Keilitz and Dunivant 1987: 134).

Ross and Fabiano (1981, 1983, 1987), on the basis of an extensive review of the literature, have developed a cognitive program that they have shown to be appropriate to the treatment of offenders based on careful assessment of the individual. The model suggests that criminal behaviour may be associated with developmental delay in the acquisition of the cognitive skills essential for effectively coping with social situations, and includes social perspective-taking, means-ends reasoning, interpersonal problem-solving, and impulsivity control. They suggest that the person who implements such programs should also be able to motivate the inmate to be involved in the program, be empathic to the inmate's thinking and feeling, be able to model effective reasoning and problem-solving, and be eclectic in his or her approach to interaction. Their own direct application of the program to an incarcerated population (Ross 1987) has shown that it is possible to teach social cognitive skills, and that mastery of these skills can transfer to positive social skills both inside and outside the institutional setting. Similar results using a program that taught delinquents to stop and think, that provided practice in 'what to think about' in a problem-solving situation, and that showed them 'how to think' has also yielded positive behaviour change after 33 hours of training with LD and low-achieving youthful offenders (Larson and Gerber 1987).

Programs such as those described above, programs that focus on academic and cognitive areas augmented by other elements, have demonstrated that the link between LD and delinquency is real and that addressing the needs of the subgroup of young offenders who are learning disabled makes good treatment sense. These programs and others like them are possible alternatives under the YOA and should be explored and developed in training schools, alternative education prorams, and public-school curricula that service young offenders.

Acknowledgment

The research described in this paper was supported in part by a grant from the Ministry of the Solicitor General of Canada.

References

Berman, A. 1978. *Delinquent Youth and Learning Disabilities*. San Raphael, CA: Academic Therapy Publications

Bill C-61. 1982. An act respecting young offenders and to repeal the Juvenile Delinquents Act. Ottawa: The House of Commons of Canada.

Broder, P., N. Dunivant, E. Smith, and L. Sutton. 1981. 'Further observations of the link between learning disabilities and juvenile delinquency,' *Journal of Educational Psychology* 73: 838–50

Canadian Association for Children with Learning Disabilities. 1981. *Definition of Learning Disabilities*. St John, NB

Child at Risk. 1980. 'A report of the standing Senate Committee on Health, Welfare and Science.' Ottawa: Minister of Supply and Services, Canada

Crawford, D. 1985. 'The link between delinquency and learning disabilities,' *Judges Journal* 24: 23

Crealock, Carol. 1978. 'Juvenile delinquency: The Canadian perspective,' *Behavioral Disorders* 3: 309–13

– 1987a. *The Learning Disabilities/Juvenile Delinquency Link: Causation or Correlation*. Ottawa: Ministry of the Solicitor General

– 1987b. 'The relationship between learning disabilities and delinquent behaviour,' *Learning Disabilities* 1: 55–8

Dalby, J.T., R.D. Schneider, and J. Arboleda-Florez. 1982. 'Learning disorders in offenders,' *International Journal of Offender Therapy and Comparative Criminology* 26 (2): 145–51

Douglas, V.I. 1972. 'Stop, look and listen: The problem of sustained attention and impulse control in hyperactive and normal children,' *Canadian Journal of Behavioural Science* 4: 259–82

Hackler, J., and W. Paranjape. 1984. 'Official reaction to juvenile theft – Comparisons across provinces,' *Canadian Journal of Criminology* 26: 179–98

Hallahan, D., and J. Kauffman. 1982. *Exceptional Children*, 3rd ed. Englewood Cliffs, NJ: Prentice-Hall

Hammill, D., and N. Bartel. *Teaching Children with Learning and Behavior Problems*, 3rd ed. Boston: Allyn and Bacon

Hardy, L., and B. Dunn-Worndl. *In Trouble with the Law: A Guide to the Young Offenders Act*. Toronto: Justice for Children

Hewitt, F., and S. Forness. 1984. *Education and Exceptional Learners*, 3rd ed. Boston: Allyn and Bacon

Ireland, J. 1987. 'Exceptional Students at the Syl Apps Training School.' Address given to the Halton County Board of Education Student Services Personnel

Keilitz, I., and N. Dunivant. 'The relationship between learning disability and juvenile delinquency: Current state of knowledge,' *Remedial and Special Education* 7 (13): 18–26

– 1987. 'The learning disabled offender,' in C. Nelson, R. Rutherford, and B. Wolford, eds, *Special Education in the Criminal Justice System*, 120–37. Toronto: Merrill

Keilitz, I., and S.L. Miller. 1980. 'Handicapped adolescents and young adults in the justice system,' *Exceptional Education Quarterly* 2: 117–26

Keilitz, I., B.A. Zaremba, and P.K. Broder. 1979. 'The link between learning disabilities and juvenile delinquency: Some issues and answers,' *Learning Disability Quarterly* 2: 2–11

Koopman, P.R.S. 1983. 'Cognitive Disorders and Syntactical Deficiencies in the Inmate Populations of Federal Penitentiaries in Canada.' Report for the Solicitor General of Canada

Kronick, D. 1983. 'Programming for social skill deficits,' *National* [CACLD newsletter] 20: 6

Larson, K. 1989. 'Task-related and interpersonal problem-solving training for increasing school success in high-risk adolescents,' *Remedial and Special Education* 10 (5): 32–42

Larson, K., and M. Gerber. 1987. 'Effects of social metacognitive training for enhancing overt behavior in learning disabled and low achieving delinquents,' *Exceptional Children* 54: 201–11

Leschied, A., M. Coolman, and S. Williams. 1984. *Addressing the Needs of School Failures in a Delinquent Population, Behavioral Disorders* 10 (1): 40–6

Lipsett, Holly. 1985. 'Reaching reluctant readers,' *Forum* 11 (4): 30–2

Mauser, A.J. 1974. 'Learning disabilities and delinquent youth,' *Academic Therapy* 9: 343–44

Milich, R., and T. Widiger. 1987. 'Differential diagnosis of attention deficit and conduct disorders using conditional probabilities,' *Journal of Consulting and Clinical Psychology* 55: 762–7

Murray, D.A. 1976. *The Link between Learning Disabilities and Juvenile Delinquency: Current Theory and Knowledge*. Washington, DC: Government Printing Office

Parker, J., and S. Asher. 1987. 'Peer relations and later personal adjustment: Are low-accepted children at risk?' *Psychological Bulletin* 102: 357–89

Pihl, R.O., and L. McLarnon. 1984. 'Learning disabled children as adolescents,' *Journal of Learning Disabilities* 17: 96–100

Podboy, J.W., and W.A. Mallory. 1978. 'Learning handicap: The underdiagnosed disability,' *Juvenile and Family Court Journal* 29: 13–16

Post, C.H. 1981. 'The link between learning disabilities and juvenile delinquency: Cause, effect and present solutions,' *Juvenile and Family Court Journal* 32: 58–68

Reid, D., and W. Hresko. 1981. 'Five faces of cognition: Theoretical influences on approaches to learning disabilities,' *Learning Disability Quarterly* 4 (3): 238–43

Reiter, M. 1982. 'School Achievement and Juvenile Delinquency: A Review of the Literature.' ED221009.

Ross, R. 1987. 'Social cognitive training for offender populations.' Paper given at the legal symposium sponsored by the Nova Scotia Ministry of Justice, Halifax

Ross, R.R., and E. Fabiano. 1981. *Time to Think: Cognition and Crime Link and Remediation*. Ottawa: Department of Criminology

– 1983. *The Cognitive Model of Crime and Delinquency, Prevention and Rehabilitation: II. Intervention Techniques*. Toronto: Ministry of Correctional Services

Ross, B., and P. Gendreau. 1979. 'Effective correctional treatment: Bibliotherapy for cynics,' *Crime and Delinquency*, October: 463–89

Sawicki, D., and B. Schaeffer. 1979. 'Affirmative approach to the LD/JD link,' *Juvenile and Family Court Journal* 30: 11–16

Scardamalia, M., and C. Bereiter. 1985. 'Written composition,' in M. Wittrock, ed, *Handbook of Research on Teaching*, 778–803. New York: Macmillan

Schumaker, J.B., J.S. Hazel, J.A. Sherman, and J. Sheldon. 1982. 'Social skill performances of learning disabled, non-learning disabled and delinquent adolescents,' *Learning Disability Quarterly* 5: 388–97

Shamsie, S.J. 1980. 'Antisocial adolescents: Our treatments do not work: Where do we go from here?' Paper presented at the annual meeting of the Canadian Psychiatric Association. Toronto.

Snyder, J., and M. White. 1979. 'The rise of cognitive self-instruction in the treatment of behaviorally disturbed adolescents,' *Behavior Therapy* 10: 227–35

Spreen, O. 1981. 'The relationship between learning disability: Neurological impairment, and delinquency,' *Journal of Nervous and Mental Disease* 169: 791–9

Swanstrom, W.J., C.W. Randle, and K. Offord. 1981. 'The frequency of learning disability: A comparison between juvenile delinquencies and seventh grade populations,' *Journal of Correctional Education* 32: 29–33

Thompson, N., et al. 1983. *Step-Up: An Eight-Year Review*. Annual Report 1982-3. Vancouver: Vancouver School District

Three Decades of Change. 1983. Toronto: Ontario Ministry of Community and Social Services

Wilgosh, L., and D. Paitich. 1982. 'Delinquency and learning disabilities: More evidence,' *Journal of Learning Disabilities* 15: 278–9

Will, M. 1986. 'Educating children with learning problems: A shared responsibility,' *Exceptional Children* 52: 411–16

Yeudall, L.T. 1979. *Neuropsychological Concomitants of Persistent Criminal Behavior*. Alberta Hospital Research Bulletin, No. 29. Edmonton

Zigmond, N., A. Kerr, B. Brown, and K. Harris. 1984. 'School survival skills in secondary aged special education students.' Paper given at the annual meeting of the American Educational Research Association, New Orleans

Zimmerman, J., W. Rich, I. Keilitz, and P. Broder. 1979. *Some Observations on the Link between Learning Disabilities and Juvenile Delinquency* (LDJD. 003). Williamsburg, VA: National Centre for State Courts, Northwestern University

13 A review of female delinquency

Marge Reitsma-Street

Although knowledge on female delinquency theory, policy, and practice is no longer a wasteland, we know little about the specific conditions under which females begin, continue, or stop committing delinquencies. Even less is known of how our laws, such as the Young Offenders Act, construct our interactions with girls labelled delinquent. We are, however, beginning to unmask the limitations of how we understand female delinquency, and to propose other ways to direct research, guide policy, and implement laws (Adelberg and Currie 1987; Adler and Simon 1979; Bertrand 1979; Campbell 1981; Davidson 1982).

One theme in the contemporary literature is a critique of sexism in our Western criminal-justice systems (Geller 1987; Smart 1976; Morris 1987). For instance, males were the major contributors to the reports, six legislative proposals, and numerous provincial and federal conferences prior to proclamation of the YOA (Reitsma-Street 1984). The data and ideas for the YOA proposals were based on male behaviours interpreted by male scholars and practitioners. The implementation of the YOA is primarily by males with males. The ordinariness of this striking fact is continually expressed in gender-exclusive language in everyday and official discourse, such as laws (Spender 1985). Thus, female delinquents are assumed to be included when section 11(1) of the YOA states a young person has a right to counsel at any stage of proceedings against *him*; female justice personnel are subsumed in the words the Attorney General or *his* delegate (s. 4[1][a]).

This chapter is not a detailed critique of the explicit or implicit sexism inherent in the YOA or its implementation. Rather, the aim is to review what is known and not known about female delinquency. Woven into the review are criticisms of that knowledge and how it came to be. It is in the context of this general picture that Canadian female young-offender policy must be analysed.

Sources for this chapter are limited to those written in English or French on female delinquency in Western industrial societies in the nineteenth or twentieth century, particularly Canada, the United States, and England. The epidemiology of female delinquency according to official and self-report data is sketched, followed by comments on what the literature tells us of the etiology and construction of delinquency in girls. After surveying the literature on interventions, the major questions in female delinquency theory, policy, and practice are posed. The chapter ends with comments on several implications of the review for analysing the interactions between the YOA and Canadian girls.

The Numbers of Delinquents and Delinquencies

Since there are various ways to define delinquencies, there are different approaches to estimating the extent of delinquency. Comments are made on the epidemiology of delinquency using cross-sectional and longitudinal Canadian data from official and self-report sources.

Official Statistics

There is consistency over time and among countries in how few girls are charged for law-breaking activities. The most frequent charges among these are for property offences or minor violations. But, there is a substantial variation over time, by place, and by race in the absolute and proportional numbers of girls who face the criminal-justice system. These patterns of consistency and variation in official statistics reveal the complexity of female delinquency and conformity, and the necessity for historically specific analysis.

From Canadian data presented in table 1, fewer than 1 per cent of Canadian girls were charged in youth courts for breaking sections of the federal Criminal Code in 1985–6.[1] The estimated total rate of court charges is closed to 2 per cent if provincial and municipal violations of, for example, traffic, liquor, or truancy laws are included. Estimates of official rates for all females in Canada and elsewhere range from 0.5 to 3 per cent of the female population at risk, depending on definitions of law-breaking, age at risk, and criminal-justice interventions (e.g., Hoffman-Bustamante 1973: 122, 125; Johnson 1986: 7; Smart 1976: 9).

TABLE 1
Variations by Canadian provinces of girls charged in youth courts for criminal code
violations, 1985–6

Province	Number	% of youth charged	% of girls at risk
Newfoundland	174	12.4	0.31
PEI	34	14.1	0.33
New Brunswick	115	10.6	0.18
Nova Scotia	297	14.8	0.41
Quebec	411	6.9	0.09
Ontario		Data not available	
Manitoba	693	17.6	0.79
Saskatchewan	428	17.8	0.56
Alberta	1689	20.5	1.02
B. Columbia	1001	17.4	0.58
Yukon	22	14.9	1.68
NWT	77	13.2	1.38
Total	4941	15.6	0.67

SOURCES: Calculated from Canadian Centre for Justice Statistics, *Preliminary Tables Youth Court Statistics*, Part I – Table 2, and Part II – Table 1 (1987)

But, whether excluding or including all types of violations, the rates vary substantially. Table 1 lists fewer than 0.41 per cent of the Canadian girls at risk in 1985–6 who were charged with Criminal Code violations coming from Quebec or the Maritimes, while the absolute numbers and rates were double or triple in the western provinces and the territories. This 1985–6 variation was also noted in other years for girls and women in different provinces and cities. For instance, despite a smaller population at risk, Winnipeg police charged 1921 girls in 1977 compared to Montreal's 874 and Ottawa's 127 (Biron and Gauvreau 1984: 72). Researchers who comment on significant differences in female delinquency or charge rates (e.g., Sarri 1976; Wolfe, Cullen, and Cullen 1984) sometimes look to variations in race and background. Others challenge the assumptions of actual differences in delinquencies and look more at policies, procedures, and attitudes in criminal-justice organizations (Cicourel 1968; Bala and Corrado 1985; Krisberg, Litsky, and Schwartz 1984; LaPrairie 1987; Sarri 1983).

Official rates over a lifetime are higher. From cross-sectional data of all age groups, Farrington estimates that 14.7 per cent of girls born in

England and Wales will have one conviction in their lifetime (1981: 174). Again rates, however, vary. Table 2 summarizes results of five longitudinal studies. The lowest rate of official delinquency is 2 per cent for English, primarily white girls, born of married parents, who went to court before their twenty-first birthday for non-status offences (Wadsworth 1979); the highest rate is 18.4 per cent for non-white girls born in Philadelphia in 1958, arrested by the police before their eighteenth birthday (Wolfgang 1983).

TABLE 2

Approximate rates of official delinquency in five longitudinal samples of girls

Study	Sample	Rate
Wadsworth (1979)	2035 mostly white born in 1946 England & Wales	2% to court for non-status by 21st birthday
Wolfgang (1983)	6943 white born in 1958 Philadelphia	4.5% arrest by 18th birthday
Werner & Smith (1977)	313 various races born in 1955 Kauai Island	11% police contact for status & criminal by 18th birthday
Roff & Wirt (1985)	565 least popular Grade 3 & 6 white two midwest Amer. cities	10% criminal records 15 years later
Wolfgang (1983)	7584 non-white born 1958 Philadelphia	18.4% arrest by 18th birthday

Since the 1960s there has been a concern that the female crime rate is rising (Adler and Simon 1979). Certainly absolute numbers are increasing. But the rate and importance of the increases over time are not clear. Canadian data on youth are not systematically recorded by sex over time. Also, Canadian youth, like their American and British sisters, have faced changes in delinquency laws in the last two decades, particularly relating to the status offences of immorality, truancy, and running away (Bala and Clarke 1981; Bottoms 1974; Lerman 1975).

None the less, there are extensive studies of changes in adult female crime such as an Australian study of sex-specific rates of populations at risk from 1900 to 1975 (Mukherjee and Fitzgerald 1981), a British analysis of 1951 to 1980 data (Box and Haly 1984), the Steffensmeiers' 1980 examination of the American Uniform Crime Reports from 1965 to 1977, and Canadian statistical summaries from 1968 through 1981 (Adams 1978; Solicitor General 1985). Authors of these studies conclude that: 1 / rates of violent crimes are strikingly constant; 2 / the longer the time frame, the more *both* increases and decreases are seen in all but violent crimes; 3 / the proportion of adult females out of total offenders is quite stable for the last eight decades, hovering around 10 per cent (although in the last two there appears to be an increase in proportion of juvenile females according to Biron and Gauvreau 1984: 10); and 4 / if only the last twenty-five years are examined, there are absolute and proportional increases of females charged for minor property offences.

More consistency than variation is also noted in types of crimes charged against females. An examination of youth-court Criminal Code charges against Canadian girls in table 3 reveals that, in each of the three years, one out of three violations was for minor theft and fewer than two of one hundred were for serious personal injury. If all violations are grouped together, more than six of ten were against property and fewer than one of ten against the person; the remaining violations were a mixture of drug,

TABLE 3
Consistency in selected criminal code charges by Canadian girls (under 18 years) in 1980, 1982, and 1985–6
(numbers are percentages of total charges)

Charge	1980 (n = 7194)	1982 (n = 9374)	1985–6 (n = 9062)
Theft under $200	36.2	34.9	32.2
Break and enter	16.0	13.0	9.6
Possess stolen goods	9.5	11.5	10.0
Assault	6.3	6.5	6.2
Mischief	6.2	6.1	4.0
Forgery, fraud	4.2	5.7	6.3
Theft over	5.0	4.9	4.4
Murder, attempt, robbery	1.4	1.7	1.1
Disorderly conduct	1.3	0.8	0.9
20 other types	13.9	14.9	25.3
Total	100.0	100.0	100.0

SOURCES: Calculated from Canadian Centre for Justice Statistics 1983: 39, 40; 1987: Part 1 – Table 3, with data not available on Ontario; West 1984: 58, 59

mischief, disorderly conduct, and other delinquencies. These proportions are similar to those reported by Johnson in her statistical review of charges laid against Canadian women in 1985 (1987: 27). If status offences such as truancy and immorality are added into the *total* charges, along with violations of drug or traffic laws, it is interesting to note that 7.2 per cent of all charges in 1980 and 5.1 per cent in 1982 are for status offences (Canadian Centre for Justice Statistics 1983: 39, 40; West 1984: 58, 59). Despite the infrequency of status offences relative to other crimes, status offences are featured in research with females. This feature is discussed later in the review of interventions.

In short, over time and place, there is consistency in the infrequency of and 'distinctly nonviolent and nonaggressive' nature of delinquencies by girls (Crites 1976: 35). The number of females who are arrested, however, varies by race, class, and residence. If the girls are non-white or from poor families, inner cities, or rural reserve, they are more likely to face charges than if white and from affluent backgrounds.

Self-report Statistics

From the self-report approach to understanding the epidemiology of female delinquency, we know that white and affluent girls do commit at least some of the delinquencies listed in the questionnaires. Real variations by race, place, or class, as noted in official statistics, are not as striking in self-report studies, although the findings are not consistent. For instance, neither Byles (1969) nor Gomme (1985) found significant correlations between socio-economic class and delinquent acts in their studies of representative Canadian urban girls. Cernovich and Giordano (1979) found few differences between races in their study of 822 mid-western urban students. In a five-year panel study of 804 randomly selected American girls age eleven to seventeen, Ageton reported more similarities than significant differences on twenty-four self-report delinquency items (1983: 561, 563). The differences were not consistent: for instance, white or suburban females reported higher mean scores on property items than did black or working-class girls, and more often said they hit their parents, while lower-class and black girls coded more gang fights or hitting fellow students.

These self-report studies challenge the amount of real variation in delinquencies by background of the girls. They also question the numbers and rates of the official statistics: the rate of official charges is infrequent, but most girls report at least one and usually more delinquencies in the previous year – whether a status or criminal offence. None the less, for most of their lives, females consistently engage in conforming behaviours. For example, in three samples with a total of more than 4000 girls altogether, the authors found that a small proportion of girls committed more than ten delinquencies in twelve months (3.3 per cent in Biron 1980: 3; fewer than 5 per cent in Canter 1982: 385; 3.5 per cent in Simons, Miller, and Aigner 1980: 46).

Consistent with official statistics are the type and ranking of delinquencies recorded in self-report studies. Girls most frequently report minor property delinquencies. They also often break alcohol and drug regulations. The girls, however, very seldom report that they harm property or persons in a substantial way (Bowker 1978: 21; Gomme, Morton, and West 1984; Hindelang, Hirschi, and Weiss 1981; Morris 1987: 34; West 1984: 85–112).

Delinquency over Time

From either official or self-report data, little is known about female recidivists. Sepsi (1974: 72) compared 105 girls returned to an Ohio correctional institution after violating parole with 105 girls in the institution for the first time. Only 18 of the 104 variables measures significantly differentiated the recidivists from the others ($p < 0.05$). That is, 86 variables showed no statistically significant difference. Of the few that did, such as previous sentence, most were part of the recidivism definition and did not help to clarify which, or under what conditions, girls continue or reduce the numbers of their delinquencies.[2] Wolfgang included 14,527 girls in his second Philadelphia birth-cohort study. Contrary to expectation, a few girls were *not* responsible for most of the crimes, and non-chronic recidivists were responsible for 42 per cent of the crimes (1983: 90, 91).

At most we know that girls appear over time to decrease their already limited involvement in most delinquencies other than drug or liquor use, traffic violations, or sexual intercourse. For example, in a two-year follow-up study of 387 Montreal girls, Biron (1980: 7) found an overall decrease in delinquencies, especially against the person, although status offences and drug use did not decrease. In her analysis of the 804 American girls in the five-year panel study, Ageton (1983: 570) also found crimes against persons fell substantially over time. As for property crimes, fewer girls reported theft, but the mean number of thefts did not decrease. Thus, Ageton (1983: 573) argued 'that as the panel ages those committing theft offenses do so more frequently.'

Summary of Epidemiology

The overwhelming majority of girls conform to the law most of the time. This statement remains true even if a girl is officially charged for primarily non-violent property crimes. It still remains true when girls reveal their more frequent participation in delinquencies, especially those associated with adolescence such as truancy or use of drugs. For those few girls who report more than the average delinquencies or who are officially caught, continued participation over time is not likely.

This consistent infrequency needs to be examined. Few theories, as reviewed in the next section, are adequate. Also needing explanation are the variations. The limited theoretical focus has been on the low delinquency rates among girls. More attention, however, is needed to understand the persistent organizational practices that mediate the processing of delinquencies by girls of backgrounds differing in class, race, and respectability (Kruttschnitt 1982). The subsequent intervention section picks up on these consistent variations.

Understanding Female Delinquency

To review what is known, I selected examples of rigorous research of various designs. In brief, some of the case studies and representative surveys emphasize the differences between delinquent and non-delinquent girls; others discover similarities. Some of the longitudinal studies and some participant observation research locates causes of delinquency within the girl and her immediate environment; others specify particular contexts in which delinquent activities and labels emerge and are negotiated. Throughout the literature, however, the implication of the girls' biological sex commands attention.

Case Studies

Common to case studies is the selection of girls who are already adjudicated or institutionalized as delinquent – defined before the 1980s as including sexual experiences outside marriage. In 1966, Konopka wrote a sensitive account of 105 adjudicated delinquents and 76 pregnant girls. Despite awareness of the double standard for the sexes, the changing cultural position of females, and their economic vulnerability, Konopka emphasizes that 'whatever her offense – whether shoplifting, truancy, or running away ... it is usually accompanied by some disturbance or unfavorable behavior in the sexual area' (1966: 4). These words echo those of Thomas in his influential book on the unadjusted girl: 'a girl destroys her value and that of her family by prostituting herself' (1969: 230).

From interviews, personality tests, diaries, and agency records, Konopka, Thomas, and others conclude that delinquent girls are relatively more unhappy, different, or disturbed in their relationships with parents, peers, schooling, and themselves in comparison with some standard of normalcy or with comparison groups (Cowie, Cowie, and Slater 1968; Richardson 1969; Gibbons 1971; Konopka 1976; Reitsma-Street, Offord, and Finch 1985; Roberts 1981; Pollack 1950; Treso 1962; Vedder and Somerville 1970). For example, in their study of 338 females admitted to Ontario's one female reformatory, Lambert and Madden state: 'The data have shown these women to be young and unrealistic, many to be highly disturbed personally, and/or products of seriously disrupted backgrounds. Their crimes, for the most part, were not dangerous to others' (1976: 324, 325).

Some recent case studies with controls continue to hypothesize differences in such variables as self-concept, maladjustment, age of first intercourse, or school performance. Few, however, found many statistically significant differences between the delinquents and non-delinquents (e.g., Bour, Young, and Henningsen 1984; Long, Sutton, and Kiefer 1984; Offord and Poushinsky 1981).

The 'delinquents are different' conclusion is further challenged in other case studies of female delinquents (Carlen 1985; Keating 1984). For instance, Gagnon and Langélier-Biron (1982) unravel the everyday universe of twenty-eight 'filles en marge.' They comment on the importance of family, love, and friends to the delinquents – concerns central to non-delinquent girls as well. In tracing five call-girls for nine months, Rosenblum argued that call girls, like all females, are 'socialized to use sexuality for gain in nonsexual interactions' (1980: 107; see also Boyer and James 1982; Smart 1985; Wilson 1978). Lowman (1987) reanalysed 272 interviews of Canadian prostitutes. Contrary to the original findings, the author did *not* find the prostitutes were pathological; rather, prostitution was a delinquency used primarily to get money to live – independently or just to avoid living in a violent home. Finally, Bowker and Klein qualitatively and quantitatively examined the difference-versus-similarity hypotheses in their study of 122 gang and 100 non-gang black girls in Los Angeles. They state that 'gang and non-gang girls, delinquent and non-delinquent, all suffer from the consequences of racism, sexism, poverty and extremely limited opportunity structures ... There were few differences of any note' (1983: 750).

Correlational Surveys

The major feature of surveys is the random selection of girls from various backgrounds at one particular time. Usually questionnaires are administered, and responses transformed into quantitative data, which are then statistically analysed, often using correlational procedures. Sometimes hypotheses are tested.

One contribution of these surveys is the conclusive finding that almost all girls are alike in that they commit a variety of delinquencies, but they do so infrequently. The Ontario Child Health Survey study, not reported earlier in the self-report section, illustrates this point. In this survey, the mental, physical, and social problems of 3294 Ontario youths were studied. The authors found only 1.7 per cent of twelve- to sixteen-year-old girls had conduct disorder – a high score on a checklist of behaviours, such as lying, stealing, hitting, adapted from Achenbach and Edelbrock (1981) as reported by parents *or* the girls. Even fewer, just 4 of 676 girls (or 0.6 per cent), had conduct disorder based on the reports of two sources (Offord et al 1984: 9, Table 6).

In using surveys to test theories such as social control or differential association, the differences-versus-similarities debate re-emerges. On the one hand, most of the surveys find delinquent behaviour in girls is statistically more frequent (using correlational, relative-odds, multiple-regression, or path-analyses statistics) if there is 1 / an increase in socio-demographic, family, child-risk factors, such as subsidized housing, domestic violence, poor friendships; 2 / weakened bonding to family, school and the law; and 3 / increased participation in subcultural groups and activities. Parental deviance, association with delinquent peers and their values, and low performance in school are weighted as more important for girls than attachment to low-income of fathers.

On the other hand, the total variance in delinquent behaviour explained by statistically significant variables is not great – as the summary of five surveys in table 4 indicates. The highest explained variance is 47 per cent (Figueria-McDonough 1985). But this outcome explains only one specific type of delinquency–adolescent, subcultural deviance, such as drug use and truancy. This subcultural deviance may not be validly explained by adolescent subcultural norms and time spent with peers. Rather, it may be a normal part of adolescent subcultural norms. Other types of delinquencies, or delinquency overall, are not as completely explained by the proposed variables, even in Figueria-McDonough's work. With so much variance unexplained, Johnson admits that 'none of the

TABLE 4
Variance of adolescent female self-reported delinquency explained in five surveys

Authors	Sample	Independent variables	Percentage of variance
Offord et al (1984)	3294 mainly white All Ontario	13	21
Jensen and Eve (1976)	4000 Richmond, California	14	27 (White) 15 (Black)
Johnson (1979)	734 Seattle, Washington	10	28 (White) 38 (Asian)
Gomme (1985)	429 mainly white South Ontario	5	35 of status 27 criminal
Figueria-McDonough (1985)	1735 American mid-west	10	47 of status

NOTE: Sample figures include male and female, students aged twelve to eighteen. Variance of delinquency explained, however, is for female *only*, except in the Jensen and Eve study. In that study, sex was considered an independent variable. In all surveys the variance explained was statistically significant with $p < 0.001$.

theories appear to be doing very well' (1979: 116). Nor is it clear how processes, such as bonding, occur or why a girl performs poorly in school even if intelligent, and how these processes lead to higher rates of delinquency (West 1984: 98). Moreover, given the limits in understanding differences in girls, it is curious that so little attention is directed to discussing the striking degree of similarity in female conformity in the surveys.

Although sexual activity is still included in some self-report delinquency scales (e.g., Ageton 1983), correlational surveys do not focus on the sexual activity of the girls. Rather, we learn that sexual activity is neither central nor singularly featured in the lives of most girls. Instead, it is one activity most girls do sometimes.

But the apparent equal treatment of the girls in most surveys is misleading. For instance, in two large projects the authors collected data on males and females. Then they relegated the females to a footnote, and developed influential delinquency theories, such as the theory of bonding and social control, using *only* the data from males (Hirschi 1969: 35, footnote 3; LeBlanc 1983: 42, footnote 5). Subsequently these male-derived theories have been used in large surveys, including several listed in table 4, to compare girls equally to boys. As discussed later, both featuring and not attending to the implication of the girls' sexuality are problematic in understanding female delinquency and conformity.

Longitudinal Studies

The longitudinal design permits a more rigorous test of hypotheses by limiting sample, time, and memory biases (Rutter 1981). Five major longitudinal studies were listed previously in table 2. There is one clear finding from longitudinal studies: as disadvantages or stresses (particularly parental quarrelling, overcrowding, school failure, or few friends) accumulate, so do delinquencies, as well as ulcers, mental hospitalizations, and unemployment (Robins 1972; Loeber 1982; Roff and Wirt 1984; Werner and Smith 1982; Whitehead 1979).

Besides this one clear finding, little else is known. If the research acknowledges the presence of girls, the authors conclude that either: there is little evidence supporting statistically significant predictors of delinquency, such as early aggressivity, awkward temperament or mental dullness, parental deviance, inconsistent or inadequate parenting, and marital tension; or predictors, such as type of parenting or parents working both in and outside the home, operate differently for girls than for boys. For instance, Wadsworth (1979) followed 2035 British female babies up to their twenty-first birthday. He found that, besides poverty and disruption in the home before the sixth birthday, little else differentiated the female delinquents and non-delinquents. In addition, Wadsworth also found that over two-thirds of the girls from homes broken by separation or divorce do *not* become delinquent.

Further study from longitudinal research results should focus on why most youth do not become delinquent – even if they have relatively disadvantaged backgrounds. The concepts needing study include resilience, invulnerability, competence, and protective factors (Garmezy 1976; Werner and Smith 1982; Rutter 1985). (However, Wadsworth discourages further studies examining background factors of delinquents and non-delinquents.) Instead, the complex situations in which particular conforming and delinquent actions start, continue, or cease need to be investigated.

Contextual Research

This type of research makes the complexity of context central to an investigation. Participatory observation, supplemented with focused conversations, questionnaires, and document review, is a method favoured in contextual research (Becker 1970). Three aspects of contextual research sharpen our understanding of female delinquency and conformity. *First, contextual research emphasizes interaction.* In particular, the 'power of the contemporary environment in determining delinquency' is analysed (Clarke 1985: 509). This focus on interaction among people and their multiple environments is fundamental to professional helping theories and practices, such as systems theory or the ecological perspective (Collins 1986; Garbarino 1982; Yelaja 1985). A focus on interaction permeates the differential treatment theories for matching environments to female delinquents who vary in interpersonal maturity or cognitive complexity (Warren 1981; Reitsma-Street and Leschied 1988). Similarly, the interaction between school environments and students was the context for an exciting, massive study of twelve inner-city London secondary schools. Rutter found that, over four years, the worst students – defined academically and behaviourally – did as well in the best schools as the best students in the worst schools (Rutter 1980). (Although half of the 1487 students in the study were females, we do not know if the findings are sex specific.)

Second, contextual research clarifies the details in interactional processes. In particular, the choices, negotiations, and meaning or symbols that interacting participants actively use to shape their environments are examined. Since 'reality is subjective, or rather, subject to social definition' (Millman and Kanter 1987: 30), contextual research investigates the meanings of person-environment interactions. These meanings are studied according to the subjective interpretations of the various participants as they act, 'no matter how badly' (Blumer 1969: 15; Cicourel 1968). Previously I mentioned several case studies chronicling the subjective universe of girl delinquents, which the authors suggested was similar to the universe of most non-delinquent girls (e.g., Carlen 1985; Gagnon and Langélier-Biron 1982).

In a major participant observation study in 1984, Anne Campbell lived with three girl Manhattan street gangs for eighteen months. She sought to share in the actions, interactions, feelings, hopes, and understandings of one key member in each gang. Campbell analysed her observations within the context of how patriarchal families and poor communities constructed the categories of aggression, paid work, housework, female roles, physical beauty and sexuality, mothering, shopping, and deviance. In conclusion, she sadly wrote: 'the gang was no alternative life for them. It was a microcosm of the society beyond. Granted, it was one that had a public image of rebellion and excitement and offered a period of distraction ... But in the end, gang or no gang, the girls remained alone with their children, still trapped in poverty and in the cultural dictate of womanhood from which there was no escape' (1984: 266).

Another giant of contextual research is Edwin M. Schur. In his many writings he argues that 'deviance is not simply a function of a person's problematic behavior; rather, it emerges as *other people define and react* to a behavior *as being* problematic' (1984: 187; emphasis in original). In his latest book analysing the literature on gender, stigma, and social control, Schur focuses on the interactional processes that label women as deviant. In everyday language, custom, laws, and organizations, females are frequently stigmatized as deviant from gender norms. They are considered less assertive, smart, strong, and creative than males; as well, they are labelled less beautiful, thin, caring, demure, nurturing *or* too bold, sexual, or aggressive than is expected of females. Schur concludes that the consistent stigmatizing as well as objectifying processes are significant tools of social control. 'Given the numerous restrictions placed on female behavior, women are highly vulnerable to being deemed out of "place" ' (Schur 1984: 197).

Schur's work also exemplifies *the third aspect of contextual research, namely, deconstruction or unmasking*. By deconstruction I mean revealing and taking apart the words, the ideas, and – above all – the processes that we use every day to make sense of our lives. In particular, those hegemonic meanings of taken-for-granted realities, such as the family, are unmasked. In deconstruction we also look at how the dominant academic, political, and economic élites maintain the taken-for-granted realities. Thus, researchers search the material base, the values, the history and future in which interacting participants find meaning and in which the researchers are themselves situated (Poff 1985). For instance, in studying how a girl shuffling down the sidewalk is documented by police as a suspected shoplifter or how wife-battering is sanitized into family violence, Dorothy Smith argues that 'facts are constructed in a context of telling' (1974a: 258). Thus, Smith (1985) proposes that research must make visible the political, economic, gender, and value contexts in which oppressive or liberating realities are constructed.

This unmasking aspect of contextual research grapples with complex and ambiguous realities within ourselves as searchers and practitioners, and in the worlds we seek to understand. Returning to Schur, we find he tries to understand not just how stigmatizing occurs, but also why. Schur agrees with feminists who proclaim that in our society male is considered normal and female is deviant. He argues that 'imputed male superiority and male social dominance *require* female "deviance" and subordination' (1984: 47, emphasis added). The constructed female deviance and subordination, then, are used to justify stigmatizing and objectifying females, which, in turn, reinforces their subordination and continued male dominance.

Although Julia and Herman Schwendinger do not focus on the process of making females deviant as does Schur, their extensive contextual research on male and female subcultures contributes significantly to our understanding of female delinquency. Also, they contextualize their research even more broadly than Schur does. A brief summary of their thinking follows.

The Schwendingers completed four years of participant observations of Southern California working-, middle-, and upper-class adolescent subcultures in the 1960s, spent four years in theory building and testing with various representative groups, and then returned in the 1980s to the original observation sites (Schwendinger and Schwendinger 1976, 1985). Central to their understanding is a theory of political economy. The Schwendingers argue that patterns of delinquencies by both sexes and all classes are not so much reactions to stress or lack of commitment to desired norms. Rather, delinquent patterns in a society are logical aspects of 1 / male pursuit of profit and economic individualism, 2 / aggravated male competitiveness and violence, 3 / male private exchange and commodity relationships, 4 / conspicuous consumption, and 5 / fetishized female sexuality. These five aspects of political economy, however, are then mediated by the life-cycle needs, morals, and markets of peer societies.

Much of their theory then develops the relationships between peer societies and delinquency. The more inclusive a peer society is, such as the socialite or street-corner group, the more delinquent are its members; youths are less delinquent if they consistently participate in intellectual or artistic types of groups. 'Stradom' is a term the Schwendingers invented to describe the inclusive nature of those peer societies that, for a time, regulate status, dress, time, interests, pursuits, spending, and relationships of the groups' members into 'parasitic styles of life encouraged by the commodification of social relations' (1985: 127). Delinquencies change over the phases of group development, beginning with consumption and ending with illegal markets and economic criminality (1985: 183).

Females in all peer societies are relegated to instrumental functions, such as love, sex, and helping. They are under 'great pressure to organize their personalities around themselves as objects that are valued as sexually attractive things' (Schwendinger and Schwendinger 1985: 167). In the stradom societies of the middle to lower classes, the Schwendingers found that girls engage in a greater variety of delinquent and non-delinquent behaviours than do girls in the stradom societies of upper classes. But in order to resist the especially strong sexist exploitation of females in stradom peer societies of all classes, girls, have to form their own clubs. The stronger their own bonding and rules, in, for instance, the socialite sororities, the more girls avoid sexual exploitation. Unfortunately, the Schwendingers do not speak as much of the implications of the context of housework, procreation, and child-care as do other authors (Clarke et al 1975; Dorn and South 1982).

One last example of contextual research is necessary to bring out a more dynamic picture of female delinquency and conformity. Like Rutter (1980), Davies (1984) and Connell et al (1982) study schools, girls, and deviance. But more like Schur and the Schwendingers, Davies and Connell broadly contextualize their research.

Connell and his colleagues analysed extensive interviews and observations of 100 students and their parents and teachers in four Australian schools for middle- and working-class students. Embedded in their analyses is an understanding of the impact of male-dominated, capitalist democracies, and the necessity for inequality so that oppressive modes of production and procreation can be maintained to the advantage of some (1982: 32, 197). But Connell and colleagues also put into context the ambiguous contradictory nature of schooling within these societies – that is, some students, parents, and teachers negotiate equality, excellence, and conformity, primarily for middle to upper class boys (and exceptional students of all backgrounds), and other students, parents, and teachers negotiate to minimize the deviance from behavioural and academic norms expected of girls and working-class boys, a deviance that promises downward mobility (1982: 62). For instance, lower-class students develop relationships of compliance or pragmatism with schooling. They try to fit in without jeopardizing their integrity. Connell et al argue that the students unfortunately do not see that schools get more selective; instead, students see the work as getting harder and blame themselves (1982: 80–94).

With complex contextual research, the lives of girls are appreciated as projects according to Connell and colleagues. These lives-as-projects may be understandable, but not predictable. Girls create their lives by choices, but choices are made within the constraints of a capitalistic, patriarchial hegemony that is in flux itself, and continually in the process of dismantling and transforming (1982: 77).

Summary of Etiology

This review of selected rigorous case studies, surveys, longitudinal investigations, and contextual research intimates that far more is not known than known about female delinquency and conformity. None the less, I submit we have learned three things.

First, we clearly do not know whether girls who are committing or are accused of a few or many delinquencies are distinguishable from those who are not. The difference position was dominant theoretically since the turn of this century and still justifies most interventions as described below. More recent research, however, strongly proposes that essential commonalities outweigh the significance of background or personal differences.

Second, with few exceptions, the etiological studies feature, hide, or integrate the implications of the girls' sexuality in relation to their delinquent and conforming behaviours. Whatever the approach, however, analysing how sex is turned into gender appears fundamental to understanding female delinquency and conformity. In the concluding pages of this chapter I expand on this point and its implications for the study of sister pairs.

Third, the focus on interaction, subjectivity, and deconstruction in contextual research is necessary to clarify the difference-similarity debate and the implications of gender in relation to female delinquency.

Criminal-Justice Interventions

In this section, a review of the literature suggests two findings. First, our societies are very effective in preventing girls from beginning or continuing to commit delinquencies. Also, there are usually minimalist reactions to most female delinquencies. This positive finding is offset by a second, nasty, one. For years, and in many countries, systematic discrimination was, and continues to be, practised against female delinquents. One element of the discrimination is the blatant inadequacy and inappropriateness of legal, social, and economic services for charged females. This concern includes the necessity for serious research on program effectiveness. The other element is more insidious. Society minimizes certain behaviours only to concentrate tenaciously on deviations from standards of femininity.

Interventions to prevent or reduce delinquencies are listed in estimated descending order of known effectiveness and humanity:

1 economic-social, such as community organizing or guaranteed income for unemployed;
2 non-programs, such as informal family or school controls, or formal suspended sentences;
3 employment training and finding of actual jobs;
4 general or specific skills and help, e.g., developing athletic programs, finding shelters, or developing cognitive problem-solving;
5 providing supervisory or therapeutic relationships; such as probation
6 evaluating and developing appropriate custodial or therapeutic institutions

Least is known about program types 1 and 2: either their effectiveness or ineffectiveness, their relevance or irrelevance, may be assumed given females' low delinquency and reconviction rates. In general, however, economic-social programs directed towards disadvantaged communities appear to have positive effects on children and families, although their specific impact on females is not known. When these programs are in operation, delinquency and school drop-out rates decrease; frictions among teachers, police, and parents decline; recreation and social facilities, especially for boys, improve; and economic viability increases. Self-help organizations grow, sometimes sufficiently to challenge systematic disadvantage, and occasionally to win (e.g., Schlossman and Sedlak 1983; Short 1979; Weissman 1969; Wharf 1979).

Most is known about institutional care, to which fewer than 17.4 per cent of Canadian girl delinquents found guilty of charges were sentenced from 1962 through 1985, as noted in table 5. (Similar institutional sentencing rates are recorded for adult females [Boyle et al 1985: 149; Johnson 1987].) Although correctional institutionalization is not often prescribed, the picture is less benign if female rates of admissions to mental-health places are included. Also the admission rates of girls in the 1970s and 1980s to all types of private facilities increased dramatically (Lerman 1984: 12, Smart 1976; Schur 1984; Schwartz, Jackson-Beeck, and Anderson 1984).

According to the research, historical and contemporary institutions are no more effective in reducing recidivism, realigning 'deviant' personalities, or reducing school and work disabilities than far less intrusive interventions. They are, however, effective in seriously disrupting the lives of girls and reinforcing their economic and social vulnerabilities (American Bar Association 1977; Ackland 1982; Brenzel 1983; Carlen 1983; Dobash, Dobash, and Gutteridge 1986; Sarri 1976; Strange 1985; Watson 1980).

TABLE 5
Distribution of sentences for three populations of Canadian girls (numbers in percentages)

Sentence	1962 (645) 16- to 19-yr-olds	1972 (1733) 16- to 19-yr-olds	1985–6 (6082) 12- to 18-yr-olds
Probation	45.2	33.7	54.9
Custody	17.4	12.3	13.1
Fine	15.3	39.3	15.1
Suspended sentence or discharge	17.7	13.0	7.4
Community service order	0.0	0.0	7.4
Compensation, restitution	0.0	0.0	7.4
Treatment	0.0	0.0	1.1
Other	4.4	1.7	0.1
Total	100.0	100.0	100.0

SOURCES: Biron and Gauvreau (1984: 94); Canadian Centre for Justice Statistics, Part 1, Table 5 (1987).

Most programs for girls since the turn of the century have involved variations on the supervisory or counselling relationship – despite sporadic efficacy (e.g., Fischer 1978; Gendreau and Ross 1987; Lipton, Martinson, and Wilks 1975; Thomlinson 1981). For instance, one-half of Canadian convicted girls are sentenced to probation. But there are very few serious studies of probation or diversion for girls, and none for women. Also, the results of the limited research are equivocal (Boyle et al 1985: 131; Ross and Fabiano 1986: 47; Ross and Gendreau 1980; Stanley and Baginsky 1984). In one study, for example, 218 problem girls were referred to an indigenous professional trained in behavioural contracting for weekly contacts for one year. The girls' arrest records for three years were compared to those of a small group of sixty-seven controls. The problem girls were *more* than twice as likely to get arrested as the controls, even though fewer than one of five in each group were arrested during the three years (O'Donnell, Lydgate, and Fo 1980). In another example, more than two hundred girls were included in the sophisticated research carried out by the 1961–9 California Differential Treatment Project. The girls were randomly assigned to intensive community probation with matched workers or to regular institutional care followed by probation. The problem girls did not do substantially better but no worse on arrests and other indicators than the controls (Palmer 1980: 263). Most discouraging, in following up the girls a decade later, Warren found few girls from either the experimental or the control group who were doing well – so many were miserable, sick, on welfare, alone, and caring for unhappy children (1982).

The limited research on combining specific skill and employment interventions suggests some effectiveness. No matter what the activity, if the girls were learning a skill or earning adequate money, their competence consistently increased. Increased competence *appears* to reduce already low rates of female delinquency. These relationships were more prominent in the context of peer support groups and behavioural contracts (Ross and Fabiano 1986; Offord and Jones 1983; Urbain and Kendall 1980; Alexander and Parsons 1980; Sultan et al 1984; Quay and Love 1980). For instance, in their extensive review of correctional programs for females, Ross and Fabiano conclude that 'employment *with adequate salary* appears to be the critical determinant of successful rehabilitation' (1986: 26, emphasis added).

In short, very little is known about the efficacy of prevention or intervention programs for females. But, because few delinquencies of girls are discovered, and official social-control reactions appear muted, an argument has been made that girls are recipients of preferential treatment, sometimes called chivalry or paternalism (Parent 1986) – that is, the agents of criminal justice and social agencies expressly limit coercive interference in the lives of girls and appear to offer a helping hand when needed. Perhaps; but why is so little serious attention paid to what seems to work so well for girls? Why have not systematic attempts been made to extend the benefits of this limited intrusiveness to youth in general as Schur recommended several years ago in his classic book on *Radical Nonintervention* (1973)?

This restrained helpfulness masks a disturbing indifference. Studies consistently note that limited money, time, creativity, and research are devoted to educational, vocational, recreational, and community programs for females, and most correctional programs are irrelevant to the economic, social, and personal realities of female delinquents (American Bar Association 1977: Boyle et al 1985; Morris 1987; Rafter and Stanko 1982; Sarri 1983; Watson 1980). For instance, in their scathing analysis of Canadian correctional programs for females, Berzins and Cooper declare that it was 'assumed that a smaller-scale version of what was available for males would suit them, and when that smaller version proved to be uneconomical, even that was no longer considered' (1982: 405).

Female delinquency may warrant more attention, money, programs, and equality. A more sophisticated unmasking of the restrained-helpfulness approach to female delinquency, however, suggest that indifference is not just forgetfulness or economics. Rather, it reflects a sexist approach 'mediated by administrative and organizational factors' (Morris 1987: 101), which, on the one hand, ignores or minimizes many behaviours or needs of females, and, on the other, inflates those behaviours or needs that threaten female gender norms. Following is some of the evidence supporting this argument, presented in numerous studies since the early 1970s.

First, 50 to 75 per cent of girls caught are cautioned by police or referred to community agencies with no charges laid. If caught running away, selling sex, truant from school, or generally behaving in a disorderly fashion, however, girls *more* likely face arrest and conviction than if caught stealing or doing burglaries or assaults, especially if accompanied by males (Datesman and Scarpitti 1977: 63; Morris 1987: 97; Smart 1976: 64; Cheaney-Lind 1979: 24; Johnston, Kennedy, and Schuman 1987: 53; Teilman and Landry 1981).

Second, sentencing appears heavier if police, judges, or counsellors consider that the females are not respectable (e.g., go out with bad friends) or are not strongly tied to a parental or marital home with child-care responsibilities. This discrimination continues even after the severity of the offence and the criminal record are controlled (Geller 1980; Kruttschnitt 1982: 231; Morris 1987: 91; Wolfe, Cullen, and Cullen 1984).

Third, girls, like youth in general, mostly commit minor property, personal, or drug delinquencies, according to both official and self-report studies. For example, more than 80 per cent of charges laid against Canadian girls in 1980 and 1982 were of these minor types (Canadian Centre for Justice Statistics 1983: 39, 40; West 1984: 58, 59). Yet, until the 1980s, fewer than 40 per cent of girls in Canadian (and other) correctional institutions were admitted for serious delinquencies.

Finally, sentences, criminal justice procedures, and programs in community or institutional settings for delinquent girls are not just inadequate. Rather, the high referrals for home investigations and counselling; repeated gynecological examinations, the perusal of sexual history; the focus on positive familial relationships; the availability of cosmetology, housekeeping, and community volunteer services – *all* reinforce the expectation that the girls should learn to become 'good girls' according to prevailing assumptions of goodness in females (Brenzel 1983; Chesney-Lind 1979; Davidson 1982; Geller 1980; Strange 1985; Watson 1980).

Summary of Interventions

In summary, the evidence above, and Parent's review of fifty-four method-ologically sound studies (1986), indicate a minimalist approach is used towards girls to prevent, or to react to, most of their infrequent delinquen-cies. Very few girls are arrested; and most who are are cautioned, while some are referred to social agencies or put on probation.

The effectiveness of this approach in preventing or reducing female delinquency, however, is neither obvious nor comforting for several reasons. We know there is little research on the effectiveness of minimalist prevention or intervention programs and no concerted effort to apply the positive effects to boys. We also know that within the minimalist approach there is a systematic indifference to the needs of female delinquents. Furthermore, there is not an indifferent, or even minimalist approach to some delinquencies: those delinquencies and attitudes that are construed as deviating from standards expected of good girls are penalized with disproportionately harsh, intrusive interventions. Finally, the minimalist, indifferent approach, with its selective harshness, is not unique to female delinquency. As Bertrand exclaims, it 'reflet d'autres non-êtres, d'autres invisibilités, d'autres impuissances [de femmes]' (1979: 9). Theoretically and practically, the definitions of female and the restricted powers of females in Western societies appear fundamental to understanding not only interventions, but also, as previously discussed, the epidemiology and etiology of female delinquency.

The Questions in Female-Delinquency Theory and Practice

We know one fact: the consistently infrequent and minor nature of female delinquency in Canada and elsewhere. Although there are those who argue that sex as a variable in explaining youth delinquency is dwarfed by other variables (e.g., Jensen and Even 1976: 446), most assume that the nature of female delinquency is a *core* fact needing explanation in any substantial theory (Hagan 1985; Harris 1977; Hindelang 1979). But the agreement ends there.

Following is a summary list of questions raised by this review of the literature. Is it more important to explain conformity or delinquency? Are female delinquents more alike or more different than non-delinquents? Are there links between conformity and delinquency (Heidensohn 1985: 199) or do explanations differ (Morris 1987: 39)? Does it make sense to isolate the relatively weak predictors of delinquency from within-the-girl or background variables, or to unravel the complex web of interactional, subjective, and structural contexts? Finally, are there relationships among 1 / the predominant minimalist approach of criminal justice to female delinquency, 2 / the persistent variations in organizational processing by type of delinquency, race, and background, and 3 / the daily insidious labelling of females as deviant from gender norms (Schur 1984)?

In short, we know little. But we are also not sure what the puzzle actually is. Although no longer a wasteland, research in female-delinquency theory and practice is just beginning to spawn concepts, hypotheses, and models that compete for attention and testing. It is a time for critical discourse – to sort out the values and knowledge pointing to which puzzles, evidence, and solutions are worth pursuing (Kuhn 1970: 6)

The Gender Debate

Through this chapter, the girls' sex was central to delinquency theories and practice. Whether featured or conspicuouly absent, it appears that the potential of females to bear babies is somehow fundamental to understanding not just delinquency and conformity, but also how we theorize, construct laws, and intervene with females.

The older theoretical voices in the debate, as well as many contemporary-practice voices, understand female delinquency in its naturalness and tendency toward 'normal femininity.' For example, Felice and Offord conclude in their review of the female-delinquency literature: 'The girl delinquent is generally a lonely girl with a warped concept of feminized identification, probably stemming from a poor, inadequate relationship with her mother' (1975: 272). The assumption is that delinquent females need help to adapt to their 'feminine' nature, to stop acting aggressively like males, to take care of their households and children, and to exchange sexual favours for domesticity, not cash (West 1984: 101).

The newer voices in the debate do not accept femininity as a natural characteristic of females. Rather, they see it as problematic. Discriminatory sentencing patterns and inadequate, indifferent interventions are rooted in femininity norms that assume 'a male's sexual behaviour was only one facet of his total character, whereas a female was actually defined by her sexuality' (Pollock 1978: 25). But the girls' sex still is central to the debate since it powerfully affects the behaviours of and reactions to girls.

These newer voices posit the debate in the context of sex turned into gender. Gender is the product of converting the biological categories of male and female into the cultural categories of masculine and feminine.

Despite the striking variations in gender characteristics over time and place, persons gendered as females are mostly less favoured than males (Broverman et al 1972). For centuries we have turned the ability of females to bear children into a liability for them. In Western societies, we have cultivated ideals of femininity based on caring, sensitivity, beauty, and passivity. These ideals are then used to justify economic, social, and political arrangements that systematically ignore the needs, uniqueness, and aspirations of females, but still maintain their domestic, sexual services within households ruled by males (Dixon 1980: 3; Jaggar 1983; Oakley 1981; O'Brien 1981).

Thus, these newer voices in the debate argue that delinquency and conformity cannot be analysed without understanding gender. Smart critiques the older voices who did not make gender problematic: they 'do not address the nature and form of social structures which place women in a subordinate and dependent position, thereby ensuring that the majority of girls and women will require material and psychological support and protection as a result of the structural limitation of access to the psychic and material resources necessary to provide for self-sufficiency and independence' (Smart 1976: 65).

Although the construction of gender is central, the newer voices vary in complexity and methodology. There are variations in how the triple articulation of female delinquency is theorized, as it is situated within three contexts: in relation to gender, in relation to age, and in relation to class and race (adapted from Clarke et al 1975: 15). There is another difference – reflecting a crucial struggle that feminist researchers are currently debating (e.g., exchange between Vickers and Eichler or non-sexist research 1987: 3–6). On the one hand, there are those, such as Figueria-McDonough (1987), Hagan (1985), Hindelang (1979), Leonard (1982), Morris (1987), and the Schwendingers (1985), who do research on both boys and girls and expressly aim to build a transformed 'non-sexist' theory of delinquency to account for sex differences that occur in a gendered (and class) society. On the other hand, there are those who focus only on girls, arguing we are far away from hypothesizing a grand 'unisex' theory (Mann 1984: 276) and that we need an 'autonomous approach' (Heidensohn 1985: 200).

In this chapter I have chosen the gender-specific approach, and thus have focused on girls. One reason is that we still have so much to learn about how, why, and when females do or do not commit delinquencies. We need good case studies, surveys, longitudinal research – all within the context of women's experiences. Another reason for the gender-specific approach is that females are usually examined in relation to males, or as males want females to be. Females have 'lower subcultural deviance' than males; females have the 'same patterns of subcultural deviance' as males; female delinquents are 'more emotional' than males; female offenders are more sexually promiscuous than they should be according to males. For instance, when Jensen and Eve (1976) unearthed the data on females that Hirschi had collected but had not used to develop his social-control theory of delinquency, they did *not* develop new theory from the data. Instead, Jensen and Eve (and others, such as Hindelang [1979]) compared the females to the males on the basis of concepts already generated from the males.

This pattern of seeing females as similar to, equal to, different from, less than, better than, the *standard of male behaviours, thoughts, and theories* is pervasive in all our sciences, laws, and practices (Spender 1985; Keller 1985). Thus, to understand the Canadian Young Offenders Act in relation to females and to contribute new ideas that may eventually transform existing practices for *both* males and females, I believe we need to consciously avoid filling our minds with the old, tenacious comparisons. As Bleneky and associates wrote: 'The male experience has been so powerfully articulated that we believed we would hear the patterns in women's voices more clearly if we held at bay the powerful templates men have etched in the literature and in our minds' (1986: 9).

Impact of the Young Offenders Act on Female Delinquency

The reason for changing the Juvenile Delinquents Act to the Young Offenders Act included the struggle to combine more equality before the law, less intrusiveness of state agencies into the lives of youths and their families, and more opportunities for accountability of all participants, especially the young offender (Bala and Clarke 1981; Macdonald 1985; Wilson 1982).

The many changes incorporated into the YOA have been reviewed elsewhere in this book. For example, to increase equality in criminal-justice practices, such as similar consequences for females and males convicted of minor offences, YOA provisions include specific charges for Criminal Code offences, the elimination of status offences, a common age range across Canada, access to due process, checks on discretion in decision making, and the principle of determinate proportionality in sentencing.

Has the YOA helped to correct the sex discrimination in criminal-justice practices? Are male and female youths held equally responsible for their behaviours and given similar treatment at all stages of the proceedings? As yet there are no convincing Canadian data supporting or disproving the press for equality. For one reason, changes such as the elimination of status offences and introduction of due-process practices have been occurring for some time in various provinces, and the YOA formalized and extended those changes to all of Canada (Trépanier 1983; Weiler 1978). Furthermore, procedures for collecting data have changed over time, making time analyses problematic; for instance, offences were not broken down by sex in official Canadian data during the early 1980s (Biron and Gauvreau 1984).

Most important to consider, however, are the multitude of minutiae in everyday organizational practices and personnel within the police, courts, agencies, and institutions that are not easily standardized and do not accurately reflect changes in official goals (Bala and Corrado 1985; Cicourel 1968; LaPraire 1987; Krisberg, Litsky, and Schwartz 1984; Teilman and Landry 1981). Research in other countries indicates that repeal of status offences and introduction of due process has had a positive impact on *decreasing incarceration of girls in* public correctional institutions. However, the change is fragile, as Chesney-Lind (1988: 157) argues, since there are also indications that status offences are being relabelled as criminal offences or medical problems (Boyle et al 1985: 144; Sarri 1983: 323). Diversion programs outside of the criminal-justice system are expanding, especially for girls who commit very minor offences or no offences, without a corresponding decrease in probation, community-service orders, or custody sentences. For example, Adler (1984: 404) reported that more than half of the referrals to California diversion programs were for status offences or general family troubles. Most disturbing is the doubling, even tripling, of female admission rates from the 1970s to 1980s to private residential programs on the recommendations of professionals or parents (Lerman 1984: Schwartz, Jackson-Beeck, and Anderson 1984; Warren 1986).

Thus, evidence and arguments in this chapter point to the centrality of gender in understanding female delinquency and reactions to it in languages, laws, attitudes, and organizational practices. We need to analyse thoroughly the totality of the YOA in relation to gender in order to grasp its intended and unintended impact. For instance, Susan Edwards's theme in her analysis of the female suspect, defendant, and offender in British law and criminal justice system is that 'gender assumptions regarding the criminality of women [are] built into the definition, procedures, and discretionary decision-making' (1984: 3).

In Canada, Boyle and her colleagues (1985) have begun this task in relation to adult women and the criminal-justice system. For instance, they argue that the use of fines and financial-restitution programs as sentences should take into account the institutionalized economic inequality females face. For young females, do probation officers and judges take into account the heavier household obligations females carry when determining hours of community service?

As a final point, the centrality of gender is essential to an understanding of the 'more control than care and more form than content' provisions of Ontario's past and current laws for delinquency and neglect (Reitsma-Street 1986). This fact goes beyond female delinquents and includes gender as it affects both males and females and their families. In the YOA a young person has 'a right to the least possible interference with freedom that is consistent with the protection of society having regards to the needs of young people and the interest of their families' (s. 3 [1][f]). This minimal intervention may have built on the minimalist approach usually used with females and expanded now to males. It also draws on the concern that the law and professionals are but 'blunt instruments' in helping families to raise their children (Goldstein, Freud, and Solnit 1973: 8). Furthermore, the restraint is a logical companion to the belief that families are the 'most satisfactory environment for children' (Canadian Council on Children and Youth 1978: 2) and the belief that parents 'view the freedom to bring up their own children without undue interference from the state not only as a legal right but a fundamental moral right deeply rooted in the traditions of our community' (Ontario Law Reform Commission 1973: 64).

But, it is the attention and the attempt at minimal intervention and support for families that are commanded, not the services. Most of the mandatory and funded YOA provisions deal with the forms of due process, such as access to a lawyer, or society's right to protection, such as fingerprinting and custody sentences. Provisions and funding reflecting minimal intervention or support for the family, such as alternative measures, intermittent custody, decreases in custody programs, treatment orders, courts sitting in the evenings, and crime-prevention programs, are optional, subject to the discretion of the attorney general or her or his delegate, as well as the participants in the process. Perhaps it is not surprising, then, that the funding and energy have gone into the mandatory court processes and correctional programs rather than into the discretional alternative dispositions or treatment programs for youths and their families (Gabor, Greene, and McCormick 1986; Leschied and Gendreau 1986; Weiler and Ward 1985).

One way to understand the strong rhetoric for minimal intervention but discretionary provisions and funding is to examine the essential relationship between gender, the family, and children in our culture. A detailed development of this relationship is a task for other books (e.g., Barrette and McIntosh 1982; Grubb and Lazerson 1982; Reitsma-Street 1986; Smith 1981; Wilson 1982). In brief, the YOA and its implications depend on the private family to implement most of its principles at minimal costs to the state. It is the personal responsibility of the family and the unpaid labour of primarily females to care for, protect, maintain, and supervise the children. When the notion of females as primarily child-rearers and homemakers was firmly entrenched at the turn of the century, the Juvenile Delinquents Act did not appear to threaten the autonomy of the family: rather this law was used to replace a few 'bad' families or to force others to own up to their responsibilities (Scott 1908). Currently, the construction of female roles in the family is more fluid with, for instance, birth control and participation in the paid labour market (Eichler 1983). Hence, more rhetoric and provisions are included in the Young Offenders Act to limit interventions by time and scope so that the state minimizes interference in the family's – i.e., primarily the females' – responsibilities for maintenance, supervision, and intimacy (Ontario Ministry of Community and Social Services 1982).

Concluding Comments

It is doubtful if the Young Offenders Act has sparked a revolution in the treatment of Canadian female young offenders. In this review of the epidemiology, etiology, and interventions, the evidence indicates a minimalist approach in criminal-justice policy, and practice mostly ignores the infrequent, minor crimes committed by females but harshly reacts to deviations from norms of femininity.

The construction of gender was the concept introduced in this chapter to debate the minimalist, contradictory, unequal approach to female delinquency through most of this century. The 1984 YOA aims to promote more fairness and accountability in juvenile justice, as well as attention to needs of youth. However, until we grapple with the fundamental implications of gender in relation to laws, policies, and practices, it is unlikely the YOA will achieve its aims for Canadian young females.

Notes

1 Calculations are based on the number of fifteen-year-old Canadian females charged, divided by the total number of fifteen-year-old Canadian females. The age was chosen since the *highest* rate of charges laid was against this age group; hence, the calculation for delinquency in the population-at-risk is as high as possible.
2 Sepsi does not emphasize the similarities as I have. He focuses on the differences between the recidivists and non-recidivists, especially the family background. He constructs a six-factor checklist to aid in early identification of recidivism.

References

Achenbach, Thomas M., and Craig S. Edelbrock. 1981. *Behavioral Problems and Competencies Reported by Parents of Normal and Disturbed Children Aged Four thru Sixteen*. Monographs of the Society for Research in Child Development, No. 188. Chicago: University of Chicago Press

Ackland, John W. 1982. *Girls in Care: A Case Study of Residential Treatment*. Hampshire, UK: Gower

Adams, Susan Gillis. 1978. *The Female Offender: A Statistical Perspective*. Ottawa: Solicitor General

Adelberg, Ellen, and Claudia Currie, eds. 1987. *Too Few to Count: Canadian Women in Conflict with the Law*. Vancouver: Press Gang

Adler, Christine 1984. 'Gender bias in juvenile diversion,' *Crime and Delinquency* 30 (3): 400–14

Adler, Freda, and Rita James Simon, eds. 1979. *The Criminology of Deviant Women*. Boston: Houghton Mifflin

Ageton, Suzanne S. 1983. 'The dynamics of female delinquency, 1976–1980,' *Criminology* 21 (4): 555–84

Alexander, J.F., and B.V. Parsons. 1980. 'Short-term behavioral intervention with delinquent families: Impact on family process and recidivism,' in R.R. Ross and P. Gendreau, eds, *Effective Correctional Treatment*, 129–41. Toronto: Butterworths

American Bar Association. 1977. *Little Sisters and the Law*. Washington, DC: Commission on Correctional Facilities and Services, Female Offender Resource Centre

Bala, Nicholas C., and Kenneth L. Clarke. 1981. *The Child and the Law*. Toronto: McGraw-Hill Ryerson

Bala, Nicholas, and Raymond Corrado. 1985. *Juvenile Justice in Canada: A Comparative Study*, Technical Report, TRS No. 5. Ottawa: Communications Group, Ministry of the Solicitor General

Barrett, Michelle, and Mary McIntosh. 1982. *The Anti-Social Family*. London: Verso

Becker, Howard S. 1970. *Sociological Work: Method and Substance*. New Brunswick, NJ: Aldine

Belenky, Mary Field, Blythe McVicker Clinchy, Nancy Rule Goldberger, and Jill Mattuck Tarule. 1986. *Women's Ways of Knowing: The Development of Self, Voice, and Mind*. New York: Basic

Bertrand, Marie-Andrée. 1979. *La femme et le crime*. Montreal: L'Aurore

Berzins, L., and S. Cooper. 1982. 'The political economy of correctional planning for women: The case of the bankrupt bureaucracy,' *Canadian Journal of Criminology* 24 (4): 399–416

Biron, Louise. 1980. 'An overview of self-reported delinquency in a sample of girls in the Montreal area,' in A. Morris and L. Gelsthrope, eds, *Women and Crime*, 1–16. Cambridge: Institute of Criminology

Biron, Louise, and Danielle Gauvreau. 1984. *Portrait of Youth Crime*. Report A84–4. Ottawa: Secretary of State, Policy-Coordination Analysis and Management Systems Branch, Social Trends Analysis Directorate

Blumer, Herbert. 1969. *Symbolic Interactionism Perspective and Method*. Englewood Cliffs, NJ: Prentice-Hall

Bottoms, A.E. 1974. 'On the decriminalization of English juvenile courts,' in R. Hood, ed, *Crime, Criminology and Public Policy*, 319–45. New York: The Free Press

Bour, Daria S., Jeanne P. Young, and Rodney Henningsen. 1984. 'A comparison of delinquent prostitutes and delinquent non-prostitutes on self-concept,' *Journal of Offender Counseling, Services and Rehabilitation* 9 (1–2): 89–102

Bowker, Lee H. 1978. *Women, Crime, and the Criminal Justice System*. Lexington, MA: D.C. Heath

Bowker, L.H., and M.W. Klein. 1983. 'The etiology of female juvenile delinquency and gang membership: A test of psychological and social structure explanations,' *Adolescence* 18 (Winter): 739–51

Box, Stephen, and Chris Haly. 1984. 'Liberation/emancipation, economic marginalization, or less chivalry,' *Criminology* 22 (4): 473–97

Boyer, Debra, and Jennifer James. 1982. 'Easy money: Adolescent involvement in prostitution,' in S. Davidson, ed, *Justice for Young Women*, 73–97. Seattle, WA: New Directions for Young Women

Boyle, Christine, Marie-Andre Bertrand, Celine Lacerte-Lamontagne, and Rebecca

Shamai. 1985. *A Feminist Review of Criminal Law*. Ottawa: Minister of Supply and Services

Brenzel, Barbara M. 1983. *Daughters of the State: A Social Portrait of the First Reform School for Girls in North America, 1856-1905*. Cambridge, MA: MIT Press

Broverman, Inge K., Susan Raymond Voget, Donald M. Broverman, Franke E. Clarkson, and Paul S. Rosenkrantz. 1972. 'Sex-role stereotypes: A current appraisal,' *Journal of Social Issues* 28 (2): 59–78

Byles, John A. 1969. *Alienation Deviance and Social Control: A Study of Adolescents in Metro Toronto*. Toronto: Interim Research Project on Unreached Youth

Campbell, Anne. 1981. *Girl Delinquents*. Oxford: Basil Blackwell

– 1984. *The Girls in the Gang: A Report from New York City*. Oxford: Basil Blackwell

Canadian Centre for Justice Statistics. 1983. *Juvenile Delinquents, 1982*. Ottawa: Statistics Canada, Ministry of Supply and Services

– 1987. *Youth Court Statistics Preliminary Tables 1985-1986*, rev. version. Ottawa: Statistics Canada, Department of Justice

Canadian Council on Children and Youth. 1978. *Admittance Restricted: The Child as Citizen in Canada*. Ottawa

Canter, Rachelle J. 1982. 'Sex differences in self-report delinquency,' *Criminology* 20 (3&4): 373–93

Carlen, Pat. 1983. *Women's Imprisonment: A Study in Social Control*. London: Routledge & Kegan Paul

– 1985. *Criminal Women: Autobiographical Accounts*. Cambridge: Polity Press

Cernkovich, Stephen A., and Peggy C. Giordano. 1979. 'A comparative analysis of male and female delinquency,' *Sociological Quarterly* 20 (1): 131–45

Chesney-Lind, Meda. 1979. 'Re-discovering Lilith: Misogyny and the "new" female crime,' in C.T. Griffiths and M. Nance, eds, *The Female Offender*, 1–35. Burnaby, BC: Simon Fraser University, Criminology Research Centre

– 1988. 'Girls and status offenses: Is juvenile justice still sexist?' *Criminal Justice Abstracts*, March: 144–65

Cicourel, Aaron V. 1968. *The Social Organization of Juvenile Justice*. New York: Wiley

Clarke, John, Stuart Hall, Tony Jefferson, and Brian Roberts. 1975. 'Subcultures, cultures and class,' in S. Hall and T. Jefferson, eds, *Resistance through Rituals*, New York: Holmes and Meier

Clarke, R.V.G. 1985. 'Jack Tizard memorial lecture: Delinquency, environment and intervention,' *Journal of Child Psychology and Psychiatry* 26 (4): 505–23

Collins, Barbara G. 1986. 'Defining feminist social work,' *Social Work* 31 (3): 214–19

Connell, R.W., D.J. Ashenden, S. Kessler, and G.W. Dowsett. 1982. *Making the Difference: Schools, Families and Social Division*. Sydney, London, Boston: George Allen and Unwin

Cowie, John, Valerie Cowie, and Elliot Slater. 1968. *Delinquency in Girls*. London: Heinemann

Crites, Laura. 1976. 'Women offenders: Myth vs. reality,' in L. Crites, ed, *The Female Offender*, 33–44. Lexington, MA: Lexington Books

Datesman, Susan K., and Frank R. Scarpitti. 1977. 'Unequal protection for males and females in the juvenile courts,' in T.N. Ferdinand, ed, *Juvenile delinquency*, 59–78. Sage Research Progress Series in Criminology, Vol. 2. Beverly Hills, CA: Sage

Davidson, Sue, ed. 1982. *Justice for Young Women: Close-up on Critical Issues*. Seattle, WA: New Directions for Young Women

Davies, Lynn. 1984. *Pupil Power: Deviance and gender in School*. London and Philadelphia: Falmer Press

Dixon, Marlene. 1980. *The Future of Women*. San Francisco: Synthesis

Dobash, Russell P., R. Emerson Dobash, and Sue Gutteridge. 1986. *The Imprisonment of Women*. Oxford, UK: Basil Blackwell

Dorn, Nicholas, and Nigel South. 1982. *Of Males and Markets: A Critical Review of 'Youth Culture' Theory*. Queensway, Enfield, Middlesex: Middlesex Polytechnic

Edwarfds, Susan M. 1984. *Women on Trial: A Study of the Female Suspect, Defendant and Offender in the Criminal Law and Criminal Justice System*. Manchester: Manchester University Press

Eichler, Margrit. 1983. *Families in Canada Today: Recent Changes and Their Policy Consequences*. Toronto: Gage

Farrington, David P. 1981. 'The prevalence of convictions,' *British Journal of Criminology* 21 (2): 173–5

Felice, Marianne, and David R. Offord. 1975. 'Girl delinquency – a review,' in Ruth Cavan, ed, *Readings in Juvenile Delinquency*, 3rd ed. 267–78. Philadelphia: J.B. Lippincott Company

Figueira-McDonough, Josefina. 1985. 'Are girls different? Gender discrepancies between delinquent behavior and control,' *Child Welfare* 64 (3): 273–89

– 1987. 'Discrimination or sex differences? Criteria for evaluating the juvenile justice system's handling of minor offenses,' *Crime and Delinquency* 33 (2): 403–24

Figueria-McDonough, Josefina, William H. Barton, and Rosmary C. Sarri. 1981. 'Normal deviance: Gender similarities in adolescent subcultures,' in Marguerite Q. Warren, ed, *Comparing Female and Male Offenders*, 17–45. Beverly Hills, CA: Sage

Fischer, Joel. 1978. 'Does anything work?' *Journal of Social Service Research* 1 (3): 215–43

Gabor, Peter, Ian Greene, and Peter McCormick. 1986. 'The Young Offenders Act in Alberta: Changes in services during the first year,' *The Social Worker* 54 (4): 150–4

Gagnon, Rosette, and Louise Langélier-Biron. 1982. *Les filles en marge: Paroles et réflexions*. Rapport No. 6. Montreal: Université de Montréal, Groupe de Recherche sur l'inadaptation juvénile

Garbarino, James. 1982. *Children and Families in the Social Environment*. New York: Aldine Publishing

Garmezy, Norman. 1976. 'The experimental study of vulnerable and invulnerable children,' in A. Davids, ed, *Child Personality and Psychopathology*, Vol. 2, 171–216. New York: Wiley

Geller, Gloria Rhea. 1980. 'Streaming of Males and Females in the Juvenile Justice System.' Doctoral diss., Ontario Institute for Studies in Education, Toronto

– 1987. 'Young women in conflict with the law,' in E. Adelberg and C. Currie, eds, *Too Few to Count*, 113–126. Vancouver: Press Gang

Gendreau, Paul, and Robert R. Ross. 1987. 'Revivification of rehabilitation: Evidence from the 1980s,' *Justice Quarterly* 4 (3): 349–407

Gibbons, T.C.N. 1971. 'Female offenders,' *British Journal of Hospital Medicine* 6: 279–86

Glueck, Sheldon, and Eleanor T. Glueck. 1934. *Five Hundred Delinquent Women*. New York: Knopf

Goldstein, Joseph, Anna Freud, and Albert J. Solnit. 1973. *Beyond the Best Interests of the Child*. New York: Free Press

Gomme, Ian M. 1985. 'Predictors of status and criminal offences among male and female adolescents in an Ontario community,' *Canadian Journal of Criminology* 27 (2): 147–60

Gomme, Ian M., Mary E. Morton, and Gordon W. West. 1984. 'Rates, types and patterns of male and female delinquency in an Ontario county,' *Canadian Journal of Criminology* 26 (3): 313–24

Grubb, W. Norton, and Marvin Lazerson. 1982. *Broken Promises: How Americans Fail Their Children*. New York: Basic Books

Hagan, John. 1985. *Modern Criminology: Crime, Criminal Behaviour and Its Control*. New York: McGraw-Hill

Harris, Anthony R. 1977. 'Sex and theories of deviance: Toward a functional theory of deviant type-scripts,' *American Sociological Review* 42 (1): 3–16

Heidensohn, Frances. 1985. *Women and Crime*. London: Macmillan

Hindelang, Michael J. 1979. 'Sex differences in criminal activity,' *Social Problems* 27: 143–56

Hindelang, Michael J., Travis Hirschi, and Joseph G. Weis. *Measuring Delinquency*. Beverly Hills, CA: Sage

Hirschi, Travis. 1969. *Causes of Delinquency*. Berkeley and Los Angeles: University of California Press

Hoffman-Bustamante, Dale. 1973. 'The nature of female criminality,' *Issues in Criminology* 8 (2): 117–36

Jaggar, Alison M. 1983. *Feminist Politics and Human Nature*. Totowa, NJ: Rowman and Allanheld

Jensen, Gary J., and Raymond Eve. 1976. 'Sex differences in delinquency,' *Criminology* 13 (4): 427–48

Johnson, Holly. 1986. *Women and Crime in Canada*. TRS No. 9. Ottawa: Communications Group, Solicitor General of Canada

– 1987. 'Getting the facts straight: A statistical overview,' in E. Adelberg and C. Currie, eds, *Too Few to Count*, 23–46. Vancouver: Press Gang

Johnson, Richard E. 1979. *Juvenile Delinquency and Its Origins*. Cambridge: Cambridge University Press

Johnston, Janet B., Thomas D. Kennedy, and I. Gayle Shuman. 1987. 'Gender differences in the sentencing of felony offenders,' *Federal Probation* 51 (1): 49–55

Keating, Colleen. 1984. 'Female Delinquency and Social Control.' Master's thesis, Centre of Criminology, University of Toronto

Keller, Evelyn Fox. 1985. *Reflections on Gender and Science*. New Haven and London: Yale University Press

Konopka, Gisela. 1966. *The Adolescent Girl in Conflict*. Englewood Cliffs, NJ: Prentice-Hall

– 1976. *Young Girls: A Portrait of Adolescence*. Englewood Cliffs, NJ: Prentice-Hall

Krisberg, Barry, Paul Litsky, and Ira Schwartz. 1984. 'Youth in confinement: Justice by geography,' *Journal Research in Crime and Delinquency* 21 (2): 153–81

Kruttschnitt, Candace. 1982. 'Respectable women and the law,' *The Sociological Quarterly* 23 (Spring): 221–34

Kuhn, Thomas S. 1970. 'Logic of discovery or psychology of research? Reflections on my critics,' in Imre Lakatos and Alan Musgrave, eds, *Criticism and the Growth of Knowledge*, 1–23, 231. Cambridge: Cambridge University Press

Lambert, Leah R., and Patrick G. Madden. 1976. 'The adult female offender: The road from institution to community life,' *Canadian Journal of Criminology and Corrections* 18 (4): 319–31

LaPrairie, Carol. 1987. 'Native women and crime in Canada: A theoretical model,' in E. Adelberg and C. Currie, eds, *Too Few to Count*, Vancouver: Press Gang

LeBlanc, Marc. 1983. 'Delinquency as an Epiphenomenon of Adolescence,' in R.R. Corrado, M. LeBlance, and J. Trépanier, eds, *Current Issues in Juvenile Justice*, 31–48. Toronto: Butterworths

Leonard, Eileen B. 1982. *Women, Crime and Society: A Critique of Theoretical Criminology*. New York: Longman

Lerman, Paul. 1975. *Community Treatment and Social Control: A Critical Analysis of*

Juvenile Correctional Policy. Chicago: University of Chicago Press

– 1984. 'Child welfare, the private sector and community-based corrections,' *Crime and Delinquency* 30 (1): 5–38

Leschied, Alan, and Paul Gendreau. 1986. 'The declining role of rehabilitation in Canadian juvenile justice: Implications of underlying theory in the YOA,' *Canadian Journal of Criminology* 28 (3): 303–14

Lipton, D., R.M. Martinson, and J. Wilks. 1975. *The Effectiveness of Correctional Treatment: A Survey of Treatment Evaluation Studies*. New York: Praeger

Loeber, Rolf. 1982. 'The stability of antisocial and delinquent child behaviour: A review,' *Child Development* 53: 1431–46

Long, Gary T., Faye E. Sultan, Stephan A. Kiefer, and David M. Schrum. 1984. 'The psychological profile of the female first offender and recidivist: A comparison,' *Journal of Offender Counseling, Services and Rehabilitation* 9 (1–2): 119–24

Lowman, J. 1987. 'Taking young prostitutes seriously,' *Canadian Review of Sociology and Anthropology* 24 (1): 99–116

MacDonald, John. 1985. 'Justice for young persons and the Young Offenders Act,' *Canadian Social Work Review* 2: 64–82

Mann, Coramae Richey. 1984. *Female Crime and Delinquency*. University, AL: University of Alabama Press

Millman, Marcia, and Rosabeth Moss Kanter. 1987. 'Introduction to another voice: Feminist perspectives on social life and social science,' in S. Harding, ed, *Feminism and Methodology*, 29–36. Bloomington: Indiana University Press

Morris, Allison. 1987. *Women, Crime and Criminal Justice*. Oxford: Basil Blackwell

Mukherjee, S.K., and R.W. Fitzgerald. 1981. 'The myth of rising female crime,' in S.K. Mukherjee and J. Scutt, eds, *Women and Crime*, 127–66. North Sydney, NSW: George Allen and Unwin

Nease, Barbara. 1966. 'Measuring juvenile delinquency in Hamilton,' *Canadian Journal of Criminology and Corrections* 8 (2): 133–45

Oakley, Ann. 1981. 'Interviewing women: A contradiction in terms,' in Helen Roberts, ed, *Doing Feminist Research*, 30–61. London: Routledge and Kegan Paul

O'Brien, Mary. 1981. *The Politics of Reproduction*. Boston, London, and Henley: Routledge and Kegan Paul

O'Donnell, C.R., T. Lydgate, and W.S. Fo. 1980. 'Community-based programs for juvenile offenders,' in R.R. Ross and P. Gendreau, eds, *Effective Correctional Treatment*, 159–68. Toronto: Butterworths

Offord, David R., and Marshall B. Jones. 1983. 'Skill development: A community intervention program for the prevention of anti-social behavior,' in S.B. Guze, F.J. earls, and J.E. barrett, eds, *Childhood Psychopathology and Development*, 165–85. New York: Raven Press

Offord, David R., R.J. Alder, M.H. Boyle, and J.A. Byles. 1984. 'The Ontario Child

Health Study: Prevalence and Selected Correlates of Conduct Disorder.' Presentation at the Joint Meeting of the American and Canadian Academies of Child Psychiatry, Toronto, October

Offord, David R., and Mary F. Poushinsky. 1981. 'School performance, IQ and female delinquency,' *International Journal of Social Psychiatry*, 27: 53–62

Ontario Law Reform Commission. 1973. *Report on Family Law – Children* (Part III). Toronto: Ministry of Attorney General

Ontario Ministry of Community and Social Services. 1982. *The Children's Act: A Consultation Paper.* Toronto

Palmer, Ted. 1980. 'The Youth Authority's community treatment project,' in R.R. Ross and P. Gendreau, eds, *Effective Correctional Treatment*, 255–78. Toronto: Butterworths

Parent, C. 1986. 'Actualités and bibliographics: La protection chevalresque ou les représentations masculines du traitement des femmes dan la justice pénale,' *Déviance et Société* 10 (2): 147–75

Poff, Deborah C. 1985. 'Feminism flies too: The principles of a feminist epistemology,' *Resources for Feminist Research* 14 (3): 6–9

Pollack, Otto. 1950. *The Criminality of Women*. Philadelphia: University of Pennsylvania Press

Pollock, Joy. 1978. 'Early theories of female criminality,' in L.H. Bowker, ed, *Women, Crime and the Criminal Justice System*, 25–55. Lexington, MA: D.C. Heath

Quay, H.C., and C.T. Love. 1980. 'The effect of a juvenile diversion program on rearrests,' in R.R. Ross and P. Gendreau, eds, *Effective Correctional Treatment*, 75–90. Toronto: Butterworths

Rae-Grant, N.J., M.H. Boyle, D.R. Offord, and H. Thomas. 1984. 'The Buffering Effect of Protective Factors in Reducing the Incidence of Common Behavioral and Emotional Disorders in Childhood. Presentation at joint meeting of the American and Canadian Academies of Child Psychiatry, Toronto, October

Rafter, Nicole Haln, and Elizabeth Anne Stanko, eds. 1982. *Judge Lawyer Victim Thief Women: Gender Roles and Criminal Justice*. Boston: Northeastern University Press

Reitsma-Street, Marge. 1984. 'Policy Formulation in the Canadian Juvenile Justice System: The Transformation of the 1980 *Juvenile Delinquents Act* into the 1982 *Young Offenders Act*.' Unpublished manuscript, Centre of Criminology, University of Toronto

– 1986. *A Feminist Analysis of Ontario Laws for Delinquency and Neglect: More Control than Care*, Working Papers on Social Welfare in Canada, No. 18. Toronto: University of Toronto, Faculty of Social Work

Reitsma-Street, Marge, and Alan Leschied. 1988. 'Conceptual level matching model in corrections,' *Criminal Justice and Behavior* 15 (1): 92–108

Reitsma-Street, Marge, David R. Offord, and Terri Finch. 1985. 'Pairs of same-sexed siblings discordant for antisocial behaviour,' *British Journal of Psychiatry* 146: 415–23

Richardson, H. 1969. *Adolescent Girls in Approved Schools*. London: Routledge and Kegan Paul

Roberts, Albert R. 1981. *Runaways and Non-runaways in an American Suburb: An Exploratory Study of Adolescent and Parental Coping*. New York: The John Jay Press

Robins, Lee N. 1972. 'Follow-up studies of behavior disorders in children,' in V.C. Quay and J.S. Werry, eds, *Psychopathological disorders of Childhood*, 483–514. New York: Wiley

– 1979. 'Longitudinal methods in the study of normal and pathological development,' in K.P. Kisker, J.E. Meyer, C. Muller, and E. Strongren, eds, *Psychiatrie der Gegenwort*, Band 1: *Grundlagen und Methoden der Psychiatrie*. Heidelberg: Springer-Verlag

Roff, J.D., and R.D. Wirt. 1984. 'Childhood aggression and social adjustment as antecedents of delinquency,' *Journal of Abnormal Child Psychology* 12 (1): 111–26

– 1985. 'The specificity of childhood problem behavior and adolescent and young adult maladjustment,' *Journal of Clinical Psychology* 41 (4): 564-71

Rosenblum, Karen E. 1980. 'Female deviance and the female sex role: A preliminary investigation,' in S. Datesman and F. Scarpitti, eds, *Women, Crime and Justice*, 106–28. New York, Oxford: Oxford University Press

Ross, Robert R., and Elizabeth A. Fabiano. 1986. *Female Offenders: Correctional Afterthought*. Jefferson, NC: London: McFarland

Ross, Robert R., and Paul Gendreau, eds. 1980. *Effective Correctional Treatment*. Toronto: Butterworths

Rutter, Michael. 1980. 'School Influences on children's behavior and development,' *Pediatrics* 65 (2): 208–20

– 1981. 'Epidemiological/longitudinal strategies and causal research in child psychiatry,' *Journal American Academy of Child Psychiatry* 20: 513–44

– 1985. 'Resilience in the face of adversity: Protective factors and resistance to psychiatric disorders,' *British Journal of Psychiatry* 147: 598–611

Sarri, Rosemary. 1976. 'Juvenile law: How it penalizes females,' in L. Crites, ed, *The Female Offender*, 67–87. Lexington, MA: Lexington Books

– 1983. 'The use of detention and alternatives in the United States since the Gault decision,' in R.R. Corrado et al, eds, *Current Issues in Juvenile Justice*, 315–34. Toronto: Butterworths

Schlossman, S., and M. Sedlak. 1983. 'The Chicago Area Project revisited,' *Crime and Delinquency*, 29 (3): 398–462

Schur, Edwin M. 1973. *Radical Non-intervention*. Englewood Cliffs, NJ: Prentice-Hall

– 1984. *Labelling Women Deviant: Gender, Stigma and Social Control*. New York: Random House

Schwartz, Ira M., Marilyn Jackson-Beeck, and Roger Anderson. 1984. 'The "hidden" system of juvenile control,' *Crime and Delinquency* 30 (3): 371–85

Schwendinger, Herman, and Julia S. Schwendinger. 1976. 'Delinquency and the collective varities of youth,' *Crime and Social Justice* 5: 7–25

Schwendinger, Herman, and Julia Siegel Schwendinger. 1985. *Adolescent Subcultures and Delinquency*, Research ed. New York: Praeger

Scott, W.L. 1908. 'The Juvenile Delinquent Act,' *The Canadian Law Times* 28: 892–904

Sepsi, Victor J. 1974. 'Girl recidivists,' *Journal of Research in Crime and Delinquency* 11 (1): 70–9

Short, James F. 1979. 'Applied Research and the Search for Knowledge: The Case of Juvenile Delinquency and Income Maintenance Experiments.' Paper presented at American Society of Criminology, Philadelphia, November

Simons, Ronald L., Martin G. Miler, and Stephen M. Aigner. 1980. 'Contemporary theories of deviance and female delinquency: An empirical test,' *Journal Research in Crime and Delinquency* 17 (1): 42–57

Smart, Carol. 1976. *Women, Crime and Criminology: A Feminist Critique*. London, Henley, and Boston: Routledge and Kegan Paul

– 1985. 'Legal subjects and sexual objects: Ideology, law and female sexuality,' in J. Brophy and C. Smart, eds, *Women-in-Law*, 50–70. London: Routledge and Kegan Paul

Smith, Dorothy E. 1974a. 'The social construction of documentary reality,' *Sociological Inquiry* 44 (4): 257–68

– 1974b. 'Women's perspective as a radical critique of sociology,' *Sociological Inquiry* 44 (1): 7–13

– 1981. 'Women's inequality and the family,' in A. Moscovitch and G. Drover, eds, *Inequality*, 156–95. Toronto: University Toronto Press

– 1985. 'Women, class and family,' in V. Burstyn and D. Smith, eds, *Women, Class, Family and the State*, 1–44. Toronto: Garamond Press, Network Basics

Solicitor General. 1985. *Canadian Crime Statistics*. Ottawa: Ministry of Supply and Services

Spender, Dale. 1985. *Man Made Language*, 2nd ed. London and New York: Routledge and Kegan Paul

Stanley, Stephen, and Mary Baginsky. 1984. *Alternatives to Prison: An Examination of Non-custodial Sentencing of Offenders*. London: Peter Owen

Statistics Division. 1985. *A Statistical Profile of Female Offenders in Canada*. Programs Branch User Report No. 8. Ottawa: Ministry of the Solicitor General

Steffensmeier, Darrell J., and Renee Hoffman Steffensmeier. 1980. 'Trends in female delinquency,' *Criminology* 18 (1): 62–85

Strange, Carolyn. 1985. ' "The criminal and fallen of their sex": The establishment of Canada's first women's prison, 1874–1901,' *Canadian Journal of Women and the Law* 1: 79–92

Sultan, Faye E., Gary T. Long, Stephan A. Kiefer, David M. Schrum, James W. Selby, and Lawrence G. Calhoun. 1984. 'The female offender's adjustment to prison life: A comparison of psychodidactic and traditional supportive approaches to treatment,' *Journal of Offender Counseling, Services and Rehabilitation* 9 (1–2): 49–56

Teilman, Katherine, and Pierre H. Landry Jr. 1981. 'Gender bias in juvenile justice,' *Journal Research in Crime and Delinquency* 18 (1): 47–80

Thomas, William I. 1969 [1923]. *The Unadjusted Girl*. Montclaire, NJ: Patterson Smith

Thomlinson, Ray J. 1981. 'Outcome effectiveness research and its implications for social work educators,' *Canadian Journal of Social Work Education* 7 (3): 55–92

Trépanier, Jean. 1983. 'The Quebec Youth Protection Act: Institutionalized diversion,' in R.R. Corrado, M. LeBlanc, and J. Trépanier, eds, *Current Issues in Juvenile Justice*, 191–201. Toronto: Butterworths

Treso, Leo J. 1962. *101 Delinquent Girls*. Notre dame, IN: Fides Publishers

Urbain, Eugene S., and Philip C. Kendall. 1980. 'Review of social-cognitive problem-solving interventions with children,' *Psychological Bulletin* 88 (1): 109–43

Vedder, C.B., and D.B. Sommerville. 1970. *The Delinquent Girl* Springfield, IL: Charles C. Thomas

Vickers, Jill, and Margrit Eichler. 1987. 'Dialogue,' *Resources for Feminist Research* 16 (4): 3–6

Wadsworth, Michael. 1979. *Roots of Delinquency*. Oxford: Martin Robertson

Warren, Carol A.B. 1986. 'New trends in the social control of juveniles: Transinstitutionalism and private profit,' in M. Brusten et al, eds, *Youth Crime, Social Control and Prevention*, 33–8. Pfaffenweiler, Germany: Centaurus-Verlagsgesellschaft

Warren, Marguerite. 1981. 'Gender comparisons in crime and delinquency,' in M. Warren, ed, *Comparing Female and Male Offenders*, 1–16. Beverly Hills, CA: Sage

– 1982. 'A follow-up study of female delinquents from the 1960's.' *The Differential View* (Proceedings of the 6th Annual Conference of International Differential Treatment Association), Issue 12: 59–68

Watson, Catherine M. 1980. 'Women Prisoners and Modern Methods of Prison Control: A Comparative Study of Two Canadian Prisons.' Doctoral diss., McGill University, Montreal

Weiler, Karen. 1978. 'Unmanageable children in Ontario: A legal review,' in H. Berkeley et al, eds, *Children's Rights*, 59–77. Toronto: Ontario Institute for Studies in Education

Weiler, Richard, and Brian Ward. 1985. 'A national overview of the implementation of YOA: One year later,' *Perception* 8 (5): 7–13

Weissman, Harold H., ed. 1969. *Justice and the Law in the Mobilization for Youth Experience*. New York: Association Press

Werner, Emmy E., and Ruth S. Smith. 1977. *Kauai's Children Come of Age*. Honolulu: University Press of Hawaii

– 1982. *Vulnerable But Invincible: A Longitudinal Study of Resilient Children*. New York: McGraw-Hill

West, Gordon W. 1984. *Young Offenders and the State: A Canadian Perspective on Delinquency*. Toronto: Butterworths

Wharf, Brian, ed. 1979. *Community Work in Canada*. Toronto: McClelland and Stewart

Whitehead, Linette. 1979. 'Sex differences in children's responses to family stress,' *Journal of Child Psychology and Psychiatry* 20: 247–54

Wilson, Deirdre. 1978. 'Sexual codes and conduct: A study of teenage girls,' in Carol Smart and Barry Smart, eds, *Women, Sexuality and Social Control*, 65–73. London, Henley, and Boston: Routledge and Kegan Paul

Wilson, S.J. (1982). *Women, the Family and the Economy*. Toronto: McGraw-Hill Ryerson

Wolfe, Nancy T., Francis T. Cullen, and John B. Cullen. 1984. 'Describing the female offender: A note on the demographies of arrest,' *Journal of Criminal Justice* 12: 483–92

Wolfgang, Marvin E. 1983. 'Delinquency in two birth cohorts,' *American Behavioral Scientist* 27 (1): 75–86

Yelaja, Shankar A. 1985. 'Concepts of social work practice,' in S.A. Yelaja, ed, *An Introduction to Social Work Practice in Canada*, 24–33. Scarborough, ON: Prentice-Hall

PART FIVE

Overview and Future Directions

14 Regaining equilibrium in the Canadian juvenile-justice system

Peter G. Jaffe, Alan W. Leschied, and Wayne Willis

The preceding chapters have examined the impact of the YOA on the Canadian juvenile-justice system. It is obvious that the shift from the JDA to the YOA had had dramatic effects on young persons as well as on the legal, mental-health, social-service, and correctional professionals who provide service for them. The purpose of this final chapter is to review current trends and speculate on the future. We plan to look ahead to what may happen as the YOA reaches adulthood in the twenty-first century. Rather than forecasting more shock waves on the justice system, we will examine the anticipated search for equilibrium among policy makers and practitioners who witnessed the birth of the YOA.

One means of examining trends is to explore major themes that have emerged over the past decade in the debate over what kind of juvenile-justice system and legislation Canada really wants and needs. The trends are apparent in analysing the nature and frequency of themes on juvenile crime that appear in a major Canadian newspaper. Naisbitt (1982) has suggested that content analysis of newspapers provides a comprehensive picture of new directions in any country. Table 1 provides an overview of major articles that have appeared in the Toronto *Globe and Mail* over the decade from 1978 to 1987.

Only articles of more than twelve lines, editorials, and feature stories were considered in a computer search by info Globe. The seventy-five articles found were categorized under one of four major themes: 1 / Resources – any discussion of programs or services; 2 / Rights of Young Persons – any discussion of critical issues and incidents related to legal process and rights of young persons; 3 / Protection of the Public – concern about the safety and protection of Canadian citizens from the crimes of young offenders; 4 / Federal-Provincial Conflicts – any expression of

TABLE 1
Globe and Mail articles* on the juvenile justice system during the decade 1978–87

Topic	1978–9	1980–1	1982–3	1984–5	1986–7
Resources	0	0	3	2	1
Rights of young persons	1	2	14	18	6
Protection of the public	0	0	0	1	2
Federal/provincial conflicts	1	3	4	14	1
Other	2	0	0	0	0
Total	4	5	21	35	10
% of total in decade	5.3	6.7	28.0	46.7	13.3

*Articles included any news story longer than twelve inches, as well as editorials and features in the 'National Edition' of the paper.

concern about differences in opinion, policies, or funding between Ottawa and any province in regard to implementation of the YOA. Articles that could not be placed in one of these categories based on the major theme or emphasis of the journalist and story were left in the 'Other' category.

A review of table 1 demonstrates that the advent of the YOA significantly raised the extent of public debate about the juvenile-justice system. Almost half of the major articles published in the decade are accounted for by the two-year period of the YOA introduction, 1984–5 (1985 is significant as the extension of the maximum age of Ontario). The period from 1982 to 1985 has more than six times as many articles as the preceding four-year period (1978–81). The dominant themes during the decade are clearly the rights of young persons and the disagreements between the federal and provincial governments about funding and implementation of the YOA. It is interesting to note that the past two years have seen less coverage, fewer federal-provincial conflicts, and a greater balance among the three remaining themes.

We will examine the nature of each of these themes, current critical issues, and speculation about future trends.

Rights of Young Persons

Bala and Kirvan draw a conclusion in chapter 4 that would find universal agreement, namely that the YOA's most notable achievement has been the provision of a clear statement on the fundamental legal rights of young persons. The birth of the YOA came at a time when all Canadians celebrated our Charter of Rights and Freedoms. In chapter 1, West dampens our enthusiasm for the real meaning of young person's rights by remind-ing us that the justice system is far removed from the social and economic conditions that trigger and maintain youthful crime. Reitsma-Street, in chapter 13, refines this point when she argues that the YOA barely acknowl-edges the needs or rights of young females. Schwartz also offers his insights, in chapter 7, that replacing *parens patriae* with an emphasis on legal rights can create a backlash exemplified by the rise of the 'get tough' movement south of our border. Great Britain experienced the same increase in crime and utilization of custodial sentence when legislators believed that they had found progressive reforms in the Children and Young Persons Act of 1969 (Rutter and Giller 1984).

No one questions the importance of young persons having the same rights as adults in any criminal proceeding (short of jury trials and preliminary hearings). However, it is vital to remain vigilant as to the unintended side-effects of new legislation such as the YOA. Even the best intentions are quickly lost in a system that depends on many players with changing roles and resources. An extreme example of excellent principles gone awry is the concept of separating young offenders from adults in detention facilities on Baffin Island. Rigid adherence to this principle is achieved by sending young persons 4000 kilometres away from their home community to Yellowknife ($1000 round trip) while they await their trial (*Globe and Mail* 1988). This is an example of what Hackler refers to in chapter 3 as the blind pursuit of legal principles that frustrates common-sense solutions for local communities.

The daily problems are far less dramatic than the example of a trip from Baffin Island to Yellowknife for the purposes of detention. An emphasis on rights and having the punishment fit the crime creates an environment in the juvenile system that models the adult system. In Ontario, for example, the same defence lawyers and judges who deal with the crimes of a thirty-year-old at 10:00 a.m. may have to change their philosophy with a sixteen-year-old young offender at 3:00 p.m. At times, only the clock changes. The result is a police force that recognizes that the most severe charge (and as many as possible) will get the most attention from the youth court. The judge who may have been a non-interventionist for serious charges under the JDA may feel the lower limits of his or her discretion challenged and provide a more severe disposition. Clearly the trends from the disposition data reviewed in chapter 8 suggests that more rights are associated with more severe consequences in the youth court.

Predictions for the future are simple. The rights that young persons have been granted under YOA will remain the most important foundation of the legislation. However, an overcrowding of youth-court dockets and open-custody facilities will lead to greater diversion through alternative measures and various early identification and prevention programs. Although the jury is still out on the effectiveness of alternative measures programs (Basta and Davidson 1988; Jaffe et al 1986), the tax-payers will find them less expensive than a formalized judicial process.

The youth court will become the place for the most severe antisocial behaviour, and it is hypothesized that existing social-service and mental-health facilities will build better bridges directly to the front lines in the community, such as the police force (e.g., Jaffe, Finlay, and Wolfe 1984). The era of the youth-court judges being part of the social conscience of the community or social-welfare advocates and co-ordinators is past. His Honour Judge Lucien Beaulieu eloquently discusses this major change in the role of youth-court judges in chapter 6.

Federal-Provincial Conflicts

What was all the fuss about? Was it Toronto's or Ottawa's fault? How much funding does the YOA really require? These and other questions appear to have become irrelevant. Reality has taken over, and increasing co-operation between federal and provincial YOA bureaucrats seems apparent. Advisory committees and federal-provincial working groups will continue to multiply like rabbits (e.g., Coflin 1988).

Some provinces, such as Ontario, couldn't believe the YOA was really happening to them and until the last moment resisted accepting the responsibility of preparing and planning an appropriate strategy for implementation. The provincial juvenile-justice systems have moved from a general mood of paralysis to reactive planning by such actions as building open-custody beds as young offenders were ordered into them.

The future holds a more mature response on the part of all the provinces in recognizing the federal responsibility for the YOA. The short-term trends will see an attempt at damage control from the impact of the initial minimal compliance to the spirit of the YOA. For example, Ontario's two-tiered system for young offenders age twelve to fifteen and sixteen and seventeen will be unified into one system following a heated discussion behind closed doors in the Ontario cabinet. The resistance to alternative measures and resulting chaos in many youth courts will blossom into well-funded and energetic diversion programs. The provinces will always want a larger slice of the federal tax dollar but the impetus for any major changes to the YOA formula has passed. Lobby groups will ensure that provinces implement not only the letter of the law but also the spirit behind the YOA (e.g., Ontario Social Development Council 1988).

Protection of the Public

Adolescents who murder or grab headlines by other heinous crimes will become the only element of youth crime widely known to the Canadian citizen. Waivers to adult court will not be frequent enough or understandable to the general public, creating intense public pressure to modify the three-year maximum sentence under the YOA. Previous research suggests that the vast majority of Canadians depend on the news media as their source of information about the justice system. The news media have a dramatic tendency to cover crimes against persons and custody sentences, and only rarely discuss reasons for sentencing (Roberts 1988).

It is no wonder that the majority of Canadians want more severe sentences. The maximum sentence of three years for murder will remain in the public eye. In the short term, resistance to changing the maximum sentence will create more and more public concern and lead to overgeneralization about dangerous young offenders running the streets (in fact, the most recent front-page stories involve young offenders killing family members). With or without free trade, we will quickly adapt the American approach to juvenile crime, which, as Schwartz outlines in chapter 7, put a capital 'T' on Tough and small 'r' on rehabilitation. We appear destined to repeat the mistakes of the American and British juvenile-justice systems (Krisburg, Swartz, and Litsky 1986; Rutter and Giller 1984). Even in the middle of the fall 1988 federal election, violent crime was a major issue. The minister of justice had to explain how 'tough' the government has been on crime in several areas (*London Free Press* 1988). Who can blame the public for their response (Cullen, Clark, and Wozniak 1985)?

Part of the concern about protection of the public will lead to increasingly longer custodial dispositions. Pressure from within the justice system will improve the quality of long-term custodial facilities that recognize the need for specialized staff and programs to deal with disturbed young offenders and special populations (e.g., sex offenders). The need for these facilities in Canada has yet to match the development of these programs in the United States (e.g., Agee 1987).

Resources

The acid test for the Canadian juvenile-justice system will be the kind of services that are available to prevent or reduce antisocial behaviour in children and adolescents. As Hackler points out in chapter 3, we stand in danger of providing more process but less meaningful outcome for young offenders.

A superficial examination of resources will point out that juvenile-justice legislation addresses only *crimes* of youth. *Needs* are the responsibility of the social-service and health systems within the community, *irrespective* of antisocial behaviour.

However, current studies suggest that only a very small percentage of youth with emotional or behavioural problems actually receive specialized interventions in the community (Ontario Ministry of Community and Social Services 1988). In fact, the group of children with the most serious behaviour problem and conduct disorders often found in a delinquent population is least likely to receive treatment (Krzanowski 1988). The youth court will be faced with the dilemma of turning its back on young offenders with special needs with the mainly false assumption that they are being looked after elsewhere in the children's services network. Or the youth court will adopt the practice of sentencing the young offender to correctional facilities that are not equipped to deal with special needs. Preliminary studies suggest that the outcome of these custodial programs for young offenders with special needs is worse under the YOA than it was under the JDA (Leschied, Austin, and Jaffe 1988).

Reid-MacNevin, in chapter 2, describes a range of theories that underlie shifting philosophies about juvenile-justice policy. The implication of her analysis is that policy and legislation change but young person's basic needs remain the same. The outcome of these changes may be to shift young persons from one system (child welfare) to another (correctional) without recognizing that the same fundamental programs will be required. The youth-service system may find itself repeating the errors of the adult mental-health system, which has witnessed a dramatic decline in the number of mental-health beds and a corresponding increase in that of custodial beds. Our colleague Dr Chris Webster, chief psychologist of the Clarke Institute of Psychiatry, has often described the ill-conceived shuffling of maladjusted individuals between hospitals and jails as 'locked-van therapy' to signify the futile nature of intervention by process and labelling alone (*Globe and Mail* 1987).

We would speculate that young persons previously in the care of child-welfare agencies or children's mental-health centres will shift to correctional facilities with uncertain mandates and without programs to meet their needs. The same children with a wide range of intellectual, emotional, social, and economic liabilities will be relabelled by a different system ill-equipped to respond to special needs.

Awad, in chapter 9, and Patterson, in chapter 10, suggest a number of modifications to the legislation or to available resources. The consent to treatment (section 22) issue in the YOA will not go away. Two solutions seem apparent. On the one hand, amendments could be made that clearly define treatment and limit the length of the intervention according to the length of a probable custody disposition for the same offence. On the other hand, custodial facilities can become 'treatment centres' if they are able to attract enough specialized staff and funding to enrich their environment. Even the most cautious legal philosophy on the YOA wishes for custody centres that offer a wide range of counselling and educational services.

We hopefully predict considerable research progress in two major areas related to resource development for young offenders: risk factors and prevention programs, and effective treatment. In the first area, it is apparent from a number of major research studies that certain factors are excellent predictors of youthful crime. Poverty, school failure, abuse, and exposure to violence and conflict in the family seem to be consistent risk factors in the youth court's clients (Rutter and Giller 1984). Programs that identify these factors at an early stage and provide co-ordinated services, such as those outlined by Crealock in chapter 12, need our immediate attention. It is obvious that the juvenile-justice system does not exist in a vacuum and needs to be part of an integrated approach to young offenders in a community (Hornick, Burrows, and Hudson 1988). Essential to an integrated approach is the education system, which appears to offer the greatest potential for addressing adjustment problems and failure at an early age (Gottfredson 1987).

In the second area, Canadian researchers need to refocus the basic questions on rehabilitation. Although we can be optimistic about the potential of many intervention programs (Basta and Davidson 1988), we need better-controlled studies with longer-term follow-up data. Rather than search for a panacea for a heterogeneous population of young offenders, we need to identify specific intervention strategies for specific clients at different stages of their development. Kazdin (1987), in his recent book on conduct disorders, emphasizes the importance of analysing the severity of problem behaviour in order to assess the impact of specific programs on mild, moderate, or severe levels of childhood and adolescent disorders. Rutter and Giller (1984) suggest that researchers clearly distinguish among young offenders at different stages of their movement into the justice system to separate the isolated incidents of adolescence from budding criminal careers. Sex differences have been ignored for too long, and the necessity of responding more appropriately to the needs of female as well as male young offenders should lead to research and program development for both populations as outlined by Reitsma-Street in chapter 13. To ignore the specificity of these research questions may lead to throwing out babies with the bath water and may encourage further cynicism about rehabilitating young offenders.

We remain desperate for quality information systems at the provincial and federal government levels. How can any meaningful planning take place without the most up-to-date information on the nature of young offenders and the dispositions that they are receiving. A recent best-seller in the business field makes this point in an urgent fashion. Tom Peters, in *Thriving on Chaos* (1987), points out that the only certainty in the world (other than death and taxes) is change. He preaches that we all need to embrace change rather than fear it. Essential to dealing with change is the availability of information for planning, daily problem solving, flexibility, and morale on the front line.

The Canadian juvenile-justice system has minimal information for any of these issues. If the youth court was a business, it would have been bankrupt by the summer of 1984. However, we remain optimistic that the commitment and creative energy visible in this book and in many youth courts across Canada will produce the information system required. Perhaps the Ontario Social Development Council's dream of a youth-justice centre promoting research and multidisciplinary training will become a reality.

Why do we remain optimistic in light of the preliminary analysis of the YOA's impact on the Canadian juvenile-justice system?

We believe fundamentally in crisis theory (Caplan 1964), which reminds us that the Chinese symbol for crisis is composed of the symbols for danger and opportunity. The advent of the YOA has represented a crisis for juvenile justice. However, the intense interest and vital debates have provided an opportunity for significant positive changes, leading to finer tuning and better balance in the future Canadian juvenile-justice system. The next decade offers considerable challenges and opportunities for the development of a more coherent and effective Canadian juvenile-justice system. The revolution is over. The YOA is here to stay, without earth-shattering amendments. The stability offered by a period of equilibrium as young persons' rights are balanced by their needs along with community reaction provides a fertile environment for innovation in program and research initiatives.

References

Agee, V. 1987. 'The Treatment Program: Paint Creek Youth Centre.' Unpublished ms. Bainbridge, Ohio

Basta, J., and W. Davidson. 1988. 'Treatment of juvenile offenders: Study outcomes since 1980,' *Behavioural Sciences and the Law* 6: 355–84

Caplan, G. 1964. *Principles of Prevention Psychiatry.* New York: Basic Books

Coflin, J. 1988. 'The federal government's role in implementing the *Young Offenders Act,*' in J. Hudson, J. Hornick, and B. Burrows, eds, *Justice and the Young Offender in Canada,* 37–50. Toronto: Wall & Thompson

Cullen, F.T., G. Clark, and J.F. Wozniak. 1985. 'Explaining the get tough movement: Can the public be blamed?' *Federal Probation* 49: 16–24

Globe & Mail. 1987. 'Treatment of criminals called wasteful, misdirected,' 31 October, p. A7

– 1988. 'Harsh rule of justice is being softened,' 24 September, 1988. p. D5

Gottfredson, G.D. 1987. 'American education: American delinquency,' *Today's Delinquent* 6: 5–70

Hornick, J., B. Burrows, and J. Hudson. 1988. 'Future directions,' in J. Hudson, J. Hornick, and B. Burrows, eds, *Justice and the Young Offender in Canada,* 169–84. Toronto: Wall & Thompson

Jaffe, P., J. Finlay, and D. Wolfe. 1984. 'Evaluating the impact of a specialized civilian family crisis unit within a police force on the resolution of family conflicts,' *Journal of Preventive Psychiatry* 2: 63–73

Jaffe, P., B. Kroeker, C. Hyatt, M. Miscevick, A. Telford, R. Chandler, C. Shanahan, and B. Sokoloff. 1986. 'Diversion in the Canadian juvenile justice system: A tale of two cities,' *Juvenile and Family Court Journal* 37: 59–66

Kazdin, A. 1987. *Conduct Disorders in Childhood and Adolescence.* Newbury Park, CA: Sage

Krisburg, B., I.M. Schwartz, and P. Litsky. 1986. 'The watershed of juvenile justice reform,' *Crime and Delinquency* 32 (1): 5–38

Krzanowska, E. 1988. 'Mental Health Status of Children in Canada.' Paper prepared for the Federal Working Group on Children and Youth. Ottawa: Health and Welfare Canada

Leschied, A., G. Austin, and P. Jaffe. 1988. 'Impact of the Young Offenders Act on recidivism of special needs youth: Clinical and policy implications,' *Canadian Journal of Behavioural Science* 20: 322–31

London Free Press. 1988. 'Violent crime edges up in Canada,' 30 September, p. 3

Naisbitt, J. 1982. *Megatrends*. New York: Warner's

Ontario Ministry of Community and Social Services. 1988. *Investing in Children*. Toronto: Queen's Park

Ontario Social Development Council. 1988. 'YOA Dispositions: Challenges and Choices: A Report of the Conference on the *Young Offenders Act* in Ontario.' 12 July

Peters, T. 1987. *Thriving on Chaos*. New York: Knopf

Roberts, J. 1988. *Sentencing in the Media: A Content Analysis of English-Language Newspapers in Canada*. Ottawa: Department of Justice, Canada

Rutter, M., and H. Giller. 1984. *Juvenile Delinquency: Trends and Perspectives*. New York: Guildford Press